The Ultimate BMAT Guide

UniAdmissions

ISBN 978-0-9935711-9-0

Published by *RAR Medical Services Limited*
www.uniadmissions.co.uk
info@uniadmissions.co.uk
Tel: 0208 068 0438

The Ultimate BMAT Guide

800 Practice Questions

Dr Rohan Agarwal

Edited by
Dr David Salt

UniAdmissions

About the Author

Rohan is the **Director of Operations** at *UniAdmissions* and is responsible for its technical and commercial arms. He graduated from Gonville and Caius College, Cambridge and is a fully qualified doctor. Over the last five years, he has tutored hundreds of successful Oxbridge and Medical applicants. He has also authored ten books on admissions tests and interviews.

Rohan has taught physiology to undergraduates and interviewed medical school applicants for Cambridge. He has published research on bone physiology and writes education articles for the Independent and Huffington Post. In his spare time, Rohan enjoys playing the piano and table tennis.

About the Editor

David is **Director of Services** at *UniAdmissions*, taking the lead in product development and customer service. David read medical sciences at Gonville and Caius College Cambridge, graduating in 2012, completed his clinical studies in the Cambridge Clinical School and now works as a medical doctor.

David is an experienced tutor, having helped students with all aspects of the university applications process. He has authored five books to help with university applications and has edited four more. Away from work, David enjoys cycling, outdoor pursuits and good food.

The Basics 6

General Advice 9

SECTION 1 14

SECTION 1: Critical Thinking 14

Critical Thinking Questions 17

SECTION 1: Problem Solving Questions 49

Problem Solving Questions 51

SECTION 1: Data Analysis 85

Data Analysis Questions 86

SECTION 2 106

SECTION 2: Biology 107

Biology Questions 108

SECTION 2: Chemistry 124

Chemistry Questions 126

SECTION 2: Physics 141

Physics Questions 143

SECTION 2: Maths 157

Maths Questions 158

SECTION 3 171

Annotated Essays 177

Mock Papers

Mock Paper A 190

Mock Paper B 203

Mock Paper C 218

ANSWERS

Answer Key 234

Worked Answers 238

Mock Paper Answers 320

Final Advice 357

Your Free Book 359

UKCAT Intensive Course 360

BMAT Intensive Course 361

Medicine Interview Course 362

The Basics

What is the BMAT?

The BioMedical Admissions Test (BMAT) is a 2-hour written exam for medical and veterinary students who are applying for competitive universities.

What does the BMAT consist of?

Section	SKILLS TESTED	Questions	Timing
ONE	Problem-solving skills, including numerical and spatial reasoning. Critical thinking skills, including understanding argument and reasoning using everyday language.	35 MCQs	60 minutes
TWO	Ability to recall, understand and apply GCSE level principles of biology, chemistry, physics and maths. Usually the section that students find the hardest.	27 MCQs	30 minutes
THREE	Ability to organise ideas in a clear and concise manner, and communicate them effectively in writing. Questions are usually but not necessarily medical.	One essay from three	30 minutes

Why is the BMAT used?

Medical and veterinary applicants tend to be a bright bunch and therefore usually have excellent grades. For example, in 2013 over 65% of students who applied to Cambridge for Medicine had UMS greater than 90% in all of their A level subjects. This means that competition is fierce – meaning that the universities must use the BMAT to help differentiate between applicants.

When do I sit BMAT?

There are two sittings for the BMAT – the second week of September and first week of November (normally Wednesday morning). You can generally sit the BMAT on either date however, some universities will ask that you sit the test on a specific date e.g. Oxford, Lee Kong Chian and Chulalongkorn University will only accept results from the November BMAT sitting. You're highly advised to check which date you should sit the BMAT depending on your university choices.

When should I sit the BMAT?

The difficulty and content of both sittings is the same so the answer will depend on how much time you have over summer and how important it is for you to know your BMAT result before you submit your UCAS application. In general, if you're applying for two or more BMAT universities, it's a good idea to sit the BMAT in September if circumstances allow.

	SEPTEMBER	NOVEMBER
Positive	Get BMAT Results before UCAS Deadline Can use the summer to prepare thoroughly	More time to prepare overall Will have coverd more science topics in school
Negative	Less time to prepare overall May conflict with UKCAT, Personal Statement etc	Hard to balance school-work with BMAT revision Won't get BMAT results until after UCAS Deadline

Who has to sit the BMAT?

Applicants to the following universities must sit the BMAT:

University	Course
University of Cambridge	Medicine and Veterinary Medicine
University of Oxford	Medicine, Graduate Medicine, Biomedical Science
University College London	Medicine
Imperial College London	Medicine, Graduate Medicine, Biomedical Science
Brighton and Sussex	Medicine
University of Leeds	Medicine, Dentistry
Lancaster University	Medicine
Keele University	Medicine, Health Foundation Year
Royal Veterinary College	Veterinary Medicine
Lee Kong Chian (Singapore)	Medicine
Thammasat University	642901(Medicine) and 642902 (Dental Surgery)
Universidad de Navarra	Medicine
Mahidol University	Medicine

Do I have to resit the BMAT if I reapply?

You only need to resit the BMAT if you are applying to a university that requires it. You cannot use your score from any previous attempts.

How is the BMAT Scored?

Section 1 and Section 2 are marked on a scale of 0 to 9. Generally, 5 is an average score, 6 is good, and 7 is excellent. Very few people (<5%) get more than 8.

The marks for sections 1 + 2 show a normal distribution with a large range. The important thing to note is that the difference between a score of 5.0 and 6.5+ is often only 3-4 questions. Thus, you can see that even small improvements in your raw score will lead to massive improvements when they are scaled.

Section 3 is marked on 2 scales: A-E for Quality of English and 0-5 for Strength of Argument

The marks for sections 3 show a normal distribution for the strength of argument; the average mark for the strength of argument is between 3 – 3.5. The quality of English marks are negatively skewed distribution. I.e. the vast majority of students will score A or B for quality of English. The ones that don't tend to be students who are not fluent in English.

This effectively means that the letter score is used to flag students who have a comparatively weaker grasp of English- i.e. it is a test of competence rather than excellence like the rest of the BMAT. This effectively means that if you get a C or below, admissions tutors are more likely to scrutinise your essay than otherwise.

Finally, section 3 is marked by two different examiners. If there is a large discrepancy between their marks, it is marked by a third examiner.

Can I resit the BMAT?

No, you can only sit the BMAT once per admissions cycle. You can resit the BMAT if you apply for medicine again in the future.

Where do I sit the BMAT?

For the September sitting, you will need to register yourself and sit the test at one of 20 authorised centres. In November, your school will normally register you and you can usually sit the BMAT at your school or college (ask your exams officer for more information). Alternatively, if your school isn't a registered test centre or you're not attending a school or college, you can sit the BMAT at an authorised test centre.

When do I get my results?

For the September sitting, you will get your results by the end of September online. You are then responsible for informing the University of your Score. For the November sitting, The BMAT results are usually released to universities in mid-late November and then to students in late November.

How is the BMAT used?

Cambridge: Cambridge interviews more than 90% of students who apply so the BMAT score isn't vital for making the interview shortlist. However, it can play a huge role in the final decision – for example, 50% of overall marks for your application may be allocated to the BMAT. Thus, it's essential you find out as much information about the college you're applying to.

Oxford: Oxford typically receives thousands of applications each year and they use the BMAT to shortlist students for interview. Typically, 450 students are invited for interview for 150 places. Thus, if you get offered an interview- you are doing very well! Oxford centralise their short listing process and use an algorithm that uses your % A*s at GCSE along with your BMAT score to rank all their applicants of which the top are invited to interview. BMAT sections 1 + 2 count for 40% each of your BMAT score whilst section 3 counts for 20% [the strength of argument (number) contributes to 13.3% and the quality of English (letter) makes up the remaining 6.7%].

UCL: UCL make offers based on all components of the application and whilst the BMAT is important there is no magic threshold that you need to meet in order to guarantee an interview. Applicants with higher BMAT scores tend to be interviewed earlier in the year.

Imperial: Imperial employs a BMAT threshold to shortlist for interview. This exact threshold changes every year but in the past has been approximately 4.5-5.0 for sections 1 + 2 and 2.5 B for section 3.

Leeds: The BMAT contributes to 15% of your academic score at Leeds. You will be allocated marks based on your rank in the BMAT. Thus, applicants in the top 20% of the BMAT will get the full quota of marks for their application and the bottom 20% will get the lowest possible mark for their application. Thus, you can still get an interview if you perform poorly in the BMAT (it' just much harder!). Leeds will calculate your BMAT score by attributing 40% to section 1, 40% to section 2 and 20% to section 3 (lower weighting as it can come up during the interview).

Brighton: Brighton started using the BMAT in 2014 so little is known about how they use it in their decision making process. They state on their website that it "may also be used as a final discriminator if needed after interview."

Royal Veterinary College: It is unclear how the RVC use the BMAT- it has influenced applications both before and after interview and it's likely that they use it on a case-by-case basis rather than as an arbitrary cut-off.

General Advice

Start Early

It is much easier to prepare if you practice little and often. Start your preparation well in advance; ideally by mid September but at the latest by early October. This way you will have plenty of time to complete as many papers as you wish to feel comfortable and won't have to panic and cram just before the test, which is a much less effective and more stressful way to learn. In general, an early start will give you the opportunity to identify the complex issues and work at your own pace.

Prioritise

Some questions in sections 1 + 2 can be long and complex – and given the intense time pressure you need to know your limits. It is essential that you don't get stuck with very difficult questions. If a question looks particularly long or complex, mark it for review and move on. You don't want to be caught 5 questions short at the end just because you took more than 3 minutes in answering a challenging multi-step physics question. If a question is taking too long, choose a sensible answer and move on. Remember that each question carries equal weighting and therefore, you should adjust your timing in accordingly. With practice and discipline, you can get very good at this and learn to maximise your efficiency.

Positive Marking

There are no penalties for incorrect answers in the BMAT; you will gain one for each right answer and will not get one for each wrong or unanswered one. This provides you with the luxury that you can always guess should you absolutely be not able to figure out the right answer for a question or run behind time. Since each question provides you with 4 to 6 possible answers, you have a 16-25% chance of guessing correctly. Therefore, if you aren't sure (and are running short of time), then make an educated guess and move on. Before 'guessing' you should try to eliminate a couple of answers to increase your chances of getting the question correct. For example, if a question has 5 options and you manage to eliminate 2 options- your chances of getting the question increase from 20% to 33%!

Avoid losing easy marks on other questions because of poor exam technique. Similarly, if you have failed to finish the exam, take the last 10 seconds to guess the remaining questions to at least give yourself a chance of getting them right.

Practice

This is the best way of familiarising yourself with the style of questions and the timing for this section. Although the BMAT tests only GCSE level knowledge, you are unlikely to be familiar with the style of questions in all 3 sections when you first encounter them. Therefore, you want to be comfortable at using this before you sit the test.

Practising questions will put you at ease and make you more comfortable with the exam. The more comfortable you are, the less you will panic on the test day and the more likely you are to score highly. Initially, work through the questions at your own pace, and spend time carefully reading the questions and looking at any additional data. When it becomes closer to the test, **make sure you practice the questions under exam conditions**.

Past Papers

Official past papers and answers from 2003 onwards are freely available online on our website at **www.uniadmissions.co.uk/bmat-past-papers** and once you've worked your way through the questions in this book, it's a good idea to attempt as many of them as you can (ideally at least 5). Keep in mind that the specification was changed in 2009 so some things asked in earlier papers may not be representative of the content that is currently examinable in the BMAT. In general, **it is worth doing at least all the papers from 2009 onwards**. Time permitting; you can work backwards from 2009 although there is little point doing the section 3 essays pre-2009 as they are significantly different to the current style of essays.

You will undoubtedly get stuck when doing some past paper questions – they are designed to be tricky and the answer schemes don't offer any explanations. Thus, **you're highly advised to acquire a copy of** *BMAT Past Paper Worked Solutions* – a free ebook is available online (see the back of this book for more details).

Scoring Tables

Use these to keep a record of your scores – you can then easily see which paper you should attempt next (always the one with the lowest score).

SECTION 1	1st Attempt	2nd Attempt		SECTION 2	1st Attempt	2nd Attempt
2003				2003		
2004				2004		
2005				2005		
2006				2006		
2007				2007		
2008				2008		
2009				2009		
2010				2010		
2011				2011		
2012				2012		
2013				2013		
2014				2014		
2015				2015		
2016				2016		

Extra Practice

If you're blessed with a good memory, you might remember the answers to certain questions in the past papers – making it less useful to repeat them again. If you want to tackle extra mock papers which are fully up-to-date then check out **www.uniadmissions.co.uk/bmat-practice-papers** for **4** x full mock papers with worked solutions.

These are normally £60 but as thanks for purchasing this book, you can get them for £40 instead (enter "*BMATWS20*" at checkout).

SECTION 1	1st Attempt	2nd Attempt		SECTION 2	1st Attempt	2nd Attempt
Practice Paper A				Practice Paper A		
Practice Paper B				Practice Paper B		
Practice Paper C				Practice Paper C		
Practice Paper D				Practice Paper D		

Repeat Questions

When checking through answers, pay particular attention to questions you have got wrong. If there is a worked answer, look through that carefully until you feel confident that you understand the reasoning, and then repeat the question without help to check that you can do it. If only the answer is given, have another look at the question and try to work out why that answer is correct. This is the best way to learn from your mistakes, and means you are less likely to make similar mistakes when it comes to the test. The same applies for questions which you were unsure of and made an educated guess which was correct, even if you got it right. When working through this book, **make sure you highlight any questions you are unsure of**, this means you know to spend more time looking over them once marked.

No Calculators

You aren't permitted to use calculators in the BMAT – thus, it is essential that you have strong numerical skills. For instance, you should be able to rapidly convert between percentages, decimals and fractions. You will seldom get questions that would require calculators but you would be expected to be able to arrive at a sensible estimate. Consider for example:

Estimate 3.962 x 2.322;

3.962 is approximately 4 and 2.323 is approximately 2.33 = 7/3.

Thus, $3.962 \times 2.322 \approx 4 \times \frac{7}{3} = \frac{28}{3} = 9.33$

Since you will rarely be asked to perform difficult calculations, you can use this as a signpost of if you are tackling a question correctly. For example, when solving a physics question, you end up having to divide 8,079 by 357- this should raise alarm bells as calculations in the BMAT are rarely this difficult.

Top tip! In general, students tend to improve the fastest in section 2 and slowest in section 1; section 3 usually falls somewhere in the middle. Thus, if you have very little time left, it's best to prioritise section 2.

A word on timing...

"If you had all day to do your BMAT, you would get 100%. But you don't."

Whilst this isn't completely true, it illustrates a very important point. Once you've practiced and know how to answer the questions, the clock is your biggest enemy. This seemingly obvious statement has one very important consequence. **The way to improve your BMAT score is to improve your speed.** There is no magic bullet. But there are a great number of techniques that, with practice, will give you significant time gains, allowing you to answer more questions and score more marks.

Timing is tight throughout the BMAT – **mastering timing is the first key to success**. Some candidates choose to work as quickly as possible to save up time at the end to check back, but this is generally not the best way to do it. BMAT questions can have a lot of information in them – each time you start answering a question it takes time to get familiar with the instructions and information. By splitting the question into two sessions (the first run-through and the return-to-check) you double the amount of time you spend on familiarising yourself with the data, as you have to do it twice instead of only once. This costs valuable time. In addition, candidates who do check back may spend 2–3 minutes doing so and yet not make any actual changes. Whilst this can be reassuring, it is a false reassurance as it is unlikely to have a significant effect on your actual score. Therefore it is usually best to pace yourself very steadily, aiming to spend the same amount of time on each question and finish the final question in a section just as time runs out. This reduces the time spent on re-familiarising with questions and maximises the time spent on the first attempt, gaining more marks.

It is essential that you don't get stuck with the hardest questions – no doubt there will be some. In the time spent answering only one of these you may miss out on answering three easier questions. If a question is taking too long, choose a sensible answer and move on. Never see this as giving up or in any way failing, rather it is the smart way to approach a test with a tight time limit. With practice and discipline, you can get very good at this and learn to maximise your efficiency. It is not about being a hero and aiming for full marks – this is almost impossible and very much unnecessary (even Oxbridge will regard any score higher than 7 as exceptional). It is about maximising your efficiency and gaining the maximum possible number of marks within the time you have.

Top tip! Ensure that you take a watch that can show you the time in seconds into the exam. This will allow you have a much more accurate idea of the time you're spending on a question. In general, if you've spent >150 seconds on a section 1 question or >90 seconds on a section 2 questions – move on regardless of how close you think you are to solving it.

Use the Options:

Some questions may try to overload you with information. When presented with large tables and data, it's essential you look at the answer options so you can focus your mind. This can allow you to reach the correct answer a lot more quickly. Consider the example below:

The table below shows the results of a study investigating antibiotic resistance in staphylococcus populations. A single staphylococcus bacterium is chosen at random from a similar population. Resistance to any one antibiotic is independent of resistance to others.

Calculate the probability that the bacterium selected will be resistant to all four drugs.

A   1 in 10^6
B   1 in 10^{12}
C   1 in 10^{20}
D   1 in 10^{25}
E   1 in 10^{30}
F   1 in 10^{35}

Antibiotic	Number of Bacteria tested	Number of Resistant Bacteria
Benzyl-penicillin	10^{11}	98
Chloramphenicol	10^9	1200
Metronidazole	10^8	256
Erythromycin	10^5	2

Looking at the options first makes it obvious that there is **no need to calculate exact values**- only in powers of 10. This makes your life a lot easier. If you hadn't noticed this, you might have spent well over 90 seconds trying to calculate the exact value when it wasn't even being asked for.

In other cases, you may actually be able to use the options to arrive at the solution quicker than if you had tried to solve the question as you normally would. Consider the example below:

A region is defined by the two inequalities: $x - y^2 > 1$ *and* $xy > 1$. Which of the following points is in the defined region?

A.   (10,3)
B.   (10,2)
C.   (-10,3)
D.   (-10,2)
E.   (-10,-3)

Whilst it's possible to solve this question both algebraically or graphically by manipulating the identities, by far **the quickest way is to actually use the options**. Note that options C, D and E violate the second inequality, narrowing down to answer to either A or B. For A: $10 - 3^2 = 1$ and thus this point is on the boundary of the defined region and not actually in the region. Thus the answer is B (as $10-4 = 6 > 1$.)

In general, it pays dividends to look at the options briefly and see if they can be help you arrive at the question more quickly. Get into this habit early – it may feel unnatural at first but it's guaranteed to save you time in the long run.

Keywords

If you're stuck on a question; pay particular attention to the options that contain key modifiers like "**always**", "**only**", "**all**" as examiners like using them to test if there are any gaps in your knowledge. E.g. the statement "arteries carry oxygenated blood" would normally be true; "All arteries carry oxygenated blood" would be false because the pulmonary artery carries deoxygenated blood.

SECTION 1

This is the first section of the BMAT and as you walk in, it is inevitable that you will feel nervous. Make sure that you have been to the toilet because once it starts you cannot simply pause and go. Take a few deep breaths and calm yourself down. Remember that panicking will not help and may negatively affect your marks- so try and avoid this as much as possible.

You have one hour to answer 35 questions in section 1. The questions fall into three categories:
- Problem solving
- Data handling
- Critical thinking

Whilst this section of the BMAT is renowned for being difficult to prepare for, there are powerful shortcuts and techniques that you can use to save valuable time on these types of questions.

You have approximately 100 seconds per question; this may sound like a lot but given that you're often required to read and analyse passages or graphs- it can often not be enough. Nevertheless, this section is not as time pressured as section 2 so most students usually finish the majority of questions in time. However, some questions in this section are very tricky and can be a big drain on your limited time. **The people who fail to complete section 1 are those who get bogged down on a particular question**.

Therefore, it is vital that you start to get a feel for which questions are going to be easy and quick to do and which ones should be left till the end. The best way to do this is through practice and the questions in this book will offer extensive opportunities for you to do so.

SECTION 1: Critical Thinking

BMAT Critical thinking questions require you to understand the constituents of a good argument and be able to pick them apart. The majority of BMAT Critical thinking questions tend to fall into 3 major categories:

1. Identifying Conclusions
2. Identifying Assumptions + Flaws
3. Strengthening and Weakening arguments

Having a good grasp of language and being able to filter unnecessary information quickly and efficiently is a vital skill in medical school – you simply do not have the time to sit and read vast numbers of textbooks cover to cover, you need to be able to filter the information and realise which part is important and this will contribute to your success in your studies. Similarly, when you have qualified and are on the wards, you need to be able to pick out key information from patient notes and make healthcare decisions from them, so getting to grips with verbal reasoning goes a long way and do not underestimate its importance.

Only use the Passage

Your answer must only be based on the information available in the passage. Do not try and guess the answer based on your general knowledge as this can be a trap. For example, if the passage says that spring is followed by winter, then take this as true even though you know that spring is followed by summer.

Top tip! Though it might initially sound counter-intuitive, it is often best to read the question *before* reading the passage. Then you'll have a much better idea of what you're looking for and are therefore more likely to find it quicker.

Take your time

Unlike the problem solving questions, critical thinking questions are less time pressured. Most of the passages are well below 300 words and therefore don't take long to read and process (unlike the UKCAT in which you should skim read passages). Thus, your aim should be to understand the intricacies of the passage and identify key information so that you don't miss key information and lose easy marks.

Identifying Conclusions

Students struggle with these type of questions because they confuse a premise for a conclusion. For clarities sake:

- A **Conclusion** is a summary of the arguments being made and is usually explicitly stated or heavily implied.
- A **Premise** is a statement from which another statement can be inferred or follows as a conclusion.

Hence a conclusion is shown/implied/proven by a premise. Similarly, a premise shows/indicates/establishes a conclusion. Consider for example: *My mom, being a woman, is clever as all women are clever.*

Premise 1: My mom is a woman + **Premise 2:** Women are clever = **Conclusion:** My mom is clever.

This is fairly straightforward as it's a very short passage and the conclusion is explicitly stated. Sometimes the latter may not happen. Consider: *My mom is a woman and all women are clever.*
Here, whilst the conclusion is not explicitly being stated, both premises still stand and can be used to reach the same conclusion.

You may sometimes be asked to identify if any of the options cannot be "reliably concluded". This is effectively asking you to identify why an option **cannot** be the conclusion. There are many reasons why but the most common ones are:

1. Over-generalising: *My mom is clever therefore all women are clever.*
2. Being too specific: All kids like candy thus my son also likes candy.
3. Confusing Correlation vs. Causation: *Lung cancer is much more likely in patients who drink water. Hence, water causes lung cancer.*
4. Confusing Cause and Effect: *Lung cancer patients tend to smoke so it follows that having lung cancer must make people want to smoke.*

Note how conjunctives like hence, thus, therefore and it follows give you a clue as to when a conclusion is being stated. More examples of these include: "it follows that, implies that, whence, entails that".
Similarly, words like "because, as indicated by, in that, given that, due to the fact that" usually identify premises.

Assumptions + Flaws:

Other types of critical thinking questions may require you to identify assumptions and flaws in a passage's reasoning. Before proceeding it is useful to define both:

- An assumption is a reasonable assertion that can be made on the basis of the available evidence.
- A flaw is an element of an argument which is inconsistent to the rest of the available evidence. It undermines the crucial components of the overall argument being made.

Consider for example: *My mom is clever because all doctors are clever.*

Premise 1: Doctors are clever. **Assumption:** My mom is a doctor. **Conclusion:** My mom is clever.

Note that the conclusion follows naturally even though there is only one premise because of the assumption. The argument relies on the assumption to work. Thus, if you are unsure if an option you have is an assumption or not, just ask yourself:

1) *Is it in the passage?* If the answer is **no** then proceed to ask:
2) *Does the conclusion rely on this piece of information in order to work?* – If the answer is **yes** – then you've identified an assumption.

You may sometimes be asked to identify flaws in an argument – it is important to be aware of the types of flaws to look out for. In general, these are broadly similar to the ones discussed earlier in the conclusion section (over-generalising, being too specific, confusing cause and effect, confusing correlation and causation). Remember that an assumption may also be a flaw.

For example consider again: *My mom is clever because all doctors are clever.*

What if the mother was not actually a doctor? The argument would then breakdown as the assumption would be incorrect or **flawed**.

> *Top tip!* Don't get confused between premises and assumptions. A **premise** is a statement that is explicitly stated in the passage. An **assumption** is an inference that is made from the passage.

Strengthening and Weakening Arguments:

You may be asked to identify an answer option that would most strengthen or weaken the argument being made in the passage. Normally, you'll also be told to assume that each answer option is true. Before we can discuss how to strengthen and weaken arguments, it is important to understand "what constitutes a good argument:

1. **Evidence:** Arguments which are heavily based on value judgements and subjective statements tend to be weaker than those based on facts, statistics and the available evidence.
2. **Logic:** A good argument should flow and the constituent parts should fit well into an overriding view or belief.
3. **Balance:** A good argument must concede that there are other views or beliefs (counter-argument). The key is to carefully dismantle these ideas and explain why they are wrong.

Thus, when asked to strengthen an argument, look for options that would: Increase the evidence basis for the argument, support or add a premise, address the counter-arguments.

Similarly, when asked to weaken an argument, look for options that would: decrease the evidence basis for the argument or create doubt over existing evidence, undermine a premise, strengthen the counter-arguments.

In order to be able to strengthen or weaken arguments, you must completely understand the passage's conclusion. Then you can start testing the impact of each answer option on the conclusion to see which one strengthens or weakens it the most i.e. is the conclusion stronger/weaker if I assume this information to be true and included in the passage.

Often you'll have to decide which option strengthens/weakens the passage most – and there really isn't an easy way to do this apart from lots of practice. Thankfully, you have plenty of time for these questions.

Critical Thinking Questions

Question 1-6 are based on the passage below:

People have tried to elucidate the differences between the different genders for many years. Are they societal pressures or genetic differences? In the past it has always been assumed that it was programmed into our DNA to act in a certain more masculine or feminine way but now evidence has emerged that may show it is not our genetics that determines the way we act, but that society pre-programmes us into gender identification. Whilst it is generally acknowledged that not all boys and girls are the same, why is it that most young boys like to play with trucks and diggers whilst young girls prefer dollies and pink?

The society we live in has always been an important factor in our identity, take cultural differences; the language we speak the food we eat, the clothes we wear. All of these factors influence our identity. New research finds that the people around us may prove to be the biggest influence on our gender behaviour. It shows our parents buying gendered toys may have a much bigger influence than the genes they gave us. Girls are being programmed to like the same things as their mothers and this has lasting effects on their personality. Young girls and boys are forced into their gender stereotypes through the clothes they are bought, the hairstyle they wear and the toys they play with.

The power of society to influence gender behaviour explains the cases where children have been born with different external sex organs to those that would match their sex determining chromosomes. Despite the influence of their DNA they identify to the gender they have always been told they are. Once the difference has been detected, how then are they ever to feel comfortable in their own skin? The only way to prevent society having such a large influence on gender identity is to allow children to express themselves, wear what they want and play with what they want without fear of not fitting in.

Question 1:
What is the main conclusion from the first paragraph?
A.   Society controls gender behaviour.
B.   People are different based on their gender.
C.   DNA programmes how we act.
D.   Boys do not like the same things as girls because of their genes.

Question 2:
Which of the following, if true, points out the flaw in the first paragraph's argument?
A.   Not all boys like trucks.
B.   Genes control the production of hormones.
C.   Differences in gender may be due to an equal combination of society and genes.
D.   Some girls like trucks.

Question 3:
According to the statement, how can culture affect identity?
A.   Culture can influence what we wear and how we speak.
B.   Our parents act the way they do because of culture.
C.   Culture affects our genetics.
D.   Culture usually relates to where we live.

Question 4:

Which of these is most implied by the statement?

A. Children usually identify with the gender they appear to be.

B. Children are programmed to like the things they do by their DNA.

C. Girls like dollies and pink because their mothers do.

D. It is wrong for boys to have long hair like girls.

Question 5:

What does the statement say is the best way to prevent gender stereotyping?

A. Mothers spending more time with their sons.

B. Parents buying gender-neutral clothes for their children.

C. Allowing children to act how they want.

D. Not telling children if they have different sex organs.

Question 6:

What, according to the statement is the biggest problem for children born with different external sex organs to those which match their sex chromosomes?

A. They may have other problems with their DNA.

B. Society may not accept them for who they are.

C. They may wish to be another gender.

D. They are not the gender they are treated as which can be distressing.

Questions 7-11 are based on the passage below:

New evidence has emerged that the most important factor in a child's development could be their napping routine. It has come to light that regular napping could well be the deciding factor for determining toddlers' memory and learning abilities. The new countrywide survey of 1000 toddlers, all born in the same year showed around 75% had regular 30-minute naps. Parents cited the benefits of their child having a regular routine (including meal times) such as decreased irritability, and stated the only downfall of occasional problems with sleeping at night. Research indicating that toddlers were 10% more likely to suffer regular night-time sleeping disturbances when they regularly napped supported the parent's view.

Those who regularly took 30-minute naps were more than twice as likely to remember simple words such as those of new toys than their non-napping counterparts, who also had higher incidences of memory impairment, behavioural problems and learning difficulties. Toddlers who regularly had 30 minute naps were tested on whether they were able recall the names of new objects the following day, compared to a control group who did not regularly nap. These potential links between napping and memory, behaviour and learning ability provides exciting new evidence in the field of child development.

Question 7:
If in 100 toddlers 5% who did not nap were able to remember a new teddy's name, how many who had napped would be expected to remember?

A. 8   B. 9   C. 10   D. 12

Question 8:
Assuming that the incidence of night-time sleeping disturbances is the same in for all toddlers independent of all characteristics other than napping, what is the percentage of toddlers who suffer regular night-time sleeping disturbances as a result of napping?

A. 7.5%   B. 10%   C. 14%   D. 20%   E. 50%

Question 9:
Using the information from the passage above, which of the following is the most plausible alternative reason for the link between memory and napping?
A. Children who have bad memory abilities are also likely to have trouble sleeping.
B. Children who regularly nap, are born with better memories.
C. Children who do not nap were unable to concentrate on the memory testing exercises for the study.
D. Parents who enforce a routine of napping are more likely to conduct memory exercises with their children.

Question 10:
Which of the following is most strongly indicated?
A. Families have more enjoyable meal times when their toddlers regularly nap.
B. Toddlers have better routines when they nap.
C. Parents enforce napping to improve their toddlers' memory ability.
D. Napping is important for parents' routines.

Question 11:
Which of the following, if true, would strengthen the conclusion that there is a causal link between regular napping and improved memory in toddlers?
A. Improved memory is also associated with regular mealtimes.
B. Parents who enforce regular napping are more inclined to include their children in studies.
C. Toddlers' memory development is so rapid that even a few weeks can make a difference to performance.
D. Among toddler playgroups where napping incidence is higher and more consistent memory performance is significantly improved compared to those that do not.

Question 12:

Tom's father says to him: 'You must work for your A-levels. That is the best way to do well in your A-level exams. If you work especially hard for Geography, you will definitely succeed in your Geography A-level exam'.

Which of the following is the best statement Tom could say to prove a flaw in his father's argument?

A.   'It takes me longer to study for my History exam, so I should prioritise that.'
B.   'I do not have to work hard to do well in my Geography A-level.'
C.   'Just because I work hard, does not mean I will do well in my A-levels.'
D.   'You are putting too much importance on studying for A-levels.'
E.   'You haven't accounted for the fact that Geography is harder than my other subjects.'

Question 13:

Today the NHS is increasingly struggling to be financially viable. In the future, the NHS may have to reduce the services it cannot afford. The NHS is supported by government funds, which come from those who pay tax in the UK. Recently the NHS has been criticised for allowing fertility treatments to be free, as many people believe these are not important and should not be paid for when there is not enough money to pay the doctors and nurses.

Which of the following is the most accurate conclusion of the statement above?

A.   Only taxpayers should decide where the NHS spends its money.
B.   Doctors and nurses should be better paid.
C.   The NHS should stop free fertility treatments.
D.   Fertility treatments may have to be cut if finances do not improve.

Question 14:

'We should allow people to drive as fast as they want. By allowing drivers to drive at fast speeds, through natural selection the most dangerous drivers will kill only themselves in car accidents. These people will not have children, hence only safe people will reproduce and eventually the population will only consist of safe drivers.'

Which one of the following, if true, most weakens the above argument?

A.   Dangerous drivers harm others more often than themselves by driving too fast.
B.   Dangerous drivers may produce children who are safe drivers.
C.   The process of natural selection takes a long time.
D.   Some drivers break speed limits anyway.

Question 15:

In the winter of 2014 the UK suffered record levels of rainfall, which led to catastrophic damage across the country. Thousands of homes were damaged and even destroyed, leaving many homeless in the chaos that followed. The Government faced harsh criticism that they had failed to adequately prepare the country for the extreme weather. In such cases the Government assess the likelihood of such events happening in the future and balance against the cost of advance measures to reduce the impact should they occur versus the cost of the event with no preparative defences in place. Until recently, for example, the risk of acts of terror taking was low compared with the vast cost anticipated should they occur. However, the risk of flooding is usually low, so it could be argued that the costs associated with anti-flooding measures would have been pre-emptively unreasonable. Should the Government be expected to prepare for every conceivable threat that could come to pass? Are we to put in place expensive measures against a seismic event as well as a possible extra-terrestrial invasion?

Which of the following best expresses the main conclusion of the statement above?
A. The Government has an obligation to assess risks and costs of possible future events.
B. The Government should spend money to protect against potential extra-terrestrial invasions and seismic events.
C. The Government should have spent money to protect against potential floods.
D. The Government was justified in not spending heavily to protect against flooding.
E. The Government should assist people who lost their homes in the floods.

Question 16:

Sadly the way in which children interact with each other has changed over the years. Where once children used to play sports and games together in the street, they now sit alone in their rooms on the computer playing games on the Internet. Where in the past young children learned human interaction from active games with their friends this is no longer the case. How then, when these children are grown up, will they be able to socially interact with their colleagues?

Which one of the following is the conclusion of the above statement?
A. Children who play computer games now interact less outside of them.
B. The Internet can be a tool for teaching social skills.
C. Computer games are for social development.
D. Children should be made to play outside with their friends to develop their social skills for later in life.
E. Adults will in the future play computer games as a means of interaction.

Question 17:

Between 2006 and 2013 the British government spent £473 million on Tamiflu antiviral drugs in preparation for a flu pandemic, despite there being little evidence to support the effectiveness of the drug. The antivirals were stockpiled for a flu pandemic that never fully materialised. Only 150,000 packs were used during the swine flu episode in 2009, and it is unclear if this improved outcomes. Therefore this money could have been much better spent on drugs that would actually benefit patients.

Which option best summarises the author's view in the passage?
A. Drugs should never be stockpiled, as they may not be used.
B. Spending millions of pounds on drugs should be justified by strong evidence showing positive effects.
C. We should not prepare for flu pandemics in the future.
D. The recipients of Tamiflu in the swine flu pandemic had no difference in symptoms or outcomes to patients who did not receive the antivirals.

Question 18:

High BMI and particularly central weight are risk factors associated with increased morbidity and mortality. Many believe the development of cheap, easily accessible fast-food outlets is partly responsible for the increase in rates of obesity. An unhealthy weight is commonly associated with a generally unhealthy lifestyle, such a lack of exercise. The best way to tackle the growing problem of obesity is for the government to tax unhealthy foods so they are no longer a cheap alternative.

Why is the solution given, to tax unhealthy foods, not a logical conclusion from the passage?

A. Unhealthy eating is not exclusively confined to low-income families.

B. A more general approach to unhealthy lifestyles would be optimal.

C. People do not only choose to eat unhealthy food because it is cheaper.

D. People need to take personal responsibility for their own health.

Question 19:

As people are living longer, care in old age is becoming a larger burden. Many people require carers to come into their home numerous times a day or need full residential care. It is not right that the NHS should be spending vast funds on the care of people who are sufficiently wealthy to fund their own care. Some argue that they want their savings kept to give to their children; however this is not a right, simply a luxury. It is not right that people should be saving and depriving themselves of necessary care, or worse, making the NHS pay the bill, so they have money to pass on to their offspring. People need to realise that there is a financial cost to living longer.

Which of the following statements is the main conclusion of the above passage?

A. We need to take a personal responsibility for our care in old age.

B. Caring for the elderly is a significant burden on the NHS.

C. The reason people are reluctant to pay for their own care is that they want to pass money onto their offspring.

D. The NHS should limit care to the elderly to reduce their costs.

E. People shouldn't save their money for old age.

Question 20:

There is much interest in research surrounding production of human stem cells from non-embryo sources for potential regenerative medicine, and a huge financial and personal gain at stake. In January 2014, a team from Japan published two papers in *Nature* that claimed to have developed totipotent stem cells from adult mouse cells by exposure to an acidic environment. However, there has since been much controversy surrounding these papers. Problems included: inability by other teams to replicate the results of the experiment, an insufficient protocol described in the paper and issues with images in one of the papers. It was dishonest of the researchers to publish the papers with such problems, and a requirement of a paper is a sufficiently detailed protocol, so that another group could replicate the experiment.

Which statement is most implied?

A. Research is fuelled mainly by financial and personal gains.

B. The researchers should take responsibility for publishing the paper with such flaws.

C. Rivalry between different research groups makes premature publishing more likely.

D. The discrepancies were in only one of the papers published in January 2014.

Question 21:

The placebo effect is a well-documented medical phenomenon in which a patient's condition undergoes improvement after being given an ineffectual treatment that they believe to be a genuine treatment. It is frequently used as a control during trials of new drugs/procedures, with the effect of the drug being compared to the effect of a placebo, and if the drug does not have a greater effect than the placebo, then it is classed as ineffective. However, this analysis discounts the fact that the drug treatment still has more of a positive effect than no action, and so we are clearly missing out on the potential to improve certain patient conditions. It follows that where there is a demonstrated placebo effect, but treatments are ineffective, we should still give treatments, as there will therefore be some benefit to the patient.

Which of the following best expresses the main conclusion of this passage?

A. In situations where drugs are no more effective than a placebo, we should still give drugs, as they will be more effective than not taking action.

B. Our current analysis discounts the fact that even if drug treatments have no more effect than a placebo, they may still be more effective than no action.

C. The placebo effect is a well-recognised medical phenomenon.

D. Drug treatments may have negative side effects that outweigh their benefit to patients.

E. Placebos are better than modern drugs.

Question 22:

The speed limit on motorways and dual carriageways has been 70mph since 1965, but this is an out-dated policy and needs to change. Since 1965, car brakes have become much more effective, and many safety features have been introduced into cars, such as seatbelts (which are now compulsory to wear), crumple zones and airbags. Therefore, it is clear that cars no longer need to be restricted to 70mph, and the speed limit can be safely increased to 80mph without causing more road fatalities.

Which of the following best illustrates an assumption in this passage?

A. The government should increase the speed limit to 80mph.

B. If the speed limit were increased to 80mph, drivers would not begin to drive at 90mph.

C. The safety systems introduced reduce the chances of fatal road accidents for cars travelling at higher speeds.

D. The roads have not become busier since the 70mph speed limit was introduced.

E. The public want the speed limit to increase.

Question 23:

Despite the overwhelming scientific proof of the theory of evolution, and even acceptance of the theory by many high-ranking religious ministers, there are still sections of many major religions that do not accept evolution as true. One of the most prominent of these in western society is the Intelligent Design movement, which promotes the religious-based (and scientifically discredited) notion of Intelligent Design as a scientific theory. Intelligent Design proponents often point to complex issues of biology as proof that god is behind the design of human beings, much as a watchmaker is inherent in the design of a watch.

One part of anatomy that has been identified as supposedly supporting Intelligent Design is fingerprints, with some proponents arguing that they are a mark of individualism created by God, with no apparent function except to identify each human being as unique. This is incorrect, as fingerprints do have a well documented function – namely channelling away of water to improve grip in wet conditions – in which hairless, smooth skinned hands otherwise struggle to grip smooth objects. The individualism of fingerprints is accounted for by the complexity of thousands of small grooves. Development is inherently affected by stochastic or random processes, meaning that the body is unable to uniformly control its development to ensure that fingerprints are the same in each human being. Clearly, the presence of individual fingerprints does nothing to support the so-called-theory of Intelligent Design.

Which of the following best illustrates the main conclusion of this passage?
A. Fingerprints have a well-established function.
B. Evolution is supported by overwhelming scientific proof.
C. Fingerprints do not offer any support to the notion of Intelligent Design.
D. The individual nature of fingerprints is explained by stochastic processes inherent in development that the body cannot uniformly control.
E. Intelligent design is a credible and scientifically rigorous theory.

Question 24:

High levels of alcohol consumption are proven to increase the risk of many non-infectious diseases, such as cancer, atherosclerosis and liver failure. James is a PhD student, and is analysing the data from a large-scale study of over 500,000 people to further investigate the link between heavy alcohol consumption and health problems. In the study, participants were asked about their alcohol consumption, and then their medical history was recorded. His analysis displays surprising results, concluding that those with high alcohol consumption have a *decreased* risk of cancer. James decides that those carrying out the study must have incorrectly recorded the data.

Which of the following is **NOT** a potential reason why the study has produced these surprising results?
A. Previous studies were incorrect, and high alcohol consumption does lower the risk of cancer.
B. The studies didn't take account of other cancer risk factors in comparing those with high and low alcohol consumption.
C. James has made some errors in his analysis, and thus his conclusions are erroneous.
D. The participants involved in the study did not truthfully report their alcohol consumption, leading to false conclusions being drawn.
E. The studies control group data was mixed up with the test group data.

Question 25:

A train is scheduled to depart from Newcastle at 3:30pm. It stops at Durham, Darlington, York, Sheffield, Peterborough and Stevenage before arriving at Kings Cross station in London, where the train completes its journey. The total length of the journey between Newcastle and Kings Cross was 230 miles, and the average speed of the train during the journey (including time spent stood still at calling stations) is 115mph. Therefore, the train will complete its journey at 5:30pm.

Which of the following is an assumption made in this passage?

A. The various stopping points did not increase the time taken to complete the journey.
B. The train left Newcastle on time.
C. The train travelled by the most direct route available.
D. The train was due to end its journey at Kings Cross.
E. There were no signalling problems encountered on the journey.

Question 26:

There have been many arguments over the last couple of decades about government expenditure on healthcare in the various devolved regions of the UK. It is often argued that, since spending on healthcare per person is higher in Scotland than in England, that therefore the people in Scotland will be healthier. However, this view fails to take account of the different needs of these 2 populations of the UK. For example, one major factor is that Scotland gets significantly colder than England, and cold weakens the immune system, leaving people in Scotland at much higher risk of infectious disease. Thus, Scotland requires higher levels of healthcare spending per person simply to maintain the health of the populace at a similar level to that of England.

Which of the following is a conclusion that can be drawn from this passage?

A. The higher healthcare spending per person in Scotland does not necessarily mean people living in Scotland are healthier.
B. Healthcare spending should be increased across the UK.
C. Wales requires more healthcare spending per person simply to maintain population health at a similar level to England.
D. It is unfair on England that there is more spending on healthcare per person in Scotland.
E. Scotland's healthcare budget is a controversial topic.

Question 27:

Vaccinations have been hugely successful in reducing the incidence of several diseases throughout the 20th century. One of the most spectacular achievements was arguably the global eradication of Smallpox, once a deadly worldwide killer, during the 1970s. Fortunately, there was a highly effective vaccine available for Smallpox, and a major factor in its eradication was an aggressive vaccination campaign. Another disease that is potentially eradicable is Polio. However, although there is a highly effective vaccine for Polio available, attempts to eradicate it have so far been unsuccessful. It follows that we should plan and execute an aggressive vaccination campaign for Polio, in order to ensure that this disease too is eradicated.

Which of the following is the main conclusion of this passage?

A. Polio is a potentially eradicable disease.
B. An aggressive vaccination campaign was a major factor in the eradication of smallpox.
C. Both Polio and smallpox have been eradicated by effective vaccination campaigns.
D. We should execute an aggressive vaccination campaign for Polio.
E. The eradication of smallpox remains one of the most spectacular achievements of medical science.

Question 28:

The Y chromosome is one of 2 sex chromosomes found in the human genome, the other being the X chromosome. As the Y chromosome is only found in males, it can only be passed from father to son. Additionally, the Y chromosome does not exchange sections with other chromosomes (as happens with most chromosomes), meaning it is passed on virtually unchanged through the generations. All of this makes the Y chromosome a fantastic tool for genetic analysis, both to identify individual lineages and to investigate historic population movements. One famous achievement of genetic research using the Y chromosome provides further evidence of its utility, namely the identification of Genghis Khan as a descendant of up to 8% of males in 16 populations across Asia.

Which of the following best illustrates the main conclusion of this passage?

A. The Y chromosome is a fantastic tool for genetic analysis.
B. Research using the Y chromosome has been able to identify Genghis Khan as the descendant of up to 8% of men in many Asian populations.
C. The Y chromosome does not exchange sections with other chromosomes.
D. The Y chromosome is a sex chromosome.
E. Genghis Khan had a staggering number of children.

Question 29:

In order for a bacterial infection to be cleared, a patient must be treated with antibiotics. Rachel has a minor lung infection, which is thought by her doctor to be a bacterial infection. She is treated with antibiotics, but her condition does not improve. Therefore, it must not be a bacterial infection.

Which of the following best illustrates a flaw in this reasoning?

A. It assumes that a bacterial infection would definitely improve after treatment with antibiotics.
B. It ignores the other potential issues that could be treated by antibiotics.
C. It assumes that antibiotics are necessary to treat bacterial infections.
D. It ignores the actions of the immune system, which may be sufficient to clear the infection regardless of what has caused it.
E. It assumes that antibiotics are the only option to treat a bacterial infection.

Question 30:

The link between smoking and lung cancer has been well established for many decades by overwhelming numbers of studies and conclusive research. The answer is clear and simple, that the single best measure that can be taken to avoid lung cancer is to not smoke, or to stop smoking if one has already started. However, despite the overwhelming evidence and clear answers, many smokers continue to smoke, and seek to minimise their risk of lung cancer by focusing on other, less important risk factors, such as exercise and healthy eating. This approach is obviously severely flawed, and the fact that some smokers feel this is a good way to reduce their risk of lung cancer shows that they are delusional.

Which of the following best illustrates the main conclusion of this passage?

A. Many smokers ignore the largest risk factor, and focus on improving less important risk factors by eating healthily and exercising.
B. Some smokers are delusional.
C. The biggest risk factor of lung cancer is smoking.
D. Overwhelming studies have proven the link between smoking and lung cancer.
E. The government should ban smoking in order to reduce the incidence of lung cancer.

Question 31:

The government should invest more money into outreach schemes in order to encourage more people to go to university. These schemes allow students to meet other people who went to university, which they may not always be able to do otherwise, even on open days.

Which of the following is the best conclusion of the above argument?

A. Outreach schemes are the best way to encourage people to go to university.
B. People will not go to university without seeing it first.
C. The government wants more people to go to university.
D. Meeting people who went to a university is a more effective method than university open days.
E. It is easier to meet people on outreach schemes than on open days.

Question 32:

The illegal drug cannabis was recently upgraded from a class C drug to class B, which means it will be taken less in the UK, because people will know it is more dangerous. It also means if people are caught, possessing the drug they will face a longer prison sentence than before, which will also discourage its use.

Which **TWO** statements if true, most weaken the above argument?

A. Class C drugs are cheaper than class B drugs.
B. Upgrading drugs in other countries has not reduced their use.
C. People who take illegal drugs do not know what class they are.
D. Cannabis was not the only class C drug before it was upgraded.
E. Even if they are caught possessing class B drugs, people do not think they will go to prison.

Question 33:

Schools with better sports programmes such as well-performing football and netball teams tend to have better academic results, less bullying and have overall happier students. Thus, if we want schools to have the best results, reduce bullying and increase student happiness, teachers should start more sports clubs.

Which one of the following best demonstrates a flaw in the above argument?

A. Teachers may be too busy to start sports clubs.
B. Better academic results may be a precondition of better sports teams.
C. Better sports programmes may prevent students from spending time with their family.
D. Some sports teams may be seen to encourage internal bullying.
E. Sport teams that do not perform well lead to increase bulling.

Question 34:

The legal age for purchasing alcohol in the UK is 18. This should be lowered to 16 because the majority of 16 year olds drink alcohol anyway without any fear of repercussions. Even if the police catch a 16-year-old buying alcohol, they are unable to enforce any consequences. If the drinking limit was lowered the police could spend less time trying to catch underage drinkers and deal with other more important crimes. There is no evidence to suggest that drinking alcohol at 16 is any more dangerous than at 18.

Which one of the following, if true, most weakens the above argument?

A. Most 16 year olds do not drink alcohol.
B. If the legal drinking age were lowered to 16, more 15 year olds would start purchasing alcohol.
C. Most 16 year olds do not have enough money to buy alcohol.
D. Most 16 year olds are able to purchase alcohol currently.

Question 35:

There has been a recent change in the way the government helps small businesses. Whilst previously small businesses were given non-repayable grants to help them grow their profits, they can now only receive government loans that must be repaid with interest when the business turns a certain amount of profit. The government wants to support small businesses but studies have shown they are less likely to prosper under the new scheme as they have been deterred from taking government money for fear of loan repayments.

Which one of the following can be concluded from the passage above?

A. Small businesses do not want government money.
B. The government cannot afford to give out grants to small businesses anymore.
C. All businesses avoid accumulating debt.
D. The action of the government is more likely to do more harm than good to small businesses.
E. Big businesses do not need government money.

Questions 36-41 are based on the passage below:

Despite the numerous safety measures in place within the practice of medicine, these can fail when the weaknesses in the layers of defence aligns to create a clear path leading to often disastrous results. This is known as the 'Swiss cheese model of accident causation'. One such occurrence occurred where the wrong kidney was removed from a patient due to a failure in the line of defences designed to prevent such an incident occurring.

When a kidney is diseased it is removed to prevent further complications, this operation, a 'nephrectomy', is regularly performed by experienced surgeons. Where normally the consultant who knew the patient would have conducted the procedure, in this case he passed the responsibility to his registrar, who was also well experienced but had not met the patient previously. The person who had copied out the patient's notes had poor handwriting had accidentally written the 'R' for 'right' in such a way that it was read as an 'L' and subsequently copied, and not noticed by anyone who further reviewed the notes.

The patient had been put asleep before the registrar had arrived and so he proceeded without checking the procedure with the patient, as he normally would have done. The nurses present noticed this error but said nothing, fearing repercussions for questioning a senior professional. A medical student was present whom, having met the patient previously in clinical, tried to alert the registrar to the mistake he was about to make. The registrar shouted at the student that she should not interrupt surgery; she did not know what she was talking about and asked her to leave. Consequently the surgery proceeded with the end result being that the patient's healthy left kidney was removed, leaving them with only their diseased right kidney, which would eventually lead to the patient's unfortunate death. Frightening as these cases appear what is perhaps scarier is the thought of how those reported may be just the 'tip of the iceberg'.

When questioned about his action to allow his registrar to perform the surgery alone, the consultant had said that it was normal to allow capable registrars to do this. 'While the public perception is that medical knowledge steadily increases over time, this is not the case with many doctors reaching their peak in the middle of their careers.' He had found that his initial increasing interest in surgery had enhanced his abilities, but with time and practice the similar surgeries had become less exciting and so his lack of interest had correlated with worsening outcomes, thus justifying his decision to devolve responsibility in this case.

Question 36:
Which of the following, if true, most weakens the argument above?

A.   If incidences are severe enough to occur they will be reported.
B.   Doctors undergo extensive training to reduce risks.
C.   Thousand of operations happen every year with no problems.
D.   Some errors are unavoidable.
E.   The patient could have passed away even if the operation had been a complete success.

Question 37:
Which one of the following is the overall conclusion of the statement?

A.   The error that occurred was a result of the failure of safety precautions in place.
B.   Surgeries should only be performed by surgeons who know their patients well.
C.   The human element to medicine means errors will always occur.
D.   The safety procedures surrounding surgical procedures need to be reviewed.
E.   Some doctors are overconfident.

Question 38:

Which of the following is attributed as the original cause of the error?

A. The medical student not having asserted herself.
B. The poor handwriting in the chart.
C. The hierarchical system of medicine.
D. The registrar not having met the patient.
E. The patient being asleep.
F. The lack of the surgical skill possessed by the registrar.
G. The registrar's poor attitude.

Question 39:

What does the 'tip of the iceberg' refer to in the passage?

A. Problems we face every day.
B. The probable large numbers of medical errors that go unreported.
C. The difficulties of surgery.
D. Reported medical errors.
E. Problems within the NHS.

You may use the graphs below once, more than once, or not at all.

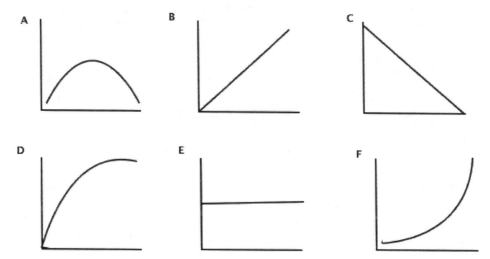

Question 40:

Which graph best describes the consultants' performance versus emotional arousal over his career?

A. A   B. B   C. C   D. D   E. E   F. F

Question 41:

Which graphs best describe the medical knowledge acquired over time?

Option	Public Perception	Consultant's Perception
A	B	B
B	B	D
C	B	F
D	D	B
E	D	D
F	D	F
G	F	B
H	F	D
I	F	F

Question 42:

Sadly, in recent times, the lack of exercise associated with sedentary lifestyles has increased in the developed world. The lack of opportunity for exercise is endemic and these countries have also seen a rise of diseases such as diabetes even in young people. In these developed countries, bodily changes such as increased blood pressure, that are usually associated with old age, are rapidly increasing. These are however still uncommon in undeveloped countries, where most people are physically active throughout the entirety of their lives.

Which one of the following can be concluded from the passage above?

A. Exercise has a greater effect on old people than young people.

B. Maintenance of good health is associated with lifelong exercise.

C. Changes in lifestyle will be necessary to cause increased life expectancies in developed countries.

D. Exercise is only beneficial when continued into old age.

E. Obesity and diabetes are the result of lack of exercise.

Questions 43 - 45 are based on the passage below:

'Midwives should now encourage women to, as often as possible, give birth at home. Not only is there evidence to suggest that normal births at home are as safe those as in hospital, but it removes the medicalisation of childbirth that emerged over the years. With the increase in availability of health resources we now, too often, use services such as a full medical team for a process that women have been completing single-handedly for thousands of years. Midwives are extensively trained to assist women during labour at home and capable enough to assess when there is a problem that requires a hospital environment. Expensive hospital births must and should move away from being standard practice, especially in an era where the NHS has far more demands on its services that it can currently afford.'

Question 43:

Which one of the following is the most appropriate conclusion from the statement?

A. People are over dependent on healthcare.

B. Some women prefer to have their babies in hospital.

C. Having a baby in hospital can actually be more risky than at home.

D. Childbirth has been over medicalised.

E. Encouraging women to have their babies at home may relieve some of the financial pressures on the NHS.

F. We should have more midwives than doctors.

Question 44:

Which one of the following if true most weakens the argument presented in the passage above?

A. Some women are scared of home births.

B. Home births are associated with poorer outcomes.

C. Midwives do not like performing home visits.

D. Some home births result in hospital births anyway.

Question 45:

Which one of the following describes what the statement cites as the cause for the 'medicalisation of childbirth'?

A. Women fear giving birth without a full medical team present.

B. Midwives are incapable of aiding childbirth without help.

C. Giving birth at home is not as safe as it used to be.

D. Excessive availability of health services.

E. Women only used to give birth at home because they could not do so at hospital.

Question 46:

We need to stop focussing so much attention on the dangers of fires. In 2011 there were only 242 deaths due to exposure to smoke, fire and flames, while there were 997 deaths from hernias. We need to think more proportionally as these statistics show that campaigns such as 'fire kills' are not necessary as comparison with the risk from the death from hernias clearly shows that fires are not as dangerous as they are perceived to be.

Which of the following statements identify a weakness in the above argument?

1. More people may die in fires if there were no campaigns about their danger and how to prevent them.
2. The smoke of a fire is more dangerous than it flames.
3. There may be more people with hernias than those in fires.

A. 1 only
B. 2 only
C. 3 only
D. 1 and 2 only
E. 1 and 3 only
F. 2 and 3 only
G. 1, 2 and 3

Question 47:

A survey of a school was taken to find out whether there was any correlation between the sports students played and the subjects they liked. The findings were as follows: some football players liked Maths and some of them liked History. All students liked English. None of the basketball players liked History, but all of them, as well as some rugby players liked Chemistry. All rugby players like Geography.

Based on the findings, which one of the below must be true?
A. Some of the footballers liked Maths and History.
B. Some of the rugby players liked three subjects.
C. Some rugby players liked History.
D. Some of the footballers liked English but did not like Maths and History.
E. Some basketball players like more than 3 subjects.

Question 48:

The control of illegal drug use is becoming increasingly difficult. New 'legal highs' are being manufactured which are slightly changed molecularly from illegal compounds so they are not technically illegal. These new 'legal drugs' are being brought onto the street at a rate of at least one per week, and so the authorities cannot keep up. Some health professionals therefore believe that the legality of drugs is becoming less relevant as to the potentially dangerous side effects. The fact that these new compounds are legal may however mean that the public are not aware of their equally high risks.

Which of the following are implied by the argument?
1. Some health professionals believe there is no value in making drugs illegal.
2. The major problem in controlling illegal drug use is the rapid manufacture of new drugs that are not classified as illegal.
3. The general public are not worried about the risks of legal or illegal highs.
4. There is no longer a good correlation between risk of drug taking and the legal status of the drug.

A. 1 only
B. 2 only
C. 1 and 4
D. 2 and 4
E. 2 and 3
F. 1,2,3 and 4

Question 49:

WilderTravel Inc. is a company which organises wilderness travel holidays, with activities such as trekking, mountain climbing, safari tours and wilderness survival courses. These activities carry inherent risks, so the directors of the company are drawing up a set of health regulations, with the aim of minimising the risks by ensuring that nobody participates in activities if they have medical complications meaning that doing so may endanger them. They consider the following guidelines:

'Persons with pacemakers, asthma or severe allergies are at significant risk of heart attack in low oxygen environments'. People undertaking mountain climbing activities with WilderTravel frequently encounter environments with low oxygen levels. The directors therefore decide that in order to ensure the safety of customers on WilderTravel holidays, one step that must be taken is to bar those with pacemakers, asthma or allergies from partaking in mountain climbing.

Which of the following best illustrates a flaw in this reasoning?

A. Participants should be allowed to assess the safety risks themselves, and should not be barred from activities if they decide the risk is acceptable.
B. They have assumed that all allergies carry an increased risk of heart attack, when the guidelines only say this applies to those with severe allergies.
C. The directors have failed to consider the health risks of people with these conditions taking part in other activities.
D. People with these conditions could partake in mountain climbing with other holiday organisers, and thus be exposed to danger of heart attack.

Question 50:

St John's Hospital in Northumbria is looking to recruit a new consultant cardiologist, and interviews a series of candidates. The interview panel determines that 3 candidates are clearly more qualified for the role than the others, and they invite these 3 candidates for a second interview. During this second interview, and upon further examination of their previous employment records, it becomes apparent that Candidate 3 is the most proficient at surgery of the 3, whilst Candidate 1 is the best at patient interaction and explaining the risks of procedures. Candidate 2, meanwhile, ranks between the other 2 in both these aspects.

The hospital director tells the interviewing team that the hospital already has a well-renowned team dedicated to patient interaction, but the surgical success record at the hospital is in need of improvement. The director issues instructions that therefore, it is more important that the new candidate is proficient at surgery, and patient interaction is less of a concern.

Which of the following is a conclusion that can be drawn from the Directors' comments?

A. The interviewing team should hire Candidate 2, in order to achieve a balance of good patient relations with good surgical records.
B. The interviewing team should hire Candidate 1, in order to ensure good patient interactions, as these are a vital part of a doctor's work.
C. The interviewing team should ignore the hospital director and assess the candidates further to see who would be the best fit.
D. The interviewing team should hire Candidate 3, in order to ensure that the new candidate has excellent surgical skills, to boost the hospital's success in this area.

Question 51:

Every winter in Britain, there are thousands of urgent callouts for ambulances in snowy conditions. The harsh conditions mean that ambulances cannot drive quickly, and are delayed in reaching patients. These delays cause many injuries and medical complications, which could be avoided with quicker access to treatment. Despite this, very few ambulances are equipped with winter tyres or special tyre coverings to help the ambulances deal with snow. Clearly, if more ambulances were fitted with winter tyres, then we could avoid many medical complications that occur each winter.

Which of the following is an assumption made in this passage?

A. Fitting winter tyres would allow ambulances to reach patients more quickly.

B. Ambulance trusts have sufficient funding to equip their vehicles with winter tyres.

C. Many medical complications could be avoided with quicker access to medical care.

D. There are no other alternatives to winter tyres that would allow ambulances to reach patients more quickly in snowy conditions.

Question 52:

Vaccinations have been one of the most outstanding and influential developments in medical history. Despite the huge successes, however, there is a strong anti-vaccination movement active in some countries, particularly the USA, who claim vaccines are harmful and ineffective.

There have been several high-profile events in recent years where anti-vaccine campaigners have been refused permission to enter countries for campaigns, or have had venues refuse to host them due to the nature of their campaigns. Many anti-vaccination campaigners have claimed this is an affront to free speech, and that they should be allowed to enter countries and obtain venues without hindrance. However, although free speech is desirable, an exception must be made here because the anti-vaccination campaign spreads misinformation to parents, causing vaccination to rates to drop.

When this happens, preventable infectious diseases often begin to increase, causing avoidable deaths of innocent members of the community, particularly so in children. Thus, in order to protect innocent people, we must continue to block the anti-vaccine campaigners from spreading misinformation freely by pressuring venues not to host anti-vaccination campaigners.

Which of the following best illustrates the principle that this argument follows?

A. Free speech is always desirable, and must not be compromised under any circumstances.

B. The right of innocent people to protection from infectious diseases is more important than the right of free speech.

C. The right of free speech does not apply when the party speaking is lying or spreading misinformation.

D. Public health programmes that achieve significant success in reducing the incidence of disease should be promoted.

Question 53:

In order for a tumour to grow larger than a few centimetres, it must first establish its own blood supply by promoting angiogenesis. Roger has a tumour in his abdomen, which is investigated at the Royal General Hospital. During the tests, they detect newly formed blood vessels in the tumour, showing that it has established its own blood supply. Thus, we should expect the tumour to grow significantly, and become larger than a few centimetres. Action must be taken to deal with this.

Which of the following best illustrates a flaw in this reasoning?

A. It assumes that the tumour in Roger's abdomen has established its own blood supply.

B. It assumes that a blood supply is necessary for a tumour to grow larger than a few centimetres.

C. It assumes that nothing can be done to stop the tumour once a blood supply has been established.

D. It assumes that a blood supply is sufficient for the tumour to grow larger than a few centimetres.

Question 54:

In this year's Great North Run, there are several dozen people running to raise money for the Great North Air Ambulance (GNAA), as part of a large national fundraising campaign. If the runners raise £500,000 between them, then the GNAA will be able to add a new helicopter to its fleet. However, the runners only raise a total of £420,000. Thus, the GNAA will not be able to get a new helicopter.

Which of the following best illustrates a flaw in this passage?

A. It has assumed that the GNAA will not be able to acquire a new helicopter without the runners raising £500,000.
B. It has assumed that that GNAA wishes to add a new helicopter to its fleet.
C. It has assumed that the GNAA does not have better things to spend the money on.
D. It has assumed that some running in the Great North Run are raising money for the GNAA.

Question 55:

Many courses, spanning Universities, colleges, apprenticeship institutions and adult skills courses should be subsidised by the government. This is because they improve the skills of those attending them. It has been well demonstrated that the more skilled people are, the more productive they are economically. Thus, government subsidies of many courses would increase overall economic productivity, and lead to increased growth.

Which of the following would most weaken this argument?

A. The UK already has a high level of growth, and does not need to accelerate this growth.
B. Research has demonstrated that higher numbers of people attending adult skills courses results in increased economic growth.
C. Research has demonstrated that the cost of many courses (to those taking them) has little effect on the number of people undertaking the courses.
D. Employers often seek to employ those with greater skill-sets, and appoint them to higher positions.

Question 56:

Pluto was once considered the 9th planet in the solar system. However, further study of the planet led to it being reclassified as a dwarf planet in 2006. One key factor in this reclassification was the discovery of many objects in the solar system with similar characteristics to Pluto, which were also placed into this new category of 'Dwarf Planet'. Some astronomers believe that Pluto should remain classified as a planet, along with the many entities similar to Pluto that have been discovered. Considering all of this, it is clear that if we were to reclassify Pluto as a planet, and maintain consistency with classification of astronomical entities, then the number of planets would significantly increase.

Which of the following best illustrates the main conclusion of this passage?

A. If Pluto is classified as a planet, then many other entities should also be planets, as they share similar characteristics.
B. Some astronomers believe Pluto should be classified as a planet.
C. Pluto should not be classified as a Planet, as this would also require many other entities to be classified as planets to ensure consistency.
D. If Pluto is to be classified as a planet, then the number of objects classified as planets should increase significantly.

Question 57:

2 trains depart from Birmingham at 5:30 pm. One of the trains is heading to London, whilst the other is heading to Glasgow. The distance from Birmingham to Glasgow is three times larger than the distance from Birmingham to London, and the train to London arrives at 6:30 pm. Thus, the train to Glasgow will arrive at 8:30pm.

Which of the following is an assumption made in this passage?

A. Both trains depart at the same time.
B. Both trains depart from Birmingham.
C. Both trains travel at the same speed.
D. The train heading to Glasgow has to travel three times as far as the train heading to London.

Question 58:

Carcinogenesis, oncogenesis and tumorigenesis are various names given to the generation of cancer, with the term literally meaning 'creation of cancer'. In order for carcinogenesis to happen, there are several steps that must occur. Firstly, a cell (or group of cells) must achieve immortality, and escape senescence (the inherent limitation of a cell's lifespan). Then they must escape regulation by the body, and begin to proliferate in an autonomous way. They must also become immune to apoptosis and other cell death mechanisms. Finally, they must avoid detection by the immune system, or survive its responses. If a single one of these steps fails to occur, then carcinogenesis will not be able to occur.

Which of the following is a conclusion that can be reliably drawn from this passage?

A. Several steps are essential for carcinogenesis.
B. If all the steps mentioned occur, then carcinogenesis will definitely occur.
C. The immune system is unable to tackle cells that have escaped regulation by the body.
D. There are various mechanisms by which carcinogenesis can occur.
E. The terminology for the creation of cancer is confusing.

Question 59:

P53 is one of the most crucial genes in the body, responsible for detecting DNA damage and halting cell replication until repair can occur. If repair cannot take place, P53 will signal for the cell to kill itself. These actions are crucial to prevent carcinogenesis, and a loss of functional P53 is identified in over 50% of all cancers. The huge importance of P53 towards protecting the cell from damaging mutations has led to it deservedly being known as 'the guardian of the genome'. The implications of this name are clear – any cell that has a mutation in P53 is at serious risk of developing a potentially dangerous mutation.

Which of the following **CANNOT** be reliably concluded from this passage?

A. P53 is responsible for detecting DNA damage.
B. Most cancers have lost functional P53.
C. P53 deserves its name 'guardian of the genome'.
D. A cell that has a mutation in P53 will develop damaging mutations.
E. None of the above.

Question 60:

Sam is buying a new car, and deciding whether to buy a petrol or a diesel model. He knows he will drive 9,000 miles each year. He calculates that if he drives a petrol car, he will spend £500 per 1,000 miles on fuel, but if he buys a diesel model he will only spend £300 per 1,000 miles on fuel. He calculates, therefore, that if he purchases a Diesel car, then this year he will make a saving of £1800, compared to if he bought the petrol car.

Which of the following is **NOT** an assumption that Sam has made?
A. The price of diesel will not fluctuate relative to that of petrol.
B. The cars will have the same initial purchase cost.
C. The cars will have the same costs for maintenance and garage expenses.
D. The cars will use the same amount of fuel.
E. All of the above are assumptions.

Question 61:

In the UK, cannabis is classified as a Class B drug, with a maximum penalty of up to 5 years imprisonment for possession, or up to 14 years for possession with intent to supply. The justification for drug laws in the UK is that classified drugs are harmful, addictive, and destructive to people's lives. However, available medical evidence indicates that cannabis is relatively safe, non-addictive and harmless. In particular, it is certainly shown to be less dangerous than alcohol, which is freely sold and advertised in the UK. The fact that alcohol can be freely sold and advertised, but cannabis, a less harmful drug, is banned highlights the gross inconsistencies in UK drugs policy.

Which of the following best illustrates the main conclusion of this passage?
A. Cannabis is a less dangerous drug than alcohol.
B. Alcohol should be banned, so we can ensure consistency in the UK drug policy.
C. Cannabis should not be banned, and should be sold freely, in order to ensure consistency in the UK drug policy.
D. The UK government's policy on drugs is grossly inconsistent.
E. Alcohol should not be advertised in the UK.

Question 62:

Every year in Britain, there are thousands of accidents at people's homes such as burns, broken limbs and severe cuts, which cause a large number of deaths and injuries. Despite this, very few households maintain a sufficient first aid kit equipped with bandages, burn treatments, splints and saline to clean wounds. If more households stocked sufficient first aid supplies, many of these accidents could be avoided.

Which of the following best illustrates a flaw in this argument?
A. It ignores the huge cost associated with maintaining good first aid supplies, which many households cannot afford.
B. It implies that presence of first aid equipment will lead to fewer accidents.
C. It ignores the many accidents that could not be treated even if first aid supplies were readily available.
D. It neglects to consider the need for trained first aid persons in order for first aid supplies to help in reducing the severity of injuries caused by accidents.

Question 63:

Researchers at SmithJones Inc., an international drug firm, are investigating a well-known historic compound, which is thought to reduce levels of DNA replication by inhibiting DNA polymerases. It is proposed that this may be able to be used to combat cancer by reducing the proliferation of cancer cells, allowing the immune system to combat them before they spread too far and become too damaging. Old experiments have demonstrated the effectiveness of the compound via monitoring DNA levels with a dye that stains DNA red, thus monitoring the levels of DNA present in cell clusters. They report that the compound is observed to reduce the rate at which DNA replicates. However, it is known that if researchers use the wrong solutions when carrying out these experiments, then the amount of red staining will decrease, suggesting DNA replication has been inhibited, even if it is not inhibited. As several researchers previously used this wrong solution, we can conclude that these experiments are flawed, and do not reflect what is actually happening.

Which of the following best illustrates a flaw in this argument?

A. From the fact that the compound inhibits DNA replication, it cannot be concluded that it has potential as an anticancer drug.
B. From the fact that the wrong solutions were used, it cannot be concluded that the experiments may produce misleading results.
C. From the fact that the experiments are old, it cannot be concluded that the wrong solutions were used.
D. From the fact that the compound is old, it cannot be concluded that it is safe.

Question 64:

Rotherham football club are currently top of the league, with 90 points. Their closest competitors are South Shields football club, with 84 points. Next week, the teams will play each other, and after this, they each have 2 games left before the end of the season. Each win is worth 3 points, a draw is worth 1 point, and a loss is worth 0 points. Thus, if Rotherham beat South Shields, they will win the league (as they will then be 9 points clear, and South Shields would only be able to earn 6 more points).

In the match of Rotherham vs. South Shields, Rotherham are winning until the 85th minute, when Alberto Simeone scores an equaliser for South Shields, and South Shields then go on to win the match. Thus, Rotherham will not win the league.

Which of the following best illustrates a flaw in this passage's reasoning?

A. It has assumed that Alberto Simeone scored the winning goal for South Shields.
B. It has assumed that beating South Shields was necessary for Rotherham to win the league, when in fact it was only sufficient.
C. Rotherham may have scored an equaliser later in the game, and not lost the match.
D. It has failed to consider what other teams might win the league.

Question 65:

Oakville Supermarkets is looking to build a new superstore, and a meeting of its directors has been convened to decide where the best place to build the supermarket would be. The Chairperson of the Board suggests that the best place would be Warrington, a town that does not currently have a large supermarket, and would thus give them an excellent share of the shopping market.

However, the CEO notes that the population of Warrington has been steadily declining for several years, whilst Middlesbrough has recently been experiencing high population growth. The CEO therefore argues that they should build the new supermarket in Middlesbrough, as they would then be within range of more people, and so of more potential customers.

Which of the following best illustrates a flaw in the CEO's reasoning?

A. Middlesbrough may already have other supermarkets, so the new superstore may get a lower share of the town's shoppers.

B. Despite the recent population changes, Warrington may still have a larger population than Middlesbrough.

C. Middlesbrough's population is projected to continue growing, whilst Warrington's is projected to keep falling.

D. Many people in Warrington travel to Liverpool or Manchester, 2 nearby major cities, in order to do their shopping.

Question 66:

Global warming is a key challenge facing the world today, and the changes in weather patterns caused by this phenomenon have led to the destruction of many natural habitats, causing many species to become extinct. Recent data has shown that extinctions have been occurring at a faster rate over the last 40 years than at any other point in the earth's history, exceeding the great Permian mass extinction, which wiped out 96% of life on earth. If this rate continues, over 50% of species on earth will be extinct by 2100. It is clear that in the face of this huge challenge, conservation programmes will require significantly increased levels of funding in order to prevent most of the species on earth from becoming extinct.

Which of the following are assumptions in this argument?

1. The rate of extinctions seen in the last 40 years will continue to occur without a step-up in conservation efforts.

2. Conservation programmes cannot prevent further extinctions without increased funding.

3. Global warming has caused many extinction events, directly or indirectly.

A. 1 only
B. 2 only
C. 3 only
D. 1 and 2
E. 1 and 3
F. 2 and 3
G. 1,2 and 3

Question 67:

After an election in Britain, the new government is debating what policy to adopt on the railway system, and whether it should be entirely privatised, or whether public subsidies should be used to supplement costs and ensure that sufficient services are run. Studies in Austria, which has high public funding for railways, have shown that the rail service is used by many people, and is highly thought of by the population. However, this is clearly down to the fact that Austria has many mountainous and high-altitude areas, which experience significant amounts of snow and ice. This makes many roads impassable, and travelling by road difficult. Thus, rail is often the only way to travel, explaining the high passenger numbers and approval ratings. Thus, the high public subsidies clearly have no effect.

Which of the following, if true, would weaken this argument?

1. France also has high public subsidy of railways, but does not have large areas where travel by road is difficult. The French railway also has high passenger numbers and approval ratings.
2. Italy also has high public subsidy of railways, but the local population dislike using the rail service, and it has poor passenger numbers.
3. There are many reasons affecting the passenger numbers and approval ratings of a given country's rail serviced.

A. 1 only
B. 2 only
C. 3 only
D. 1 and 2
E. 1 and 3
F. 2 and 3

Question 68:

In 2001-2002, 1,019 patients were admitted to hospital due to obesity. This figure was more than 11 times higher by 2011-12 when there were 11,736 patients admitted to hospital with the primary reason for admission being obesity. Data has shown higher percentages of both men and women were either obese or overweight in 2011 compared to 1993, with male obesity climbing from 58% to 65%, and female from 49% to 58%. Rates of adult obesity have increased even more steeply within this period – 13% to 24% for men and 16% to 26% for women.

Studies in 2011 found that nearly a third of children between 2 – 15 years were either overweight or obese, however this was not significantly different from 2010. Lifestyles are also becoming less healthy, with a decline in both children and adults eating the recommended number of fruit and vegetables each day and taking the recommended amount of exercise each week. The ease of availability of fast-food outlets may be partly to blame for the rising number of obese people. Education is required to teach people the importance of a healthy lifestyle, however people must take some personal responsibility for their health.

Using only information from the passage, which of the following statements is correct?

A. In 2011, there was a higher proportion of obese men than women.
B. Obesity rates are rising steeply for both males and females of all age groups.
C. Responsibility needs to be taken by both individuals and local authorities to effectively tackle the epidemic.
D. The main reason people eat fast food is because it's cheaper in times of reducing income.

Question 69:

Tobacco companies sell cigarettes despite being fully aware that cigarettes cause significant harm to the wellbeing of those that smoke them. Diseases caused or aggravated by smoking cost billions of pounds for the NHS to treat each year. This is despicable behaviour from the tobacco companies. Tobacco companies should be taxed, and the money raised put towards funding the NHS.

Which of the following conclusions **CANNOT** be drawn from the above?
A. There is a connection between lung cancer and smoking.
B. There is a connection between liver disease and smoking.
C. There is a connection between oral cancer and smoking.
D. All smokers drink excessively.
E. All of the above.

Question 70:

Investigations in the origins of species suggest that humans and the great apes have the same ancestors. This is suggested by the high degree of genetic similarity between humans and chimpanzees (estimated at 99%). At the same time there is an 84% homology between the human genome and that of pigs. This raises the interesting question of whether it would be possible to use pig or chimpanzee organs for the treatment of human disease.

Which conclusion can be reasonably drawn from the above article?
A. Pigs and chimpanzees have a common ancestor.
B. Pigs and humans have a common ancestor.
C. It can be assumed that chimpanzees will develop into humans if given enough time.
D. There seems to be great genetic homology across a variety of species.
E. Organs from pigs or chimpanzees present a good alternative for human organ donation.

Question 71:

Poor blood supply to a part of the body can cause damage of the affected tissue - i.e. lead to an infarction. There are a variety of known risk factors for vascular disease. Diabetes is a major risk factor. Other risk factors are more dependent on the individual as they represent individual choices such as smoking, poor dietary habits as well as little to no exercise. In some cases infarction of the limbs and in particular the feet can become very bad and extensive with patches of tissue dying. This is known as necrosis and is marked by affected area of the body turning black. Necrotic tissue is usually removed in surgery.

Which of the following statements **CANNOT** be concluded from the information in the above passage?
A. Smoking causes vascular disease.
B. Diabetes causes vascular disease.
C. Vascular disease always leads to infarctions.
D. Necrotic tissue must be removed surgically.
E. Necrotic tissue only occurs following severe infarction.
F. All of the above.

Question 72:

People who can afford to pay for private education should not have access to the state school system. This would allow more funding for students from lower income backgrounds. More funding will provide better resources for students from lower income backgrounds, and will help to bridge the gap in educational attainment between students from higher income and lower income backgrounds.

Which of the following statements, if true, would most strengthen the above argument?

A. Educational attainment is a significant factor in determining future prospects.

B. Providing better resources for students has been demonstrated to lead to an increase in educational attainment.

C. Most people who can afford to do so choose to purchase private education for their children.

D. A significant gap exists in educational attainment between students from high income and low-income backgrounds.

E. Most schools currently receive a similar amount of funding relative to the number of students in the school.

Question 73:

Increasing numbers of people are choosing to watch films on DVD in recent years. In the past few years, cinemas have lost customers, causing them to close down. Many cinemas have recently closed, removing an important focal point for many local communities and causing damage to those communities. Therefore, we should ban DVDs in order to help local communities.

Which of the following best states an assumption made in this argument?

A. The cinemas that have recently closed have done so because of reduced profits due to people choosing to watch DVDs instead.

B. Cinemas being forced to close causes damage to local communities.

C. DVDs are improving local communities by allowing people to meet up and watch films together.

D. Sales of DVDs have increased due to economic growth.

E. Local communities have called for DVDs to be banned.

Question 74:

Aeroplanes are the fastest form of transport available. An aeroplane can travel a given distance in less time than a train or a car. John needs to travel from Glasgow to Birmingham. If he wants to arrive as soon as possible, he should travel by aeroplane.

Which of the following best illustrates a flaw in this argument?

A. One day, there could be faster cars built that could travel as fast as aeroplanes.

B. Travelling by air is often more expensive.

C. It ignores the time taken to travel to an airport and check in to a flight, which may mean he will arrive later if travelling by aeroplane.

D. John may not own a car, and thus may not have any option.

E. John may not be legally allowed to make the journey.

Question 75:

During autumn, spiders frequently enter people's homes to escape the cold weather. Many people dislike spiders and seek ways to prevent them from entering properties, leading to spider populations falling as they struggle to cope with the cold weather. Studies have demonstrated that when spider populations fall, the population of flies rises. Higher numbers of flies are associated with an increase in food poisoning cases. Therefore, people must not seek to prevent spiders from entering their homes.

Which of the following best illustrates the main conclusion of this argument?

A. People should not dislike spiders being present in their homes.

B. People should seek methods to prevent flies from entering their homes.

C. People should actively encourage spiders to occupy their homes to increase biodiversity.

D. People should accept the presence of spiders in their homes to reduce the incidence of food poisoning.

E. Spiders should be cultivated and used as a biological pest control to combat flies.

Question 76:

Each year, thousands of people acquire infections during prolonged stays at hospital. Concurrently, bacteria are becoming resistant to antibiotics at an ever-increasing rate. In spite of this, progressively less pharmaceutical companies are investing in research into new antibiotics, and the number of antibiotics coming onto the market is decreasing. As a result, the number of antibiotics that can be used to treat infections is falling. If pharmaceutical companies were pressured into investing in new antibiotic research, many lives could be saved.

Which of the following best illustrates a flaw in this argument?

A. It assumes the infections acquired during stays at hospital are resulting in deaths.

B. It ignores the fact that many people never have to stay in hospital.

C. It does not take into account the fact that antibiotics do not produce much profit for pharmaceutical companies.

D. It ignores the fact that some hospital-acquired infections are caused by organisms that cannot be treated by antibiotics, such as viruses.

E. It assumes that bacterial resistance to antibiotics has not been happening for some time.

Question 77:

Katherine has shaved her armpits most of her adult life, but has now decided to stop. She explains her reasons for this to John, saying she does not like the pressures society puts on women to be shaven in this area. John listens to her reasons, but ultimately responds 'just because you explain why I should find your hairiness attractive, it does not mean I will. I find you unattractive, as I do not like girls with hair on their arm pits.'

What assumption has John made?

A. That just because he finds Katherine unattractive, he would find other girls with unshaven arm pits unattractive.

B. That Katherine is trying to make John find her armpit hair attractive.

C. That Katherine will never conceal her armpit hair.

D.   Katherine must be wrong, because she is a woman.

E. That Katherine thinks women should stop shaving.

Question 78:

Medicine has improved significantly over the last century. Better medicine causes a reduction in the death rate from all causes. However, as people get older, they suffer from infectious disease more readily.

Many third world countries have a high rate of deaths from infectious disease. Sunita argues that this high death rate is caused by better medicine, which has given an ageing population, thus giving a high rate of deaths from infectious disease as elderly people suffer from infectious disease more readily. Sunita believes that better medicine is thus indirectly responsible for this high death rate from infectious disease.

However, this cannot be the case. In third world countries, most people do not live to old age, often dying from infectious disease at a young age. Therefore, an ageing population cannot be the reason behind the high rate of death from infectious disease. As better medicine causes a reduction in the death rate from all causes, it is clear that better medicine will lead to a reduction in the death rate from infectious disease in third world countries.

Which of the following best states the main conclusion of this argument?
A. We can expect that improvements in medicine seen over the last century will improve.
B. Better medicine is not responsible for the increased prevalence of infectious disease in third world countries.
C. Better medicine has caused the overall death rate of third world countries to increase.
D. Better medicine will cause a decrease in the rate of death from infectious disease in third world countries.
E. As people get older, they suffer from infectious disease more readily.

Question 79:

Bristol and Cardiff are 2 cities with similar demographics, and located in a roughly similar area of the country. Bristol has higher demand for housing than Cardiff. Therefore, a house in Bristol will cost more than a similar house in Cardiff.

Which of the following best illustrates an assumption in the statement above?
A. House prices will be higher if demand for housing is higher.
B. People can commute from Cardiff to Bristol.
C. Supply of housing in Cardiff will not be lower than in Bristol.
D. Bristol is a better place to live.
E. Cardiff has sufficient housing to provide for the needs of its communities.

Question 80:

Jellicoe Motors is a small motor company in Sheffield, employing 3 people. The company is hiring a new mechanic and interviews several candidates. New research into production lines has indicated that having employees with a good ability to work as part of a team boosts a company's productivity and profits. Therefore, Jellicoe motors should hire a candidate with good team-working skills.

Which of the following best illustrates the main conclusion of this argument?
A. Jellicoe Motors should not hire a new mechanic.
B. Jellicoe motors should hire a candidate with good team-working skills in order to boost their productivity and profits.
C. Jellicoe motors should hire several new candidates in order to form a good team, and boost their productivity.
D. If Jellicoe motors does not hire a candidate with good team-working skills, they may struggle to be profitable.
E. Jellicoe motors should not listen to the new research.

Question 81:

Research into new antibiotics does not normally hold much profit for pharmaceutical firms. As a consequence many firms are not investing in antibiotic research, and very few new antibiotics are being produced. However, with bacteria becoming increasingly resistant to current antibiotics, new ones are desperately needed to avoid running the risk of thousands of deaths from bacterial infections. Therefore, the UK government must provide financial incentives for pharmaceutical companies to invest in research into new antibiotics.

Which of the following best expresses the main conclusion of this argument?

A. If bacteria continue to become resistant to antibiotics, there could be thousands of deaths from bacterial infections.

B. Pharmaceutical firms are not investing in new antibiotic research due to a lack of potential profit.

C. If the UK government invests in research into new antibiotics, thousands of lives will be saved.

D. The pharmaceutical firms should invest in areas of research that are profitable, and ignore antibiotic research.

E. The UK government must provide financial incentives for pharmaceutical firms to invest into antibiotic research if it wishes to avoid risking thousands of deaths from bacterial infections.

Question 82:

People in developing countries use far less water per person than those in developed countries. It is estimated that at present, people in the developing world use an average of 30 litres of water per person per day, whilst those in developed countries use on average 70 litres of water per person per day. It is estimated that for the current world population, an average water usage of 60 litres per person per day would be sustainable, but any higher than this would be unsustainable.

The UN has set development targets such that in 20 years, people living in developing countries will be using the same amount of water per person per day as those living in developed countries. Assuming the world population stays constant for the next 20 years, if these targets are met the world's population will be using water at an unsustainable rate.

Which of the following, if true, would most weaken the argument above?

A. The prices of water bills are dropping in developed countries like the UK.

B. The level of water usage in developed countries is falling, and may be below 60 litres per person per day in 20 years.

C. The population of all developing countries is less than the population of all developed countries.

D. Climate change is likely to decrease the amount of water available for human use over the next 20 years.

E. The UN's development targets are unlikely to be met.

Question 83:

In this Senior Management post we need someone who can keep a cool head in a crisis and react quickly to events. The applicant says he suffers from a phobia about flying, and panics especially when an aircraft is landing and that therefore he would prefer not to travel abroad on business if it could be avoided. He is obviously a very nervous type of person who would clearly go to pieces and panic in an emergency and fail to provide the leadership qualities necessary for the job. Therefore this person is not a suitable candidate for the post.

Which of the following highlights the biggest flaw in the argument above?
A. It falsely assumes that phobias are untreatable or capable of being eliminated.
B. It falsely assumes that the person appointed to the job will need to travel abroad.
C. It falsely assumes that a specific phobia indicates a general tendency to panic.
D. It falsely assumes that people who stay cool in a crisis will be good leaders.
E. It fails to take into account other qualities the person might have for the post.

Question 84:

There are significant numbers of people attending university every year, as many as 45% of 18 year olds. As a result, there are many more graduates entering the workforce with better skills and better earning potential. Going to university makes economic sense and we should encourage as many people to go there as possible.

Which of the following highlights the biggest flaw in the argument above?
A. There are no more university places left.
B. Students can succeed without going to university.
C. Not all degrees equip students with the skills needed to earn higher salaries.
D. Some universities are better than others.

Question 85:

Young people spend too much time watching television, which is bad for them. Watching excessive amounts of TV is linked to obesity, social exclusion and can cause eye damage. If young people were to spend just one evening a week playing sport or going for a walk the benefits would be manifold. They would lose weight, feel better about themselves and it would be a sociable activity. Exercise is also linked to strong performance at school and so young people would be more likely to perform well in their exams.

Which of the following highlights the biggest flaw in the argument above?
A. Young people can watch sport on television.
B. There are many factors that affect exam performance.
C. Television does not necessarily have any damaging effect.
D. Television and sport are not linked.

Question 86:

Campaigners pushing for legalisation of cannabis have many arguments for their cause. Most claim there is little evidence of any adverse affects to health caused by cannabis usage, that many otherwise law-abiding people are users of cannabis and that in any case, prohibition of drugs does not reduce their usage. Legalising cannabis would also reduce crime associated with drug trafficking and would provide an additional revenue stream for the government.

Which of the following best represents the conclusion of the passage?

A. Regular cannabis users are unlikely to have health problems.
B. Legalising cannabis would be good for cannabis users.
C. There are multiple reasons to legalise cannabis.
D. Prohibition is an effective measure to reduce drugs usage.
E. Drug associated crime would reduce if cannabis was legal.

Question 87:

Mohan has been offered a new job in Birmingham, starting in several months with a fixed salary. In order to ensure he can afford to live in Birmingham on his new salary, Mohan compares the prices of some houses in Birmingham. He finds that a 2 bedroomed house will cost £200,000. A 3 bedroomed house will cost £250,000. A 4 bedroomed house with a garden will cost £300,000.

Mohan's bank tells him that if he is earning the salary of the job he has been offered, they will grant him a mortgage for a house costing up to £275,000. After a month of deliberation, Mohan accepts the job and decides to move to Wolverhampton. He begins searching for a house to buy. He reasons that he will not be able to purchase a 4-bedroomed house.

Which of the following is NOT an assumption that Mohan has made?

A. A house in Wolverhampton will cost the same as a similar house in Birmingham.
B. A different bank will not offer him a mortgage for a more expensive house on the same salary.
C. The salary for the job could increase, allowing him to purchase a more expensive house.
D. A 4-bedroomed house without a garden will not cost less than a 4-bedroomed house with a garden.
E. House prices in Birmingham will not have fall in the time between now and Mohan purchasing a house.

Question 88:

We should teach the Holocaust in schools. It is important that young people see what it was like for Jewish people under Nazi rule. If we expose the harsh realities to impressionable people then this will help improve tolerance of other races. It will also prevent other such terrible events happening again.

Which is the best conclusion?

A. We should teach about the Holocaust in schools.
B. The Holocaust was a tragedy.
C. The Nazis were evil.
D. We should not let terrible events happen again.
E. Educating people is the best solution to the world's problems.

Question 89:

The popular series 'Game of Thrones' should not be allowed on television because it shows scenes of a disturbing nature, in particular scenes of rape. Children may find themselves watching the programme on TV, and then going on to commit the terrible crime of rape, mimicking what they have watched.

Which of the following best illustrates a flaw in this argument?
A. Children may also watch the show on DVD.
B. Adults may watch the show on television.
C. Watching an action does not necessarily lead to recreating the action yourself.
D. There are lots of non-violent scenes in the show.

Question 90:

The TV series 'House of Cards' teaches us all a valuable lesson: the world is not a place that rewards kind behaviour. The protagonist of the series, Frank Underwood, uses intrigue and guile to achieve his goals, and through clever political tactics he is able to climb in rank. If he were to be kinder to people, he would not be able to be so successful. Success is predicated on his refusal to conform to conventional morality. The TV series should be shown to small children in schools, as it could teach them how to achieve their dreams.

Which of the following is an assumption made in the argument?
A. Children pay attention to school lessons.
B. The TV series is sufficiently entertaining.
C. One cannot both obey a moral code and succeed.
D. Frank Underwood is a likable character.

Question 91:

Freddy makes lewd comments on a female passer-by's body to his friend, Neil, loud enough for the woman in question to hear. Neil is uncomfortable with this, and states that it is inappropriate for Freddy to do so, and that Freddy is being sexist. Freddy refutes this, and Neil retorts that Freddy would not make these comments about a man's body. Freddy replies by saying 'it is not sexist, I am a feminist, I believe in equality for men and women.'

Which of the following describes a flaw made in Freddy's logic?
A. A self-proclaimed feminist could still say a sexist thing.
B. The female passer-by in question felt uncomfortable.
C. Neil, too, considers himself a feminist.
D. It would still not be OK to make lewd comments at male passers-by.
E. Lewd comments are always inappropriate.

Question 92:

The release of CO_2 from consumption of fossil fuels is the main reason behind global warming, which is causing significant damage to many natural environments throughout the world. One significant source of CO_2 emissions is cars, which release CO_2 as they use up petrol. In order to tackle this problem, many car companies have begun to design cars with engines that do not use as much petrol. However, engines which use less petrol are not as powerful, and less powerful cars are not attractive to the public. If a car company produces cars which are not attractive to the public, they will not be profitable.

Which of the following best illustrates the main conclusion of this argument?
A. Car companies which produce cars that use less petrol will not be profitable.
B. The public prefer more powerful cars.
C. Car companies should prioritise profits over helping the environment.
D. Car companies should seek to produce engines that use less petrol but are still just as powerful.
E. The public are not interested in helping the environment.

SECTION 1: Problem Solving Questions

Section 1 problem solving questions are arguably the hardest to prepare for. However, there are some useful techniques you can employ to solve some types of questions much more quickly:

Construct Equations

Some of the problems in Section 1 are quite complex and you'll need to be comfortable with turning prose into equations and manipulating them. For example, when you read "Mark is twice as old as Jon" – this should immediately register as M = 2J. Once you get comfortable forming equations, you can start to approach some of the harder questions in this book (and past papers) which may require you to form and solve simultaneous equations. Consider the example:

Nick has a sleigh that contains toy horses and clowns and counts 44 heads and 132 legs in his sleigh. Given that horses have one head and four legs, and clowns have one head and two legs, calculate the difference between the number of horses and clowns.

A. 0
B. 5
C. 22
D. 28
E. 132
F. More information is needed.

To start with, let C= Clowns and H= Horses.
For Heads: $C + H = 44$; For Legs: $2C + 4H = 132$
This now sets up your two equations that you can solve simultaneously.
$C = 44 - H$ so $2(44 - H) + 4H = 132$
Thus, $88 - 2H + 4H = 132$;
Therefore, $2H = 44$; $H = 22$
Substitute back in to give $C = 44 - H = 44 - 22 = 22$
Thus the difference between horses and clowns $= C - H = 22 - 22 = 0$

It's important you are able to do these types of questions quickly (and **without resorting to trial & error** as they are commonplace in section 1.

Diagrams

When a question asks about timetables, orders or sequences, draw out diagrams. By doing this, you can organise your thoughts and help make sense of the question.

"Mordor is West of Gondor but East of Rivendale. Lorien is midway between Gondor and Mordor. Erebus is West of Mordor. Eden is not East of Gondor."

*Which of the following **cannot** be concluded?*

A. Lorien is East of Erebus and Mordor.
B. Mordor is West of Gondor and East of Erebus.
C. Rivendale is west of Lorien and Gondor.
D. Gondor is East of Mordor and East of Lorien.
E. Erebus is West of Mordor and West of Rivendale.

Whilst it is possible to solve this in your head, it becomes much more manageable if you draw a quick diagram and plot the positions of each town:

Now, it's a simple case of going through each option and seeing if it is correct according to the diagram. You can now easily see that Option E- Erebus cannot be west of Rivendale.

Don't feel that you have to restrict yourself to linear diagrams like this either – for some questions you may need to draw tables or even Venn diagrams. Consider the example:

Slifers and Osiris are not legendary. Krakens and Minotaurs are legendary. Minotaurs and Lords are both divine. Humans are neither legendary nor divine.

A.   Krakens may be only legendary or legendary and divine.
B.   Humans are not divine.
C.   Slifers are only divine.
D.   Osiris may be divine.
E.   Humans and Slifers are the same in terms of both qualities.

Constructing a Venn diagram allows us to quickly see that the position of Osiris and Krakens aren't certain. Thus, A and D must be true. Humans are neither so B is true. Krakens may be divine so A is true. E cannot be concluded as Slifers are divine but are humans are not. Thus, E is False.

Spatial Reasoning

There are usually 1-2 spatial reasoning questions every year. They usually give nets for a shape or a patterned cuboid and ask which options are possible rotations. Unfortunately, they are extremely difficult to prepare for because the skills necessary to solve these types of questions can take a very long time to improve. The best thing you can do to prepare is to familiarise yourself with the basics of how cube nets work and what the effect of transformations are e.g. what happens if a shape is reflected in a mirror etc.

It is also a good idea to try to learn to draw basic shapes like cubes from multiple angles if you can't do so already. Finally, remember that if the shape is straightforward like a cube, it might be easier for you to draw a net, cut it out and fold it yourself to see which of the options are possible.

Problem Solving Questions

Question 93:

Pilbury is south of Westside, which is south of Harrington. Twotown is north of Pilbury and Crewville but not further north than Westside. Crewville is:

A. South of Westside, Pilbury and Harrington but not necessarily Twotown.
B. North of Pilbury, and Westside.
C. South of Westside and Twotown, but north of Pilbury.
D. South of Westside, Harrington and Twotown but not necessarily Pilbury.
E. South of Harrington, Westside, Twotown and Pilbury.

Question 94:

The hospital coordinator is making the rota for the ward for next week; two of Drs Evans, James and Luca must be working on weekdays, none of them on Sundays and all of them on Saturdays. Dr Evans works 4 days a week including Mondays and Fridays. Dr Luca cannot work Monday or Thursday. Only Dr James can work 4 days consecutively, but he cannot do 5.

What days does Dr James work?

A. Saturday, Sunday and Monday.
B. Monday, Tuesday, Wednesday, Thursday and Saturday.
C. Monday, Thursday Friday and Saturday.
D. Tuesday, Wednesday, Friday and Saturday.
E. Monday, Tuesday, Wednesday, Thursday and Friday.

Question 95:

Michael, a taxi driver, charges a call out rate and a rate per mile for taxi rides. For a 4 mile ride he charges £11, and for a 5 mile ride, £13.

How much does he charge for a 9-mile ride?

A. £15   B. £17   C. £19   D. £20   E. £21

Question 96:

Goblins and trolls are not magical. Fairies and goblins are both mythical. Elves and fairies are magical. Gnomes are neither mythical nor magical.

Which of the following is **FALSE**?

A. Elves may be only magical or magical and mythical.
B. Gnomes are not mythical.
C. Goblins are only mythical.
D. Trolls may be mythical.
E. Gnomes and goblins are the same in terms of both qualities.

Question 97:

Jessica runs a small business making bespoke wall tiles. She has just had a rush order for 100 tiles placed that must be ready for today at 7pm. The client wants the tiles packed all together, a process which will take 15 minutes. Only 50 tiles can go in the kiln at any point and they must be put in the kiln to heat for 45 minutes. The tiles then sit in the kiln to cool before they can be packed, a process which takes 20 minutes. While tiles are in the kiln Jessica is able to decorate more tiles at a rate of 1 tile per minute.

What is the latest time Jessica can start making the tiles?

A. 2:55pm   B. 3:15pm   C. 3:30pm   D. 3:45pm

Question 98:

Pain nerve impulses are twice as fast as normal touch impulses. If Yun touches a boiling hot pan this message reaches her brain, 1 metre away, in 1 millisecond.

What is the speed of a normal touch impulse?

A. 5 m/s   B. 20 m/s   C. 50 m/s   D. 200m/s   E. 500 m/s

Question 99:

A woman has two children Melissa and Jack, yearly, their birthdays are 3 months apart, both being on the 22nd. The woman wishes to continue the trend of her children's names beginning with the same letter as the month they were born. If her next child, Alina is born on the 22nd 2 months after Jack's birthday, how many months after Alina is born will Melissa have her next birthday?

A. 2 months   B. 4 months   C. 5 months   D. 6 months   E. 7 months

Question 100:

Policemen work in pairs. PC Carter, PC Dirk, PC Adams and PC Bryan must work together but not for more than seven days in a row, which PC Adams and PC Bryan now have. PC Dirk has worked with PC Carter for 3 days in a row. PC Carter does not want to work with PC Adams if it can be avoided.

Who should work with PC Bryan?

A. PC Carter
B. PC Dirk
C. PC Adams
D. Nobody is available under the guidelines above.

Question 101:

My hair-dressers charges £30 for a haircut, £50 for a cut and blow-dry, and £60 for a full hair dye. They also do manicures, of which the first costs £15, and includes a bottle of nail polish, but are subsequently reduced by £5 if I bring my bottle of polish. The price is reduced by 10% if I book and pay for the next 5 appointments in advance and by 15% if I book at least the next 10.

I want to pay for my next 5 cut and blow-dry appointments, as well as for my next 3 manicures. How much will it cost?

A. £170   B. £255   C. £260   D. £285   E. £305

Question 102:

Alex, Bertha, David, Gemma, Charlie, Elena and Frankie are all members of the same family consisting of three children, two of whom, Frankie and Gemma are girls. No other assumption of gender based on name can be established. There are also four adults. Alex is a doctor and is David's brother. One of them is married to Elena, and they have two children. Bertha is married to David; Gemma is their child.
Who is Charlie?

A. Alex's daughter
B. Frankie's father
C. Gemma's brother
D. Elena's son
E. Gemma's sister

Question 103:

At 14:30 three medical students were asked to examine a patient's heart. Having already watched their colleague, the second two students were twice as fast as the first to examine. During the 8 minutes break after the final student had finished, they were told by their consultant that they had taken too long and so should go back and do the examinations again. The second time all the students took half as long as they had taken the first time with the exception of the first student who, instead took the same time as his two colleagues' second attempt. Assuming there was a one minute change over time between each student and they were finished by 15:15, how long did the second student take to examine the first time?

A. 3 minutes   B. 4 minutes   C. 6 minutes   D. 7 minutes   E. 8 minutes

Question 104:

I pay for 2 chocolate bars that cost £1.65 each with a £5 note. I receive 8 coins change, only 3 of which are the same.

Which **TWO** coins do I not receive in my change?

A. 1p   C. 5p   E. 20p   G. £1

B. 2p   D. 10p   F. £2

Question 105:

Two 140m long trains are running at the same speed in opposite directions. If they cross each other in 14 seconds then what is speed of each train?

A. 10 km/hr   B. 18 km/hr   C. 32 km/hr   D. 36 km/hr   E. 42 km/hr

Question 106:

Anil has to refill his home's swimming pool. He has four hoses which all run at different speeds. Alone, the first would completely fill the pool with water in 6 hours, the second in two days, the third in three days and the fourth in four days.

Using all the hoses together, how long will it take to fill the pool to the nearest quarter of an hour?

A. 4 hours 15 minutes

B. 4 hours 30 minutes

C. 4 hours 45 minutes

D. 5 hours

E. 5 hours 15 minutes

Question 107:

An ant is stuck in a 30 cm deep ditch. When the ant reaches the top of the ditch he will be able to climb out straight away. The ant is able to climb 3 cm upwards during the day, but falls back 2 cm at night.

How many days does it take for the ant to climb out of the ditch?

A. 27   B. 28   C. 29   D. 30   E. 31

Question 108:

When buying his ingredients a chef gets a discount of 10% when he buys 10 or more of each item, and 20% discount when he buys 20 or more. On one order he bought 5 sausages and 10 Oranges and paid £8.50. On another, he bought 10 sausages and 10 apples and paid £9, on a third he bought 30 oranges and paid £12.

How much would an order of 2 oranges, 13 sausages and 12 apples cost?

A. £12.52   B. £12.76   C. £13.52   D. £13.76   E. £13.80

Question 109:

My hairdressers encourage all of its clients to become members. By paying an annual member fee, the cost of haircuts decreases. VIP membership costs £125 annually with a £10 reduction on haircuts. Executive VIP membership costs £200 for the year with a £15 reduction per haircut. At the moment I am not a member and pay £60 per haircut. I know how many haircuts I have a year, and I work out that by becoming a member on either programme it would work out cheaper, and I would save the same amount of money per year on either programme.

How much will I save this year by buying membership?

A. £10   B. £15   C. £25   D. £30   E. £50

Question 110:

If criminals, thieves and judges are represented below:

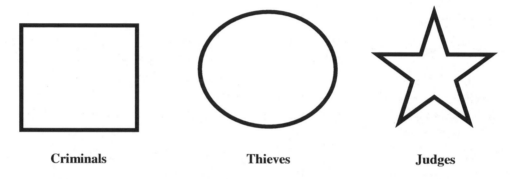

| **Criminals** | **Thieves** | **Judges** |

Assuming that judges must have clean record, all thieves are criminals and all those who are guilty are convicted of their crimes, which of one of the following best represents their interaction?

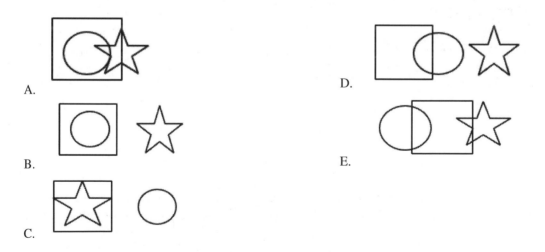

A.

B.

C.

D.

E.

Question 111:

The months of the year have been made into number codes. The code is comprised of three factors, including two of these being related the letters that make up the name of the month. No two months would have the same first number. But some such as March, which has the code 3513, have the same last number as others, such as May, which has the code 5313. October would be coded as 10715 while February is 286.

What would be the code for April?

A. 154   B. 441   C. 451   D. 514   E. 541

Question 112:

A mother gives yearly birthday presents of money to her children based on the age and their exam results. She gives them £5 each plus £3 for every year they are older than 5, and a further £10 for every A* they achieved in their results. Josie is 16 and gained 9 A*s in her results. Although Josie's brother Carson is 2 years older he receives £44 less a year for his birthday.

How many more A*s did Josie get than Carson?

A. 2   B. 3   C. 4   D. 5   E. 10

Question 113:

Apples are more expensive than pears, which are more expensive than oranges. Peaches are more expensive than oranges. Apples are less expensive than grapes.

Which two of the following must be true?

A. Grapes are less expensive than oranges.
B. Peaches may be less expensive than pears.
C. Grapes are more expensive than pears.
D. Pears and peaches are the same price.
E. Apples and peaches are the same price.

Question 114:

What is the minimum number of straight cutting motions needed to slice a cylindrical cake into 8 equally sized pieces?

A. 2   B. 3   C. 4   D. 5   E. 6   F. 8

Question 115

Three friends, Mark, Russell and Tom had agreed to meet for lunch at 12 PM on Sunday. Daylight saving time (GMT+1) had started at 2 AM the same day, where clocks should be put forward by one hour. Mark's phone automatically changes the time but he does not realise this so when he wakes up he puts his phone forward an hour and uses his phone to time his arrival to lunch. Tom puts all of his clocks forward one hour at 7 AM. Russell forgets that the clocks should go forward, wakes at 10 AM doesn't change his clocks. All of the friends arrive on time as far as they are concerned.

Assuming that none of the friends realise any errors before arriving, which **TWO** of the following statements are **FALSE**?

A. Tom arrives at 12 PM (GMT +1).
B. All three friends arrive at the same time.
C. There is a 2 hour difference between when the first and last friend arrive.
D. Mark arrives late.
E. Mark arrives at 1 PM (GMT+3).
F. Russell arrives at 12 PM (GMT+0).

Question 116:

A class of young students has a pet spider. Deciding to play a practical joke on their teacher, one day during morning break one of the students put the spider in their teachers' desk. When first questioned by the head teacher, Mr Jones, the five students who were in the classroom during morning break all lied about what they saw. Realising that the students were all lying, Mr Jones called all 5 students back individually and, threatened with suspension, all the students told the truth. Unfortunately Mr Jones only wrote down the student's statements not whether they had been told in the truthful or lying questioning.

The students' two statements appear below:

Archie: "It wasn't Edward. "

      "It was Bella."

Charlotte: "It was Edward."

      "It wasn't Archie"

Darcy: "It was Charlotte"

      "It was Bella"

Bella: "It wasn't Charlotte."

      "It wasn't Edward."

Edward: "It was Darcy"

      "It wasn't Archie"

Who put the spider in the teacher's desk?

A. Edward
B. Bella
C. Darcy

D. Charlotte
E. More information needed.

Question 117:

Dr Massey wants to measure out 0.1 litres of solution. Unfortunately the lab assistant dropped the 200 ml measuring cylinder, and so the scientist only has a 300 ml and a half litre-measuring beaker. Assuming he cannot accurately use the beakers to measure anything less than their full capacity, what is the minimum volume he will have to use to be able to ensure he measures the right amount?

A. 100 ml
B. 200 ml

C. 300 ml
D. 400 ml

E. 500 ml
F. 600 ml

Question 118:

Francis lives on a street with houses all consecutively numbered evenly. When one adds up the value of all the house numbers it totals 870.

In order to determine Francis' house number:

1. The relative position of Francis' house must be known.
2. The number of houses in the street must be known.
3. At least three of the house numbers must be known.

A. 1 only
B. 2 only
C. 3 only

D. 1 and 2
E. 2 and 3

Question 119:

There were 20 people exercising in the cardio room of a gym. Four people were about to leave when suddenly a man collapsed on one of the machines. Fortunately a doctor was on the machine beside him. Emerging from his office, one of the personal trainers called an ambulance. In the 5 minutes that followed before the two paramedics arrived, half of the people who were leaving, left upon hearing the commotion, and eight people came in from the changing rooms to hear the paramedics pronouncing the man dead.

How many living people were left in the room?

A. 25   B. 26   C. 27   D. 28   E. 29   F. 30

Question 120:

A man and woman are in an accident. They both suffer the same trauma, which causes both of them to lose blood at a rate of 0.2 Litres/minute. At normal blood volume the man has 8 litres and the woman 7 litres, and people collapse when they lose 40% of their normal blood volume.

Which **TWO** of the following are true?

A. The man will collapse 2 minutes before the woman.
B. The woman collapses 2 minutes before the man.
C. The total blood loss is 5 litres.
D. The woman has 4.2 litres of blood in her body when she collapses.
E. The man's blood loss is 4.8 litres when he collapses.
F. Blood loss is at a rate of 2 litres every 12 minutes.

Question 121:

Jenny, Helen and Rachel have to run a distance of 13 km. Jenny runs at a pace of 8 kmph, Helen at a pace of 10 kmph, and Rachel 11 kmph.

If Jenny sets off 15 minutes before Helen, and 25 minutes before Rachel, what order will they arrive at the destination?

A. Jenny, Helen, Rachel.
B. Helen, Rachel, Jenny.
C. Helen, Jenny, Rachel.
D. Rachel, Helen, Jenny.
E. Jenny, Rachel, Helen.
F. None of the above.

Question 122:

On a specific day at a GP surgery 150 people visited the surgery and common complaints were recorded as a percentage of total patients. Each patient could use their appointment to discuss up to 2 complaints. 56% flu-like symptoms, 48% pain, 20% diabetes, 40% asthma/COPD and 30% high blood pressure.

Which statement **must** be true?
A. A minimum of 8 patients complained of pain and flu-like symptoms.
B. No more than 45 patients complained of high blood pressure and diabetes.
C. There were a minimum of 21 patients who did not complain about flu-like symptoms or high blood pressure.
D. There were actually 291 patients who visited the surgery.
E. None of the above.

Question 123:

All products in a store were marked up by 15%. They were subsequently reduced in a sale with quoted saving of 25% from the higher price. What is the true reduction from the original price?
A. 5%
B. 10%
C. 13.75%
D. 18.25%
E. 20%
F. None of the above.

Question 124:

A recipe states it makes 12 pancakes and requires the following ingredients: 2 eggs, 100g plain flour, and 300ml milk. Steve is cooking pancakes for 15 people and wants to have sufficient mixture for 3 pancakes each.

What quantities should Steve use to ensure this whilst using whole eggs?
A. 2½ eggs, 125g plain flour, 375ml milk
B. 3 eggs , 150g plain flour, 450 ml milk
C. 7½ eggs, 375g plain flour, 1125 ml milk
D. 8 eggs, 400g plain flour, 1200 ml milk
E. 12 eggs, 600g plain flour, 1800 ml milk
F. None of the above.

Question 125:

Spring Cleaning cleaners buy industrial bleach from a warehouse and dilute it twice before using it domestically. The first dilution is by 9:1 and then the second, 4:1.

If the cleaners require 6 litres of diluted bleach, how much warehouse bleach do they require?
A. 30 ml
B. 120 ml
C. 166 ml
D. 666 ml
E. 1,200 ml
F. None of the above

Question 126:

During a GP consultation in 2015, Ms Smith tells the GP about her grandchildren. Ms Smith states that Charles is the middle grandchild and was born in 2002. In 2010, Bertie was twice the age of Adam and that in 2015 there are 5 years between Bertie and Adam. Charles and Adam are separated by 3 years.

How old are the 3 grandchildren in 2015?
A. Adam = 16, Bertie = 11, Charles = 13
B. Adam = 5, Bertie = 10, Charles = 8
C. Adam = 10, Bertie = 15, Charles = 13
D. Adam = 10, Bertie = 20, Charles = 13
E. Adam = 11, Bertie = 10, Charles = 8
F. More information needed.

Question 127:

Kayak Hire charges a fixed flat rate and then an additional half-hourly rate. Peter hires the kayak for 3 hours and pays £14.50, and his friend Kevin hires 2 kayaks for 4hrs30mins each and pays £41. How much would

Tom pay to hire one kayak for 2 hours?
A. £8
B. £10.50
C. £15
D. £33.20
E. £35.70
F. None of the above.

Question 128:

A ticketing system uses a common digital display of numbers 0 – 9. The number 7 is showing. However, a number of the light elements are not currently working.

Which set of the following digits is possible?
A. 3, 4, 7
B. 0, 1, 9
C. 2, 7, 8
D. 0, 5, 9
E. 3, 8, 9
F. 3, 4, 9

Question 129:

A team of 4 builders take 12 days of 7 hours work to complete a house. The company decides to recruit 3 extra builders.

How many 8 hour days will it take the new workforce to build a house?

A. 2 days
B. 6 days
C. 7 days

D. 10 days
E. 12 days
F. More information needed

Question 130:

All astragalus are fabacaea as are all gummifer. Acacia are not astragalus. Which of the following statements is true?

A. Acacia are not fabacaea.
B. No astragalus are also gummifer.
C. All fabacae are astragalus or gummifer.
D. Some acacia may be fabacaea.
E. Gummifer are all acacia.
F. None of the above.

Question 131:

The Smiths want to reupholster both sides of their seating cushions (dimensions shown on diagram). The fabric they are using costs £10/m, can only be bought in whole metre lengths and has a standard width of 1m. Each side of a cushion must be made from a single piece of fabric. The seamstress changes a flat rate of £25 per cushion. How much will it cost them to reupholster 4 cushions?

A. £ 20
B. £ 80
C. £ 110
D. £ 130
E. £ 150
F. £ 200

30 cm / 75 cm / 50 cm / Negligible Thickness

Question 132:

Lisa buys a cappuccino from either Milk or Beans Coffee shops each day. The quality of the coffee is the same but she wishes to work out the relative costs once the loyalty scheme has been taken into account. In Milk, a regular cappuccino is £2.40, and in Beans, £2.15. However, the loyalty scheme in Milk gives Lisa a free cappuccino for every 9 she buys, whereas Beans use a points system of 10 points per full pound spent (each point is worth 1p) which can be used to cover the cost of a full cappuccino.

If Lisa buys a cappuccino each day of September, which coffee shop would work out cheaper, and by how much?

A. Milk, by £4.60
B. Beans by £6.30

C. Beans, by £4.60
D. Beans, by £2.45

E. Milk, by £2.45
F. Milk, by £6.25

Question 133:

Paula needs to be at a meeting in Notting Hill at 11am. The route requires her to walk 5 minutes to the 283 bus which takes 25 minutes, and then change to the 220 bus which takes 14 minutes. Finally she walks for 3 minutes to her meeting. If the 283 bus comes every 10 minutes, and the 220 bus at 0 minutes, 20 minutes and 40 minutes past the hour, what is the latest time she can leave and still be at her meeting on time?

A. 09.45   B. 09.58   C. 10.01   D. 10.05   E. 10.10   F. 10.15

Question 134:

Two trains, a high speed train A and a slower local train B, travel from Manchester to London. Train A travels the first 20 km at 100 km/hr and then at an average speed of 150km/hr. Train B travels at a constant average speed of 90 km/hr. If train B leaves 20 minutes before train A, at what distance will train A pass train B?

A. 75 km   B. 90 km   C. 100 km   D. 120 km   E. 150 km

Question 135:

The university gym has an upfront cost of £35 with no contract fee, but classes are charged at £3 each. The local gym has no joining fee and is £15 per month. What is the minimum number of classes I need to attend in a 12 month period to make the local gym cheaper than the university gym?

A. 40   B. 48   C. 49   D. 50   E. 55   F. 60

Question 136:

"All medicines are drugs, but not all drugs are medicines", goes a well-known saying. If we accept this statement as true, and consider that all antibiotics are medicines, but no herbal drugs are medicines, then which of the following is definitely **FALSE**?

A. Some herbal drugs are not medicines.
B. All antibiotics are drugs.

C. Some herbal drugs are antibiotics.
D. Some medicines are antibiotics

Question 137:

Sonia has been studying the paths taken by various trains travelling between London and Edinburgh on the East coast. Trains can stop at the following stations: Newark, Peterborough, Doncaster, York, Northallerton, Darlington, Durham and Newcastle.

She notes the following:

-   All trains stop at Peterborough, York, Darlington and Newcastle.
-   All trains which stop at Northallerton also stop at Durham.
-   Each day, 50% of the trains stop at both Newark *and* Northallerton.
-   All designated "Fast" trains make less than 5 stops. All other trains make 5 stops or more.
-   On average, 16 trains run each day.

Which of the following can be reliably concluded from these observations?
A. All trains, which are not designated "fast" trains, must stop at Durham.
B. No more than 8 trains on any 1 day will stop at Northallerton.
C. No designated "Fast" trains will stop at Durham.
D. It is possible for a train to make 5 stops, including Northallerton.
E. A train which stops at Newark will also stop at Durham.

Question 138:

Rakton is 5 miles directly north of Blueville. Gallford is 8 miles directly south of Haston. Lepstone is situated 5 miles directly east of Blueville, and 5 miles directly west of Gallford.

Which of the following **CANNOT** be reliably concluded from this information?
A. Lepstone is South of Rakton
B. Haston is North of Rakton
C. Gallford is East of Rakton
D. Blueville is East of Haston
E. Haston is North of Lepstone

Question 139:

The Eastminster Parliament is undergoing a new set of elections. There are 600 seats up for election, each of which will be elected separately by the people living in that constituency. 6 parties win at least 1 seat in the election, the Blue Party, the Red party, the Orange party, the Yellow party, the Green party and the Purple party. In order to form a government, a party (or coalition) must hold *over* 50% of the seats. After the election, a political analysis committee produces the following report:

- No party has gained more than 45% of the seats, so nobody is able to form a government by themselves.
- The red and the blue party each gained over 40% of the seats.
- No other party gained more than 4% of the seats.
- The Yellow party did not win the fewest seats

The red party work out that if they collaborate with the green party and the orange party, between the 3 of them, they will have enough seats to form a coalition government.

What is the minimum number of seats that the green party could have?

A. 5	C. 7	E. 9
B. 6	D. 8	F. 10

Questions 140-144 are based on the following information:

A grandmother wants to give her 5 grandchildren £100 between them for Christmas this year. She wants to grade the money she gives to each grandchild exactly so that the older children receive more than the younger ones. She wants share the money such that she will give the 2nd youngest child as much more than the youngest, as the 3rd youngest gets than the 2nd youngest, as the 4th youngest gets from the 3rd youngest and so on. The result will be that the two youngest children together will get seven times as less money than the three oldest.

M is the amount of money the youngest child receives, and D the difference between the amount the youngest and 2nd youngest children receive.

Question 140:

What is the expression for the amount the oldest child receives?

A. M	C. $2M$	E. $M + 4D$
B. $M + D$	D. $4M^2$	F. None of the above.

Question 141:

What is the correct expression for the total money received?

A. $5M = £100$

B. $5D + 10M = £100$

C. $D = \frac{M}{100}$

D. $5M + 10D = £100$

E. $M = \frac{2D}{11}$

Question 142:

"The two youngest children together will get seven times less money than the three oldest."

Which one of the following best expresses the above statement?

A. $7(3M + 9D) = 2M + D$

B. $7D = M$

C. $7(2M + D) = 3M + 9D$

D. $2(7M + D) = 3M + 9D$

Question 143

Using the statement in the previous question, what is the correct expression for M?

A. $\frac{2D}{11}$	B. $\frac{2}{11}$	C. $\frac{10D}{11}$	D. $\frac{120}{11}$

Question 144:

Express £100 in terms of D.

A. $£100 = \frac{120D}{11}$

B. $£100 = \frac{120D}{10}$

C. $£100 = \frac{120}{11D}$

D. $£100 = 21D$

E. $£100 = 5M + 10D$

Question 145:

Four young girls entered a local baking competition. Though a bit burnt, Ellen's carrot cake did not come last. The girl who baked a Madeira sponge had practiced a lot, and so came first, while Jaya came third with her entry. Aleena did better than the girl who made the Tiramisu, and the girl who made the Victoria sponge did better than Veronica.

Which **TWO** of the following were **NOT** results of the competition?

A. Veronica made a tiramisu

B. Ellen came second

C. Aleena made a Victoria sponge

D. The Victoria sponge came in 3rd place

E. The carrot cake came 3rd

Question 146:

In a young children's football league of 5 teams were; Celtic Changers, Eire Lions, Nordic Nesters, Sorten Swipers and the Whistling Winners. One of the boys playing in the league, after being asked by his parents, said that while he could remember the other teams' total points he could not remember his own, the Eire Lions, score. He said that all the teams played each other and when teams lost they were given 0 points, when they drew, 1 point, and 3 for a win. He remembered that the Celtic Changers had a total of 2 points; the Sorten Swipers had 5; the Nordic Nesters had 8, and the Whistling Winners 1.

How many did the boy's team score?

A. 1

B. 4

C. 8

D. 10

E. 11

F. None of the above.

Question 147:

T is the son of Z, Z and J are sisters, R is the mother of J and S is the son of R.

Which one of the following statements is correct?

A. T and J are cousins

B. S and J are sisters

C. J is the maternal uncle of T

D. S is the maternal uncle of T

E. R is the grandmother of Z.

Question 148:

John likes to shoot bottles off a shelf. In the first round he places 16 bottles on the shelf and knocks off 8 bottles. 3 of the knocked off bottles are damaged and can no longer be used, whilst 1 bottle is lost. He puts the undamaged bottles back on the shelf before continuing. In the second round he shoots six times and misses 50% of these shots. He damages two bottles with every shot which does not miss. 2 bottles also fall off the shelf at the end. He puts up 2 new bottles before continuing. In the final round, John misses all his shots and in frustration, knocks over gets angry and knocks over 50% of the remaining bottles.

How many bottles were left on the wall after the final round?

A. 2

B. 3

C. 4

D. 5

E. 6

F. More information needed.

Questions 149 - 155 are based on the information below:

All lines are named after a station they serve, apart from the Oval and Rectangle lines, which are named for their recognisable shapes. Trains run in both directions.

➢ There are express trains that run from end to end of the St Mark's and Straightly lines in 5 and 6 minutes respectively.

➢ It takes 2 minutes to change between St Mark's and both Oval and Rectangle lines, 1 minute between Rectangle and Oval.

➢ It takes 3 minutes to change between the Straightly and all other lines, except with the St Mark's line which only takes 30 seconds

➢ The Straightly line is a fast line and takes only 2 minutes between stops apart from to and from Keyton, which only takes 1 minute, and to and from Lime St which takes 3 minutes.

➢ The Oval line is much slower and takes 4 minutes between stops, apart from between Baxton and Marven, and also Archite and West Quays, which takes 5 minutes.

➢ The Rectangle line a reliable line; never running late but as a consequence is much slower taking 6 minutes between stops.

➢ The St Mark's line is fast and takes 2 and half minutes between stations.

➢ If a passenger reaches the end of the line, it takes three minutes to change onto a train travelling back in the opposite direction.

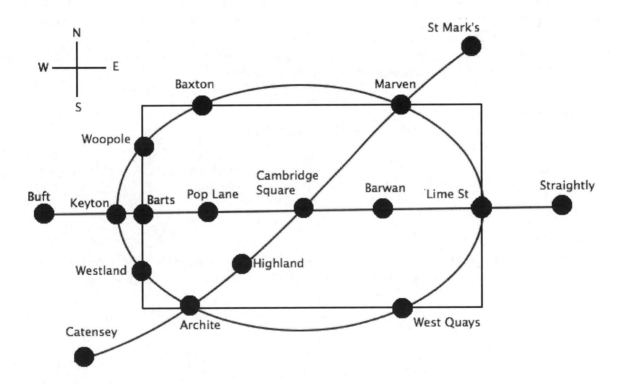

Question 149:

Assuming all lines are running on time, how long does it take to go from St Mark's to Archite on the St Mark's line?

A. 5 minutes

B. 6 minutes

C. 7.5 minutes

D. 10 minutes

E. 12.5 minutes

Question 150:

Assuming all lines are running on time, what's the shortest time it will take to go from Buft to Straightly?

A. 6 minutes

B. 10 minutes

C. 12 minutes

D. 14 minutes

E. 16 minutes

Question 151:

What is the shortest time it will take to go from Baxton to Pop Lane?

A. 11 minutes

B. 12 minutes

C. 13 minutes

D. 14 minutes

E. 15 minutes

Question 152

Which station, even at the quickest journey time, is furthest in terms of time from Cambridge Square?

A. Catensey   B. Buft   C. Woopole   D. Westland

Questions 153-155 use this additional information:

On a difficult day there are signal problems whereby all lines except the reliable line are delayed, such that train travel times between stations are doubled. These delays have caused overcrowding at the platforms which means that while changeover times between lines are still the same, passengers always have to wait an extra 5 minutes on all of the platforms before catching the next train.

Question 153

At best, how long will it now take to go from Westland to Marven?

A. 25 minutes

B. 29 minutes

C. 30 minutes

D. 33 minutes

E. 35 minutes

Question 154:

There is a bus that goes from Baxton to Archite and takes 27-31 minutes. Susan lives in Baxton and needs to get to her office in Archite as quickly as possible. With all the delays and lines out of service,

How should you advise Susan best to get to work?

A. Baxton to Archite via Barts using the Rectangle line.

B. Baxton to Woopole on the Rectangle line, then Oval to Archite via Keyton.

C. It is not possible to tell between the fastest two options.

D. Baxton to Woopole on the Rectangle line, then Oval to Archite via Keyton.

E. Baxton to Archite on the Oval line.

F. Baxton to Archite using the bus.

Question 155:

In addition to the delays the Oval line signals fail completely, so the line falls out of service. How long will it now take to go from St Mark's to West Quays as quickly as possible?

A. 35 minutes

B. 30 minutes

C. 33 minutes

D. 29 minutes

E. 30.5 minutes

F. None of the above.

Question 156:

In an unusual horserace, only 4 horses, each with different racing colours and numbers competed. Simon's horse wore number 1. Lila's horse wasn't painted yellow nor blue, and the horse that wore 3, which was wearing red, beat the horse that came in third. Only one horse wore the same number as the position it finished in. Arthur's horse beat Simon's horse, whereas Celia's horse beat the horse that wore number 1. The horse wearing green, Celia's, came second, and the horse wearing blue wore number 4. Which one of the following must be true?

A. Simon's horse was yellow and placed 3rd.
B. Celia's horse was red.
C. Celia's horse was in third place.
D. Arthur's horse was blue.
E. Lila's horse wore number 4.

Question 157:

Jessie plants a tree with a height of 40 cm. The information leaflet states that the plant should grow by 20% each year for the first 2 years, and then 10% each year thereafter.

What is the expected height at 4 years?

A. 58.08 cm
B. 64.89 cm
C. 69.696 cm
D. 89.696 cm
E. 82.944 cm
F. None of the above

Question 158

A company is required to pay each employee 10% of their wage into a pension fund if their annual total wage bill is above £200,000. However, there is a legal loophole that if the company splits over two sites, the £200,000 bill is per site. The company therefore decides to have an east site, and a west site.

Name	Annual Salary (£)
Luke	47,000
John	78,400
Emma	68,250
Nicola	88,500
Victoria	52,500
Daniel	63,000

Which employees should be grouped at the same site to minimise the cost to the company?

A. John, Nicola, Luke
B. Nicola, Victoria, Daniel
C. Nicola, Daniel, Luke
D. John, Daniel, Emma
E. Luke, Victoria, Emma

Question 159:

A bus takes 24 minutes to travel from White City to Hammersmith with no stops. Each time the bus stops to pick up and/or drop off passengers, it takes approximately 90 seconds. This morning, the bus picked up passengers from 5 stops, and dropped off passengers at 7 stops.

What is the minimum journey time from White City to Hammersmith this morning?

A. 28 minutes
B. 34 minutes
C. 34.5 minutes
D. 36 minutes
E. 37.5 minutes
F. 42 minutes

Question 160:

Sally is making a Sunday roast for her family and is planning her schedule regarding cooking times. The chicken takes 15 minutes to prepare, 75 minutes to cook, and needs to stand for exactly 5 minutes after cooking. The potatoes take 18 minutes to prepare, 5 minutes to boil, then 50 minutes to roast, and must be roasted immediately after boiling, and then served immediately. The vegetables require only 5 minutes preparation time and 8 minutes boiling time before serving, and can be kept warm to be served at any time after cooking. Given that the cooker can only be cooking two items at any given time and Sally can prepare only one item at a time, what should Sally's schedule be if she wishes to serve dinner at 4pm and wants to start cooking each item as late as possible?

A. Chicken 2.25, potatoes 2.47, vegetables 2.42
B. Chicken 2.25, potatoes 2.47, vegetables 3.47
C. Chicken 2.35, potatoes 3.47, vegetables 2.47

D. Chicken 2.35, potatoes 2.47, vegetables 3.47
E. Chicken 2.45, potatoes 3.47, vegetables 2.47
F. Chicken 2.45, potatoes 2.47, vegetables 3.47

Question 161:

The Smiths have 4 children whose total age is 80. Paul is double the age of Jeremy. Annie is exactly half way between the ages of Jeremy and Paul, and Rebecca is 2 years older than Paul. How old are each of the children?

A. Paul 23, Jeremy 12, Rebecca 26, Annie 19.
B. Paul 22, Jeremy, 11, Rebecca 24, Annie 16.
C. Paul 24, Jeremy 12, Rebecca 26, Annie 18.

D. Paul 28, Jeremy 14, Rebecca 30, Annie 21.
E. More information needed.

Question 162:

Sarah has a jar of spare buttons that are a mix of colours and sizes. The jar contains the following assortment of buttons:

	10mm	25mm	40mm
Cream	15	22	13
Red	6	15	7
Green	9	19	8
Blue	20	6	15
Yellow	4	8	26
Black	17	16	14
Total	**71**	**86**	**83**

Sarah wants to use a 25mm diameter button, but doesn't mind if it is cream or yellow. What is the maximum number of buttons she will have to remove in order to guarantee to pick a suitable button on the next attempt?

A. 210
B. 218
C. 219
D. 239
E. None of the above

Question 163:

Ben wants to optimise his score with one throw of a dart. 50% of the time he hits a segment to either side of the one he is aiming at. With this in mind, which segment should he aim for?

[Ignore all double/triple modifiers]

A. 15
B. 16
C. 17

D. 18
E. 19
F. 20

Question 164:

Victoria is completing her weekly shop, and the total cost of the items is £8.65. She looks in her purse and sees that she has a £5 note, and a large amount of change, including all types of coins. She uses the £5 note, and pays the remainder using the maximum number of coins possible in order to remove some weight from the purse. However, the store has certain rules she has to follow when paying:

- No more than 20p can be paid in "bronze" change (the name given to any combination of 1p pieces and 2p pieces)
- No more than 50p can be paid using any combination of 5p pieces and 10p pieces.
- No more than £1.50 can be paid using any combination of 20p pieces and 50p pieces.

Victoria pays the exact amount, and does not receive any change. Under these rules, what is the *maximum* number of coins that Victoria can have paid with?

A. 30   B. 31   C. 36   D. 41   E. 46

Question 165:

I look at the clock on my bedside table, and I see the following digits:

However, I also see that there is a glass of water between me and the clock, which is in front of 2 adjacent figures. I know that this means these 2 figures will appear reversed. For example, 10 would appear as 01, and 20 would appear as 05 (as 5 on a digital clock is a reversed image of a 2). Some numbers, such as 3, cannot appear reversed because there are no numbers which look like the reverse of 3.

Which of the following could be the actual time?

A. 15:52   B. 21:25   C. 12:55   D. 12:22   E. 21:52

Question 166:

Slavica has invaded Worsid, whilst Nordic has invaded Lorkdon. Worsid, spotting an opportunity to bolster its amount of land and natural resources, invades Nordic. Each of these countries is either a dictatorship or a democracy. Slavica is a dictatorship, but Lorkdon is a democracy. 10 years ago, a treaty was signed which guaranteed that no democracy would invade another democracy. No dictatorship has both invaded another dictatorship *and* been invaded by another dictatorship.

Assuming the aforementioned treaty has been upheld, what style of government is practiced in Worsid?

A. Worsid is a Dictatorship.
B. Worsid is a Democracy.
C. Worsid does not practice either of these forms of government.
D. It is impossible to tell.

Question 167:

Sheila is on a shift at the local supermarket. Unfortunately, the till has developed a fault, meaning it cannot tell her how much change to give each customer. A customer is purchasing the following items, at the following costs:

- A packet of grated cheese priced at £3.25
- A whole cucumber, priced at 75p
- A fish pie mix, priced at £4.00
- 3 DVDs, each priced at £3.00

Sheila knows there is an offer on DVDs in the store at present, in which 3 DVDs bought together will only cost £8.00. The customer pays with a £50 note.

How much change will Sheila need to give the customer?

A. £4   B. £33   C. £34   D. £36   E. £38

Question 168:

Ryan is cooking breakfast for several guests at his hotel. He is frying most of the items using the same large frying pan, to get as much food prepared in as little time as possible. Ryan is cooking Bacon, Sausages, and eggs in this pan. He calculates how much room is taken up in the pan by each item. He calculates the following:

- Each rasher of bacon takes up 7% of the available space in the pan
- Each sausage takes up 3% of the available space in the pan.
- Each egg takes up 12% of the available space in the pan.

Ryan is cooking 2 rashers of bacon, 4 sausages and 1 egg for each guest. He decides to cook all the food for each guest at the same time, rather than cooking all of each item at once.

How many guests can he cook for at once?

A. 1   B. 2   C. 3   D. 4   E. 5

Question 169:

SafeEat Inc. is a national food development testing agency. The Manchester-based laboratory has a system for recording all the laboratory employees' birthdays, and presenting them with cake on their birthday, in order to keep staff morale high. Certain amounts of petty cash are set aside each month in order to fund this. 40% of the staff have their birthday in March, and the secretary works out that £60 is required to fund the birthday cake scheme during this month.

If all birthdays cost £2 to provide a cake for, how many people work at the laboratory?

A. 45   B. 60   C. 75   D. 100   E. 150

Question 170:

Many diseases, such as cancer, require specialist treatment, and thus cannot be treated by a general practitioner. Instead, these diseases must be *referred* to a specialist after an initial, more generalised, medical assessment. Bob has had a biopsy on the 1st of August on a lump found in his abdomen. The results show that it is a tumour, with a slight chance of becoming metastatic, so he is referred to a waiting list for specialist radiotherapy and chemotherapy. The average waiting time in the UK for such treatment is 3 weeks, but in Bob's local district, high demand means that it takes 50% longer for each patient to receive treatment. As he is a lower risk case, with a low risk of metastasis, his waiting time is extended by another 20%.

How many weeks will it be before Bob receives specialist treatment?

A. 4.5   B. 4.6   C. 5.0   D. 5.1   E. 5.4   F. 5.6

Question 171:

In a class of 30 seventeen year old students, 40% drink alcohol at least once a month. Of those who drink alcohol at least once a month, 75% drink alcohol at least once a week. 1 in 3 of the students who drink alcohol at least once a week also smoke marijuana. 1 in 3 of the students who drink alcohol less than once a month also smoke marijuana.

How many of the students in total smoke marijuana?

A. 3   B. 4   C. 6   D. 9   E. 10   F. 15

Question 172:

Complete the following sequence of numbers: 1, 4, 10, 22, 46, …

A. 84   B. 92   C. 94   D. 96   E. 100

Question 173:

If the mean of 5 numbers is 7, the median is 8 and the mode is 3, what must the two largest numbers in the set of numbers add up to?

A. 14   C. 24   E.   35
B. 21   D. 26   F.   More information needed.

Question 174:

Ahmed buys 1kg bags of potatoes from the supermarket. 1kg bags have to weigh between 900 and 1100 grams. In the first week, there are 10 potatoes in the bag. The next week, there are only 5. Assuming that the potatoes in the bag in week 1 are all the same weight as each other, and the potatoes in the bag in week 2 are all the same weight as each other, what is the maximum possible difference between the heaviest and lightest potato in the two bags?

A. 50g   B. 70g   C. 90g   D. 110g   E. 130g

Question 175:

A football tournament involves a group stage, then a knockout stage. In the group stage, groups of four teams play in a round robin format (i.e. each team plays every other team once) and the team that wins the most matches in each group proceeds through to a knockout stage. In addition, the single best performing second place team across all the groups gains a place in the knockout stage. In the knockout stage, sets of two teams play each other and the one that wins proceeds to the next round until there are two teams left, who play the final.

If we start with 60 teams, how many matches are played altogether?

A. 75   B. 90   C. 100   D. 105   E. 165

Question 176:

The last 4 digits of my card number are 2 times my PIN number, plus 200. The last 4 digits of my husband's card number are the last four digits of my card number doubled, plus 200. My husband's PIN number is 2 times the last 4 digits of his card number, plus 200. Given that all these numbers are 4 digits long, whole numbers, and cannot begin with 0, what is the largest number my PIN number can be?

A. 1,074   C. 2,348   E. 9,999
B. 1,174   D. 4,096   F. More information needed.

Question 177:

All women between 50 and 70 in the UK are invited for breast cancer screening every 3 years. Patients at Doddinghurst Surgery are invited for screening for the first time at any point between their 50th and 53rd birthday. If they ignore an invitation, they are sent reminders every 5 months. We can assume that a woman is screened exactly 1 month after she is sent the invitation or reminder that she accepts. The next invitation for screening is sent exactly 3 years after the previous screening.

If a woman accepts the screening on the second reminder each time, what is the youngest she can be when she has her 4th screening?

A. 60   B. 61   C. 62   D. 63   E. 64   F. 65

Question 178:

Ellie gets a pay rise of k thousand pounds on every anniversary of joining the company, where k is the number of years she has been at the company. She currently earns £40,000, and she has been at the company for 5.5 years. What was her salary when she started at the company?

A. £25,000   C. £28,000   E. £31,000

B. £27,000   D. £30,000   F. £32,000

Question 179:

Northern Line trains arrive into Kings Cross station every 8 minutes, Piccadilly Line trains every 5 minutes and Victoria Line trains every 2 minutes. If trains from all 3 lines arrived into the station exactly 15 minutes ago, how long will it be before they do so again?

A. 24 minutes   C. 40 minutes   E. 65 minutes

B. 25 minutes   D. 60 minutes   F. 80 minutes

Question 180:

If you do not smoke or drink alcohol, your risk of getting Disease X is 1 in 12. If you smoke, you are half as likely to get Disease X as someone who does not smoke. If you drink alcohol, you are twice as likely to get Disease X. A new drug is released that halves anyone's total risk of getting Disease X for each tablet taken. How many tablets of the drug would someone who drinks alcohol have to take to reduce their risk to the same level as someone who smoked but did not take the drug?

A. 0   B. 1   C. 2   D. 3   E. 4   F. 5

Questions 181 – 183 refer to the following information:

There are 20 balls in a bag. 1/2 are red. 1/10 of those that are not red are yellow. The rest are green except 1, which is blue.

Question 181:

If I draw 2 balls from the bag (without replacement), what is the most likely combination to draw?

A. Red and green   C. Red and red

B. Red and yellow   D. Blue and yellow

Question 182:

If I draw 2 balls from the bag (without replacement), what is the least likely (without being impossible) combination to draw?

A. Blue and green   C. Yellow and yellow

B. Blue and yellow   D. Yellow and green

Question 183:

How many balls do you have to draw (without replacement) to guarantee getting at least one of at least three different colours?

A. 5   B. 12   C. 13   D. 17   E. 18   F. 19

Question 184:

A general election in the UK resulted in a hung parliament, with no single party gaining more than 50% of the seats. Thus, the main political parties are engaged in discussion over the formation of a coalition government. The results of this election are shown below:

Political Party	Seats won
Conservatives	260
Labour	270
Liberal Democrats	50
UKIP	35
Green Party	20
Scottish National Party	17
Plaid Cymru	13
Sinn Fein	9
Democratic Unionist Party (DUP)	11
Other	14 (14 other parties won 1 seat each)

There are a total of 699 seats, meaning that in order to form a government, any coalition must have at least 350 seats between them. Several of the party leaders have released statements about who they are and are not willing to form a coalition with, which are summarised as follows:

– The Conservative party and Labour are not willing to take part in a coalition together.
– The Liberal Democrats refuse to take part in any coalition which also involves UKIP.
– The Labour party will only form a coalition with UKIP if the Green party are also part of this coalition.
– The Conservative party are not willing to take part in any coalition with UKIP unless the Liberal Democrats are also involved.

Considering this information, what is the minimum number of parties required to form a coalition government?

A) 2   B) 3   C) 4   D) 5   E) 6

Question 185:

On Tuesday, 360 patients attend appointments at Doddinghurst Surgery. Of the appointments that are booked in, only 90% are attended. Of the appointments that are booked in, 1 in 2 are for male patients, the remaining appointments are for female patients. Male patients are three times as likely to miss their booked appointment as female patients.

How many male patients attend appointments at Doddinghurst Surgery on Tuesday?

A. 30   B. 60   C. 130   D. 150   E. 170

Question 186:

Every A Level student at Greentown Sixth Form studies Maths. Additionally, 60% study Biology, 50% study Economics and 50% study Chemistry. The other subject on offer at Greentown Sixth Form is Physics. Assuming every student studies 3 subjects and that there are 60 students altogether, how many students study Physics?

A. 15   C. 30   E. 60
B. 24   D. 40   F. More information needed

Question 187:

100,000 people are diagnosed with chlamydia each year in the UK. An average of 0.6 sexual partners are informed per diagnosis. Of these, 80% have tests for chlamydia themselves. Half of these tests come back positive.

Assuming that each of the people diagnosed has had an average of 3 sexual partners (none of them share sexual partners or have sex with each other) and that the likelihood of having chlamydia is the same for those partners who are tested and those who are not, how many of the sexual partners who were not tested (whether they were informed or not) have chlamydia?

A. 120,000	C. 136,000	E. 240,000
B. 126,000	D. 150,000	F. 252,000

Question 188:

In how many different positions can you place an additional tile to make a straight line of 3 tiles?

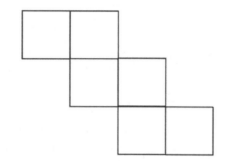

A. 6
B. 7
C. 8
D. 9
E. 10
F. 11
G. 12

Question 189:

Harry is making orange squash for his daughter's birthday party. He wants to have a 200ml glass of squash for each of the 20 children attending and a 300ml glass of squash for him and each of 3 parents who are helping him out. He has 1,040ml of the concentrated squash.

What ratio of water: concentrated squash should he use in the dilution to ensure he has the right amount to go around?

A. 2:1	C. 4:1	E. 6:1
B. 3:1	D. 5:1	F. 5:2

Question 190:

4 children, Alex, Beth, Cathy and Daniel are each sitting on one of the 4 swings in the park. The swings are in a straight line. One possible arrangement of the children is, left to right, Alex, Beth, Cathy, Daniel.

How many other possible arrangements are there?

A. 5	C. 23	E. 64
B. 12	D. 24	F. 256

Question 191:

A delivery driver is looking to make deliveries in several towns. He is given the following map of the various towns in the area. The lines indicate roads between the towns, along with the lengths of these roads.

The delivery driver's vehicle has a black box which records the distance travelled and locations visited. At the end of the day, the black box recording shows that he has travelled a total of 14 miles. It also shows that he has visited one town twice, but has not visited any other town more than once. Which of the following is a possible route the driver could have taken?

A. Snayton → Baleford→ Grassford → Snayton→ Kirkelby
B. Baleford → Kirkelby→ Hondale → Grassford→ Baleford→ Snayton
C. Kirkelby → Hondale→ Baleford →Grassford→ Snayton
D. Baleford → Hondale→ Grassford → Baleford→ Hondale→ Kirkelby
E. Snayton → Baleford→ Kirkelby → Hondale→ Grassford
F. None of the above.

Question 192:

Ellie, her brother Tom, her sister Georgia, her mum and her dad line up in height order from shortest to tallest for a family photograph. Ellie is shorter than her dad but taller than her mum. Georgia is shorter than both her parents. Tom is taller than both his parents.

If 1 is shortest and 5 is tallest, what position is Ellie in the line?
A. 1   B. 2   C. 3   D. 4   E. 5

Question 193:

Miss Briggs is trying to arrange the 5 students in her class into a seating plan. Ashley must sit on the front row because she has poor eyesight. Danielle disrupts anyone she sits next to apart from Caitlin, so she must sit next to Caitlin and no-one else. Bella needs to have a teaching assistant sat next to her. The teaching assistant must be sat on the left hand side of the row, near to the teacher. Emily does not get on with Bella, so they need to be sat apart from one another. The teacher has 2 tables which each sit 3 people, which are arranged 1 behind the other.

Who is sitting in the front right seat?
A. Ashley   B. Bella   C. Caitlin   D. Danielle   E. Emily

Question 194:

My aunt runs the dishwasher twice a week, plus an extra time for each person who is living in the house that week. When her son is away at university, she buys a new pack of dishwasher tablets every 6 weeks, but when her son is home she has to buy a new one every 5 weeks. How many people are living in the house when her son is home?

A. 2   C. 4   E. 6
B. 3   D. 5   F. 7

Question 195:

Dates can be written in an 8 digit form, for example 26-12-2014. How many days after 26-12-2014 would be the next time that the 8 digits were made up of exactly 4 different integers?

A. 6   C. 10   E. 24

B. 8   D. 16   F. 30

Question 196:

Redtown is 4 miles east of Greentown. Bluetown is 5 miles north of Greentown. If every town is due North, South, East or West of at least two other towns, and the only other town is Yellowtown, how many miles away from Yellowtown is Redtown, and in what direction?

A. 4 miles east of Yellowtown.   D. 4 miles west of Yellowtown.

B. 5 miles south of Yellowtown.   E. 5 miles west of Yellowtown.

C. 5 miles north of Yellowtown.   F. None of the above.

Question 197:

Jenna pours wine from two 750ml bottles into glasses. The glasses hold 250ml, but she only fills them to 4/5 of capacity, except the last glass, where she puts whatever she has left. How full is the last glass compared to its capacity?

A. 1/5   B. 2/5   C. 3/5   D. 4/5   E. 5/5

Question 198:

There are 30 children in Miss Ellis's class. Two thirds of the girls in Miss Ellis's class have brown eyes, and two thirds of the class as a whole have brown hair. Given that the class is half boys and half girls, what is the difference between the minimum and maximum number of girls that could have brown eyes and brown hair?

A. 0   C. 5   E. 10

B. 2   D. 7   F. More information needed.

Question 199:

A biased die with the numbers 1 to 6 on it is rolled twice. The resulting numbers are multiplied together, and then their sum subtracted from this result to get the 'score' of the dice roll. If the probability of getting a negative (non-zero) score is 0.75, what is the probability of rolling a 1 on a third throw of the die?

A. 0.1   C. 0.3   E. 0.5

B. 0.2   D. 0.4   F. More information needed.

Questions 200 - 202 are based on the following information:

Fares on the number 11 bus are charged at a number of pence per stop that you travel, plus a flat rate. Emma, who is 21, travels 15 stops and pays £1.70. Charlie, who is 43, travels 8 stops and pays £1.14. Children (under 16) pay half the adult flat rate plus a quarter of the adult charge "per stop".

Question 200:

How much does 17 year old Megan pay to travel 30 stops to college?

A. £0.85
B. £2.40
C. £2.90

D. £3.40
E. More information needed.

Question 201:

How much does 14 year old Alice pay to travel 25 stops to school?

A. £0.50
B. £0.75
C. £1.25

D. £2.50
E. More information needed.

Question 202:

James, who is 24, wants to get the bus into town. The town stop is the 25th stop along a straight road from his house, but he only has £2.

Assuming he has to walk past the stop nearest his house, how many stops will he need to walk past before he gets to the stop he can afford to catch the bus from?

A. 4
B. 6

C. 7
D. 8

E. 9
F. 10

Questions 203 -205 are based on the following information:

Emma mounts and frames paintings. Each painting needs a mount which is 2 inches bigger in each dimension than the painting, and a wooden frame which is 1 inch bigger in each dimension than the mount. Mounts are priced by multiplying 50p by the largest dimension of the mount, so a mount which is 8 inches in one direction and 6 in the other would be £4. Frames are priced by multiplying £2 by the smallest dimension of the frame, so a frame which is 8 inches in one direction and 6 in the other would be £12.

Question 203:

How much would mounting and framing a painting that is 10 x 14 inches cost?

A. £8   B. £26   C. £27   D. £34   E. £42

Question 204:

How much more would mounting and framing a 10 x 10 inch painting cost than mounting and framing an 8 x 8 inch painting?

A. £ 3.00   B. £ 4.00   C. £ 5.00   D. £ 6.00   E. £ 7.00

Question 205:

What is the largest square painting that can be framed for £40?

A. 12 inches
B. 13 inches
C. 14 inches

D. 15 inches
E. 16 inches

Question 206:

If the word 'CREATURES' is coded as 'FTEAWUTEV', which itself would be coded as 'HWEAYUWEX'. What would be the second coding of the word 'MAGICAL'?

A. QCKIGAN

B. OCIIEAN

C. PAJIFAN

D. RALIHAQ

E. RCIMGEP

Question 207:

Jane's mum has asked Jane to go to the shops to get some items that they need. She tells Jane that she will pay her per kilometre that she cycles on her bike to get to the shop, plus a flat rate payment for each place she goes to. Jane receives £6 to go to the grocers, a distance of 5 km, and £4.20 to go the supermarket, a distance of 3km.

How much would she earn if she then cycles to the library to change some books, a distance of 7 km?

A. £7.50

B. £7.70

C. £7.80

D. £8.00

E. £8.10

F. £8.20

Question 208:

In 2001-2002, 1,019 patients were admitted to hospital due to obesity. This figure was more than 11 times higher by 2011-12 when there were 11,736 patients admitted to hospital with the primary reason for admission being obesity.

If the rate of admissions due to obesity continues to increase at the same linear rate as it has from 2001/2 to 2011/12, how many admissions would you expect in 2031/32?

A. 22,453

B. 23,437

C. 33,170

D. 134,964

E. 269,928

F. 300,000

Question 209:

A shop puts its dresses on sale at 20% off the normal selling price. During the sale, the shop makes a 25% profit over the price at which they bought the dresses. What is the percentage profit when the dresses are sold at full price?

A. 36%

B. 42.5%

C. 56.25%

D. 64%

E. 77%

F. 80%

Question 210:

The 'Keys MedSoc committee' is made up of 20 students from each of the 6 years at the university. However, the president and vice-president are sabbatical roles (students take a year out from studying). There must be at least two general committee students from each year, as well as the specialist roles. Additionally, the social and welfare officers must be pre-clinical students (years 1-3) but not first years, and the treasurer must be a clinical student (years 4-6).

Which **TWO** of the following statements must be true?

1. There can be a maximum of 13 preclinical (years 1-3) students on the committee.
2. There must be a minimum of 6 2nd and 3rd years.
3. There is an unequal distribution of committee members over the different year groups.
4. There can be a maximum of 10 clinical (years 4-6) students on the committee.
5. There can be a maximum of 2 first year students on the committee.
6. General committee members are equally spread across the 6 years.

A. 1 and 4

B. 2 and 3

C. 2 and 4

D. 3 and 6

E. 4 and 5

F. 4 and 6

Question 211:

Friday the 13th is superstitiously considered an 'unlucky' day. If 13th January 2012 was a Friday, when would the next Friday the 13th be?

A. March 2012
B. April 2012
C. May 2012
D. June 2012

E. July 2012
F. August 2012
G. September 2012
H. January has the only Friday 13th in 2012.

Question 212:

A farmer has 18 sheep, 8 of which are male. Unfortunately, 9 sheep die, of which 5 were female. The farmer decides to breed his remaining sheep in order to increase the size of his herd. Assuming every female gives birth to two lambs, how many sheep does the farmer have after all the females have given birth once?

A. 10   B. 14   C. 15   D. 16   E. 19

Question 213:

Piyanga writes a coded message for Nishita. Each letter of the original message is coded as a letter a specific number of characters further on in the alphabet (the specific number is the same for all letters). Piyanga's coded message includes the word "PJVN". What could the original word say?

A. CAME   B. DAME   C. FAME   D. GAME   E. LAME

Question 214:

A number of people get on the bus at the station, which is considered the first stop. At each subsequent stop, 1/2 of the people on the bus get off and then 2 people get on. Between the 4th and 5th stop after the station, there are 5 people on the bus.

How many people got on at the station?

A. 4   B. 6   C. 20   D. 24   E. 30

Question 215:

I have recently moved into a new house, and I am looking to repaint my new living room. The price of several different colours of paint is displayed in the table below. A small can contains enough to paint 10 m^2 of wall. A large can contains enough to paint 25 m^2 of wall.

Colour	Cost for a Small Can	Cost for a Large Can
Red	£4	£12
Blue	£8	£15
Black	£3	£9
White	£2	£13
Green	£7	£15
Orange	£5	£20
Yellow	£10	£12

I decide to paint my room a mixture of blue and white, and I purchase some small cans of blue paint and white paint. The cost of blue paint accounts for 50% of the total cost. I paint a total of 100 m^2 of wall space. I use up all the paint. How many m^2 of wall space have I painted blue?

A. 10 m^2 B. 20 m^2 C. 40 m^2 D. 50 m^2 E. 80 m^2

Question 216:

Cakes usually cost 42p at the bakers. The bakers want to introduce a new offer where the amount in pence you pay for each cake is discounted by the square of the number of cakes you buy. For example, buying 3 cakes would mean each cake costs 33p. Isobel says that this is not a good offer from the baker's perspective as it would be cheaper to buy several cakes than just 1. How many cakes would you have to buy for the total cost to fall below 40p?

A. 2   B. 3   C. 4   D. 5   E. 6

Question 217:

The table below shows the percentages of students in two different universities who take various courses. There are 800 students in University A and 1200 students in University B. Biology, Chemistry and Physics are counted as "Sciences".

	University A	University B
Biology	23.50	13.25
Economics	10.25	14.5
Physics	6.25	14.75
Mathematics	11.50	17.25
Chemistry	30.25	7.00
Psychology	18.25	33.25

Assuming each student only takes one course, how many more students in University A than University B study a "Science"?

A. 10   B. 25   C. 60   D. 250   E. 600

Question 218:

Traveleasy Coaches charge passengers at a rate of 50p per mile travelled, plus an additional charge of £5.00 for each international border crossed during the journey. Europremier Coaches charge £15 for every journey, plus 10p per mile travelled, with no charge for crossing international borders. Sonia is travelling from France to Germany, crossing 1 international border. She finds that both companies will charge the same price for this journey.

How many miles is Sonia travelling?

A. 10   B. 20   C. 25   D. 35   E. 40

Question 219:

Lauren, Amy and Chloe live in different cities across England. They decide to meet up together in London and have a meal together. Lauren departs from Southampton at 2:30pm, and arrives in London at 4pm. Amy's journey lasts twice as long as Lauren's journey and she arrives in London at 4:15pm. Chloe departs from Sheffield at 1:30pm, and her journey lasts an hour longer than Lauren's journey.

Which of the following statements is definitely true?

A. Chloe's journey took the longest time.
B. Amy departed after Lauren.
C. Chloe arrived last.
D. Everybody travelled by train.
E. Amy departed before Chloe.

Question 220:

Emma is packing to go on holiday by aeroplane. On the aeroplane, she can take a case of dimension 50cm by 50cm by 20cm, which, when fully packed, can weigh up to 20kg. The empty suitcase weighs 2kg. In her suitcase, she needs to take 3 books, each of which is 0.2m by 0.1m by 0.05m in size, and weighs 1000g. She would also like to take as many items of clothing as possible. Each item of clothing has volume 1500cm^3 and weighs 400 g.

Assuming each item of clothing can be squashed so as to fill any shape gap, how many items of clothing can she take in her case?

A. 28   B. 31   C. 34   D. 37   E. 40

Question 221:

Alex is buying a new bed and mattress. There are 5 bed shops Alex can buy the bed and mattress he wants from, each of which sells the bed and mattress for a different price as follows:

➢ **Bed Shop A:** Bed £120, Mattress £70
➢ **Bed Shop B:** All beds and mattresses £90 each
➢ **Bed Shop C:** Bed £140, Mattress £60. Mattress half price when you buy a bed and mattress together.
➢ **Bed Shop D:** Bed £140, Mattress £100. Get 33% off when you buy a bed and mattress together.
➢ **Bed Shop E:** Bed £175. All beds come with a free mattress.

Which is the cheapest place for Alex to buy the bed and mattress from?

A. Bed Shop A   C. Bed Shop C   E. Bed Shop E
B. Bed Shop B   D. Bed Shop D

Question 222:

In Joseph's sock drawer, there are 21 socks. 4 are blue, 5 are red, 6 are green and the rest are black. How many socks does he need to take from the drawer in order to guarantee he has a matching pair?

A. 3   B. 4   C. 5   D. 6   E. 7

Question 223:

Printing a magazine uses 1 sheet of card and 25 sheets of paper. It also uses ink. Paper comes in packs of 500 and card comes in packs of 60 which are twice the price of a pack of paper. Each ink cartridge prints 130 sheets of either paper or card. A pack of paper costs £3. Ink cartridges cost £5 each.

How many complete magazines can be printed with a budget of £300?

A. 210   B. 220   C. 230   D. 240   E. 250

Question 224:

Rebecca went swimming yesterday. After a while she had covered one fifth of her intended distance. After swimming six more lengths of the pool, she had covered one quarter of her intended distance. How many lengths of the pool did she intend to complete?

A. 40   B. 72   C. 80   D. 100   E. 120

Question 225:

As a special treat, Sammy is allowed to eat five sweets from his very large jar which contains many sweets of each of three flavours – Lemon, Orange and Strawberry. He wants to eat his five sweets in such a way that no two consecutive sweets have the same flavour.

In how many ways can he do this?

A. 32   B. 48   C. 72   D. 108   E. 162

Question 226:

Granny and her granddaughter Gill both had their birthday yesterday. Today, Granny's age in years is an even number and 15 times that of Gill. In 4 years' time Granny's age in years will be the square of Gill's age in years.

How many years older than Gill is Granny today?

A. 42　　　　　B. 49　　　　　C. 56　　　　　D. 60　　　　　E. 64

Question 227:

Pierre said, "Just one of us is telling the truth". Qadr said, "What Pierre says is not true". Ratna said, "What Qadr says is not true". Sven said, "What Ratna says is not true". Tanya said, "What Sven says is not true".

How many of them were telling the truth?

A. 0　　　　　B. 1　　　　　C. 2　　　　　D. 3　　　　　E. 4

Question 228:

Two entrants in a school's sponsored run adopt different tactics. Angus walks for half the time and runs for the other half, whilst Bruce walks for half the distance and runs for the other half. Both competitors walk at 3 mph and run at 6 mph. Angus takes 40 minutes to complete the course.

How many minutes does Bruce take?

A. 30　　　　　B. 35　　　　　C. 40　　　　　D. 45　　　　　E. 50

Question 229:

Dr Song discovers two new alien life forms on Mars. Species 8472 have one head and two legs. Species 24601 have four legs and one head. Dr Song counts a total of 73 heads and 290 legs in the area. How many members of Species 8472 are present?

A. 0　　　　　　　　C. 72　　　　　　　　E. 145
B. 1　　　　　　　　D. 73　　　　　　　　F. More information needed.

Question 230:

A restaurant menu states that:

"All chicken dishes are creamy and all vegetable dishes are spicy. No creamy dishes contain vegetables."

Which of the following **must** be true?

A.　Some chicken dishes are spicy.
B.　All spicy dishes contain vegetables.
C.　Some creamy dishes are spicy.
D.　Some vegetable dishes contain tomatoes.
E.　None of the above

Question 231:

Simon and his sister Lucy both cycle home from school. One day, Simon is kept back in detention so Lucy sets off for home first. Lucy cycles the 8 miles home at 10 mph. Simon leaves school 20 minutes later than Lucy. How fast must he cycle in order to arrive home at the same time as Lucy?

A. 10 mph　　　　B. 14 mph　　　　C. 17 mph　　　　D. 21 mph　　　　E. 24 mph

Question 232:

Dr. Whu buys 2000 shares in a company at a rate of 50p per share. He then sells the shares for 58p per share. Subsequently he buys 1000 shares at 55p per share then sells them for 61p per share. There is a charge of £20 for each transaction of buying or selling shares. What is Dr. Whu's total profit?

A. £140   B. £160   C. £180   D. £200   E. £220

Question 233:

Jina is playing darts. A dartboard is composed of equal segments, numbered from 1 to 20. She takes three throws, and each of the darts lands in a numbered segment. None land in the centre or in double or triple sections. What is the probability that her total score with the three darts is odd?

A. $\frac{1}{4}$ B. $\frac{1}{3}$ C. $\frac{1}{2}$ D. $\frac{3}{5}$ E. $\frac{2}{3}$

Question 234:

John Morgan invests £5,000 in a savings bond paying 5% interest per annum. What is the value of the investment in 5 years' time?

A. £6,250   B. £6,315   C. £6,381   D. £6,442   E. £6,570

Question 235:

Joe is 12 years younger than Michael. In 5 years the sum of their ages will be 62. How old was Michael two years ago?

A. 20   B. 24   C. 26   D. 30   E. 32

Question 236:

A book has 500 pages. Vicky tears every page out that is a multiple of 3. She then tears out every remaining page that is a multiple of 6. Finally, she tears out half of the remaining pages. If the book measures 15 cm x 30cm and is made from paper of weight 110 gm^{-2}, how much lighter is the book now than at the start?

A. 1,648 g   B. 1,698 g   C. 1,722 g   D. 1,790 g   E. 1,848 g

Question 237:

A farmer is fertilising his crops. The more fertiliser is used, the more the crops grow. Fertiliser costs 80p per kilo. Fertilising at a rate of 0.2 kgm^{-2} increases the crop yield by £1.30 m^{-2}. For each additional 100g of fertiliser above 200g, the extra yield is 30% lower than the linear projection of the stated rate. At what rate of fertiliser application is it no longer cost effective to increase the dose

A. 0.5 kgm^{-2} B. 0.6 kgm^{-2} C. 0.7 kgm^{-2} D. 0.8 kgm^{-2} E. 0.9 kgm^{-2}

Question 238:

Pet-Star, Furry Friends and Creature Cuddles are three pet shops, which each sell food for various types of pets.

Type of pet food	Amount of food required per week	Price per Kg in:		
		Pet-star	Furry Friends	Creature Cuddles
Guinea Pig	3 Kg	£2	£1	£1.50
Cat	6 Kg	£4	£6	£5
Rabbit	4 Kg	£3	£1	£2.50
Dog	8 Kg	£5	£8	£6
Chinchilla	2 Kg	£1.50	£0.50	£1

Given the information above, which of the following statements can we state is definitely *not* true?

A. Regardless of which of these shops you use, the most expensive animal to provide food for will be a dog.
B. If I own a mixture of cats and rabbits, it will be cheaper for me to shop at Pet-star.
C. If I own 3 cats and a dog, the cheapest place for me to shop is at Pet-star
D. Furry Friends sells the cheapest food for the type of pet requiring the most food
E. If I only have one pet, Creature Cuddles will not be the cheapest place to shop regardless of which type of pet I have.

Question 239:

I record my bank balance at the start of each month for six months to help me see how much I am spending each month. My salary is paid on the 10th of each month. At the start of the year, I earn £1000 a month but from March inclusive I receive a pay rise of 10%.

Date	Bank balance
January 1st	1,200
February 1st	1,029
March 1st	1,189
April 1st	1,050
May 1st	925
June 1st	1,025

In which month did I spend the most money?
A. January
B. February
C. March
D. April
E. May

Question 240:

Amy needs to travel from Southtown station to Northtown station, which are 100 miles apart. She can travel by 3 different methods: train, aeroplane or taxi. The tables below show the different times for these 3 methods. The taxi takes 1 minute to cover a distance of 1 mile. Aeroplane passengers must be at the airport 30 minutes before their flight. Southtown airport is 10 minutes travelling time from Southtown station and Northtown airport is 30 minutes travelling time from Northtown station.

If Amy wants to arrive by 1700 and wants to set off as late as possible, what method of travel should she choose and what time will she leave Southtown station?

Train	Departs Southtown station	1400	1500	1600
	Arrives Northtown station	1615	1650	1715
Flights	Departs Southtown airport	1610		
	Arrives Northtown airport	1645		

A. Flight, 1530
B. Train, 1600
C. Taxi, 1520
D. Train, 1500
E. Flight, 1610

Question 241:

In the multiplication grid below, a, b, c and d are all integers. What does d equal?

A. 18
B. 24
C. 30
D. 40
E. 45

	c	d
a	168	720
b	119	510

Question 242:

A sixth form college has 1,500 students. 48% are girls. 80 of the girls are mixed race.

If an equal proportion of boys and girls are mixed race, how many mixed race boys are there in the college to the nearest 10?

A. 50
B. 60
C. 70
D. 80
E. 90

Question 243:

Christine is a control engineer at the Browdon Nuclear Power Plant. On Wednesday, she is invited to a party on the Friday, and asks her manager if she can take the Friday off. She acknowledged that this will mean she will have worked less than the required number of hours this week, and offers to make this up by working extra hours next week. Her manager suggests that instead, she works 5 hours this Sunday, and 3 extra hours next Thursday to make up the required hours. Christine accepts this proposal. Christine's amended schedule for the week is shown below:

Day	Monday	Tuesday	Wednesday	Thursday	Friday	Saturday	Sunday
Hours worked	8	7	9	6	0	0	5

How many hours was Christine supposed to have worked this week, if she had completed her usual Friday shift?

A. 34
B. 35
C. 36
D. 38
E. 40
F. 42

Question 244:

Leonidas notes that the time on a normal analogue clock is 0340. What is the smaller angle between the hands on the clock?

A. 110°
B. 120°
C. 130°
D. 140°
E. 150°

Question 245:

Sheila is on a shift at the local supermarket. Unfortunately, the till has developed a fault, meaning it cannot tell her how much change to give each customer. A customer is purchasing the following items, at the following costs:

-    A packet of grated cheese priced at £3.25
-    A whole cucumber, priced at 75p
-    A fish pie mix, priced at £4.00
-    3 DVDs, each priced at £3.00

Sheila knows there is an offer on DVDs in the store at present, in which 3 DVDs bought together will only cost £8.00.The customer pays with a £50 note. How much change will Sheila need to give the customer?

A.   £33
B.   £34
C.   £35
D.   £36
E.   £37

SECTION 1: Data Analysis

Data analysis questions show a great variation in type and difficulty. The best way to improve with these questions is to do lots of practice questions in order to familiarise yourself with the style of questions.

Options First

Despite the fact that you may have lots of data to contend with, the rule about looking at the options first still stands in this section. This will allow you to register what type of calculation you are required to make and what data you might need to look at for this. Remember, Options → Question → Data/Passage.

Working with Numbers

Percentages frequently make an appearance in this section and it's vital that you're able to work comfortably with them. For example, you should be comfortable increasing and decreasing by percentages, and working out inverse percentages too. When dealing with complex percentages, break them down into their components. For example, $17.5\% = 10\% + 5\% + 2.5\%$.

Graphs and Tables

When you're working with graphs and tables, it's important that you take a few seconds to check the following before actually extracting data from it.

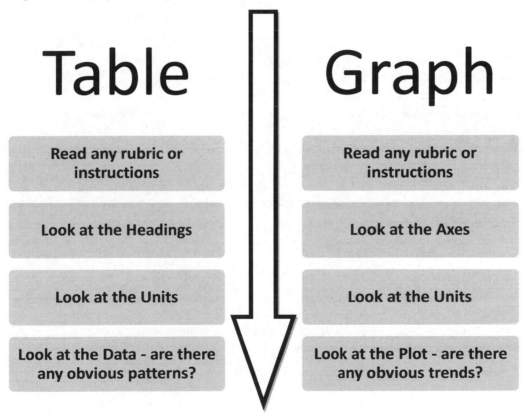

Get into the habit of doing this whenever you are faced with data and you'll find it much easier to approach these questions under time pressure.

Data Analysis Questions

Questions 246 to 248 are based on the following passage:

It has recently been questioned as to whether the recommended five fruit and vegetables a day is sufficient or if it would be more beneficial to eat 7 fruit and vegetable portions each day. A study at UCL looked at the fruit and vegetables eating habits of 65,000 people in England. Analysis of the data showed that eating more portions was beneficial and vegetables seemed to have a greater protective effect than fruit. The study however did not distinguish whether vegetables themselves have a greater protective effect, or whether these people tend to eat an overall healthier diet. A meta-analysis carried out by researchers across the world complied data from 16 studies which encompassed over 800,000 participants, of whom 56,423 had died.

They found a decline in death of around 5% from all causes for each additional portion of fruit or vegetables eaten, however they recorded no further decline for people who ate over 5 portions. Rates of cardiovascular disease, heart disease or stroke, were shown to decline 4% for each portion up to five, whereas the number of portions of fruit and vegetables eaten seemed to have little impact on cancer rates. The data from these studies points in a similar direction, that eating as much fruit and vegetables a day is preferable, but that five portions is sufficient to have a significant impact on reduction in mortality. Further studies need to look into the slight discrepancies, particularly why the English study found vegetables more protective, and if any specific cancers may be affected by fruit and vegetables even if the general cancer rates more greatly depend on other lifestyle factors.

Question 246:

Which of the following statements is correct?

A. The UCL study found no additional reduction in mortality in those who eat 7 rather than 5 portions of fruit and vegetables a day.

B. People who eat more fruit and vegetables are assumed to have an overall healthier diet which is what gives them the beneficial effect.

C. The meta analysis found fruit and vegetables are more protective against cancer than cardiovascular disease

D. The English study showed fruit had more protective effects than vegetables.

E. The meta-analysis found no additional reduction in mortality in those who eat 7 rather than 5 portions of fruit and vegetables a day.

F. The meta-analysis suggests people who eat 7 portions would have a 10% lower risk of death from any cause than those who eat 5 portions.

G. Fruit and vegetables are not protective against any specific cancers.

Question 247:

If rates of death were found to be 1% lower in the UCL study than the meta-analysis, approximately how many people died in the UCL study?

A. 3,000   B. 3,200   C. 3,900   D. 4,550   E. 5,200

Question 248

Which statement does the article **MOST** agree with?

A. Eating more fruit and vegetables does not particularly lower the risk of any specific cancers.

B. The UCL research suggests that the guideline should be 7 fruit and vegetables a day for England.

C. The results found by the UCL study and the meta-analysis were contradictory.

D. Many don't eat enough vegetables due to cost and taste.

E. Fruit and vegetables are only protective against cardiovascular disease.

F. The UCL study and meta-analysis use a similar sample of participants.

G. People should aim to eat 7 portions of fruit and vegetables a day.

Questions 249-251 relate to the following table regarding average alcohol consumption in 2010.

Country	Total	Recorded Consumption	Unrecorded consumption	Beer (%)	Wine (%)	Spirits (%)	Other (%)	2020 Consumption Projection
Belarus		14.4	3.2	17.3	5.2	46.6	30.9	17.1
Lithuania	15.4	12.9	2.5		7.8	34.1	11.6	16.2
Andorra	13.8		1.4	34.6		20.1	0	9.1
Grenada	12.5	11.9	0.7	29.3	4.3		0.2	10.4
Czech Republic	13	11.8	1.2	53.5	20.5	26	0	14.1
France	12.2	11.8		18.8	56.4	23.1	1.7	11.6
Russia		11.5	3.6	37.6	11.4	51	0	14.5
Ireland	11.9	11.4	0.5	48.1	26.1	18.7	7.7	10.9

NB: Some data is missing.

Question 249:

Which of the following countries had the highest total beer and wine consumption for 2010?

A. Belarus
B. Lithuania
C. Ireland
D. France
E. Andorra

Question 250:

Which country has the greatest difference for spirit consumption in 2010 and 2020 projection, assuming percentages stay the same?

A. Russia
B. Belarus
C. Lithuania
D. Grenada
E. Ireland

Question 251:

It was later found that some of the percentages of types of alcohol consumed had been mixed up. If the actual amount of beer consumed by each person in the Czech Republic was on average 4.9L, which country were the percentage figures mixed up with?

A. Lithuania
B. Grenada
C. Russia
D. France
E. Ireland
F. Belarus
G. Andorra

Questions 252-255 are based on the following information:

The table below shows the incidence of 6 different types of cancer in Australia:

	Prostate	Lung	Bowel	Bladder	Breast	Uterus
Men	40,000	25,000	20,000	8,000	1,000	0
Women	0	20,000	18,000	4,000	50,000	9,000

Question 252:

Supposing there are 10 million men and 10 million women in Australia, how many percentage points higher is the incidence of cancer amongst women than amongst men?

A. 0.007 %   B. 0.07 %   C. 0.093 %   D. 0.7 %   E. 0.93 %

Question 253:

Now suppose there are 11.5 million men and 10 million women in Australia. Assuming all men are equally likely to get each type of cancer and all women are equally likely to get each type of cancer, how many of the types of cancer are you more likely to develop if you are a man than if you are a woman?

A. 1   B. 2   C. 3   D. 4

Question 254:

Suppose that prostate, bladder and breast cancer patients visit hospital 1 time during the first month of 2015 and patients for all other cancers visit hospital 2 times during the first month of 2015. 10% of cancer patients in Australia are in Sydney, and patients in Sydney are not more or less likely to have certain types of cancer than other patients.

How many hospital visits are made by patients in Sydney with these 6 cancers during the first month of 2015?

A. 10,300   C. 19,500   E. 195,000
B. 18,400   D. 28,700   F. 287,000

Question 255:

Which of the graphs correctly represents the combined proportion of men versus women with bladder cancer?

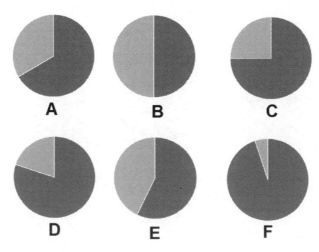

Questions 256 – 258 are based on the following information:

Units of alcohol are calculated by multiplying the alcohol percentage by the volume of liquid in litres, for example a 0.75 L bottle of wine which is 12% alcohol contains 9 units. 1 pint = 570 ml.

	Volume in bottle/barrel	Standard drinks per bottle/barrel	Percentage
Vodka	1250 ml	50	40%
Beer	10 pints	11.4	3%
Cocktail	750 ml	3	8%
Wine	750 ml	3.75	12.5%

Question 256:

Which standard drink has the most units of alcohol in?

A. Vodka
B. Beer
C. Cocktail
D. Wine

Question 257:

Some guidance suggests the recommended maximum number of units of alcohol per week for women is 14. In a week, Hannah drinks 4 standard drinks of wine, 3 standard drinks of beer, 2 standard cocktails and 5 standard vodkas. This guidance states the recommended maximum number of units per week for men is 21. In a week, Mark drinks 2 standard drinks of wine, 6 standard drinks of beer, 3 standard cocktails and 10 standard vodkas.

Who has exceeded their recommended maximum number of units by more and by how many units more have they exceeded it by than the other person?

A. Hannah, by 1 unit
B. Hannah, by 0.5 units
C. Both by the same
D. Mark, by 0.5 units
E. Mark, by 1 unit

Question 258:

How many different combinations of drinks that total 4 units are there (the same combination in a different order doesn't count).

A. 2
B. 3
C. 4
D. 5
E. 6

Questions 259-261 relate to the table below which shows information about Greentown's population:

	Female	Male	Total
Under 20	1,930		
20-39	1,960	3,760	5,720
40-59		4,130	
60 and over	2,350	2,250	4,600
Total	11,430	12,890	24,320

Question 259:

How many males under 20 are there in Greentown?

A. 2,650
B. 2,700
C. 2,730
D. 2,750
E. 2,850

Question 260:

How many females aged 40-59 are there in Greentown?

A. Between 3,000 and 4,000
B. Between 4,000 and 5,000
C. Between 5,000 and 6,000
D. Between 6,000 and 7,000

Question 261:

Which is the approximate ratio of females:males in the age group that has the highest ratio of males:females?

A. 1.4:1
B. 1.9:1
C. 1:1.9
D. 1:1.4

Questions 262-264 relate to the follow graph:

The graph below shows the average temperatures in London (top trace) and Newcastle (bottom trace).

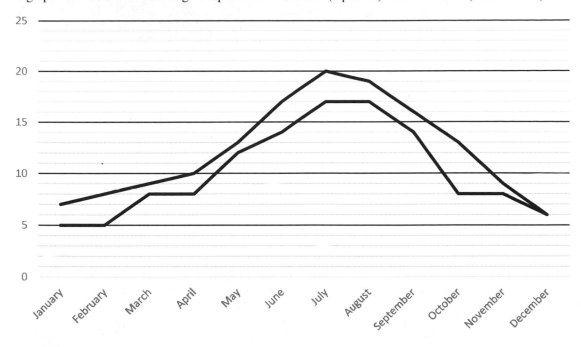

Question 262:

If the average monthly temperature is the same in every year, how many times during the period May 2007 to September 2013 inclusive is the average temperature the same in 2 consecutive months in Newcastle?

A. 20
B. 24
C. 25
D. 30

Question 263:

In how many months in the period specified in the previous question is the average temperature in London AND Newcastle lower than the previous month?

A. 19
B. 21
C. 25
D. 32

Question 264:

To the nearest 0.5 degrees Celsius, what is the average temperature difference between Newcastle and London?

A. 1.5°C
B. 2°C
C. 2.5 °C
D. 3 °C

Questions 265-267 concern the following data:

The pie chart to the right shows sales of ice cream across the four quarters of a year from January to December. Sales are lowest in the month of February. From February they increase in every subsequent month until they get to the maximum sales and from that point they decrease in every subsequent month until the end of the year.

Sales of ice cream

Question 265:

In which month are the sales highest?

A. June   B. July   C. August   D. Cannot tell

Question 266:

If total sales of ice cream were £354,720 for the year, how much of this was taken during Q1?

A. 29,480   B. £29,560   C. £29,650   D. £29,720   E. £29,800

Question 267:

Assuming total sales revenue (i.e. before costs are taken off) is £180,000, and that each tub of ice cream is sold for £2 and costs the manufacturer £1.50 in total production and transportation costs, how much profit is made during Q2?

A. £15,000   B. £30,000   C. £45,000   D. £60,000

Question 268:

Data on the amount families spend on food per month to the nearest £100 was collected for families with 1, 2 and 3 children. The percentage of families with different spending sizes is displayed below:

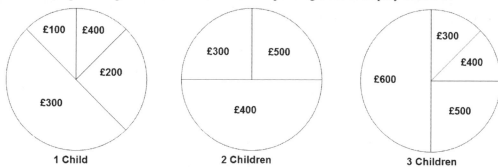

Which of the following statements is definitely true?

A. More families with 1 child than families with 2 children spent £300 a month on food.
B. The overall fraction of families spending £600 was 1/6.
C. All of the families with 2 children spent under £4000 on food per year.
D. The fraction of families with 1 child spending £400 on food per month is the same as the fraction of families with 3 children spending this amount.
E. The average amount spent on food by families with 2 children is £410 a month.

Questions 269-272 are based on the passage below:

A big secondary school recently realised that there were a large number of incidences of bullying occurring that were going unnoticed by teachers. It is possible that some believe bullying to be as much a part of student life as lessons and homework. In order to tackle the problem, the school emailed out a questionnaire to all students' parents and asked them to question their children about where they had experienced or seen bullying in school. Those children that answered yes were then asked if they had told their teachers about it, and asked why they did not if they had not. Those that had told their teacher were asked whether they had seen the teacher act upon the information and whether the bullying had stopped as a result.

Of the 2500 school students surveyed 2210 filled in the online questionnaire. The results were that, 1121 students, almost exactly half (50.7%) had seen bullying in school. Only 396 (35%) of these students told a teacher about the bullying. Of the students who told a teacher, 286 did not witness any action following sharing of the information and of those that did, 60% did not notice any direct action with the bully involved. From those students who did not report the bullying, 146 gave the reason that they didn't think it was important. 427 cited fears of being found out. 212 students said they did not tell because they didn't think the teachers would do anything about it even if they did know. Assume that all the students who filled out the survey did so honestly.

Question 269:
To the nearest integer, what percentage of students did not respond?
A. 10%   B. 12%   C. 18%   D. 8%   E. 5%

Question 270:
If a student saw bullying occur and did not tell a teacher about it, what is the probability that the reasoning for this is that they thought it to be unimportant?

A. 0.1   B. 0.15   C. 0.2   D. 0.35   E. 0.13

Question 271:
After reporting the bullying, how many students saw the teacher act on the information directly with the bully?

A. 66
B. 44
C. 178
D. 104
E. 118

Question 272:
Which of the following does the questionnaire indicate is the best explanation for why students at the school did not report bullying?

A. Students do not think bullying happens at their school.
B. Students think the teachers will do nothing with the information.
C. Students think that bullying is a part of school life.
D. The student's were worried about others finding out.

Question 273:

The obesity epidemic is growing rapidly with reports of a three-fold rise in the period from 2007 to 2012. The rates of hospital admission have also been found to vary massively across different areas of England with the highest rates in the North-East (56 per 100,000 people), and the lowest rates in the East of England (12 per 100,000). During almost every year from 2001-12, there were around twice as many women admitted for obesity as men. The reason for this is however unclear and does not imply there are twice as many obese women as men.

What was the approximate number of admissions per 100 000 women in the North-East in 2011-12?

A. 18   B. 26   C. 37   D. 56   E. 62   F. 74

Question 274:

Health professionals are becoming increasingly worried by the decline in exercise being taken by both children and adults. Around only 40% of adults take the recommended amount of exercise which is 150 minutes per week. As well as falling rates of exercise, a shockingly low number of individuals eat five portions of fruit and vegetables a day. Figures for children aged 5-15 fell to only 16% for boys, and 20% for girls in 2011. Data for adults was only slightly better with 29% of women and 24% of men eating the recommended number of portions.

Using a figure of 8 million children between 5-15 years (equal ratio of girls to boys) in England in 2011, how many more girls than boys ate 5 portions of fruit and vegetables a day?

A. 80,000   B. 120,000   C. 160,000   D. 320,000   E. 640,000

Question 275:

The table below shows the leading causes of death in the UK.

	WOMEN		MEN	
Rank	**Cause of Death**	**Number of Deaths**	**Cause of Death**	**Number of Deaths**
1	Dementia and Alzheimer's	31,850	Coronary Heart Disease	37,797
2	Coronary Heart Disease	26,075	Lung Cancer	16,818
3	Stroke	20,706	Dementia and Alzheimer's	15,262
4	Flu and Pneumonia	15,361	Lower Respiratory Disease	15,021
5	Lower Respiratory Disease	14,927	Stroke	14,058
6	Lung Cancer	13,619	Flu and Pneumonia	11,426
7	Breast Cancer	10,144	Prostate Cancer	9,726
8	Colon Cancer	6,569	Colon Cancer	7,669
9	Urinary Infections	5,457	Lymphatic Cancer	6,311
10	Heart Failure	5,012	Liver Disease	4,661
	Total	**261,205**	**Total**	**245,585**

Using information from the table only, which of the following statements is correct?

A.   More women died from cancers than men.

B.   More than 30,000 women died due to respiratory causes.

C.   Dementia and Alzheimer's is more common in women than men.

D.   No cause of death is of the same ranking for both men and women.

Question 276 is based on the passage below:

The government has recently released a campaign leaflet saying that last year waiting times in NHS A&E departments decreased 20% compared to the year before. The opposition has criticised this statement, saying that there are several definitions which can be described as "waiting times", and the government's campaign leaflet does not make it clear what they mean by "waiting times in A&E".

The NHS watchdog has recently released the following figures describing different aspects of A&E departments, and the change from last year:

Assessment Criterion	2014	2013
Average time spent before being seen in A&E	1 hour	90 minutes
Average time between dialling 999 and receiving treatment in A&E	2 hours	3 hours
Number of people waiting for over 4 hours in A&E	3200	4000
Number of high-priority cases waiting longer than 1 hour	900	1000
Average waiting time for those seen in under 4 hours	50 minutes	40 minutes

Question 276:

Assuming these figures are correct, which criterion of assessment have the government described as "waiting times in A&E" on their campaign leaflet?

A. Number of people waiting for over 4 hours in A&E.
B. Number of people waiting for under 4 hours in A&E.
C. Number of high-priority cases waiting longer than 1 hour.
D. Average time spent before being seen in A&E.
E. Average time between dialling 999 and receiving treatment in A&E.
F. Average waiting time for those seen in less than 4 hours.

Questions 277– 279 refer to the following information:

The table below shows the final standings at the end of the season, after each team has played all the other teams twice each (once at home, once away). The teams are listed in order of how many points they got during the season. Teams get 3 points for a win, 1 point for a draw and 0 points for a loss. No team got the same number of points as another team. Some of the information in the table is missing.

Team	W	D	L
United	8	1	
Athletic	7		
City	7	2	
Town	1	4	
Rovers		0	9
Rangers		2	8

Question 277:

How many points did Rovers get?

A. 0
B. 3
C. 6
D. 9
E. More information needed.

Question 278:

How many games did Athletic lose?

A. 0
B. 1
C. 2
D. 3
E. More information needed.

Question 279:

How many more points did United get than Rangers?

A. 7
B. 15
C. 23
D. 25
E. More information needed.

Questions 280-282 use information from the graph recording A&E attendances and response times for NHS England from 2004 to 2014. Type 1 departments are major A&E units, type 2&3 are urgent care centres or minor injury units. The old target (2004 – June 2010) was 97.5%; the new target (July 2010 – 2015) is 95%.

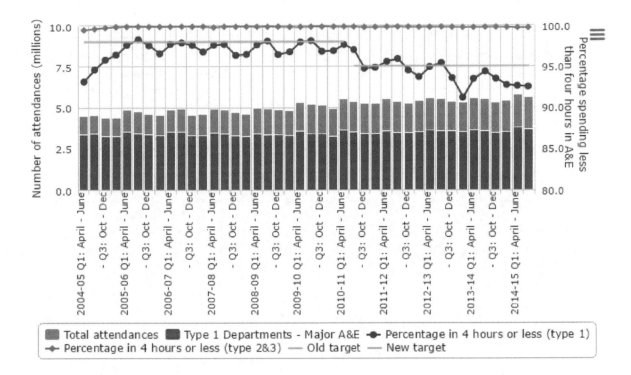

Question 280:

Which of the following statements is **FALSE**?

A. There has been an overall increase in total A&E attendances from 2004-2014.
B. The number of attendances in type 1 departments has been fairly constant from 2004-2014.
C. The new target of 4 hours waiting time has only been reached in two quarters by type 1 departments.
D. The change in attendances is largely due to an in increase people going to type 2&3 departments.

Question 281:

What percentage has the number of total attendances changed from Q1 2004-5 to Q1 2008-9?

A. +5%   C. +10%   E. +15%
B. –5%   D. –10%   F. –15%

Question 282:

If the new target was achieved by type 1 departments 4 times, in what percentage of the quarters was the target missed?

A. 25%
B. 60%
C. 75%
D. 90%

Questions 283-284 relate to the following data:

Ranjna is travelling from Manchester to Bali. She is required to make a stopover in Singapore for which he wants to allow at least 2 hours. It takes 14 hours to fly from Manchester to Singapore, and 2 hours from Singapore to Bali. The table below shows the departure times in local time [Manchester GMT, Singapore GMT + 8, Bali GMT + 8]:

Manchester to Singapore			Singapore to Bali			
Monday	Wednesday	Thursday	Monday	Tuesday	Wednesday	Thursday
08.00	09.30	02.30	13.00	00.00	15.30	13.00
10.45	14.00	08.30	15.30	07.30	18.00	16.00
13.30	18.00	12.30	21.00	08.30	20.30	19.00
15.00	20.00	19.00		12.00		

Question 283:

What is the latest flight Ranjna can take from Manchester to ensure she arrives at Bali Airport by Thursday 22:00?

A. 18:00 Tuesday
B. 14:00 Wednesday
C. 18:00 Wednesday
D. 20:00 Wednesday
E. 02:30 Thursday
F. 08:30 Thursday

Question 284:

Ranjna takes the 08:00 flight from Manchester to Singapore on Monday. She allows 1 hour to clear customs and collect her luggage at Bali Airport and another 45 minutes for the taxi to her hotel. At what time will she arrive at the hotel?

A. 16.45 Monday
B. 04:15 Tuesday
C. 10:30 Tuesday
D. 12:15 Tuesday
E. 12:30 Tuesday
F. 20:30 Tuesday

Question 285:

The graph below represents the percentage of adult smokers in the UK from 1974 to 2010. The top trace represents men and the bottom trace represents women. The middle trace is for both men and women.

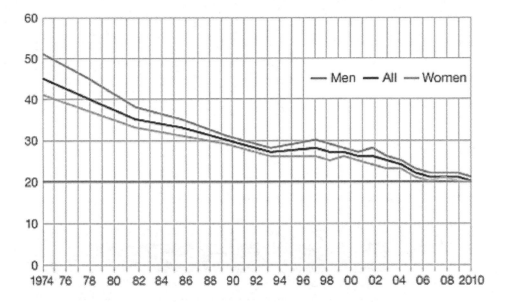

Which of the following statements can be concluded from the graph?

A. The 2007 smoking ban increased the rate in decline of smokers.
B. There has been a constant reduction in percentage of smoker since 1974.
C. The highest rate in decline in smoking for women was 2004-2006.
D. From 1974 to 2010, the smoking rate in men decreased by a half.
E. There has always been a significant difference between the smoking habits of men and women.

Question 286:

The name, age, height, weight and IQ of 11 people were recorded below in a table and a scatter plot. However, the axis labels were left out by mistake. Scale breaks are permitted.

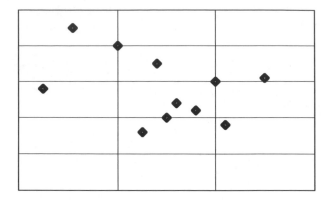

Name	Age	Height (cm)	Weight (kg)	IQ
Alice	18	180	68	110
Ben	12	160	79	120
Camilla	14	170	62	100
David	25	145	98	108
Eliza	29	165	75	96
Rohan	15	190	92	111
George	20	172	88	104
Hannah	22	168	68	115
Ian	13	182	86	98
James	17	176	90	102
Katie	27	151	66	125

Which variants are possible for the X and Y axis?

	X axis	Y axis
A	Height	Weight
B	IQ	Height
C	Age	IQ
D	Height	IQ
E	Height	Age
F	IQ	Weight

Question 287:

A group of students looked at natural variation in height and arm span within their group and got the following results:

Name	Arm span (cm)	Height (cm)
Adam	175	168
Tom	188	175
Shiv	172	184
Mary	148	142
Alice	165	156
Sarah	166	168
Emily	159	160
Matthew	165	172
Michael	185	183

They then drew a scatter plot, but forgot to include names for each point. They also forgot to plot one student.

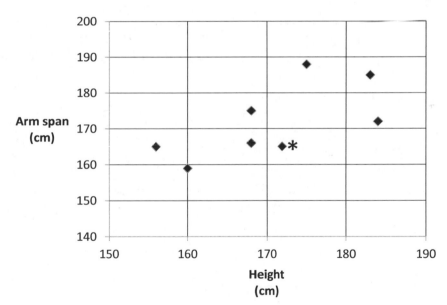

Which student is represented by the point marked with a *?

A. Alice
B. Sarah
C. Matthew
D. Adam
E. Emily
F. Michael

Questions 288 - 294 are based on the following information:

The rectangle represents women. The circle represents those that have children. The triangle represents those that work, and the square those that went to university.

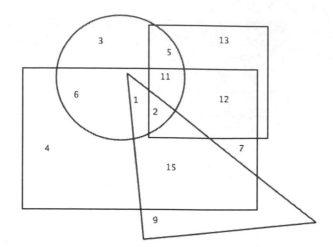

Question 288:

What is the number of non-working women who have children and who did not go to university?

A. 3   B. 5   C. 6   D. 7   E. 9

Question 289:

What is the total number of women who have children and work?

A. 1   B. 2   C. 3   D. 11   E. 14

Question 290:

How many women were surveyed in total?

A. 49   C. 58   E. 85

B. 51   D. 67   F. None of the above.

Question 291:

What is the number of people who went to university and had children?

A. 5   C. 13   E. 18

B. 11   D. 16   F. None of the above.

Question 292:

What is the total number of people who went to university, or have children but not both?

A. 18   C. 35   E. 53

B. 28   D. 41   F. None of the above.

Question 293:

The total number of men who went to university and had children was?

A. 3   B. 4   C. 5   D. 12   E. 13   F. 18

Question 294:

Which of the following people were not surveyed? Choose **TWO** options.

A. A non-working woman who went to university but did not have children.

B. A working man who went to university and has children.

C. A working woman who had children but did not go to university.

D. A non-working man who did not have children and did not go to university.

E. A working woman who went to university but did not have children.

Question 295:

Savers"R"Us is national chain of supermarkets. The price of several items in the supermarket is displayed below:

Item	Price
Beef roasting joint	£8.00
Chicken breast fillet	£6.00
Lamb shoulder	£7.00
Pork belly meat portion	£4.00
Sausages – 10 pack	£3.50

This week the supermarket has a sale on, with 50% off the normal price of all meat products. Alfred visits the supermarket during this sale and purchases a beef roasting joint, a 10 pack of sausages and a lamb shoulder, paying with a £20 note.

How much change does Alfred get?

A. £1.50
B. £5.00

C. £10.75
D. £11.75

E. £12.50
F. None of the above.

Question 296:

The local football league table is shown below, but the number of goals scored against Wilmslow is missing. Each team played the other teams in the league once at home and once away during the season.

Team Name	Points	Goals For	Goals Against
Sale	20	16	2
Wilmslow	16	11	?
Timperley	14	8	7
Altrincham	13	7	9
Mobberley	10	8	12
Hale	8	4	14

How many goals must Wilmslow have conceded?

A. 8
B. 9

C. 10
D. 11

E. 12
F. 14

Question 297:

The heights and weights of three women with BMI's 21, 22 and 23 were measured. If Julie and Lydia had different weights but the same height of 154 cm, and the weight of Emma, Lydia and Julie combined was 345 lbs, what was Emma's height?

Weight (lbs)

	100	105	110	115	120
152	19	20	22	24	26
154	18	19	21	23	25
156	17	18	20	22	24
158	15	17	19	21	23
160	14	15	18	20	22
162	13	14	17	19	21
164	12	13	15	18	20
166	11	12	14	17	19
168	10	11	13	15	18
170	9	10	12	14	17

Height (cm) is shown to the left of the table rows.

A. 158 cm
B. 162 cm
C. 160 cm
D. 164 cm
E. 165 cm

Question 298:

The measurements for different types of fish appear below:

	Length (cm)	Weight (lbs)
Bluecup	78	40
Silverfinn	96	60
Starbug	98	98
Jawless	100	56
Lamprene	108	92
Scarfynne	118	40
Rayfish	122	136
Lobefin	126	108
Eringill	146	124
Whaler	148	154
Magic fish	176	124
Blondeye	188	72

Which fish is shown by the point marked **X**?

A. Silverfinn   B. Starbug   C. Lobefin   D. Blondeye   E. Eringill

The following graphs are required for questions 299-300:

The graph below shows the price of crude oil in US Dollars during 2014:

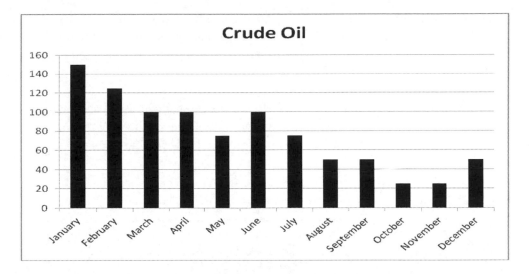

The graph below shows total oil production, in millions of barrels per day:

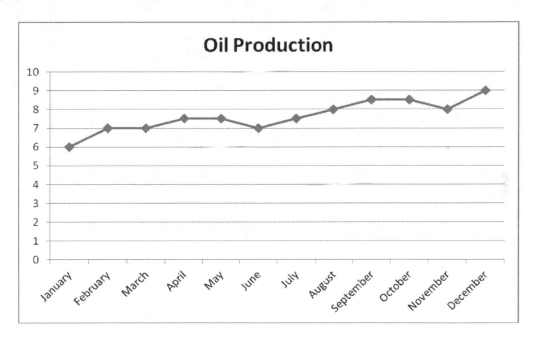

Question 299:

What was approximate total oil production in 2014?

A.   1,750 million barrels

B.   2,146 million barrels

C.   2,300 million barrels

D.   2,700 million barrels

E.   3,500 million barrels

Question 300:

How much did oil sales total in July 2014?

A. $0.56 Billion   B. $16.9 Billion   C. $17.4 Billion   D. $21.1 Billion

SECTION 2

Section 2 is undoubtedly the most time-pressured section of the BMAT. This section tests GCSE biology, chemistry, physics and maths. You have to answer 27 questions in 30 minutes. The questions can be quite difficult and it's easy to get bogged down. However, it's also the section in which you can improve the most quickly in so it's well worth spending time on it.

Although the vast majority of questions in section 2 aren't particularly difficult, the intense time pressure of having to do one question every minute makes this section the hardest in the BMAT. As with section 1, the trick is to identify and do the easy questions whilst leaving the hard ones for the end.

In general, the biology and chemistry questions in the BMAT require the least amount of time per question whilst the maths and physics are more time-draining as they usually consist of multi-step calculations.

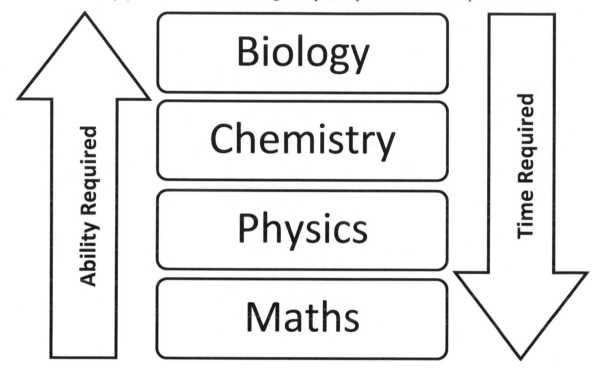

Gaps in Knowledge

The BMAT only tests GCSE level knowledge. However, there is a large variation in content between the GCSE exam boards meaning that you may not have covered some topics that are examinable. This is more likely if you didn't carry on with Biology or physics to AS level (e.g. Newtonian mechanics and parallel circuits in physics; hormones and stem cells in biology). If you fall into this category, you are highly advised to go through the BMAT Specification and ensure that you have covered all examinable topics. An electronic copy of this can be obtained from the official BMAT website at www.admissionstestingservice.org/bmat.

The questions in this book will help highlight any particular areas of weakness or gaps in your knowledge that you may have. Upon discovering these, make sure you take some time to revise these topics before carrying on – there is little to be gained by attempting section 2 questions with huge gaps in your knowledge.

Maths

Being confident with maths is extremely important for section 2. Many students find that improving their numerical and algebraic skills usually results in big improvements in their section 1 and 2 scores. Remember that maths in section 2 not only comes up in the maths question but also in physics (manipulating equations and standard form) and chemistry (mass calculations). So if you find yourself consistently running out of time in section 2, spending a few hours on brushing up your basic maths skills may do wonders for you.

SECTION 2: Biology

Thankfully, the biology questions tend to be fairly straightforward and require the least amount of time. You should be able to do the majority of these within the 60 second limit (often far less). This means that you should be aiming to make up time in these questions. In the majority of cases – you'll either know the answer or not i.e. they test advanced recall so the trick is to ensure that there are no obvious gaps in your knowledge.

Before going onto to do the practice questions in this book, ensure you are comfortable with the following commonly tested topics:

➤ Structure of animal, plant and bacterial cells

➤ Osmosis, Diffusion and Active Transport

➤ Cell Division (mitosis + meiosis)

➤ Family pedigrees and Inheritance

➤ DNA structure and replication

➤ Gene Technology & Stem Cells

➤ Enzymes – Function, mechanism and examples of digestive enzymes

➤ Aerobic and Anaerobic Respiration

➤ The central vs. peripheral nervous system

➤ The respiratory cycle including movement of ribs and diaphragm

➤ The Cardiac Cycle

➤ Hormones

➤ Basic immunology

➤ Food chains and food webs

➤ The carbon and nitrogen cycles

Top tip! If you find yourself getting less than 50% of biology questions correct in this book, make sure you revisit the syllabus before attempting more questions as this is the best way to maximise your efficiency. In general, there is no reason why you shouldn't be able to get the vast majority of biology questions correct (and in well under 60 seconds) with sufficient practice.

Biology Questions

Question 301:

In relation to the human genome, which of the following are correct?

1. The DNA genome is coded by 4 different bases.
2. The sugar backbone of the DNA strand is formed of glucose.
3. DNA is found in the nucleus of bacteria.

A. 1 only	C. 3 only	E. 1 and 3	G. 1, 2 and 3
B. 2 only	D. 1 and 2	F. 2 and 3	

Question 302:

Animal cells contain organelles that take part in vital processes. Which of the following is true?

1. The majority of energy production by animal cells occurs in the mitochondria.
2. The cell wall protects the animal cell membrane from outside pressure differences.
3. The endoplasmic reticulum plays a role in protein synthesis.

A. 1 only	C. 3 only	E. 2 and 3	G. 1, 2 and 3
B. 2 only	D. 1 and 2	F. 1 and 3	

Question 303:

With regards to animal mitochondria, which of the following is correct?

A. Mitochondria are not necessary for aerobic respiration.
B. Mitochondria are the sole cause of sperm cell movement.
C. The majority of DNA replication happens inside mitochondria.
D. Mitochondria are more abundant in fat cells than in skeletal muscle.
E. The majority of protein synthesis occurs in mitochondria.
F. Mitochondria are enveloped by a double membrane.

Question 304:

In relation to bacteria, which of the following is **FALSE**?

A. Bacteria always lead to disease.
B. Bacteria contain plasmid DNA.
C. Bacteria do not contain mitochondria.
D. Bacteria have a cell wall and a plasma membrane.
E. Some bacteria are susceptible to antibiotics.

Question 305:

In relation to bacterial replication, which of the following is correct?

A. Bacteria undergo sexual reproduction.
B. Bacteria have a nucleus.
C. Bacteria carry genetic information on circular plasmids.
D. Bacterial genomes are formed of RNA instead of DNA.
E. Bacteria require gametes to replicate.

Question 306

Which of the following are correct regarding active transport?

A. ATP is necessary and sufficient for active transport.
B. ATP is not necessary but sufficient for active transport.
C. The relative concentrations of the material being transported have little impact on the rate of active transport.
D. Transport proteins are necessary and sufficient for active transport.
E. Active transport relies on transport proteins that are powered by an electrochemical gradient.

Question 307:

Concerning mammalian reproduction, which of the following is **FALSE**?

A. Fertilisation involves the fusion of two gametes.
B. Reproduction is sexual and the offspring display genetic variation.
C. Reproduction relies upon the exchange of genetic material.
D. Mammalian gametes are diploid cells produced via meiosis.
E. Embryonic growth requires carefully controlled mitosis.

Question 308:

Which of the following apply to Mendelian inheritance?

1. It only applies to plants.
2. It treats different traits as either dominant or recessive.
3. Heterozygotes have a 25% chance of expressing a recessive trait.

A. 1 only	C. 3 only	E. 1 and 3	G. All of the
B. 2 only	D. 1 and 2	F. 2 and 3	above

Question 309:

Which of the following statements are correct?

A. Hormones are secreted into the blood stream and act over long distances at specific target organs.
B. Hormones are substances that almost always cause muscles to contract.
C. Hormones have no impact on the nervous or enteric systems.
D. Hormones are always derived from food and never synthesised.
E. Hormones act rapidly to restore homeostasis.

Question 310:

With regard to neuronal signalling in the body, which of the following are true?

1. Neuronal transmission can be caused by both electrical and chemical stimulation.
2. Synapses ultimately result in the production of an electrical current for signal transduction.
3. All synapses in humans are electrical and unidirectional.

A. 1 only	C. 3 only	E. 1 and 3	G. 1, 2 and 3
B. 2 only	D. 1 and 2	F. 2 and 3	

Question 311:
What is the **primary** reason that pH is controlled so tightly in humans?

A. To allow rapid protein synthesis.
B. To allow for effective digestion throughout the GI tract.
C. To ensure ions can function properly in neural signalling.
D. To prevent changes in electrical charge in polypeptide chains.
E. To prevent changes in core body temperature.

Question 312:
Which of the following statements are correct regarding bacterial cell walls?

1. It confers bacteria protection against external environmental stimuli.
2. It is an evolutionary remnant and now has little functional significance in most bacteria.
3. It is made up primarily of glucose in bacteria.

A. Only 1	C. Only 3	E. 2 and 3	G. 1, 2 and 3
B. Only 2	D. 1 and 2	F. 1 and 3	

Question 313:
Which of the following statements are correct regarding mitosis?

1. It is important in sexual reproduction.
2. A single round of mitosis results in the formation of 2 genetically distinct daughter cells.
3. Mitosis is vital for tissue growth, as it is the basis for cell multiplication.

A. Only 1	C. Only 3	E. 2 and 3	G. 1, 2 and 3
B. Only 2	D. 1 and 2	F. 1 and 3	

Question 314:
Which of the following is the best definition of a mutation?

A. A mutation is a permanent change in DNA.
B. A mutation is a permanent change in DNA that is harmful to an organism.
C. A mutation is a permanent change in the structure of intra-cellular organelles caused by changes in DNA/RNA.
D. A mutation is a permanent change in chromosomal structure caused by DNA/RNA changes.

Question 315:
In relation to mutations, which of the following are correct?

1. Mutations always lead to discernible changes in the phenotype of an organism.
2. Mutations are central to natural processes such as evolution.
3. Mutations play a role in cancer.

A. Only 1	C. Only 3	E. 2 and 3	G. 1, 2 and 3
B. Only 2	D. 1 and 2	F. 1 and 3	

Question 316:
Which of the following is the most accurate definition of an antibody?

A. An antibody is a molecule that protects red blood cells from changes in pH.
B. An antibody is a molecule produced only by humans and has a pivotal role in the immune system.
C. An antibody is a toxin produced by a pathogen to damage the host organism.
D. An antibody is a molecule that is used by the immune system to identify and neutralize foreign objects and molecules.
E. Antibodies are small proteins found in red blood cells that help increase oxygen carriage.

Question 317:
Which of the following statements about the kidney are correct?

1. The kidneys filter the blood and remove waste products from the body.
2. The kidneys are involved in the digestion of food.
3. In a healthy individual, the kidneys produce urine that contains high levels of glucose.

A. Only 1   C. Only 3   E. 2 and 3   G. 1, 2 and 3
B. Only 2   D. 1 and 2   F. 1 and 3

Question 318:
Which of the following statements are correct?

1. Hormones are slower acting than nerves.
2. Hormones act for a very short time.
3. Hormones act more generally than nerves.
4. Hormones are released when you get a scare.

A. 1 only
B. 1 and 3 only
C. 2 and 4 only
D. 1, 3 and 4 only
E. 1, 2, 3 and 4

Question 319:
Which statements about homeostasis are correct?

1. Homeostasis is about ensuring the inputs within your body exceed the outputs to maintain a constant internal environment.
2. Homeostasis is about ensuring the inputs within your body are less than the outputs to maintain a constant internal environment.
3. Homeostasis is about balancing the inputs within your body with the outputs to ensure your body fluctuates with the needs of the external environment.
4. Homeostasis is about balancing the inputs within your body with the outputs to maintain a constant internal environment.

A. 1 only   C. 3 only   E. 1 and 3 only   G. 2 and 3 only
B. 2 only   D. 4 only   F. 2 and 4 only

Question 320:

Which of the following statement is true?

A. There is more energy and biomass each time you move up a trophic level.
B. There is less energy and biomass each time you move up a trophic level.
C. There is more energy but less biomass each time you move up a trophic level.
D. There is less energy but more biomass each time you move up a trophic level.
E. There is no difference in the energy or biomass when you move up a trophic level.

Question 321:

Which of the following statements are true about asexual reproduction?

1. There is no fusion of gametes.
2. There are two parents.
3. There is no mixing of chromosomes.
4. There is genetic variation.

A. 1 and 3 only   C. 2 and 3 only   E. 2 and 4 only
B. 1 and 4 only   D. 3 and 4 only   F. 1, 2, 3 and 4

Question 322:

Put the following in the order which they occur when Jonas sees a bowl of chicken and moves towards it.

1. Retina   3. Sensory neuron   5. Muscle
2. Motor neuron   4. Brain

A. 1 - 3 - 4 - 5 - 2   D. 1 - 3 - 2 - 4 - 5
B. 1 - 2 - 3 - 4 - 5   E. 1 - 3 - 4 - 2 - 5
C. 5 - 1 - 3 - 2 - 4   F. 4 - 1 - 3 - 2 - 5

Question 323:

What path does blood take from the kidney to the liver?

1. Pulmonary artery   3. Hepatic artery   5. Pulmonary vein
2. Inferior vena cava   4. Aorta   6. Renal vein

A. 2 - 1 - 4 - 3 - 5 - 6   D. 6 - 2 - 1 - 5 - 4 - 3
B. 1 - 2 - 3 - 4 - 5 - 6   E. 3 - 2 - 1 - 4 - 6 - 5
C. 6 - 2 - 5 - 1 - 4 - 3   F. 3 - 6 - 2 - 4 - 1 – 5

Question 324:

Which of the following statements are true about animal cloning?

1. Animals cloned from embryo transplants are genetically identical.
2. The genetic material is removed from an unfertilised egg during adult cell cloning.
3. Cloning can cause a reduced gene pool.
4. Cloning is only possible with mammals.

A. 1 only   C. 3 only   E. 1 and 2 only   G. 1, 2, 3 and 4
B. 2 only   D. 4 only   F. 1, 2 and 3 only
H.

Question 325:
Which of the following statements are true with regard to evolution?

1. Individuals within a species show variation because of differences in their genes.
2. Beneficial mutations will accumulate within a population.
3. Gene differences are caused by sexual reproduction and mutations.
4. Species with similar characteristics never have similar genes.

A. 1 only
B. 1 and 4 only
C. 2 and 3 only
D. 2 and 4 only
E. 3 and 4 only
F. 1, 2 and 3 only

Question 326:
Which of the following genetic statements are correct?

1. Alleles are a similar version of different cells.
2. If you are homozygous for a trait, you have three alleles the same for that particular gene.
3. If you are heterozygous for a trait, you have two different alleles for that particular gene.
4. To show the characteristic that is caused by a recessive allele, both carried alleles for the gene have to be recessive.

A. 1 only
B. 2 only
C. 3 only
D. 4 only
E. 1 and 2 only
F. 3 and 4 only
G. 1, 2, and 3 only

Question 327:
Which of the following statements are correct about meiosis?

1. The DNA content of a gamete is half that of a human red blood cell.
2. Meiosis requires ATP.
3. Meiosis only takes place in reproductive tissue.
4. In meiosis, a diploid cell divides in such a way so as to produce two haploid cells.

A. 1 only
B. 3 only
C. 1 and 2 only
D. 2 and 3 only
E. 2 and 4 only
F. 1, 2, 3 and 4

Question 328:
Put the following statements in the correct order of events for when there is too little water in the blood.

1. Urine is more concentrated
2. Pituary gland releases ADH
3. Blood water level returns to normal
4. Hypothalamus detects too little water in blood
5. Kidney affects water level

A. 1 - 2 - 3 - 4 - 5
B. 5 - 4 - 3 - 2 - 1
C. 4 - 2 - 5 - 1 - 3
D. 3 - 2 - 4 - 1 - 5
E. 5 - 2 - 3 - 4 - 1
F. 4 - 2 – 1- 5 - 3

Question 329:
The pH of venous blood is 7.35. Which of the following is the likely pH of arterial blood?

A. 4.4
B. 5.2
C. 6.5
D. 7.0
E. 7.4
F. 7.95

Question 330:

Which of the following are true of the cytoplasm?

1. The vast majority of the cytoplasm is made up of water.
2. All contents of animal cells are contained in the cytoplasm.
3. The cytoplasm contains electrolytes and proteins.

A. 1 only   C. 3 only   E. 1 and 3 only
B. 2 only   D. 1 and 2 only   F. 1, 2 and 3

Question 331:

ATP is produced in which of the following organelles?

1. The golgi apparatus
2. The rough endoplasmic reticulum
3. The mitochondria
4. The nucleus

A. 1 only   C. 3 only   E. 1 and 2   G. 3 and 4 only
B. 2 only   D. 4 only   F. 2 and 3 only   H. 1, 2, 3 and 4

Question 332:

The cell membrane:

A. Is made up of a phospholipid bilayer which only allows active transport across it.
B. Is not found in bacteria.
C. Is a semi-permeable barrier to ions and organic molecules.
D. Consists purely of enzymes.

Question 333:

Cells of the *Polyommatus atlantica* butterfly of the Lycaenidae family have 446 chromosomes. Which of the following statements about a *P. atlantica* butterfly are correct?

1. Mitosis will produce 2 daughter cells each with 223 pairs of chromosomes
2. Meiosis will produce 4 daughter cells each with 223 chromosomes
3. Mitosis will produce 4 daughter cells each with 446 chromosomes
4. Meiosis will produce 2 daughter cells each with 223 pairs of chromosomes

A. 1 and 2 only   C. 2 and 3 only   E. 1, 2 and 3 only
B. 1 and 3 only   D. 3 and 4 only   F. 1, 2, 3 and 4

Questions 334-336 are based on the following information:

Assume that hair colour is determined by a single allele. The R allele is dominant and results in black hair. The r allele is recessive for red hair. Mary (red hair) and Bob (black hair) are having a baby girl.

Question 334:

What is the probability that she will have red hair?

A. 0% only   C. 50% only   E. 0% or 50%
B. 25% only   D. 0% or 25%   F. 25% or 50%

Question 335:

Mary and Bob have a second child, Tim, who is born with red hair. What does this confirm about Bob?

A. Bob is heterozygous for the hair allele.
B. Bob is homozygous dominant for the hair allele.
C. Bob is homozygous recessive for the hair allele.
D. Bob does not have the hair allele.

Question 336:

Mary and Bob go on to have a third child. What are the chances that this child will be born homozygous for black hair?

A. 0%   B. 25%   C. 50%   D. 75%   E. 100%

Question 337:

Why does air flow into the chest on inspiration?

1. Atmospheric pressure is smaller than intra-thoracic pressure during inspiration.
2. Atmospheric pressure is greater than intra-thoracic pressure during inspiration.
3. Anterior and lateral chest expansion decreases absolute intra-thoracic pressure.
4. Anterior and lateral chest expansion increases absolute intra-thoracic pressure.

A. 1 only   C. 2 and 3   E. 1 and 3
B. 2 only   D. 1 and 4   F. 2 and 4

Question 338:

Which of the following components of a food chain represent the largest biomass?

A. Producers   D. Secondary consumers
B. Decomposers   E. Tertiary consumers
C. Primary consumers

Question 339:

Concerning the nitrogen cycle, which of the following are true?

1. The majority of the Earth's atmosphere is nitrogen.
2. Most of the nitrogen in the Earth's atmosphere is inert.
3. Bacteria are essential for nitrogen fixation.
4. Nitrogen fixation occurs during lightning strikes.

A. 1 and 2   C. 2 and 3   E. 3 and 4
B. 1 and 3   D. 2 and 4   F. 1, 2, 3 and 4

Question 340:

Which of the following statement are correct regarding mutations?

1. Mutations always cause proteins to lose their function.
2. Mutations always change the structure of the protein encoded by the affected gene.
3. Mutations always result in cancer.

A. Only 1   D. 1 and 2   G. 1, 2 and 3
B. Only 2   E. 2 and 3   H. None of the above
C. Only 3   F. 1 and 3

Question 341:
Which of the following is not a function of the central nervous system?

A. Coordination of movement
B. Decision making and executive functions
C. Control of heart rate

D. Cognition
E. Memory

Question 342:
Which of the following control mechanisms are involved in modulating cardiac output?

1. Voluntary control.
2. Sympathetic control to decrease heart rate.
3. Parasympathetic control to increase heart rate.

A. Only 1
B. Only 2
C. Only 3

D. 1 and 2
E. 2 and 3
F. 1 and 3

G. 1, 2 and 3
H. None of the above

Question 343:
Vijay goes to see his GP with fatty, smelly stools that float on water. Which of the following enzymes is most likely to be malfunctioning?

A. Amylase
B. Lipase
C. Protease

D. Sucrase
E. Lactase

Question 344:
Which of the following statements concerning the cardiovascular system is correct?

A. Oxygenated blood from the lungs flows to the heart via the pulmonary artery.
B. All arteries carry oxygenated blood.
C. All animals have a double circulatory system.
D. The superior vena cava contains oxygenated blood
E. All veins have valves.
F. None of the above.

Question 345:
Which part of the GI tract has the least amount of enzymatic digestion occurring?

A. Mouth
B. Stomach
C. Small intestine

D. Large intestine
E. Rectum

Question 346:
Oge touches a hot stove and immediately moves her hand away. Which of the following components are **NOT** involved in this reaction?

1. Thermo-receptor
2. Brain

3. Spinal Cord
4. Sensory nerve

5. Motor nerve
6. Muscle

A. 1 only
B. 2 only

C. 3 only
D. 1 and 2 only

E. 1, 2 and 3 only
F. 3, 4, 5 and 6

Question 347:
Which of the following represents a scenario with an appropriate description of the mode of transport?

1. Water moving from a hypotonic solution outside of a potato cell, across the cell wall and cell membrane and into the hypertonic cytoplasm of the potato cell→ Osmosis.
2. Carbon dioxide moving across a respiring cell's membrane and dissolving in blood plasma →Active transport.
3. Reabsorption of amino acids against a concentration gradient in the glomeruluar apparatus → Diffusion.

A. 1 only
B. 2 only
C. 3 only
D. 1 and 2 only
E. 2 and 3 only
F. 1 and 3 only
G. 1, 2 and 3

Question 348:
Which of the following equations represents anaerobic respiration?

1. Carbohydrate + Oxygen → Energy + Carbon Dioxide + Water
2. Carbohydrate → Energy + Lactic Acid + Carbon dioxide
3. Carbohydrate → Energy + Lactic Acid
4. Carbohydrate → Energy + Ethanol + Carbon dioxide

A. 1 only
B. 2 only
C. 3 only
D. 4 only
E. 1 and 2
F. 1 and 3
G. 1 and 4
H. 2 and 4 only
I. 3 and 4 only

Question 349:
Which of the following statements regarding respiration are correct?

1. The mitochondria are the centres for both aerobic and anaerobic respiration.
2. The cytoplasm is the main site of anaerobic respiration.
3. For every two moles of glucose that is respired aerobically, 12 moles of CO_2 are liberated.
4. Anaerobic respiration is more efficient than aerobic respiration.

A. 1 and 2
B. 1 and 4
C. 2 and 3
D. 2 and 4
E. 3 and 4

Question 350:
Which of the following statements are true?

1. The nucleus contains the cell's chromosomes.
2. The cytoplasm consists purely of water.
3. The plasma membrane is a single phospholipid layer.
4. The cell wall prevents plants cells from lysing due to osmotic pressure.

A. 1 and 2
B. 1 and 4
C. 1, 3 and 4
D. 1, 2 and 3
E. 1, 2 and 4
F. 2, 3 and 4

Question 351:

Which of the following statements are true about osmosis?

1. If a medium is hypertonic relative to the cell cytoplasm, the cell will gain water through osmosis.
2. If a medium is hypotonic relative to the cell cytoplasm, the cell will gain water through osmosis.
3. If a medium is hypotonic relative to the cell cytoplasm, the cell will lose water through osmosis.
4. If a medium is hypertonic relative to the cell cytoplasm, the cell will lose water through osmosis.
5. The medium's tonicity has no impact on the movement of water.

A. 1 only   C. 1 and 3   E. 5 only
B. 2 only   D. 2 and 4

Question 352:

Which of the following statements are true about stem cells?

1. Stem cells have the ability to differentiate into other mature types of cells.
2. Stem cells are unable to maintain their undifferentiated state.
3. Stem cells can be classified as embryonic stem cells or adult stem cells.
4. Stem cells are only found in embryos.

A. 1 and 3   C. 2 and 3   E. 2 and 4
B. 3 and 4   D. 1 and 2

Question 353:

Which of the following are **NOT** examples of natural selection?

1. Giraffes growing longer necks to eat taller plants.
2. Antibiotic resistance developed by certain strains of bacteria.
3. Pesticide resistance among locusts in farms.
4. Breeding of horses to make them run faster.

A. 1 only   C. 1 and 3   E. 2 and 4
B. 4 only   D. 1 and 4

Question 354:

Which of the following statements are true?

1. Enzymes stabilise the transition state and therefore lower the activation energy.
2. Enzymes distort substrates in order to lower activation energy.
3. Enzymes decrease temperature to slow down reactions and lower the activation energy.
4. Enzymes provide alternative pathways for reactions to occur.

A. 1 only   C. 1 and 4   E. 3 and 4
B. 1 and 2   D. 2 and 4

Question 355:
Which of the following are examples of negative feedback?

1. Salivating whilst waiting for a meal.
2. Throwing a dart.

3. The regulation of blood pH.
4. The regulation of blood pressure.

A. 1 only
B. 1 and 2

C. 3 and 4
D. 2, 3, and 4

E. 1, 2, 3 and 4

Question 356:
Which of the following statements about the immune system are true?

1. White blood cells defend against bacterial and fungal infections.
2. White blood cells can temporarily disable but not kill pathogens.
3. White blood cells use antibodies to fight pathogens.
4. Antibodies are produced by bone marrow stem cells.

A. 1 and 3
B. 1 and 4

C. 2 and 3
D. 2 and 4

E. 1, 2, and 3
F. 1, 3, and 4

Question 357:
The cardiovascular system does **NOT**:

A. Deliver vital nutrients to peripheral cells.
B. Oxygenate blood and transports it to peripheral cells.
C. Act as a mode of transportation for hormones to reach their target organ.
D. Facilitate thermoregulation.
E. Respond to exercise by increasing cardiac output to exercising muscles.

Question 358:
Which of the following statements is correct?

A. Adrenaline can sometimes decrease heart rate.
B. Adrenaline is rarely released during flight or fight responses.
C. Adrenaline causes peripheral vasoconstriction.
D. Adrenaline only affects the cardiovascular system.
E. Adrenaline travels primarily in lymphatic vessels.
F. None of the above.

Question 359:
Which of the following statements is true?

A. Protein synthesis occurs solely in the nucleus.
B. Each amino acid is coded for by three DNA bases.
C. Each protein is coded for by three amino acids.
D. Red blood cells can create new proteins to prolong their lifespan.
E. Protein synthesis isn't necessary for mitosis to take place.
F. None of the above.

Question 360:

A solution of amylase and carbohydrate is present in a beaker, where the pH of the contents is 6.3. Assuming amylase is saturated, which of the following will increase the rate of production of the product?

1. Add sodium bicarbonate
2. Add carbohydrate
3. Add amylase
4. Increase the temperature to 100° C

A. 1 only
B. 2 only
C. 3 only
D. 4 only
E. 1 and 2
F. 1 and 3
G. 1, 2 and 3
H. 1, 3 and 4

Question 361:

Celestial Necrosis is a newly discovered autosomal recessive disorder. A female carrier and a male with the disease produce two boys. What is the probability that neither boy's genotype contains the celestial necrosis allele?

A. 100%
B. 75%
C. 50%
D. 25%
E. 0%

Question 362:

Which among the following has no endocrine function?

A. The thyroid
B. The ovary
C. The pancreas
D. The adrenal gland
E. The testes
F. None of the above.

Question 363:

Which of the following statements are true?

1. Increasing levels of insulin cause a decrease in blood glucose levels.
2. Increasing levels of glycogen cause an increase in blood glucose levels.
3. Increasing levels of adrenaline decrease the heart rate.

A. 1 only
B. 2 only
C. 3 only
D. 1 and 2
E. 2 and 3
F. 1 and 3
G. 1, 2 and 3

Question 364:

Which of the following rows is correct?

	Oxygenated Blood		Deoxygenated Blood	
A.	Left atrium	Left ventricle	Right atrium	Right ventricle
B.	Left atrium	Right atrium	Left ventricle	Right ventricle
C.	Left atrium	Right ventricle	Right atrium	Right ventricle
D.	Right atrium	Right ventricle	Left atrium	Left ventricle
E.	Left ventricle	Right atrium	Left atrium	Right ventricle

Questions 365-367 are based on the following information:
The pedigree below shows the inheritance of a newly discovered disease that affects connective tissue called Nafram syndrome. Individual 1 is a normal homozygote.

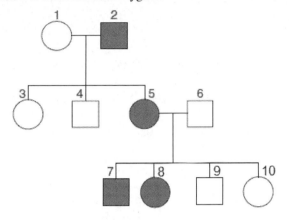

Question 365:
What is the inheritance of Nafram syndrome?

A. Autosomal dominant
B. Autosomal recessive
C. X-linked dominant
D. X-linked recessive
E. Co-dominant

Question 366:
Which individuals must be heterozygous for Nafram syndrome?

A. 1 and 2
B. 8 and 9
C. 2 and 5
D. 5 and 6
E. 6 and 8
F. 6 and 10

Question 367:
Taking N to denote a diseased allele and n to denote a normal allele, which of the following are **NOT** possible genotypes for 6's parents?

1. NN x NN
2. NN x Nn
3. Nn x nn
4. Nn x Nn
5. nn x nn

A. 1 and 2
B. 1 and 3
C. 2 and 3
D. 2 and 5
E. 3 and 4
F. 4 and 5

Question 368:
Which of the following correctly describes the passage of urine through the body?

	1st	2nd	3rd	4th
A	Kidney	Ureter	Bladder	Urethra
B	Kidney	Urethra	Bladder	Ureter
C	Urethra	Bladder	Ureter	Kidney
D	Ureter	Kidney	Bladder	Urethra

Question 369:

Which of the following best describes the passage of blood from the body, through the heart, back to the body?

A. Aorta → Left Ventricle → Left Atrium → Inferior Vena Cava → Right Atrium → Right Ventricle → Lungs → Aorta

B. Inferior vena cava → Left Atrium → Left Ventricle → Lungs → Right Atrium → Right Ventricle → Aorta

C. Inferior vena cava → Right Ventricle → Right Atrium → Lungs → Left Atrium → Left Ventricle → Aorta

D. Aorta → Left Atrium → Left Ventricle → Lungs → Right Atrium → Right Ventricle → Inferior Vena Cava

E. Right Atrium → Left Atrium → Inferior vena cava → Lungs → Left Atrium → Right Ventricle → Aorta

F. None of the above.

Question 370:

Which of the following best describes the events during inspiration?

	Intrathoracic Pressure	Intercostal Muscles	Diaphragm
A	Increases	Contract	Contracts
B	Increases	Relax	Contracts
C	Increases	Contract	Relaxes
D	Increases	Relax	Relaxes
E	Decreases	Contract	Contracts
F	Decreases	Relax	Contracts
G	Decreases	Contract	Relaxes
H	Decreases	Relax	Relaxes

Questions 371-372 are based on the following information:

DNA is made up of the four nucleotide bases: adenine, cytosine, guanine and thymine. A triplet repeat or codon is a sequence of three nucleotides which code for an amino acid. While there are only 20 amino acids there are 64 different combinations of the four DNA nucleotide bases. This means that more than one combination of 3 DNA nucleotides sequences code for the same amino acid.

Question 371:

Which property of the DNA code is described above?

A. The code is unambiguous.
B. The code is universal.
C. The code is non-overlapping.

D. The code is degenerate.
E. The code is preserved.
F. The code has no punctuation.

Question 372:

Which type of mutation does the described property protect against the most?

A. An insertion - where a single nucleotide is inserted.
B. A point mutation - where a single nucleotide is replaced for another.
C. A deletion - where a single nucleotide is deleted.
D. A repeat expansion - where a repeated trinucleotide sequence is added.
E. A duplication - where a piece of DNA is abnormally copied.

Question 373:

Which row of the table below describes what happens when external temperature decreases?

	Temperature Change Detected by	Sweat Gland Secretion	Cutaneous Blood Flow
A	Hypothalamus	Increases	Increases
B	Hypothalamus	Increases	Decreases
C	Hypothalamus	Decreases	Increases
D	Hypothalamus	Decreases	Decreases
E	Cerebral Cortex	Increases	Increases
F	Cerebral Cortex	Increases	Decreases
G	Cerebral Cortex	Decreases	Increases
H	Cerebral Cortex	Decreases	Decreases

Question 374:

Which of the following processes involve active transport?

1. Reabsorption of glucose in the kidney.
2. Movement of carbon dioxide into the alveoli in the lungs.
3. Movement of chemicals in a neural synapse.

A. 1 only
B. 2 only
C. 3 only
D. 1 and 2
E. 1 and 3
F. 2 and 3
G. 1, 2 and 3

Question 375:

Which of the following statements is correct about enzymes?

A. All enzymes are made up of amino acids only.
B. Enzymes can sometimes slow the rate of reactions.
C. Enzymes have no impact on reaction temperatures.
D. Enzymes are heat sensitive but resistant to changes in pH.
E. Enzymes are unspecific in their substrate use.
F. None of the above.

SECTION 2: Chemistry

Most students don't struggle with BMAT chemistry as they'll be studying it at A2. However, there are certain questions that even good students tend to struggle with under time pressure e.g. balancing equations and mass calculations. It is essential that you're able to do these quickly as they take up by far the most time in the chemistry questions.

Balancing Equations

For some reason, most students are rarely shown how to formally balance equations – including those studying it at A-level. Balancing equations intuitively or via trial and error will only get you so far in the BMAT as the equations you'll have to work with will be fairly complex. To avoid wasting valuable time, it is essential you learn a method that will allow you to solve these in less than 60 seconds on a consistent basis. The method shown below is the simplest way and requires you to be able to do quick mental arithmetic (which is something you should be aiming for anyway). The easiest way to do learn it is through an example:

The following equation shows the reaction between Iodic acid, hydrochloric acid and copper Iodide:

$$\mathbf{a}\ HIO_3 + \mathbf{b}\ CuI_2 + \mathbf{c}\ HCl \rightarrow \mathbf{d}\ CuCl_3 + \mathbf{e}\ ICl + \mathbf{f}\ H_2O$$

What values of $\mathbf{a}$, $\mathbf{b}$, $\mathbf{c}$, $\mathbf{d}$, $\mathbf{e}$ and $\mathbf{f}$ are needed in order to balance the equation?

	a	b	c	d	e	f
A	5	4	25	4	13	15
B	5	4	20	4	8	15
C	5	6	20	6	8	15
D	2	8	10	8	8	15
E	6	8	24	10	16	15
F	6	10	22	10	16	15

<u>Step 1:</u> Pick an element and see how many atoms there are on the left and right sides.

<u>Step 2:</u> Form an equation to represent this. For Cu: b = d

<u>Step 3:</u> See if any of the answer options don't satisfy b=d. In this case, for option E, b is 8 and d is 10. This allows us to eliminate option E.

Once you've eliminated as many options as possible, go back to <u>step 1</u> and pick another element.
For Hydrogen (H): a + c = 2f

Then see if any of the answer options don't satisfy a + c = 2f.

➢   Option A: 5 + 25 is equal to 2 x 15

➢   Option B: 5 + 20 is not equal to 2 x 15

➢   Option C: 5 + 20 is not equal to 2 x 15

➢   Option D: 2 + 10 is not equal to 2 x 15

This allows us to eliminate option B, C and D. E has already been eliminated. Thus, the only solution possible is A.

This method works best when you get given a table above as this allows you to quickly eliminate options. However, it is still a viable method even if you don't get this information.

Chemistry Calculations

Equations you **MUST** know:

–   Atomic Mass = Mass/Moles
–   Amount (mol) = Concentration (mol/dm^3) x Volume (dm^3)

Avogadro's Constant:
One mole of anything contains 6×10^{23} of it e.g. 5 Moles of water contain $5 \times 6 \times 10^{23}$ number of water molecules.

Abundances:
The average atomic mass takes the abundances of all isotopes into account. Thus:
A_r = (Abundance of Isotope 1) x (Mass of Isotope 1) + (Abundance of Isotope 2) x (Mass of Isotope 2) +…

It's easier to understand this by working through examples e.g. **questions 406, 412 and 439**.

> ***Top tip!*** Ensure you're able convert between **Litres, dm^3, cm^3 and mm^3** quickly and accurately so that you don't make silly mistakes in the real exam when under time pressure.

Chemistry Questions

Question 376:
Which of the following most accurately defines an isotope?

A. An isotope is an atom of an element that has the same number of protons in the nucleus but a different number of neutrons orbiting the nucleus.
B. An isotope is an atom of an element that has the same number of neutrons in the nucleus but a different number of protons orbiting the nucleus.
C. An isotope is any atom of an element that can be split to produce nuclear energy.
D. An isotope is an atom of an element that has the same number of protons in the nucleus but a different number of neutrons in the nucleus.
E. An isotope is an atom of an element that has the same number of protons in the nucleus but a different number of electrons orbiting it.

Question 377:
Which of the following is an example of a displacement reaction?

1. $Fe + SnSO4 \rightarrow FeSO_4 + Sn$
2. $Cl_2 + 2KBr \rightarrow Br_2 + 2KCl$
3. $H_2SO_4 + Mg \rightarrow MgSO_4 + H_2$
4. $NaHCO_3 + HCl \rightarrow NaCl + CO_2 + H_2O$

A. 1 only
B. 1 and 2 only
C. 2 and 3 only
D. 3 and 4 only
E. 1, 2 and 3 only
F. 1, 2, 3 and 4

Question 378:
What values of **a**, **b** and **c** are needed to balance the equation below?

$$aCa(OH)_2 + bH_3PO_4 \rightarrow Ca_3(PO_4)_2 + cH_2O$$

A. $a = 3$ $b = 2$ $c = 6$
B. $a = 2$ $b = 2$ $c = 4$
C. $a = 3$ $b = 2$ $c = 1$
D. $a = 1$ $b = 2$ $c = 3$
E. $a = 4$ $b = 2$ $c = 6$
F. $a = 3$ $b = 2$ $c = 4$

Question 379:
What values of **s**, **t** and **u** are needed to balance the equation below?

$$sAgNO_3 + tK_3PO_4 \rightarrow 3Ag_3PO_4 + uKNO_3$$

A. $s = 9$ $t = 3$ $u = 9$
B. $s = 6$ $t = 3$ $u = 9$
C. $s = 9$ $t = 3$ $u = 6$
D. $s = 9$ $t = 6$ $u = 9$
E. $s = 3$ $t = 3$ $u = 9$
F. $s = 9$ $t = 3$ $u = 3$

Question 380:
Which of the following statements are true with regard to displacement?

1. A less reactive halogen can displace a more reactive halogen.
2. Chlorine cannot displace bromine or iodine from an aqueous solution of its salts.
3. Bromine can displace iodine because of the trend of reactivity.
4. Fluorine can displace chlorine as it is higher up the group.
5. Lithium can displace francium as it is higher up the group.

A. 3 only
B. 5 only
C. 1 and 2 only

D. 3 and 4 only
E. 2 , 3 and 5 only
F. 3, 4 and 5 only

Question 381:
What mass of magnesium oxide is produced when 75g of magnesium is burned in excess oxygen?
Relative Atomic Masses: Mg = 24, O = 16

A. 80g   B. 100g   C. 125g   D. 145g   E. 175g   F. 225g

Question 382:
Hydrogen can combine with hydroxide ions to produce water. Which process is involved in this?

A. Hydration
B. Oxidation

C. Reduction
D. Dehydration

E. Evaporation
F. Precipitation

Question 383:
Which of the following statements about Ammonia are correct?

1. It has a formula of NH_3.
2. Nitrogen contributes 82% to its mass.
3. It can be broken down again into nitrogen and hydrogen.
4. It is covalently bonded.
5. It is used to make fertilisers.

A. 1 and 2 only
B. 1 and 4 only
C. 1, 2 and 3 only

D. 1, 2 and 5 only
E. 3, 4 and 5 only
F. 1, 2, 3, 4 and 5

Question 384:
What colour will a universal indicator change to in a solution of milk and lipase?

A. From green to orange.
B. From red to green.
C. From purple to green.

D. From purple to orange.
E. From yellow to purple.
F. From purple to red.

Question 385:
Vitamin C [$C_6H_8O_6$] can be artificially synthesised from glucose [$C_6H_{12}O_6$]. What type of reaction is this likely to be?

A. Dehydration
B. Hydration

C. Oxidation
D. Reduction

E. Displacement
F. Evaporation

Question 386:
Which of the following statements are true?

1. Cu^{64} will undergo oxidation faster than Cu^{65}.
2. Cu^{65} will undergo reduction faster than Cu^{64}.
3. Cu^{65} and Cu^{64} have the same number of electrons.

A. 1 only	C. 3 only	E. 1 and 3 only
B. 2 only	D. 2 and 3 only	F. 1, 2 and 3

Question 387:
6g of Mg^{24} is added to a solution containing 30g of dissolved sulphuric acid (H_2SO_4). Which of the following statements are true?
Relative Atomic Masses: S = 32, Mg = 24, O = 16, H = 1

1. In this reaction, the magnesium is the limiting reagent
2. In this reaction, sulphuric acid is the limiting reagent
3. The mass of salt produced equals the original mass of sulphuric acid

A. 1 only	C. 3 only	E. 1 and 3 only
B. 2 only	D. 1 and 2 only	F. 2 and 3 only

Question 388:
In which of the following mixtures will a displacement reaction occur?

1. $Cu + 2AgNO_3$
2. $Cu + Fe(NO_3)_2$
3. $Ca + 2H_2O$
4. $Fe + Ca(OH)_2$

A. 1 only	C. 3 only	E. 1 and 2 only	G. 1, 2 and 3
B. 2 only	D. 4 only	F. 1 and 3 only	H. 1, 2, 3 and 4

Question 389:
Which of the following statements is true about the following chain of metals?

$$Na \rightarrow Ca \rightarrow Mg \rightarrow Al \rightarrow Zn$$

Moving from left to right:

1. The reactivity of the metals increases.
2. The likelihood of corrosion of the metals increases.
3. More energy is required to separate these metals from their ores.
4. The metals lose electrons more readily to form positive ions.

A. 1 and 2 only	C. 2 and 3 only	E. 2, 3 and 4 only	G. None of the
B. 1and 3 only	D. 1 and 4 only	F. 1, 2, 3 and 4	above

Question 390:
In which of the following mixtures will a displacement reaction occur?

1. $I_2 + 2KBr$
2. $Cl_2 + 2NaBr$
3. $Br_2 + 2KI$

A. 1 only	C. 3 only	E. 1 and 3 only	G. 1, 2 and 3
B. 2 only	D. 1 and 2 only	F. 2 and 3 only	

Question 391:
Which of the following statements about Al and Cu are true?

1. Al is used to build aircraft because it is lightweight and resists corrosion.
2. Cu is used to build electrical wires because it is a good insulator.
3. Both Al and Cu are good conductors of heat.
4. Al is commonly alloyed with other metals to make coins.
5. Al is resistant to corrosion because of a thin layer of aluminium hydroxide on its surface.

A. 1 and 3 only

B. 1 and 4 only

C. 1, 3 and 5 only

D. 1, 3, 4, 5 only

E. 2, 4 and 5 only

F. 2, 3, 4, 5 only

Question 392:
21g of Li^7 reacts completely with excess water. Given that the molar gas volume is 24 dm^3 under the conditions, what is the volume of hydrogen produced?

A. 12 dm^3

B. 24 dm^3

C. 36 dm^3

D. 48 dm^3

E. 72 dm^3

F. 120 dm^3

Question 393:
Which of the following statements regarding bonding are true?

1. NaCl has stronger ionic bonds than $MgCl_2$.
2. Transition metals are able to lose varying numbers of electrons to form multiple stable positive ions.
3. All covalently bonded structures have lower melting points than ionically bonded compounds.
4. All covalently bonded structures do not conduct electricity.

A. 1 only

B. 2 only

C. 3 only

D. 4 only

E. 1 and 2 only

F. 2 and 3 only

G. 3 and 4 only

H. 1, 2 and 4 only

Question 394:
Consider the following two equations:

A. $C + O_2 \rightarrow CO_2$ $\Delta H = -394$ kJ per mole

B. $CaCO_3 \rightarrow CaO + CO_2$ $\Delta H = +178$ kJ per mole

Which of the following statements are true?

1. Reaction **A** is exothermic and Reaction **B** is endothermic.
2. CO_2 has less energy than C and O_2.
3. CaO is more stable than $CaCO_3$.

A. 1 only

B. 2 only

C. 3 only

D. 1 and 2

E. 1 and 3

F. 2 and 3

G. 1, 2 and 3

Question 395:
Which of the following are true of regarding the oxides formed by Na, Mg and Al?

1. All of the metals and their solid oxides conduct electricity.
2. MgO has stronger bonds than Na_2O.
3. Metals are extracted from their molten ores by fractional distillation.

A. 1 only

B. 2 only

C. 3 only

D. 1 and 2 only

E. 2 and 3 only

F. 1, 2 and 3

Question 396:
Which of the following pairs have the same electronic configuration?

1. Li^+ and Na^+
2. Mg^{2+} and Ne
3. Na^{2+} and Ne
4. O^{2-} and a Carbon atom

A. 1 only
B. 1 and 2 only
C. 1 and 3 only
D. 2 and 3 only
E. 2 and 4 only
F. 1, 2, 3 and 4

Question 397:
In relation to reactivity of elements in group 1 and 2, which of the following statements is correct?

1. Reactivity decreases as you go down group 1.
2. Reactivity increases as you go down group 2.
3. Group 1 metals are generally less reactive than group 2 metals.

A. Only 1
B. Only 2
C. Only 3
D. 1 and 2
E. 2 and 3
F. 1 and 3

Question 398:
What role do catalysts fulfil in an endothermic reaction?

A. They increase the temperature, causing the reaction to occur at a faster rate.
B. They decrease the temperature, causing the reaction to occur at a faster rate.
C. They reduce the energy of the reactants in order to trigger the reaction.
D. They reduce the activation energy of the reaction.
E. They increase the activation energy of the reaction.

Question 399:
Tritium H^3 is an isotope of Hydrogen. Why is tritium commonly referred to as 'heavy hydrogen'?

A. Because H^3 contains 3 protons making it heavier than H^1 that contains 1 proton.
B. Because H^3 contains 3 neutrons making it heavier than H^1 that contains 1 neutron.
C. Because H^3 contains 1 neutron and 2 protons making it heavier than H^1 that contains 1 neutron and 1 proton.
D. Because H^3 contains 1 proton and 2 neutrons making it heavier than H^1 that contains 1 proton.
E. Because H^3 contains 3 electrons making it heavier than H^1 that contains 1 electron.

Question 400:
In relation to redox reactions, which of the following statements are correct?

1. Oxidation describes the loss of electrons.
2. Reduction increases the electron density of an ion, atom or molecule.
3. Halogens are powerful reducing agents.

A. Only 1
B. Only 2
C. Only 3
D. 1 and 2
E. 2 and 3
F. 1 and 3

Question 401:

Which of the following statements is correct?

A. At higher temperatures, gas molecules move at angles that cause them to collide with each other more frequently.
B. Gas molecules have lower energy after colliding with each other.
C. At higher temperatures, gas molecules attract each other resulting in more collisions.
D. The average kinetic energy of gas molecules is the same for all gases at the same temperature.
E. The momentum of gas molecules decreases as pressure increases.

Question 402:

Which of the following are exothermic reactions?

1. Burning Magnesium in pure oxygen
2. The combustion of hydrogen
3. Aerobic respiration
4. Evaporation of water in the oceans
5. Reaction between a strong acid and a strong base

A. 1, 2 and 4   C. 1, 3 and 5   E. 1, 2, 3 and 5
B. 1, 2 and 5   D. 2, 3 and 4   F. 1, 2, 3, 4 and 5

Question 403:

Ethene reacts with oxygen to produce water and carbon dioxide. Which elements are oxidised/reduced?

A. Carbon is reduced and oxygen is oxidised.
B. Hydrogen is reduced and oxygen is oxidised.
C. Carbon is oxidised and hydrogen is reduced.
D. Hydrogen is oxidised and carbon is reduced.
E. Carbon is oxidised and oxygen is reduced.
F. None of the above.

Question 404:

In the reaction between Zinc and Copper (II) sulphate which elements act as oxidising + reducing agents?

A. Zinc is the reducing agent while sulfur is the oxidizing agent.
B. Zinc is the reducing agent while copper in $CuSO_4$ is the oxidizing agent.
C. Copper is the reducing agent while zinc is the oxidizing agent.
D. Oxygen is the reducing agent while copper in $CuSO_4$ is the oxidizing agent.
E. Sulfur is the reducing agent while oxygen is the oxidizing agent.
F. None of the above.

Question 405:

Which of the following statements is true?

A. Acids are compounds that act as proton acceptors in aqueous solution.
B. Acids only exist in a liquid state.
C. Strong acids are partially ionized in a solution.
D. Weak acids generally have a pH or 6 - 7.
E. The reaction between a weak and strong acid produces water and salt.

Question 406:

An unknown element, Z, has 3 isotopes: Z^5, Z^6 and Z^8. Given that the atomic mass of Z is 7, and the relative abundance of Z^5 is 20%, which of the following statements are correct?

1. Z^5 and Z^6 are present in the same abundance.
2. Z^8 is the most abundant of the isotopes.
3. Z^8 is more abundant than Z^5 and Z^6 combined.

A. 1 only
B. 2 only
C. 3 only
D. 1 and 2 only

E. 2 and 3 only
F. 1 and 3 only
G. 1, 2 and 3
H. None of the statements are correct.

Question 407:

Which of following best describes the products when an acid reacts with a metal that is more reactive than hydrogen?

A. Salt and hydrogen
B. Salt and ammonia
C. Salt and water

D. A weak acid and a weak base
E. A strong acid and a strong base
F. No reaction would occur.

Question 408:

Choose the option which balances the following equation:

$$\textbf{a } FeSO_4 + \textbf{b } K_2Cr_2O_7 + \textbf{c } H_2SO_4 \rightarrow \textbf{d } (Fe)_2(SO_4)_3 + \textbf{e } Cr_2(SO_4)_3 + \textbf{f } K_2SO_4 + \textbf{g } H_2O$$

	a	b	c	d	e	f	g
A	6	1	8	3	1	1	7
B	6	1	7	3	1	1	7
C	2	1	6	2	1	1	6
D	12	1	14	4	1	1	14
E	4	1	12	4	1	1	12
F	8	1	8	4	2	1	8

Question 409:

Which of the following statements is correct?

A. Matter consists of atoms that have a net electrical charge.
B. Atoms and ions of the same element have different numbers of protons and electrons but the same number of neutrons.
C. Over 80% of an atom's mass is provided by protons.
D. Atoms of the same element that have different numbers of neutrons react at significantly different rates.
E. Protons in the nucleus of atoms repel each other as they are positively charged.
F. None of the above.

Question 410:

Which of the following statements is correct?

A. The noble gasses are chemically inert and therefore useless to man.
B. All the noble gasses have a full outer electron shell.
C. The majority of noble gasses are brightly coloured.
D. The boiling point of the noble gasses decreases as you progress down the group.
E. Neon is the most abundant noble gas.

Question 411:

In relation to alkenes, which of the following statements is correct?

1. They all contain double bonds.
2. They can all be reduced to alkanes.
3. Aromatic compounds are also alkenes as they contain double bonds.

A. Only 1
B. Only 2
C. Only 3

D. 1 and 2
E. 2 and 3
F. 1 and 3

G. All of the above.
H. None of the above.

Question 412:

Chlorine is made up of two isotopes, Cl^{35} (atomic mass 34.969) and Cl^{37} (atomic mass 36.966). Given that the atomic mass of chlorine is 35.453, which of the following statements is correct?
A. Cl^{35} is about 3 times more abundant than Cl^{37}.
B. Cl^{35} is about 10 times more abundant than Cl^{37}.
C. Cl^{37} is about 3 times more abundant than Cl^{35}.
D. Cl^{37} is about 10 times more abundant than Cl^{35}.
E. Both isotopes are equally abundant.

Question 413:

Which of the following statements regarding transition metals is correct?

A. Transition metals form ions that have multiple colours.
B. Transition metals usually form covalent bonds.
C. Transition metals cannot be used as catalysts as they are too reactive.
D. Transition metals are poor conductors of electricity.
E. Transition metals are frequently referred to as f-block elements.

Question 414:

20 g of impure Na^{23} reacts completely with excess water to produce 8,000 cm^3 of hydrogen gas under standard conditions. What is the percentage purity of sodium?
[Under standard conditions 1 mole of gas occupies 24 dm^3]

A. 88.0%   B. 76.5%   C. 66.0%   D. 38.0%   E. 15.3%

Question 415:

An organic molecule contains 70.6% Carbon, 5.9% Hydrogen and 23.5% Oxygen. It has a molecular mass of 136. What is its chemical formula?

A. C_4H_4O B. C_5H_4O C. $C_8H_8O_2$ D. $C_{10}H_8O_2$ E. C_2H_2O

Question 416:

Choose the option which balances the following reaction:

$$aS + bHNO_3 \rightarrow cH_2SO_4 + dNO_2 + eH_2O$$

	a	b	c	d	e
A	3	5	3	5	1
B	1	6	1	6	2
C	6	14	6	14	2
D	2	4	2	4	4
E	2	3	2	3	2
F	4	4	4	4	2

Question 417:

Which of the following statements is true?

1. Ethane and ethene can both dissolve in organic solvents.
2. Ethane and ethene can both be hydrogenated in the presence of Nickel.
3. Breaking C=C requires double the energy needed to break C-C.

A. 1 only
B. 2 only
C. 3 only
D. 1 and 2 only
E. 2 and 3 only
F. 1 and 3 only
G. 1, 2 and 3

Question 418:

Diamond, Graphite, Methane and Ammonia all exhibit covalent bonding. Which row adequately describes the properties associated with each?

	Compound	Melting Point	Able to conduct electricity	Soluble in water
1.	Diamond	High	Yes	No
2.	Graphite	High	Yes	No
3.	$CH_{4(g)}$	Low	No	No
4.	$NH_{3(g)}$	Low	No	Yes

A. 1 and 2 only
B. 2 and 3 only
C. 1 and 3 only
D. 1 and 4 only
E. 1, 2 and 3
F. 2, 3 and 4
G. 1,2 and 4
H. 1, 2, 3 and 4

Question 419:

Which of the following statements about catalysts are true?

1. Catalysts reduce the energy required for a reaction to take place.
2. Catalysts are used up in reactions.
3. Catalysed reactions are almost always exothermic.

A. 1 only
B. 2 only
C. 1 and 2
D. 2 and 3
E. 1, 2 and

Question 420:

What is the name of the molecule below?

A. But-1-ene
B. But-2-ene
C. Pent-3-ene
D. Pent-1-ene
E. Pent-2-ene
F. Pentane
G. Pentanoic acid

Question 421:

Which of the following statements is correct regarding Group 1 elements? [Excluding Hydrogen]

A. The oxidation number of Group 1 elements usually decreases in most reactions.
B. Reactivity decreases as you progress down Group 1.
C. Group 1 elements do not react with water.
D. All Group 1 elements react instantaneously with oxygen.
E. All of the above.
F. None of the above.

Question 422:
Which of the following statements about electrolysis are correct?

1. The cathode attracts negatively charged ions.
2. Atoms are reduced at the anode.
3. Electrolysis can be used to separate mixtures.

A. Only 1
B. Only 2
C. Only 3

D. 1 and 2
E. 2 and 3
F. 1 and 3

G. 1, 2 and 3
H. None of the above.

Question 423:
Which of the following is **NOT** an isomer of pentane?

A. $CH_3CH_2CH_2CH_2CH_3$
B. $CH_3C(CH_3)CH_3CH_3$

C. $CH_3(CH_2)_3CH_3$
D. $CH_3C(CH_3)_2CH_3$

Question 424:
Choose the option which balances the following reaction:

$Cu + HNO_3 \rightarrow Cu(NO_3)_2 + NO + H_2O$

A. $8\ Cu + 3\ HNO_3 \rightarrow 8\ Cu(NO_3)_2 + 4\ NO + 2\ H_2O$
B. $3\ Cu + 8\ HNO_3 \rightarrow 2\ Cu(NO_3)_2 + 3\ NO + 4\ H_2O$
C. $5Cu + 7HNO_3 \rightarrow 5\ Cu(NO_3)_2 + 4\ NO + 8\ H_2O$
D. $6\ Cu + 10\ HNO_3 \rightarrow 6\ Cu(NO_3)_2 + 3\ NO + 7\ H_2O$
E. $3\ Cu + 8\ HNO_3 \rightarrow 3\ Cu(NO_3)_2 + 2\ NO + 4\ H_2O$

Question 425:
What of the following statements regarding alkenes is correct?

A. Alkenes are an inorganic homologous series.
B. Alkenes always have three times as many hydrogen atoms as they do carbon atoms.
C. Bromine water changes from clear to brown in the presence of an alkene.
D. Alkenes are more reactive than alkanes because they are unsaturated.
E. Alkenes frequently take part in subtraction reactions.
F. All of the above.

Question 426:
Which of the following statements is correct regarding Group 17?

A. All Group 17 elements are electrophilic and therefore form negatively charged ions.
B. All Group 17 elements are gasses a room temperature.
C. The reaction between Sodium and Fluorine is less vigorous than Sodium and Iodine.
D. All Group 17 elements are non-coloured.
E. Some Group 17 elements are found naturally as unbonded atoms.
F. All of the above.
G. None of the above.

Question 427:

Why does the electrolysis of NaCl solution (brine) require the strict separation of the products of anode and cathode?

A. To prevent the preferential discharge of ions.
B. In order to prevent spontaneous combustion.
C. In order to prevent production of H_2.
D. In order to prevent the formation of HCl.
E. In order to avoid CO poisoning.
F. All of the above.

Question 428:

In relation to the electrolysis of brine (NaCl), which of the following statements are correct?

1. Electrolysis results in the production of hydrogen and chlorine gas.
2. Electrolysis results in the production of sodium hydroxide.
3. Hydrogen gas is released at the anode and chlorine gas is released at the cathode.

A. Only 1   C. Only 3   E. 1 and 3   G. All of the above
B. Only 2   D. 1 and 2   F. 2 and 3

Question 429:

Which of the following statements is correct?

A. Alkanes consist of multiple C-H bonds that are very weak.
B. An alkane with 14 hydrogen atoms is called Heptane.
C. All alkanes consist purely of hydrogen and carbon atoms.
D. Alkanes burn in excess oxygen to produce carbon monoxide and water.
E. Bromine water is decolourised in the presence of an alkane.
F. None of the above.

Question 430:

Which of the following statements are correct?

1. All alcohols contain a hydroxyl functional group.
2. Alcohols are highly soluble in water.
3. Alcohols are sometimes used a biofuels.

A. Only 1   C. Only 3   E. 2 and 3   G. 1, 2 and 3
B. Only 2   D. 1 and 2   F. 1 and 3

Question 431:

Which row of the table below is correct?

	Non-Reducible Hydrocarbon			Reducible Hydrocarbon		
A	C_nH_{2n}	$Br_{2(aq)}$ remains brown	Saturated	C_nH_{2n+2}	Turns $Br_{2(aq)}$ colourless	Unsaturated
B	C_nH_{2n+2}	Turns $Br_{2(aq)}$ colourless	Unsaturated	C_nH_{2n}	$Br_{2(aq)}$ remains brown	Saturated
C	C_nH_{2n}	$Br_{2(aq)}$ remains brown	Unsaturated	C_nH_{2n+2}	Turns $Br_{2(aq)}$ colourless	Saturated
D	C_nH_{2n+2}	Turns $Br_{2(aq)}$ colourless	Saturated	C_nH_{2n}	$Br_{2(aq)}$ remains brown	Unsaturated
E	C_nH_{2n+2}	$Br_{2(aq)}$ remains brown	Saturated	C_nH_{2n}	Turns $Br_{2(aq)}$ colourless	Unsaturated

~ 136 ~

Question 432:

How many grams of magnesium chloride are formed when 10 grams of magnesium oxide are dissolved in excess hydrochloric acid? Relative atomic masses: $Mg = 24$, $O = 16$, $H = 1$, $Cl = 35.5$

A.   10.00
B.   14.95

C.   20.00
D.   23.75

E.   47.55
F.   More information needed

Question 433:

Pentadecane has the molecular formula $C_{15}H_{32}$. Which of the following statements is true?

A.   Pentadecane has a lower boiling point than pentane.
B.   Pentadecane is more flammable than pentane.
C.   Pentadecane is more volatile than pentane.
D.   Pentadecane is more viscous than pentane.
E.   All of the above.
F.   None of the above.

Question 434:

The rate of reaction is normally dependent upon:
1.   The temperature.
2.   The concentration of reactants.
3.   The concentration of the catalyst.
4.   The surface area of the catalyst.

A.   1 and 2
B.   2 and 3

C.   2, 3 and 4
D.   1, 3 and 4

E.   1, 2 and 3
F.   1, 2, 3 and 4

Question 435:

The equation below shows the complete combustion of a sample of unknown hydrocarbon in excess oxygen.

$$C_aH_b + O_2 \rightarrow cCO_2 + dH_2O$$

The product yielded 176 grams of CO_2 and 108 grams of H_2O. What is the most likely formula of the unknown hydrocarbon? Relative atomic masses: $H = 1$, $C = 12$, $O = 16$.

A. CH_4
B. CH_3

C. C_2H_6
D. C_3H_9

E. C_2H_4
F. C_4H_{10}

Question 436:

What type of reaction must ethanol undergo in order to be converted to ethylene oxide (C_2H_4O)?

A.   Oxidation
B.   Reduction

C.   Dehydration
D.   Hydration

E.   Redox
F.   All   of   the   above

Question 437:

What values of a, b and c balance the equation below?

$$a \ Ba_3N_2 + 6H_2O \rightarrow b \ Ba(OH)_2 + c \ NH_3$$

	a	b	c
A	1	2	3
B	1	3	2
C	2	1	3
D	2	3	1
E	3	1	2
F	3	2	1

Question 438:

What values of *a, b* and *c* balance the equation below?

$$a\ FeS + 7O_2 \rightarrow b\ Fe_2O_3 + c\ SO_2$$

	a	b	c
A	3	2	2
B	2	4	1
C	3	1	5
D	4	1	3
E	4	2	4

Question 439:

Magnesium consists of 3 isotopes: Mg^{23}, Mg^{25}, and Mg^{26} which are found naturally in a ratio of 80:10:10. Calculate the relative atomic mass of magnesium.

A. 23.3   B. 23.4   C. 23.5   D. 23.6   E. 24.6   F. 25.2   G. 25.5

Question 440:

Consider the three reactions:
1. $Cl_2 + 2Br^- \rightarrow 2Cl^- + Br_2$
2. $Cu^{2+} + Mg \rightarrow Cu + Mg^{2+}$
3. $Fe_2O_3 + 3CO \rightarrow 2Fe + 3CO_2$

Which of the following statements are correct?

A. Cl_2 and Fe_2O_3 are reducing agents.
B. CO and Cu^{2+} are oxidising agents.
C. Br_2 is a stronger oxidising agent than Cl_2.
D. Mg is a stronger reducing agent than Cu.
E. All of the above.
F. None of the above.

Question 441:

Which row best describes the properties of NaCl?

	Melting Point	Solubility in Water	Conducts electricity?	
			As solid	In solution
A	High	Yes	Yes	Yes
B	High	No	Yes	No
C	High	Yes	No	Yes
D	High	No	No	No
E	Low	Yes	Yes	Yes
F	Low	No	Yes	No
G	Low	Yes	No	Yes
H	Low	No	No	No

Question 442:

80g of Sodium hydroxide reacts with excess zinc nitrate to produce zinc hydroxide. Calculate the mass of zinc hydroxide produced. Relative atomic mass: N = 14, Zn = 65, O = 16, Na = 23.

A. 49g
B. 95g

C. 99g
D. 100g

E. 198g
F. More information needed.

Question 443:

Which of the following statements is correct?

A. The reaction between all Group 1 metals and water is exothermic.
B. All Group 1 metals react with water to produce a metal oxide.
C. All Group 1 metals react with water to produce elemental hydrogen.
D. Sodium reacts more vigorously with water than Potassium.
E. All of the above.
F. None of the above.

Question 444:

Which of the following statements is correct?

A. NaCl can be separated using sieves.
B. CO_2 can be separated using electrolysis.
C. Dyes in a sample of ink can be separated using chromatography.
D. Oil and water can be separated using fractional distillation.
E. Methane and diesel can be separated using a separating funnel.
F. None of the above.

Question 445:

Which of the following statements about the reaction between caesium and fluoride are correct?

1. It is an exothermic reaction and therefore requires catalysts.
2. It results in the formation of a salt.
3. The addition of water will make the reaction safer.

A. Only 1
B. Only 2
C. Only 3

D. 1 and 2
E. 2 and 3
F. 1 and 3

G. All of the above.
H. None of the above.

Question 446:

Which of the following statements is generally true about stable isotopes?
1. The nucleus contains an equal number of neutrons and protons.
2. The nuclear charge is equal and opposite to the peripheral charge due to the orbiting electrons.
3. They can all undergo radioactive decay into more stable isotopes.

A. Only 1
B. Only 2
C. Only 3

D. 1 and 2
E. 2 and 3
F. 1 and 3

G. All of the above.
H. None of the above.

Question 447:

Why do most salts have very high melting temperatures?
A. Their surface is able to radiate away a significant portion of heat to their environment.
B. The ionic bonds holding them together are very strong.
C. The covalent bonds holding them together are very strong.
D. They tend to form large macromolecules as each salt molecule bonds with multiple other molecules.
E. All of the above.

Question 448:

A bottle of water contains 306ml of pure deionised water. How many protons are in the bottle from the water? Avogadro Constant = 6×10^{23}.

A. 1×10^{22} B. 1×10^{23} C. 1×10^{24} D. 1×10^{25} E. 1×10^{26}

Question 449:

On analysis, an organic substance is found to contain 41.4% Carbon, 55.2% Oxygen and 3.45% Hydrogen by mass. Which of the following could be the empirical formula of this substance?

A. $C_3O_3H_6$ C. $C_4O_2H_4$ E. $C_4O_2H_8$

B. $C_3O_3H_{12}$ D. $C_4O_4H_4$ F. More information needed.

Question 450:

A is a Group 2 element and B is a Group 17 element. Which row best describes what happens when A reacts with B?

	B is	Formula
A	Reduced	AB
B	Reduced	A_2B
C	Reduced	AB_2
D	Oxidised	AB
E	Oxidised	A_2B
F	Oxidised	AB_2

SECTION 2: Physics

If you haven't done physics at AS then you'll have to ensure that you are confident with commonly examined topics like Newtonian mechanics, electrical circuits and radioactive decay as you may not have covered these at GCSE depending on the specification you did.

The first step to improving in this section is to memorise by rote all the equations listed on the next page.

The majority of the physics questions involve a fair bit of maths – this means you need to be comfortable with converting between units and also powers of 10. **Most questions require two step calculations**. Consider the example:

A metal ball is released from the roof a 20 metre building. Assuming air resistance equals is negligible; calculate the velocity at which the ball hits the ground. [$g = 10ms^{-2}$]

A. 5 ms^{-1}
B. 10 ms^{-1}
C. 15 ms^{-1}
D. 20 ms^{-1}
E. 25 ms^{-1}

When the ball hits the ground, all of its gravitational potential energy has been converted to kinetic energy. Thus, $E_p = E_k$:

$$mg\Delta h = \frac{mv^2}{2}$$

Thus, $v = \sqrt{2gh} = \sqrt{2 \times 10 \times 20}$

$$= \sqrt{400} = 20ms^{-1}$$

Here, you were required to not only recall two equations but apply and rearrange them very quickly to get the answer; all in under 60 seconds. Thus, it is easy to understand why the physics questions are generally much harder than the biology and chemistry ones.

Note that if you were comfortable with basic Newtonian mechanics, you could have also solved this using a single suvat equation: $v^2 = u^2 + 2as$

$$v = \sqrt{2 \times 10 \times 20} = 20ms^{-1}$$

This is why you're **strongly advised to learn the 'suvat' equations** on the next page even if they're technically not on the syllabus.

SI Units

Remember that in order to get the correct answer you must always work in SI units i.e. do your calculations in terms of metres (not centimetres) and kilograms (not grams), etc.

Top tip! Knowing SI units is extremely useful because they allow you to **'work out' equations** if you ever forget them e.g. The units for density are kg/m^3. Since Kg is the SI unit for mass, and m^3 is represented by volume –the equation for density must be = Mass/Volume.

This can also work the other way, for example we know that the unit for Pressure is Pascal (Pa). But based on the fact that Pressure = Force/Area, a Pascal must be equivalent to N/m^2. Some physics questions will test your ability to manipulate units like this so it's important you are comfortable converting between them.

Formulas you MUST know:

Equations of Motion:

➢ $s = ut + 0.5at^2$
➢ $v = u + at$
➢ $a = (v-u)/t$
➢ $v^2 = u^2 + 2as$

Equations relating to Force:

➢ Force = mass x acceleration
➢ Force = Momentum/Time
➢ Pressure = Force / Area
➢ Moment of a Force = Force x Distance
➢ Work done = Force x Displacement

For objects in equilibrium:

➢ Sum of Clockwise moments = Sum of Anti-clockwise moments
➢ Sum of all resultant forces = 0

Equations relating to Energy:

➢ Kinetic Energy = $0.5 \, mv^2$
➢ Δ in Gravitational Potential Energy = $mg\Delta h$
➢ Energy Efficiency = (Useful energy/ Total energy) x 100%

Equations relating to Power:

➢ Power = Work done / time
➢ Power = Energy transferred / time
➢ Power = Force x velocity

Electrical Equations:

➢ $Q = It$
➢ $V = IR$
➢ $P = IV = I^2R = V^2/R$
➢ V = Potential difference (V, Volts)

➢ R = Resistance (Ohms)
➢ P = Power (W, Watts)
➢ Q = Charge (C, Coulombs)
➢ t = Time (s, seconds)

For Transformers: $\dfrac{V_p}{V_s} = \dfrac{n_p}{n_s}$ where:

➢ V: Potential difference
➢ n: Number of turns
➢ p: Primary
➢ s: Secondary

Other:

➢ Weight = mass x g
➢ Density = Mass / Volume
➢ Momentum = Mass x Velocity
➢ $g = 9.81 \, \text{ms}^{-2}$ (unless otherwise stated)

Factor	Text	Symbol
10^{12}	Tera	T
10^9	Giga	G
10^6	Mega	M
10^3	Kilo	k
10^2	Hecto	h
10^{-1}	Deci	d
10^{-2}	Centi	c
10^{-3}	Milli	m
10^{-6}	Micro	μ
10^{-9}	Nano	n
10^{-12}	Pico	p

Physics Questions

Question 451:
Which of the following statements are **FALSE**?

A. Electromagnetic waves cause things to heat up.
B. X-rays and gamma rays can knock electrons out of their orbits.
C. Loud sounds can make objects vibrate.
D. Wave power can be used to generate electricity.
E. Since waves carry energy away, the source of a wave loses energy.
F. The amplitude of a wave determines its mass.

Question 452:
A spacecraft is analysing a newly discovered exoplanet. A rock of unknown mass falls on the planet from a height of 30 m. Given that $g = 5.4$ ms^{-2} on the planet, calculate the speed of the rock when it hits the ground and the time it took to fall.

	Speed (ms^{-1})	Time (s)
A	18	3.3
B	18	3.1
C	12	3.3
D	10	3.7
E	9	2.3
F	1	0.3

Question 453:
A canoe floating on the sea rises and falls 7 times in 49 seconds. The waves pass it at a speed of 5 ms^{-1}. How long are the waves?
A. 12 m   B. 22 m   C. 25 m   D. 35 m   E. 57 m   F. 75 m

Question 454:
Miss Orrell lifts her 37.5 kg bike for a distance of 1.3 m in 5 s. The acceleration of free fall is 10 ms^{-2}. What is the average power that she develops?

A. 9.8 W   C. 57.9 W   E. 97.5W
B. 12.9 W   D. 79.5 W   F. 98.0 W

Question 455:
A truck accelerates at 5.6 ms^{-2} from rest for 8 seconds. Calculate the final speed and the distance travelled in 8 seconds.

	Final Speed (ms^{-1})	Distance (m)
A	40.8	119.2
B	40.8	129.6
C	42.8	179.2
D	44.1	139.2
E	44.1	179.7
F	44.2	129.2
G	44.8	179.2
H	44.8	179.7

Question 456:
Which of the following statements is true when a sky diver jumps out of a plane?

A. The sky diver leaves the plane and will accelerate until the air resistance is greater than their weight.
B. The sky diver leaves the plane and will accelerate until the air resistance is less than their weight.
C. The sky diver leaves the plane and will accelerate until the air resistance equals their weight.
D. The sky diver leaves the plane and will accelerate until the air resistance equals their weight squared.
E. The sky diver will travel at a constant velocity after leaving the plane.

Question 457:
A 100 g apple falls on Isaac's head from a height of 20 m. Calculate the apple's momentum before the point of impact. Take $g = 10$ ms^{-2}

A. 0.1 kgms^{-1} C. 1 kgms^{-1} E. 10 kgms^{-1}
B. 0.2 kgms^{-1} D. 2 kgms^{-1} F. 20 kgms^{-1}

Question 458:
Which of the following do all electromagnetic waves all have in common?

1. They can travel through a vacuum.
2. They can be reflected.
3. They are the same length.
4. They have the same amount of energy.
5. They can be polarised.

A. 1, 2 and 3 only   C. 4 and 5 only   E. 1, 2 and 5 only
B. 1, 2, 3 and 4 only   D. 3 and 4 only   F. 1 and 5 only

Question 459:
A battery with an internal resistance of 0.8 Ω and e.m.f of 36 V is used to power a drill with resistance 1 Ω. What is the current in the circuit when the drill is connected to the power supply?

A. 5 A   B. 10 A   C. 15 A   D. 20 A   E. 25 A   F. 30 A

Question 460:
Officer Bailey throws a 20 g dart at a speed of 100 ms^{-1}. It strikes the dartboard and is brought to rest in 10 milliseconds. Calculate the average force exerted on the dart by the dartboard.

A. 0.2 N   C. 20 N   E. 2,000 N
B. 2 N   D. 200 N   F. 20,000 N

Question 461:
Professor Huang lifts a 50 kg bag through a distance of 0.7 m in 3 s. What average power does she develop to 3 significant figures? Take $g = 10$ms^{-2}

A. 112 W   C. 114 W   E. 116 W
B. 113 W   D. 115 W   F. 117 W

Question 462:
An electric scooter is travelling at a speed of 30 ms^{-1} and is kept going against a 50 N frictional force by a driving force of 300 N in the direction of motion. Given that the engine runs at 200 V, calculate the current in the scooter.

A. 4.5 A   C. 450 A   E. 45,000 A
B. 45 A   D. 4,500 A   F. More information needed.

Question 463:
Which of the following statements about the physical definition of work are correct?

1. $Work\ done = \frac{Force}{distance}$
2. The unit of work is equivalent to $Kgms^{-2}$.
3. Work is defined as a force causing displacement of the body upon which it acts.

A. Only 1
B. Only 2
C. Only 3
D. 1 and 2
E. 2 and 3
F. 1 and 3

Question 464:
Which of the following statements about kinetic energy are correct?

1. It is defined as $E_k = \frac{mv^2}{2}$
2. The unit of kinetic energy is equivalent to $Pa \times m^3$.
3. Kinetic energy is equal to the amount of energy needed to decelerate the body in question from its current speed.

A. Only 1
B. Only 2
C. Only 3
D. 1 and 2
E. 2 and 3
F. 1 and 3
G. 1, 2 and 3

Question 465:
In relation to radiation, which of the following statements is **FALSE**?

A. Radiation is the emission of energy in the form of waves or particles.
B. Radiation can be either ionizing or non-ionizing.
C. Gamma radiation has very high energy.
D. Alpha radiation is of higher energy than beta radiation.
E. X-rays are an example of wave radiation.

Question 466:
In relation to the physical definition of half-life, which of the following statements are correct?

1. In radioactive decay, the half-life is independent of atom type and isotope.
2. Half-life is defined as the time required for exactly half of the entities to decay.
3. Half-life applies to situations of both exponential and non-exponential decay.

A. Only 1
B. Only 2
C. Only 3
D. 1 and 2
E. 2 and 3
F. 1 and 3

Question 467:
In relation to nuclear fusion, which of the following statements is **FALSE**?

A. Nuclear fusion is initiated by the absorption of neutrons.
B. Nuclear fusion describes the fusion of hydrogen atoms to form helium atoms.
C. Nuclear fusion releases great amounts of energy.
D. Nuclear fusion requires high activation temperatures.
E. All of the statements above are false.

Question 468:
In relation to nuclear fission, which of the following statements is correct?

A. Nuclear fission is the basis of many nuclear weapons.
B. Nuclear fission is triggered by the shooting of neutrons at unstable atoms.
C. Nuclear fission can trigger chain reactions.
D. Nuclear fission commonly results in the emission of ionizing radiation.
E. All of the above.

Question 469:

Two identical resistors (R_a and R_b) are connected in a series circuit. Which of the following statements are true?

1. The current through both resistors is the same.
2. The voltage through both resistors is the same.
3. The voltage across the two resistors is given by Ohm's Law.

A. Only 1   D. 1 and 2   G. 1, 2 and 3
B. Only 2   E. 2 and 3   H. None of the above.
C. Only 3   F. 1 and 3

Question 470:

The Sun is 8 light-minutes away from the Earth. Estimate the circumference of the Earth's orbit around the Sun. Assume that the Earth is in a circular orbit around the Sun. Speed of light = 3×10^8 ms^{-1}

A. 10^{24} m   C. 10^{18} m   E. 10^{12} m
B. 10^{21} m   D. 10^{15} m   F. 10^9 m

Question 471:

Which of the following statements about the physical definition of speed are true?

1. Speed is the same as velocity.
2. The internationally standardised unit for speed is ms^{-2}.
3. Velocity = distance/time.

A. Only 1   D. 1 and 2   G. 1, 2 and 3
B. Only 2   E. 2 and 3   H. None of the above
C. Only 3   F. 1 and 3

Question 472:

Which of the following statements best defines Ohm's Law?

A. The current through an insulator between two points is indirectly proportional to the potential difference across the two points.
B. The current through an insulator between two points is directly proportional to the potential difference across the two points.
C. The current through a conductor between two points is inversely proportional to the potential difference across the two points.
D. The current through a conductor between two points is proportional to the square of the potential difference across the two points.
E. The current through a conductor between two points is directly proportional to the potential difference across the two points.

Question 473:

Which of the following statements regarding Newton's Second Law are correct?

1. For objects at rest, Resultant Force must be 0 Newtons
2. Force = Mass x Acceleration
3. Force = Rate of change of Momentum

A. Only 1   C. Only 3   E. 2 and 3   G. 1, 2 and 3
B. Only 2   D. 1 and 2   F. 1 and 3

Question 474:
Which of the following equations concerning electrical circuits are correct?

1. $Charge = \dfrac{Voltage \; x \; time}{Resistance}$

2. $Charge = \dfrac{Power \; x \; time}{Voltage}$

3. $Charge = \dfrac{Current \; x \; time}{Resistance}$

A. Only 1
B. Only 2
C. Only 3
D. 1 and 2

E. 2 and 3
F. 1 and 3
G. 1, 2 and 3
H. None of the equations are correct.

Question 475:
An elevator has a mass of 1,600 kg and is carrying passengers that have a combined mass of 200 kg. A constant frictional force of 4,000 N retards its motion upward. What force must the motor provide for the elevator to move with an upward acceleration of 1 ms^{-2}? Assume: $g = 10$ ms^{-2}

A. 1,190 N
B. 11,900 N
C. 18,000 N

D. 22,000 N
E. 23,800 N

Question 476:
A 1,000 kg car accelerates from rest at 5 ms^{-2} for 10 s. Then, a braking force is applied to bring it to rest within 20 seconds. What distance has the car travelled?

A. 125 m
B. 250 m

C. 650 m
D. 750 m

E. 1,200 m
F. More information needed

Question 477:
An electric heater is connected to 120 V mains by a copper wire that has a resistance of 8 ohms. What is the power of the heater?

A. 90 W
B. 180 W
C. 900 W
D. 1800 W

E. 9,000W
F. 18,000 W
G. More information needed

Question 478:
In a particle accelerator electrons are accelerated through a potential difference of 40 MV and emerge with an energy of 40MeV (1 MeV = 1.60 x 10^{-13} J). Each pulse contains 5,000 electrons and constitutes a current of 250 μA. The current is zero between pulses. Assuming that the electrons have zero energy prior to being accelerated what is the power delivered by the electron beam?

A. 1 kW
B. 10 kW

C. 100 kW
D. 1,000 kW

E. 10,000 kW
F. More information needed

Question 479:
Which of the following statements is true?

A. When an object is in equilibrium with its surroundings, there is no energy transferred to or from the object and so its temperature remains constant.
B. When an object is in equilibrium with its surroundings, it radiates and absorbs energy at the same rate and so its temperature remains constant.
C. Radiation is faster than convection but slower than conduction.
D. Radiation is faster than conduction but slower than convection.
E. None of the above.

Question 480:

A 6kg block is pulled from rest along a horizontal frictionless surface by a constant horizontal force of 12 N. Calculate the speed of the block after it has moved 300 cm.

A. $2\sqrt{3}\ ms^{-1}$ C. $4\sqrt{3}\ ms^{-1}$

B. $4\sqrt{3}\ ms^{-1}$ D. $12\ ms^{-1}$ E. $\sqrt{\frac{3}{2}}\ ms^{-1}$

Question 481:

A 100 V heater heats 1.5 litres of pure water from 10°C to 50°C in 50 minutes. Given that 1 kg of pure water requires 4,000 J to raise its temperature by 1°C, calculate the resistance of the heater.

A. 12.5 ohms   C. 125 ohms   E. 500 ohms

B. 25 ohms   D. 250 ohms   F. 850 ohms

Question 482:

Which of the following statements are true?

1. Nuclear fission is the basis of nuclear energy.
2. Following fission, the resulting atoms are a different element to the original one.
3. Nuclear fission often results in the production of free neutrons and photons.

A. Only 1   D. 1 and 2   G. 1, 2 and 3

B. Only 2   E. 2 and 3   H. None of the above

C. Only 3   F. 1 and 3

Question 483:

Which of the following statements are true? Assume $g = 10\ \text{ms}^{-2}$.

1. Gravitational potential energy is defined as $E_p = m \times g \times \Delta h$.
2. Gravitational potential energy is a measure of the work done against gravity.
3. A reservoir situated 1 km above ground level with 10^6 litres of water has a potential energy of 1 Giga Joule.

A. Only 1   D. 1 and 2   G. 1, 2 and 3

B. Only 2   E. 2 and 3   H. None of the above

C. Only 3   F. 1 and 3

Question 484:

Which of the following statements are correct in relation to Newton's 3rd law?

1. For every action there is an equal and opposite reaction.
2. According to Newton's 3rd law, there are no isolated forces.
3. Rockets cannot accelerate in deep space because there is nothing to generate an equal and opposite force.

A. Only 1   C. Only 3   E. 2 and 3

B. Only 2   D. 1 and 2   F. 1 and 3

Question 485:

Which of the following statements are correct?
1. Positively charged objects have gained electrons.
2. Electrical charge in a circuit over a period of time can be calculated if the voltage and resistance are known.
3. Objects can be charged by friction.

A. Only 1   C. Only 3   E. 2 and 3   G. 1, 2 and 3

B. Only 2   D. 1 and 2   F. 1 and 3

Question 486:
Which of the following statements is true?

A. The gravitational force between two objects is independent of their mass.
B. Each planet in the solar system exerts a gravitational force on the Earth.
C. For satellites in a geostationary orbit, acceleration due to gravity is equal and opposite to the lift from engines.
D. Two objects that are dropped from the Eiffel tower will always land on the ground at the same time if they have the same mass.
E. All of the above.
F. None of the above.

Question 487:
Which of the following best defines an electrical conductor?

A. Conductors are usually made from metals and they conduct electrical charge in multiple directions.
B. Conductors arc usually made from non-metals and they conduct electrical charge in multiple directions.
C. Conductors are usually made from metals and they conduct electrical charge in one fixed direction.
D. Conductors are usually made from non-metals and they conduct electrical charge in one fixed direction.
E. Conductors allow the passage of electrical charge with zero resistance because they contain freely mobile charged particles.
F. Conductors allow the passage of electrical charge with maximal resistance because they contain charged particles that are fixed and static.

Question 488:
An 800 kg compact car delivers 20% of its power output to its wheels. If the car has a mileage of 30 miles/gallon and travels at a speed of 60 miles/hour, how much power is delivered to the wheels? 1 gallon of petrol contains 9×10^8 J.

A. 10 kW   B. 20 kW   C. 40 kW   D. 50 kW   E. 100 kW

Question 489:
Which of the following statements about beta radiation are true?

1. After a beta particle is emitted, the atomic mass number is unchanged.
2. Beta radiation can penetrate paper but not aluminium foil.
3. A beta particle is emitted from the nucleus of the atom when an electron changes into a neutron.

A. 1 only   C. 1 and 3   E. 2 and 3
B. 2 only   D. 1 and 2   F. 1, 2 and 3

Question 490:
A car with a weight of 15,000 N is travelling at a speed of 15 ms^{-1} when it crashes into a wall and is brought to rest in 10 milliseconds. Calculate the average braking force exerted on the car by the wall. Take $g = 10$ ms^{-2}

A. $1.25 \times 10^4 N$ C. $1.25 \times 10^6 N$ E. $2.25 \times 10^5 N$
B. $1.25 \times 10^5 N$ D. $2.25 \times 10^4 N$ F. $2.25 \times 10^6 N$

Question 491:
Which of the following statements are correct?

1. Electrical insulators are usually metals e.g. copper.
2. The flow of charge through electrical insulators is extremely low.
3. Electrical insulators can be charged by rubbing them together.

A. Only 1   C. Only 3   E. 2 and 3   G. 1, 2 and 3
B. Only 2   D. 1 and 2   F. 1 and 3

The following information is needed for Questions 492 and 493:

The graph below represents a car's movement. At t=0 the car's displacement was 0 m.

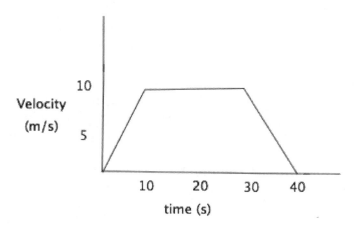

Question 492:
Which of the following statements are not true?

1. The car is reversing after t = 30.
2. The car moves with constant acceleration from t = 0 to t = 10.
3. The car moves with constant speed from t = 10 to t = 30.

A. 1 only   D. 1 and 3   G. 1, 2 and 3
B. 2 only   E. 1 and 2
C. 3 only   F. 2 and 3

Question 493:
Calculate the distance travelled by the car.

A. 200 m   C. 350 m   E. 500 m
B. 300 m   D. 400 m   F. More information needed

Question 494:
A 1,000 kg rocket is launched during a thunderstorm and reaches a constant velocity 30 seconds after launch. Suddenly, a strong gust of wind acts on it for 5 seconds with a force of 10,000 N in the direction of movement. What is the resulting change in velocity?

A. 0.5 ms^{-1} C. 50 ms^{-1} E. 5000 ms^{-1}
B. 5 ms^{-1} D. 500 ms^{-1} F. More information needed

Question 495:
A 0.5 tonne crane lifts a 0.01 tonne wardrobe by 100 cm in 5,000 milliseconds.
Calculate the average power developed by the crane. Take $g = 10$ ms^{-2}.

A. 0.2 W   C. 5 W   E. 50 W
B. 2 W   D. 20 W   F. More information needed

Question 496:

A 20 V battery is connected to a circuit consisting of a 1 Ω and 2 Ω resistor in parallel. Calculate the overall current of the circuit.

A. 6.67 A   B. 8 A   C. 10 A   D. 12 A   E. 20 A   F. 30 A

Question 497:

Which of the following statements is correct?

A. The speed of light changes when it enters water.
B. The speed of light changes when it leaves water.
C. The direction of light changes when it enters water.
D. The direction of light changes when it leaves water.
E. All of the above.
F. None of the above.

Question 498:

In a parallel circuit, a 60 V battery is connected to two branches. Branch A contains 6 identical 5 Ω resistors and branch B contains 2 identical 10 Ω resistors.

Calculate the current in branches A and B.

	I_A (A)	I_B (A)
A	0	6
B	6	0
C	2	3
D	3	2
E	3	3
F	1	5
G	5	1

Question 499:

Calculate the voltage of an electrical circuit that has a power output of 50,000,000,000 nW and a current of 0.000000004 GA.

A. 0.0125 GV   C. 0.0125 kV   E. 0.0125 mV   G. 0.0125 nV
B. 0.0125 MV   D. 0.0125 V   F. 0.0125 μV

Question 500:

Which of the following statements about radioactive decay is correct?

A. Radioactive decay is highly predictable.
B. An unstable element will continue to decay until it reaches a stable nuclear configuration.
C. All forms of radioactive decay release gamma rays.
D. All forms of radioactive decay release X-rays.
E. An atom's nuclear charge is unchanged after it undergoes alpha decay.
F. None of the above.

Question 501:

A circuit contains three identical resistors of unknown resistance connected in series with a 15 V battery. The power output of the circuit is 60 W.
Calculate the overall resistance of the circuit when two further identical resistors are added to it.

A. 0.125 Ω   C. 3.75 Ω   E. 18.75 Ω
B. 1.25 Ω   D. 6.25 Ω   F. More information needed.

Question 502:

A 5,000 kg tractor's engine uses 1 litre of fuel to move 0.1 km. 1 ml of the fuel contains 20 kJ of energy. Calculate the engine's efficiency. Take $g = 10$ ms^{-2}

A. 2.5 %

B. 25 %

C. 38 %

D. 50 %

E. 75 %

F. More information needed.

Question 503:

Which of the following statements are correct?

1. Electromagnetic induction occurs when a wire moves relative to a magnet.
2. Electromagnetic induction occurs when a magnetic field changes.
3. An electrical current is generated when a coil rotates in a magnetic field.

A. Only 1

B. Only 2

C. Only 3

D. 1 and 2

E. 2 and 3

F. 1 and 3

G. 1, 2 and 3

Question 504:

Which of the following statements are correct regarding parallel circuits?
1. The current flowing through a branch is dependent on the branch's resistance.
2. The total current flowing into the branches is equal to the total current flowing out of the branches.
3. An ammeter will always give the same reading regardless of its location in the circuit.

A. Only 1

B. Only 2

C. Only 3

D. 1 and 2

E. 2 and 3

F. 1 and 3

G. All of the above

Question 505:

Which of the following statements regarding series circuits are true?
1. The overall resistance of a circuit is given by the sum of all resistors in the circuit.
2. Electrical current moves from the positive terminal to the negative terminal.
3. Electrons move from the positive terminal to the negative terminal.

A. Only 1

B. Only 2

C. Only 3

D. 1 and 2

E. 2 and 3

F. 1 and 3

Question 506:

The graphs below show current vs. voltage plots for 4 different electrical components.

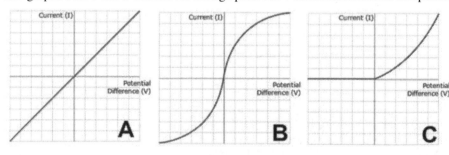

Which of the following graphs represents a resistor at constant temperature, and which a filament lamp?

	Fixed Resistor	Filament Lamp
A	A	B
B	A	C
C	A	D
D	C	A
E	C	C
F	C	D

Question 507:
Which of the following statements are true about vectors?

A. Vectors can be added or subtracted.
B. All vector quantities have a defined magnitude.
C. All vector quantities have a defined direction.
D. Displacement is an example of a vector quantity.
E. All of the above.
F. None of the above.

Question 508:
The acceleration due to gravity on the Earth is six times greater than that on the moon. Dr Tyson records the weight of a rock as 250 N on the moon.

Calculate the rock's density given that it has a volume of 250 cm³. Take $g_{Earth} = 10$ ms^{-2}

A. 0.2 kg/cm³   C. 0.6 kg/cm³   E. 0.8 kg/cm³
B. 0.5 kg/cm³   D. 0.7 kg/cm³   F. More information needed.

Question 509:
A radioactive element X_{78}^{225} undergoes alpha decay. What is the atomic mass and atomic number after 5 alpha particles have been released?

	Mass Number	Atomic Number
A	200	56
B	200	58
C	205	64
D	205	68
E	215	58
F	215	73
G	225	78
H	225	83

Question 510:
A 20 A current passes through a circuit with resistance of 10 Ω. The circuit is connected to a transformer that contains a primary coil with 5 turns and a secondary coil with 10 turns. Calculate the potential difference exiting the transformer.

A. 100 V   D. 500 V   G. 5,000 V
B. 200 V   E. 2,000 V
C. 400 V   F. 4,000 V

Question 511:
A metal sphere of unknown mass is dropped from an altitude of 1 km and reaches terminal velocity 300 m before it hits the ground. Given that resistive forces do a total of 10 kJ of work for the last 100 m before the ball hits the ground, calculate the mass of the ball. Take $g = 10$ms^{-2}.

A. 1 kg   C. 5 kg   E. 20 kg
B. 2 kg   D. 10 kg   F. More information needed.

Question 512:
Which of the following statements is true about the electromagnetic spectrum?

A. The wavelength of ultraviolet waves is shorter than that of x-rays.
B. For waves in the electromagnetic spectrum, wavelength is directly proportional to frequency.
C. Most electromagnetic waves can be stopped with a thin layer of aluminium.
D. Waves in the electromagnetic spectrum travel at the speed of sound.
E. Humans are able to visualise the majority of the electromagnetic spectrum.
F. None of the above.

Question 513:
In relation to the Doppler Effect, which of the following statements are true?

1. If an object emitting a wave moves towards the sensor, the wavelength increases and frequency decreases.
2. An object that originally emitted a wave of a wavelength of 20 mm followed by a second reading delivering a wavelength of 15 mm is moving towards the sensor.
3. The faster the object is moving away from the sensor, the greater the increase in frequency.

A. Only 1
B. Only 2
C. Only 3
D. 1 and 2

E. 1 and 3
F. 2 and 3
G. 1, 2 and 3
H. None of the above statements are true.

Question 514:
A 5 g bullet is travels at 1 km/s and hits a brick wall. It penetrates 50 cm before being brought to rest 100 ms after impact. Calculate the average braking force exerted by the wall on the bullet.

A. 50 N
B. 500 N

C. 5,000 N
D. 50,000 N

E. 500,000 N
F. More information needed.

Question 515:
Polonium (Po) is a highly radioactive element that has no known stable isotope. Po^{210} undergoes radioactive decay to Pb^{206} and Y. Calculate the number of protons in 10 moles of Y. [Avogadro's Constant = 6 x 10^{23}]

A. 0
B. 1.2 x 10^{24}

C. 1.2 x 10^{25}
D. 2.4 x 10^{24}

E. 2.4 x 10^{25}
F. More information needed

Question 516:
Dr Sale measures the background radiation in a nuclear wasteland to be 1,000 Bq. He then detects a spike of 16,000 Bq from a nuclear rod made up of an unknown material. 300 days later, he visits and can no longer detect a reading higher than 1,000 Bq from the rod, even though it hasn't been disturbed.
What is the longest possible half-life of the nuclear rod?

A. 25 days
B. 50 days

C. 75 days
D. 100 days

E. 150 days
F. More information needed

Question 517:

A radioactive element Y_{89}^{200} undergoes a series of beta (β^-) and gamma decays. What are the number of protons and neutrons in the element after the emission of 5 beta particles and 2 gamma waves?

	Protons	Neutrons
A	79	101
B	84	111
C	84	116
D	89	111
E	89	106
F	94	111
G	94	106
H	109	111

Question 518:

Most symphony orchestras tune to 'standard pitch' (frequency = 440 Hz). When they are tuning, sound directly from the orchestra reaches audience members that are 500 m away in 1.5 seconds.
Estimate the wavelength of 'standard pitch'.

A. 0.05 m

B. 0.5 m

C. 0.75 m

D. 1.5 m

E. 15 m

F. More information needed

Question 519:

A 1 kg cylindrical artillery shell with a radius of 50 mm is fired at a speed of 200 ms^{-1}. It strikes an armour plated wall and is brought to rest in 500 μs.

Calculate the average pressure exerted on the entire shell by the wall at the time of impact.

A. 5×10^6 Pa

B. 5×10^7 Pa

C. 5×10^8 Pa

D. 5×10^9 Pa

E. 5×10^{10} Pa

F. More information needed

Question 520:

A 1,000 W display fountain launches 120 litres of water straight up every minute. Given that the fountain is 10% efficient, calculate the maximum possible height that the stream of water could reach.
Assume that there is negligible air resistance and $g = 10$ ms^{-2}.

A. 1 m

B. 5 m

C. 10 m

D. 20 m

E. 50m

F. More information needed

Question 521

In relation to transformers, which of the following is true?
1. Step up transformers increase the voltage leaving the transformer.
2. In step down transformers, the number of turns in the primary coil is smaller than in the secondary coil.
3. For transformers that are 100% efficient: $I_p V_p = I_s V_s$

A. Only 1

B. Only 2

C. Only 3

D. 1 and 2

E. 1 and 3

F. 2 and 3

G. 1, 2 and 3

H. None of the above.

Question 522:

The half-life of Carbon-14 is 5,730 years. A bone is found that contains 6.25% of the amount of C^{14} that would be found in a modern one. How old is the bone?

A. 11,460 years

B. 17,190 years

C. 22,920 years

D. 28,650 years

E. 34,380 years

F. 40,110 years

Question 523:

A wave has a velocity of 2,000 mm/s and a wavelength of 250 cm. What is its frequency in MHz?

A. 8×10^{-3} MHz

B. 8×10^{-4} MHz

C. 8×10^{-5} MHz

D. 8×10^{-6} MHz

E. 8×10^{-7} MHz

F. 8×10^{-8} MHz

Question 524:

A radioactive element has a half-life of 25 days. After 350 days it has a count rate of 50. What was its original count rate?

A. 102,400

B. 162,240

C. 204,800

D. 409,600

E. 819,200

F. 1,638,400

G. 3,276,800

Question 525:

Which of the following units is **NOT** equivalent to a Volt (V)?

A. $A\Omega$

B. WA^{-1}

C. $Nms^{-1}A^{-1}$

D. NmC

E. JC^{-1}

F. $JA^{-1}s^{-1}$

SECTION 2: Maths

BMAT Maths questions are designed to be time draining- if you find yourself consistently not finishing, it might be worth leaving the maths (and probably physics) questions until the very end.

Good students sometimes have a habit of making easy questions difficult; remember that the BMAT only tests GCSE level knowledge so you are not expected to know or use calculus or trigonometry in any part of the exam.

Formulas you **MUST** know:

2D Shapes		3D Shapes		
	Area		**Surface Area**	**Volume**
Circle	πr^2	**Cuboid**	Sum of all 6 faces	Length x width x height
Parallelogram	Base x Vertical height	**Cylinder**	$2\pi r^2 + 2\pi rl$	πr^2 x l
Trapezium	0.5 x h x (a+b)	**Cone**	$\pi r^2 + \pi rl$	πr^2 x (h/3)
Triangle	0.5 x base x height	**Sphere**	$4\pi r^2$	$(4/3)\pi r^3$

Even good students who are studying maths at A2 can struggle with certain BMAT maths topics because they're usually glossed over at school. These include:

Quadratic Formula

The solutions for a quadratic equation in the form $ax^2 + bx + c = 0$ are given by: $x = \frac{-b \pm \sqrt{b^2 - 4ac}}{2a}$

Remember that you can also use the discriminant to quickly see if a quadratic equation has any solutions:

$$If\ b^2 - 4ac < 0: No\ solutions$$
$$If\ b^2 - 4ac = 0: One\ solution$$
$$If\ b^2 - 4ac > 2: Two\ solutions$$

Completing the Square

If a quadratic equation cannot be factorised easily and is in the format $ax^2 + bx + c = 0$ then you can rearrange it into the form $a\left(x + \frac{b}{2a}\right)^2 + [c - \frac{b^2}{4a}] = 0$

This looks more complicated than it is – remember that in the BMAT, you're extremely unlikely to get quadratic equations where $a > 1$ and the equation doesn't have any easy factors. This gives you an easier equation:

$\left(x + \frac{b}{2}\right)^2 + [c - \frac{b^2}{4}] = 0$ and is best understood with an example.

Consider: $x^2 + 6x + 10 = 0$

This equation cannot be factorised easily but note that: $x^2 + 6x - 10 = (x + 3)^2 - 19 = 0$

Therefore, $x = -3 \pm \sqrt{19}$. Completing the square is an important skill – make sure you're comfortable with it.

Difference between 2 Squares

If you are asked to simplify expressions and find that there are no common factors but it involves square numbers – you might be able to factorise by using the 'difference between two squares'.

For example, $x^2 - 25$ can also be expressed as $(x + 5)(x - 5)$.

Maths Questions

Question 526:

Robert has a box of building blocks. The box contains 8 yellow blocks and 12 red blocks. He picks three blocks from the box and stacks them up high. Calculate the probability that he stacks two red building blocks and one yellow building block, in **any** order.

A. $\frac{8}{20}$
B. $\frac{44}{95}$
C. $\frac{11}{18}$
D. $\frac{8}{19}$
E. $\frac{12}{20}$
F. $\frac{35}{60}$

Question 527:

Solve $\frac{3x+5}{5} + \frac{2x-2}{3} = 18$

A. 12.11
B. 13.49
C. 13.95
D. 14.2
E. 19
F. 265

Question 528:

Solve $3x^2 + 11x - 20 = 0$

A. 0.75 and $-\frac{4}{3}$
B. -0.75 and $\frac{4}{3}$
C. -5 and $\frac{4}{3}$
D. 5 and $\frac{4}{3}$
E. 12 only
F. -12 only

Question 529:

Express $\frac{5}{x+2} + \frac{3}{x-4}$ as a single fraction.

A. $\frac{15x-120}{(x+2)(x-4)}$
B. $\frac{8x-26}{(x+2)(x-4)}$
C. $\frac{8x-14}{(x+2)(x-4)}$
D. $\frac{15}{8x}$
E. 24
F. $\frac{8x-14}{x^2-8}$

Question 530:

The value of p is directly proportional to the cube root of q. When p = 12, q = 27. Find the value of q when p = 24.

A. 32
B. 64
C. 124
D. 128
E. 216
F. 1728

Question 531:

Write 72^2 as a product of its prime factors.

A. $2^6 \times 3^4$
B. $2^6 \times 3^5$
C. $2^4 \times 3^4$
D. 2×3^3
E. $2^6 \times 3$
F. $2^3 \times 3^2$

Question 532:

Calculate: $\frac{2.302 \times 10^5 + 2.302 \times 10^2}{1.151 \times 10^{10}}$

A. 0.0000202

B. 0.00020002

C. 0.00002002

D. 0.00000002

E. 0.000002002

F. 0.000002002

Question 533:

Given that $y^2 + \mathbf{a}y + \mathbf{b} = (y + 2)^2 - 5$, find the values of **a** and **b**.

	a	b
A	-1	4
B	1	9
C	-1	-9
D	-9	1
E	4	-1
F	4	1

Question 534:

Express $\frac{4}{5} + \frac{m-2n}{m+4n}$ as a single fraction in its simplest form:

A. $\frac{6m+6n}{5(m+4n)}$

B. $\frac{9m+26n}{5(m+4n)}$

C. $\frac{20m+6n}{5(m+4n)}$

D. $\frac{3m+9n}{5(m+4n)}$

E. $\frac{3(3m+2n)}{5(m+4n)}$

F. $\frac{6m+6n}{3(m+4n)}$

Question 535:

A is inversely proportional to the square root of B. When A = 4, B = 25.

Calculate the value of A when B = 16.

A. 0.8   B. 4   C. 5   D. 6   E. 10   F. 20

Question 536:

S, T, U and V are points on the circumference of a circle, and O is the centre of the circle.

Given that angle SVU = 89°, calculate the size of the smaller angle SOU.

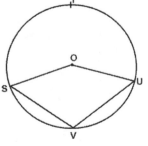

A. 89°   B. 91°   C. 102°   D. 178°   E. 182°   F. 212°

Question 537:

Open cylinder A has a surface area of 8π cm^2 and a volume of 2π cm^3. Open cylinder B is an enlargement of A and has a surface area of 32π cm^2. Calculate the volume of cylinder B.

A. 2π cm^3

B. 8π cm^3

C. 10π cm^3

D. 14π cm^3

E. 16π cm^3

F. 32π cm^3

Question 538:

Express $\frac{8}{x(3-x)} - \frac{6}{x}$ in its simplest form.

A. $\frac{3x-10}{x(3-x)}$

C. $\frac{6x-10}{x(3-2x)}$

E. $\frac{6x-10}{x(3-x)}$

B. $\frac{3x+10}{x(3-x)}$

D. $\frac{6x-10}{x(3+2x)}$

F. $\frac{6x+10}{x(3-x)}$

Question 539:

A bag contains 10 balls. 9 of those are white and 1 is black. What is the probability that the black ball is drawn in the tenth and final draw if the drawn balls are not replaced?

A. 0   B. $\frac{1}{10}$ C. $\frac{1}{100}$ D. $\frac{1}{10^{10}}$ E. $\frac{1}{362,880}$

Question 540:

Gambit has an ordinary deck of 52 cards. What is the probability of Gambit drawing 2 Kings (without replacement)?

A. 0

B. $\frac{1}{169}$

C. $\frac{1}{221}$

D. $\frac{4}{663}$

E. None of the above

Question 541:

I have two identical unfair dice, where the probability that the dice get a 6 is twice as high as the probability of any other outcome, which are all equally likely. What is the probability that when I roll both dice the total will be 12?

A. 0

B. $\frac{4}{49}$

C. $\frac{1}{9}$

D. $\frac{2}{7}$

E. None of the above

Question 542:

A roulette wheel consists of 36 numbered spots and 1 zero spot (i.e. 37 spots in total).

What is the probability that the ball will stop in a spot either divisible by 3 or 2?

A. 0   B. $\frac{25}{37}$ C. $\frac{25}{36}$ D. $\frac{18}{37}$ E. $\frac{24}{37}$

Question 543:

I have a fair coin that I flip 4 times. What is the probability I get 2 heads and 2 tails?

A. $\frac{1}{16}$

B. $\frac{3}{16}$

C. $\frac{3}{8}$

D. $\frac{9}{16}$

E. None of the above

Question 544:

Shivun rolls two fair dice. What is the probability that he gets a total of 5, 6 or 7?

A. $\frac{9}{36}$

B. $\frac{7}{12}$

C. $\frac{1}{6}$

D. $\frac{5}{12}$

E. None of the above

Question 545:

Dr Savary has a bag that contains x red balls, y blue balls and z green balls (and no others). He pulls out a ball, replaces it, and then pulls out another. What is the probability that he picks one red ball and one green ball?

A. $\frac{2(x+y)}{x+y+z}$

B. $\frac{xz}{(x+y+z)^2}$

C. $\frac{2xz}{(x+y+z)^2}$

D. $\frac{(x+z)}{(x+y+z)^2}$

E. $\frac{4xz}{(x+y+z)^4}$

F. More information necessary

Question 546:

Mr Kilbane has a bag that contains x red balls, y blue balls and z green balls (and no others). He pulls out a ball, does **NOT** replace it, and then pulls out another. What is the probability that he picks one red ball and one blue ball?

A. $\frac{2xy}{(x+y+z)^2}$

B. $\frac{2xy}{(x+y+z)(x+y+z-1)}$

C. $\frac{2xy}{(x+y+z)^2}$

D. $\frac{xy}{(x+y+z)(x+y+z-1)}$

E. $\frac{4xy}{(x+y+z\ 1)^2}$

F. More information needed

Question 547:

There are two tennis players. The first player wins the point with probability p, and the second player wins the point with probability 1-p. The rules of tennis say that the first player to score four points wins the game, unless the score is 4-3. At this point the first player to get two points ahead wins.

What is the probability that the first player wins in exactly 5 rounds?

A. $4p^4(1-p)$

B. $p^4(1-p)$

C. $4p(1-p)$

D. $4p(1-p)^4$

E. $4p^5(1-p)$

F. More information needed.

Question 548:

Solve the equation $\frac{4x+7}{2} + 9x + 10 = 7$

A. $\frac{22}{13}$

B. $-\frac{22}{13}$

C. $\frac{10}{13}$

D. $-\frac{10}{13}$

E. $\frac{13}{22}$

F. $-\frac{13}{22}$

Question 549:

The volume of a sphere is $V = \frac{4}{3}\pi r^3$, and the surface area of a sphere is $S = 4\pi r^2$. Express S in terms of V

A. $S = (4\pi)^{2/3}(3V)^{2/3}$

B. $S = (8\pi)^{1/3}(3V)^{2/3}$

C. $S = (4\pi)^{1/3}(9V)^{2/3}$

D. $S = (4\pi)^{1/3}(3V)^{2/3}$

E. $S = (16\pi)^{1/3}(9V)^{2/3}$

Question 550:

Express the volume of a cube, V, in terms of its surface area, S.

A. $V = (S/6)^{3/2}$

B. $V = S^{3/2}$

C. $V = (6/S)^{3/2}$

D. $V = (S/6)^{1/2}$

E. $V = (S/36)^{1/2}$

F. $V = (S/36)^{3/2}$

Question 551:

Solve the equations $4x + 3y = 7$ and $2x + 8y = 12$

A. $(x,y) = \left(\frac{17}{13}, \frac{10}{13}\right)$

B. $(x,y) = \left(\frac{10}{13}, \frac{17}{13}\right)$

C. $(x,y) = (1,2)$

D. $(x,y) = (2,1)$

E. $(x,y) = (6,3)$

F. $(x,y) = (3,6)$

G. No solutions possible.

Question 552:

Rearrange $\frac{(7x+10)}{(9x+5)} = 3y^2 + 2$, to make x the subject.

A. $\dfrac{15\,y^2}{7 - 9(3y^2+2)}$

B. $\dfrac{15\,y^2}{7 + 9(3y^2+2)}$

C. $-\dfrac{15\,y^2}{7 - 9(3y^2+2)}$

D. $-\dfrac{15\,y^2}{7 + 9(3y^2+2)}$

E. $-\dfrac{5\,y^2}{7 + 9(3y^2+2)}$

F. $\dfrac{5\,y^2}{7 + 9(3y^2+2)}$

Question 553:

Simplify $3x\left(\dfrac{3x^7}{x^{\frac{1}{3}}}\right)^3$

A. $9x^{20}$

B. $27x^{20}$

C. $87x^{20}$

D. $9x^{21}$

E. $27x^{21}$

F. $81x^{21}$

Question 554:

Simplify $2x[(2x)^7]^{\frac{1}{14}}$

A. $2x\sqrt{2\,x^4}$

B. $2x\sqrt{2x^3}$

C. $2\sqrt{2\,x^4}$

D. $2\sqrt{2x^3}$

E. $8x^3$

F. $8x$

Question 555:

What is the circumference of a circle with an area of 10π?

A. $2\pi\sqrt{10}$

B. $\pi\sqrt{10}$

C. 10π

D. 20π

E. $\sqrt{10}$

F. More information needed.

Question 556:

If $a.b = (ab) + (a + b)$, then calculate the value of $(3.4).5$

A. 19　　　　B. 54　　　　C. 100　　　　D. 119　　　　E. 132

Question 557:

If $a.b = \dfrac{a^b}{a}$, calculate $(2.3).2$

A. $\dfrac{16}{3}$　　　B. 1　　　C. 2　　　D. 4　　　E. 8

Question 558:

Solve $x^2 + 3x - 5 = 0$

A. $x = -\dfrac{3}{2} \pm \dfrac{\sqrt{11}}{2}$

B. $x = \dfrac{3}{2} \pm \dfrac{\sqrt{11}}{2}$

C. $x = -\dfrac{3}{2} \pm \dfrac{\sqrt{11}}{4}$

D. $x = \dfrac{3}{2} \pm \dfrac{\sqrt{11}}{4}$

E. $x = \dfrac{3}{2} \pm \dfrac{\sqrt{29}}{2}$

F. $x = -\dfrac{3}{2} \pm \dfrac{\sqrt{29}}{2}$

Question 559:

How many times do the curves $y = x^3$ and $y = x^2 + 4x + 14$ intersect?

A. 0　　　　B. 1　　　　C. 2　　　　D. 3　　　　E. 4

Question 560:

Which of the following graphs **do not** intersect?

1. $y = x$　　　2. $y = x^2$　　　3. $y = 1 - x^2$　　　4. $y = 2$

A. 1 and 2

B. 2 and 3

C. 3 and 4

D. 1 and 3

E. 1 and 4

F. 2 and 4

Question 561:

Calculate the product of 897,653 and 0.009764.

A. 87646.8

B. 8764.68

C. 876.468

D. 87.6468

E. 8.76468

F. 0.876468

Question 562:

Solve for x: $\frac{7x+3}{10} + \frac{3x+1}{7} = 14$

A. $\frac{929}{51}$ 　　　　 B. $\frac{949}{47}$ 　　　　 C. $\frac{949}{79}$ 　　　　 D. $\frac{980}{79}$

Question 563:

What is the area of an equilateral triangle with side length x.

A. $\frac{x^2\sqrt{3}}{4}$ 　　 B. $\frac{x\sqrt{3}}{4}$ 　　 C. $\frac{x^2}{2}$ 　　 D. $\frac{x}{2}$ 　　 E. x^2 　　 F. x

Question 564:

Simplify $3 - \frac{7x(25x^2 - 1)}{49x^2(5x+1)}$

A. $3 - \frac{5x-1}{7x}$ 　　　　 C. $3 + \frac{5x-1}{7x}$ 　　　　 E. $3 - \frac{5x^2}{49}$

B. $3 - \frac{5x+1}{7x}$ 　　　　 D. $3 + \frac{5x+1}{7x}$ 　　　　 F. $3 + \frac{5x^2}{49}$

Question 565:

Solve the equation $x^2 - 10x - 100 = 0$

A. $-5 \pm 5\sqrt{5}$ 　　　　 C. $5 \pm 5\sqrt{5}$ 　　　　 E. $5 \pm 5\sqrt{125}$

B. $-5 \pm \sqrt{5}$ 　　　　 D. $5 \pm \sqrt{5}$ 　　　　 F. $-5 \pm \sqrt{125}$

Question 566:

Rearrange $x^2 - 4x + 7 = y^3 + 2$ to make x the subject.

A. $x = 2 \pm \sqrt{y^3 + 1}$

B. $x = 2 \pm \sqrt{y^3 - 1}$

C. $x = -2 \pm \sqrt{y^3 - 1}$

D. $x = -2 \pm \sqrt{y^3 + 1}$

E. x cannot be made the subject for this equation.

Question 567:

Rearrange $3x + 2 = \sqrt{7x^2 + 2x + y}$ to make y the subject.

A. $y = 4x^2 + 8x + 2$ 　　　 C. $y = 2x^2 + 10x + 2$ 　　　 E. $y = x^2 + 10x + 2$

B. $y = 4x^2 + 8x + 4$ 　　　 D. $y = 2x^2 + 10x + 4$ 　　　 F. $y = x^2 + 10x + 4$

Question 568:

Rearrange $y^4 - 4y^3 + 6y^2 - 4y + 2 = x^5 + 7$ to make y the subject.

A. $y = 1 + (x^5 + 7)^{1/4}$

C. $y = 1 + (x^5 + 6)^{1/4}$

B. $y = -1 + (x^5 + 7)^{1/4}$

D. $y = -1 + (x^5 + 6)^{1/4}$

Question 569:

The aspect ratio of my television screen is 4:3 and the diagonal is 50 inches. What is the area of my television screen?

A. $1,200$ inches^2

C. 120 inches^2

E. More information needed.

B. $1,000$ inches^2

D. 100 inches^2

Question 570:

Rearrange the equation $\sqrt{1 + 3x^{-2}} = y^5 + 1$ to make x the subject.

A. $x = \frac{(y^{10} + 2y^5)}{3}$

C. $x = \sqrt{\frac{3}{y^{10} + 2y^5}}$

E. $x = \sqrt{\frac{y^{10} + 2y^5 + 2}{3}}$

B. $x = \frac{3}{(y^{10} + 2y^5)}$

D. $x = \sqrt{\frac{y^{10} + 2y^5}{3}}$

F. $x = \sqrt{\frac{3}{y^{10} + 2y^5 + 2}}$

Question 571:

Solve $3x - 5y = 10 \; and \; 2x + 2y = 13$.

A. $(x, y) = (\frac{19}{16}, \frac{85}{16})$

D. $(x, y) = (-\frac{85}{16}, -\frac{19}{16})$

B. $(x, y) = (\frac{85}{16}, -\frac{19}{16})$

E. No solutions possible.

C. $(x, y) = (\frac{85}{16}, \frac{19}{16})$

Question 572:

The two inequalities $x + y \leq 3 \; and \; x^3 - y^2 < 3$ define a region on a plane. Which of the following points is inside the region?

A. $(2, 1)$

C. $(1, 2)$

E. $(1, 2.5)$

B. $(2.5, 1)$

D. $(3, 5)$

F. None of the above.

Question 573:

How many times do $y = x + 4 \; and \; y = 4x^2 + 5x + 5$ intersect?

A. 0

B. 1

C. 2

D. 3

E. 4

Question 574:

How many times do $y = x^3$ and $y = x$ intersect?

A. 0   B. 1   C. 2   D. 3   E. 4

Question 575:

A cube has unit length sides. What is the length of a line joining a vertex to the midpoint of the opposite side?

A. $\sqrt{2}$

B. $\sqrt{\frac{3}{2}}$

C. $\sqrt{3}$

D. $\sqrt{5}$

E. $\frac{\sqrt{5}}{2}$

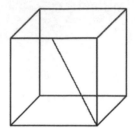

Question 576:

Solve for x, y, and z.

1. $x + y - z = -1$

2. $2x - 2y + 3z = 8$

3. $2x - y + 2z = 9$

	x	y	z
A	2	-15	-14
B	15	2	14
C	14	15	-2
D	-2	15	14
E	2	-15	14
F	No solutions possible		

Question 577:

Fully factorise: $3a^3 - 30a^2 + 75a$

A. $3a(a-3)^3$

B. $a(3a-5)^2$

C. $3a(a^2 - 10a + 25)$

D. $3a(a-5)^2$

E. $3a(a+5)^2$

Question 578:

Solve for x and y:

$$4x + 3y = 48$$
$$3x + 2y = 34$$

	x	y
A	8	6
B	6	8
C	3	4
D	4	3
E	30	12
F	12	30
G	No solutions possible	

Question 579:

Evaluate: $\dfrac{-\left(5^2 - 4 \times 7\right)^2}{-6^2 + 2 \times 7}$

A. $-\dfrac{3}{50}$ B. $\dfrac{11}{22}$ C. $-\dfrac{3}{22}$ D. $\dfrac{9}{50}$ E. $\dfrac{9}{22}$ F. 0

Question 580:

All license plates are 6 characters long. The first 3 characters consist of letters and the next 3 characters of numbers. How many unique license plates are possible?

A. 676,000
B. 6,760,000
C. 67,600,000
D. 1,757,600
E. 17,576,000
F. 175,760,000

Question 581:

How many solutions are there for: $2(2(x^2 - 3x)) = -9$

A. 0
B. 1
C. 2
D. 3
E. Infinite solutions.

Question 582:

Evaluate: $\left(x^{\frac{1}{2}} y^{-3}\right)^{\frac{1}{2}}$

A. $\dfrac{x^{\frac{1}{2}}}{y}$ B. $\dfrac{x}{y^{\frac{3}{2}}}$ C. $\dfrac{x^{\frac{1}{4}}}{y^{\frac{3}{2}}}$ D. $\dfrac{y^{\frac{1}{4}}}{x^{\frac{3}{2}}}$

Question 583:

Bryan earned a total of £ 1,240 last week from renting out three flats. From this, he had to pay 10% of the rent from the 1-bedroom flat for repairs, 20% of the rent from the 2-bedroom flat for repairs, and 30% from the 3-bedroom flat for repairs. The 3-bedroom flat costs twice as much as the 1-bedroom flat. Given that the total repair bill was £ 276 calculate the rent for each apartment.

	1 Bedroom	2 Bedrooms	3 Bedrooms
A	280	400	560
B	140	200	280
C	420	600	840
D	250	300	500
E	500	600	1,000

Question 584:

Evaluate: $5 [5(6^2 - 5 \times 3) + 400^{\frac{1}{2}}]^{1/3} + 7$

A. 0   B. 25   C. 32   D. 49   E. 56   F. 200

Question 585:

What is the area of a regular hexagon with side length 1?

A. $3\sqrt{3}$ C. $\sqrt{3}$ E. 6

B. $\frac{3\sqrt{3}}{2}$ D. $\frac{\sqrt{3}}{2}$ F. More information needed

Question 586:

Dexter moves into a new rectangular room that is 19 metres longer than it is wide, and its total area is 780 square metres. What are the room's dimensions?

A. Width = 20 m; Length = -39 m   D. Width = -39 m; Length = 20 m

B. Width = 20 m; Length = 39 m   E. Width = -20 m; Length = 39 m

C. Width = 39 m; Length = 20 m

Question 587:

Tom uses 34 meters of fencing to enclose his rectangular lot. He measured the diagonals to 13 metres long. What is the length and width of the lot?

A. 3 m by 4 m   C. 6 m by 12 m   E. 9 m by 15 m

B. 5 m by 12 m   D. 8 m by 15 m   F. 10 m by 10 m

Question 588:

Solve $\frac{3x-5}{2} + \frac{x+5}{4} = x + 1$

A. 1

B. 1.5

C. 3

D. 3.5

E. 4.5

F. None of the above

Question 589:

Calculate: $\frac{5.226 \times 10^6 + 5.226 \times 10^5}{1.742 \times 10^{10}}$

A. 0.033

B. 0.0033

C. 0.00033

D. 0.000033

E. 0.0000033

Question 590:

Calculate the area of the triangle shown to the right:

A. $3 + \sqrt{2}$

B. $\frac{2 + 2\sqrt{2}}{2}$

C. $2 + 5\sqrt{2}$

D. $3 - \sqrt{2}$

E. 3

F. 6

$2 + \sqrt{2}$

$4 - \sqrt{2}$

Question 591:

Rearrange $\sqrt{\frac{4}{x} + 9} = y - 2$ to make x the subject.

A. $x = \frac{11}{(y-2)^2}$

B. $x = \frac{9}{(y-2)^2}$

C. $x = \frac{4}{(y+1)(y-5)}$

D. $x = \frac{4}{(y-1)(y+5)}$

E. $x = \frac{4}{(y+1)(y+5)}$

F. $x = \frac{4}{(y-1)(y-5)}$

Question 592:

When 5 is subtracted from 5x the result is half the sum of 2 and 6x. What is the value of x?

A. 0

B. 1

C. 2

D. 3

E. 4

F. 6

Question 593:

Estimate $\frac{54.98 + 2.25^2}{\sqrt{905}}$

A. 0

B. 1

C. 2

D. 3

E. 4

F. 5

Question 594:

At a Pizza Parlour, you can order single, double or triple cheese in the crust. You also have the option to include ham, olives, pepperoni, bell pepper, meat balls, tomato slices, and pineapples. How many different types of pizza are available at the Pizza Parlour?

A. 10

B. 96

C. 192

D. 384

E. 768

F. None of the above

Question 595:

Solve the simultaneous equations $x^2 + y^2 = 1$ and $x + y = \sqrt{2}$, for x, y > 0

A. $(x,y) = (\frac{\sqrt{2}}{2}, \frac{\sqrt{2}}{2})$

B. $(x,y) = (½, \frac{\sqrt{3}}{2})$

C. $(x,y) = (\sqrt{2} - 1, 1)$

D. $(x,y) = (\sqrt{2}, ½)$

Question 596:

Which of the following statements is **FALSE**?

A. Congruent objects always have the same dimensions and shape.

B. Congruent objects can be mirror images of each other.

C. Congruent objects do not always have the same angles.

D. Congruent objects can be rotations of each other.

E. Two triangles are congruent if they have two sides and one angle of the same magnitude.

Question 597:

Solve the inequality $x^2 \geq 6 - x$

A. $x \leq -3$ and $x \leq 2$

B. $x \leq -3$ and $x \geq 2$

C. $x \geq -3$ and $x \leq 2$

D. $x \geq -3$ and $x \geq 2$

E. $x \geq 2$ only

F. $x \geq -3$ only

Question 598:

The hypotenuse of an equilateral right-angled triangle is x cm. What is the area of the triangle in terms of x?

A. $\frac{\sqrt{x}}{2}$

B. $\frac{x^2}{4}$

C. $\frac{x}{4}$

D. $\frac{3x^2}{4}$

E. $\frac{x^2}{10}$

Question 599:

Mr Heard derives a formula: $Q = \frac{(X+Y)^2 A}{3B}$. He doubles the values of X and Y, halves the value of A and triples the value of B. What happens to value of Q?

A. Decreases by $\frac{1}{3}$

B. Increases by $\frac{1}{3}$

C. Decreases by $\frac{2}{3}$

D. Increases by $\frac{2}{3}$

E. Increases by $\frac{4}{3}$

F. Decreases by $\frac{4}{3}$

Question 600:

Consider the graphs $y = x^2 - 2x + 3$, and $y = x^2 - 6x - 10$. Which of the following is true?

A. Both equations intersect the x-axis.

B. Neither equation intersects the x-axis.

C. The first equation does not intersect the x-axis; the second equation intersects the x-axis.

D. The first equation intersects the x-axis; the second equation does not intersect the x-axis.

SECTION 3

The Basics

In section 3, you have to write a one A4 page essay on one of three essay titles. Whilst different questions will inevitably demand differing levels of comprehension and knowledge, it is important to realise that one of the major skills being tested is actually your ability to construct a logical and coherent argument- and to convey it to the lay-reader.

Section 3 of the BMAT is frequently neglected by lots of students, who choose to spend their time on sections 1 & 2 instead. However, it has the highest returns per hour of work out of all three sections so is well worth putting time into.

The aim of section 3 is not to write as much as you can. Rather, the examiner is looking for you to make interesting and well supported points, and tie everything neatly together for a strong conclusion. Make sure you're writing critically and concisely; not rambling on. **Irrelevant material can actually lower your score.** You only get one side of A4 for your BMAT essay, so make it count!

Essay Structure

Most BMAT essays consist of 3 parts:

1) Explain what a quote or a statement means.
2) Argue for or against the statement.
3) Ask you "to what extent" you agree with the statement.

Number 1 should be the smallest portion of the essay (no more than 4 lines) and be used to provide a smooth segue into the rather more demanding "argue for/against" part of the question. This main part requires a firm grasp of the concept being discussed and the ability to strengthen and support the argument with a wide variety of examples from multiple fields. This section should give a balanced approach to the question, exploring **at least two distinct ideas.** Supporting evidence should be provided throughout the essay, with examples referred to when possible.

The final part effectively asks for your personal opinion and is a chance for you to shine- be brave and make an **innovative yet firmly grounded conclusion** for an exquisite mark. The conclusion should bring together all sides of the argument, in order to reach a clear and concise answer to the question. There should be an obvious logical structure to the essay, which reflects careful planning and preparation.

Paragraphs

Paragraphs are an important formatting tool which show that you have thought through your arguments and are able to structure your ideas clearly. A new paragraph should be used every time a new idea is introduced. There is no single correct way to arrange paragraphs, but it's important that each paragraph flows smoothly from the last. A slick, interconnected essay shows that you have the ability to communicate and organise your ideas effectively.

Given that you only have a limit of one A4 page to write in – **you shouldn't have more than 5 paragraphs** (use indents to show paragraphs – don't leave empty lines!). In general, 2 of these 5 will be taken up by the introduction and conclusion respectively.

Remember- the emphasis should remain on quality and not quantity. An essay with fewer paragraphs, but with well-developed ideas, is much more effective than a number of short, unsubstantial paragraphs that fail to fully grasp the question at hand.

Approaching the Essay

Section 3 can be broken down into 3 components; selecting your essay title, planning and writing it.

Most students think that the "writing" component is most important. This is simply not true.

The vast **majority of problems are caused by a lack of planning and essay selection**- usually because students just want to get writing as they are worried about finishing on time. Thirty minutes is long enough to be able to plan your essay well and *still* have time to write it so don't feel pressured to immediately start writing.

Step 1: Selecting

Selecting your essay is crucial- make sure you're comfortable with the topic and ensure you understand the actual question- it sounds silly but about 25% of essays that we mark score poorly because they don't actually answer the question!

Take two minutes to read all the questions. Whilst one essay might originally seem the easiest, if you haven't thought through it you might quickly find yourself running out of ideas. Likewise, a seemingly difficult essay might actually offer you a good opportunity to make interesting points.

Use this time to carefully select which question you will answer by gauging how accessible and comfortable you are with it given your background knowledge. Section 3, however, is not a test of knowledge but rather a test of how well you are able to argue.

It's surprisingly easy to change a question into something similar, but with a different meaning. Thus, you may end up answering a completely different essay title. Once you've decided which question you're going to do, read it very carefully through a few times to make sure you fully understand it. Answer all aspects of the question. Keep reading it as you answer to ensure you stay on track!

Step 2: Planning

Why should I plan my essay?

There are multiple reasons you should plan your essay for the first 5-10 minutes of section 3:

* As you don't have much space to write, make the most of it by writing a very well organised essay.
* It allows you to get all your thoughts ready before you put pen to paper.
* You'll write faster once you have a plan.
* You run the risk of missing the point of the essay or only answering part of it if you don't plan adequately.

How much time should I plan for?

There is no set period of time that should be dedicated to planning, and everyone will dedicate a different length of time to the planning process. You should spend as long planning your essay as you require, but it is essential that you leave enough time to write the essay. As a rough guide, it is **worth spending about 5-10 minutes to plan** and the remaining time on writing the essay. However, this is not a strict rule, and you are advised to tailor your time management to suit your individual style.

How should I go about the planning process?

There are a variety of methods that can be employed in order to plan essays (e.g. bullet-points, mind-maps etc). If you don't already know what works best, it's a good idea to experiment with different methods.

Generally, the first step is to gather ideas relevant to the question, which will form the basic arguments around which the essay is to be built. You can then begin to structure your essay, including the way that points will be linked. At this stage it is worth considering the balance of your argument, and confirming that you have considered arguments from both sides of the debate. Once this general structure has been established, it is useful to consider any examples or real world information that may help to support your arguments. Finally, you can begin to assess the plan as a whole, and establish what your conclusion will be based on your arguments.

Step 3: Writing

Introduction

Why are introductions important?

An introduction provides tutors with their first opportunity to examine your work. The introduction is where first impressions are formed, and these can be extremely important in producing a convincing argument. A well-constructed introduction shows that you have really thought about the question, and can indicate the logical flow of arguments that is to come.

What should an introduction do?

A good introduction should **briefly explain the statement or quote** and give any relevant background information in a concise manner. However, don't fall into the trap of just repeating the statement in a different way. The introduction is the first opportunity to suggest an answer to the question posed- the main body is effectively your justification for this answer.

Main Body

How do I go about making a convincing point?

Each idea that you propose should be supported and justified, in order to build a convincing overall argument. A point can be solidified through a basic Point → Evidence → Evaluation process. By following this process, you can be assured each sentence within a paragraph builds upon the last, and that all the ideas presented are well solidified.

How do I achieve a logical flow between ideas?

One of the most effective ways of displaying a good understanding of the question is to keep a logical flow throughout your essay. This means linking points effectively between paragraphs, and creating a congruent train of thought for the examiner as the argument develops. A good way to generate this flow of ideas is to provide ongoing comparisons of arguments, and discussing whether points support or dispute one another.

Should I use examples?

In short – yes! Examples can help boost the validity of arguments, and can help display high quality writing skills. Examples can add a lot of weight to your argument and make an essay much more relevant to the reader. When using examples, you should ensure that they are relevant to the point being made, as they will not help to support an argument if they are not.

Some questions will provide more opportunities to include examples than others so don't worry if you aren't able to use as many examples as you would have liked. There is no set rule about how many examples should be included!

> ***Top tip!*** Remember that there is no single correct answer to these questions and you're not expected to be able to fit everything onto one page. Instead it's better to pick a few key points to focus on.

Conclusion

The conclusion provides an opportunity to emphasise the **overall sentiment of your essay** which readers can then take away. It should summarise what has been discussed during the main body and give a definitive answer to the question.

Some students use the conclusion to **introduce a new idea that hasn't been discussed**. This can be an interesting addition to an essay, and can help make you stand out. However, it is by no means, a necessity. In fact, a well-organised, 'standard' conclusion is likely to be more effective than an adventurous but poorly executed one.

Medical Ethics

There is normally a medical ethics questions in most years so it's well worth knowing the basics. Whilst there are huge ethical textbooks available– you only need to be familiar with the basic principles for the purposes of the BMAT. **These principles can be applied to all cases** regardless what the social/ethnic background the healthcare professional or patient is from. In addition to being helpful in the BMAT, you'll need to know them for the interview stages anyway so they're well worth learning now. The principles are:

Beneficence: The wellbeing of the patient should be the doctor's first priority. In medicine this means that one must act in the patient's best interests to ensure the best outcome is achieved for them i.e. 'Do Good'.

Non-Maleficence: This is the principle of avoiding harm to the patient (i.e. Do no harm). There can be a danger that in a willingness to treat, doctors can sometimes cause more harm to the patient than good. This can especially be the case with major interventions, such as chemotherapy or surgery. Where a course of action has both potential harms and potential benefits, non-maleficence must be balanced against beneficence.

Autonomy: The patient has the right to determine their own health care. This therefore requires the doctor to be a good communicator, so that the patient is sufficiently informed to make their own decisions. 'Informed consent' is thus a vital precursor to any treatment. A doctor must respect a patient's refusal for treatment even if they think it is not the correct choice. Note that patients cannot <u>demand</u> treatment – only refuse it, e.g. an alcoholic patient can refuse rehabilitation but cannot demand a liver transplant.

There are many situations where the application of autonomy can be quite complex, for example:
➢ **Treating Children**: Consent is required from the parents, although the autonomy of the child is taken into account increasingly as they get older.
➢ **Treating adults without the capacity** to make important decisions. The first challenge with this is in assessing whether or not a patient has the capacity to make the decisions. Just because a patient has a mental illness does not necessarily mean that they lack the capacity to make decisions about their health care. Where patients do lack capacity, the power to make decisions is transferred to the next of kin (or Legal Power of Attorney, if one has been set up).

Justice: This principle deals with the fair distribution and allocation of healthcare resources for the population.

Consent: This is an extension of Autonomy- patients must agree to a procedure or intervention. For consent to be valid, it must be **voluntary informed consent.** This means that the patient must have sufficient mental capacity to make the decision and must be presented with all the relevant information (benefits, side effects and the likely complications) in a way they can understand.

Confidentiality: Patients expect that the information they reveal to doctors will be kept private- this is a key component in maintaining the trust between patients and doctors. You must ensure that patient details are kept confidential. Confidentiality can be broken if you suspect that a patient is a risk to themselves or to others e.g. Terrorism, suicides.

When answering a question on medical ethics, you need to ensure that you show an appreciation for the fact that there are often two sides to the argument. Where appropriate, you should outline both points of view and how they pertain to the main principles of medical ethics and then come to a reasoned judgement.

Common Mistakes

Ignoring the other side of the argument
Although you're normally required to support one side of the debate, it is important to **consider arguments against your judgement** in order to get the higher marks. A good way to do this is to propose an argument that might be used against you, and then to argue why it doesn't hold true or seem relevant. You may use the format: *"some may say that...but this doesn't seem to be important because..."* in order to dispel opposition arguments, whilst still displaying that you have considered them. For example, *"some may say that fox hunting shouldn't be banned because it is a tradition. However, witch hunting was also once a tradition – we must move on with the times"*.

Answering the topic/Answering only part of the question
One of the most common mistakes is to only answer a part of the question whilst ignoring the rest of it as it's inaccessible. According to the official mark scheme, **in order to get a score of 3 or more, you must write "...*an answer that addresses ALL aspects of the question*"**. This should be your minimum standard- anything else that you write should then point you towards achieving 4/5.

Long Introductions
Some students can start rambling and make introductions too long and unfocussed. Although background information about the topic can be useful, it is normally not necessary. Instead, the **emphasis should be placed on responding to the question**. Some students also just **rephrase the question** rather than actually explaining it. The examiner knows what the question is, and repeating it in the introduction is simply a waste of space in an essay where you are limited to just one A4 side.

Not including a Conclusion
An essay that lacks a conclusion is incomplete and can signal that the answer has not been considered carefully or that your organisation skills are lacking. **The conclusion should be a distinct paragraph** in its own right and not just a couple of rushed lines at the end of the essay.

Sitting on the Fence
Students sometimes don't reach a clear conclusion. You need to **ensure that you give a decisive answer to the question** and clearly explain how you've reached this judgement. Essays that do not come to a clear conclusion generally have a smaller impact and score lower.

Exceeding the one page limit
The page limit is there for a reason – don't exceed it under any circumstances as any material over the limit won't be marked and it will appear that you haven't read the instructions.

Not using all the available space
Remember that you only have one A4 side to write on so ensure you make the maximum use of the space available to you. Don't leave lines to show paragraphs – instead, you should use indents. Similarly, you should also use the top-most line in the response sheet and avoid crossing entire sentences out.

Marking your Essays

Practicing section 3 can be tricky because most students don't know how to mark their essay. However, if you have a willing friend/family member, it is fairly easy to mark your own work. You can use the diagram below to get an idea of your score – keep in mind that this is just a very rough guide – examiners will look at several other factors when deciding on your overall score.

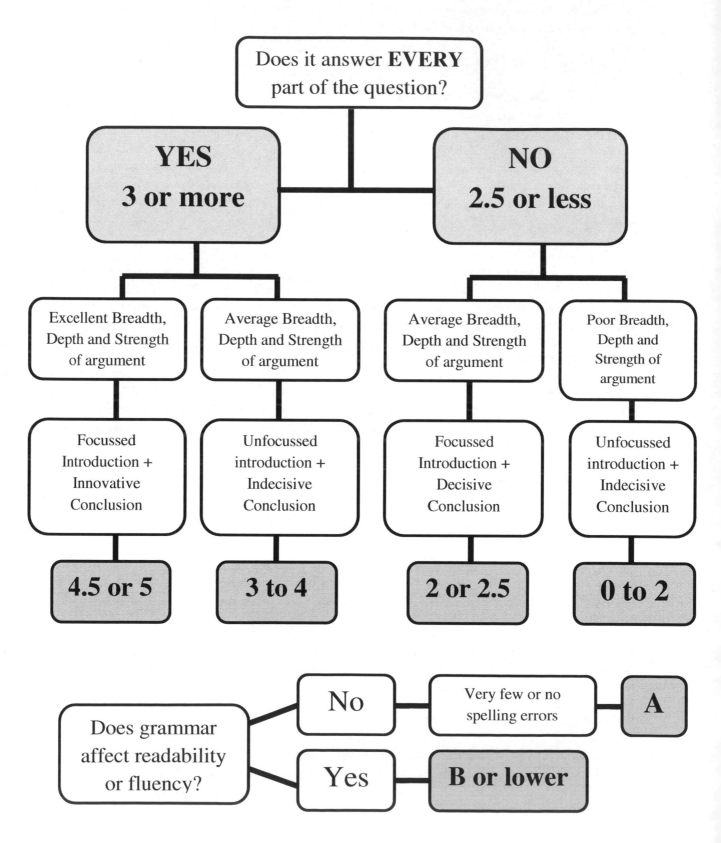

Annotated Essays

Example Essay 1:

"A doctor should never disclose medical information about his patients"
What does this statement mean? Argue to the contrary using examples to strengthen your response.
To what extent do you agree with this statement?

The statement suggests that one of a doctor's most vital qualities is maintaining confidentiality of a patient's medical record. This involves all doctors with various specialities in different work places such as the clinics.

Disclosing medical informations regarding to their patients by doctors is considered as an unacceptable act within the medical society. For Example, by informing unrelated people about the patient might result in the individual's most embarrased health situation to be exposed. For example, suffering pain from their private parts and this may disgust other. This situation would inevitably upset the patient as their health privacy has been breached by others without consent leading to a sence of distrust towards doctors.

However, disclosing such matters to certain suitable people such as family and relatives may be crucial. For example, if the patient is the head of the family or the guardian to the children. As these individuals are in charge of leading and taking are of the family, they need to be able to perform mundane task (such as providing good support to the children) at their optimum. Also, to ensure that the members realise that the patient should not over exert him or herself despite their health conditions. Also, a sudden collapse will reduce shock when the family is to rush the patient back to the hospital knowing that the illness is related to the situation.

Overall, a patient's confidentially should not be disclosed without consent or any importance by all means. This is to respect their health privacy and to avoid any inconvenience within the medical society.

Examiner's Comments:

Introduction: The student appears to have an understanding of the topic but frequently makes statements that don't add much to the argument e.g. the second sentence of the first paragraph. The introduction would be better used to set up the counter arguments that will form the bulk of the main body.

Main Body: The first paragraph actually supports the statement and is therefore not actually answering the question. The example doesn't really add much either. The key issue that needed to be discussed was a doctor's duty to the patient – not about "disgusting others". The last sentence of the first paragraph is good and starts to address the question but it comes far too late.

The second paragraph is better but misses the key points of the essay that were necessary to discuss i.e. when can patient confidentiality be broken? Examples would include suspected terrorism, notifiable diseases and criminal activity, suicides etc.

Conclusion: The conclusion doesn't really address the counter-arguments for breaking confidentiality or give a balanced answer. It also contains confusing terminology e.g. one discloses confidential information, not 'confidentiality'. The sentence concerning "inconvenience within the medical community" is also somewhat ambiguous.

Language: The grammar hinders the points that the student is trying to make throughout the essay e.g. "suffering pain from their private parts and this may disgust other". There are also frequent spelling mistakes like "embarrased" and "sence" that reduce the fluency significantly.

Score: D2

Example Essay 2

"A doctor should never disclose medical information about his patients"
What does this statement mean? Argue to the contrary using examples to strengthen your response.
To what extent do you agree with this statement?

This statement is one of the duties set out by the General Medical Council for doctors to comply with, which is to respect patient's autonomy. It means that a doctor cannot share patient's medical information to other parties unless the patients, themselves, have granted permissions to do so.

The ethical principle of respecting patients' autonomy cannot be applied in all cases, as some cases require doctors to disclose medical information about patients. First, when it involves a criminal act that has been comitted by a patient, a doctor has to report to any appropriate authority, such as the police. This is because the patient may potentially cause even more harm to others and as doctors, they have to prevent that from happening. An example of a case would be if a patient has suffered from a gunshot wound and he had told his doctor that he had gotten it when he murdered someone.

Next, another incident when a doctor has no choice but to disclose patients' medical information is when it may affect the health of society and could potentially cause an epidemic. Such patients might have an infectious disease and do not wish to let other people know about it. For instance, there has been many cases in West Africa where people who have Ebola are afraid to let their neighbours or friends find out because they do not want to be stigmatised and ostrilised from the society. However, these patients could spread the disease and so a doctor must not withold the information. Last of all, if a patient is underage, then he/ she is still not competent enough to make her own decision. Therefore, any medical information must be shared with his/ her legal guardian.

Respecting patient's autonomy by never disclosing their information is also important because patients have the right to chose who gets to know about it. It is his own body. He is the only person who knows the consequences of sharing this sensitive information. In conclusion, I believe that never disclosing patients' medical information cannot be complied in every incident. Respecting their autonomy is important but we have to treat each case separately.

Examiner's Comments:

Introduction: The introduction is well written but could be improved by making it explicitly clear that confidentiality can be breached in certain circumstances. This would then set up the main body nicely as the student would then be able to go straight into giving examples.

Main Body: The first sentence of the second paragraph is well written but should have gone in the introduction. There is good breadth of argument with the important points being covered like a doctor's duty to prevent harm to others, 'public good' and the issue of 'capacity'. However, there is unnecessary padding that doesn't add much e.g. there was no need to expand on your example of infectious diseases. The extra space from avoiding this would have allowed the student to write about the fact that although confidentiality must sometimes be breached, a doctor has certain professional duties. For example, informing the patient both before and after and explaining why they have disclosed what they have to try and mitigate any damage to the doctor patient relationship. In this way public trust in medical professionals would be maintained.

Conclusion: The conclusion concisely summarises the arguments put forth in the main body and offers a nice resolution by saying that each case is different.

Language: Whilst it is clear that the student understands the question – there is some confusion as to the difference between "autonomy" and "confidentiality" (It's important to know the basics of medical ethics as they'll be helpful for the interview stage as well).Furthermore, there are minor spelling mistakes like "comitted" and "withold". In the conclusion, they also assume that patients are only male – "it is his own body" vs. "it is their own body".

Score: B3.5

Example Essay 3

"A doctor should never disclose medical information about his patients"
What does this statement mean? Argue to the contrary using examples to strengthen your response.
To what extent do you agree with this statement?

Confidentiality is a basic patient right. The patient provides information to the doctor not to be unnecessarily shared with others without their knowledge or permission. On this basis, the statement argues that a doctor should never reveal the medical data, such as results from tests or prescriptions given.

However, it can be argued that there are many circumstances whereby it is necesary to breach patient confidentiality and disclose medical information. More specifically, if the patient poses a threat to the public health, their medical situation should be disclosed immediately so that actions can be taken to prevent the spread. For instance, under the Public Health Act 1988, if a patient is suspected of communicable diseases such as tuberculosis, the doctor is required to inform the local health authorities immediately so that they can make precautions to protect the other citizens. In addition, a doctor should also disclose medical information if the patient has broken the law. For instance, the doctor should reveal medical data to the detectives and other relevant professionals if they request for it, to enable them to come to a conclusion of the case more quickly and accurately.

However, I agree with this statement to a large extent. After all, the patient should have the right over what happens to his medical documents and information. Revealing information about the patient unnecessarily will take this basic right away, and it is extremely unfair for the patient. Furthermore, this unprofessional decision may undermine the confidence between the patient and doctor. The patient may be less willing to reveal vital personal information to the doctor in the future, in fear that he might release this information as well. This would be extremely detrimental to the diagnoses and treatment for the patient or the doctor might not be able to gain sufficient information to make a more informed decision.

In conclusion, a doctor should never disclose medical information about his patients unless there are other external circumstances that oblige the doctor to do so. Breaking this confidentiality will cause the patient-doctor relationship to collapse, compromising the trust between them. However, in some cases, the decision to disclose is not that clear-cut; if a patient had sexually-transmitted infections, should the doctor disclose this information to his spouse? Such situations have to be decided on a case-by-case basis.

Examiner's Comments:

Introduction: This is a bold introduction that catches one's attention and gets straight to the point. The student however does make a rather generalised statement - "confidentiality is a basic patient right". A pedantic examiner could easily challenge this and thus, it's important to be careful with your wording.

Main Body: There is a good level of breadth and depth of argument here. However, there are again some generalising statements that are incorrect e.g. doctors don't need to break confidentiality if a patient has broken ANY law – just serious ones e.g. committed or intend to commit murder/terrorism etc. There is however, excellent discussion of the consequences of breaking confidentiality and a good level of detail (e.g. Public health act 1988).

Conclusion: An excellent conclusion that not only summarises the main arguments from both sides but also builds upon these to offer a solution as to when to break confidentiality by treating it on a case-by-case basis.

Language: There is only one spelling mistake (*"necessry"*) and although the somewhat general phrases stop this from being a perfect A5, it is still an excellent essay that displays good insight. Spend time making sure that you write exactly what you mean, instead of being loose with your words and conveying an incorrect message.

Score: A4.5

Example Essay 4

"Medicine is a science; not an art."
Explain what this statement means. Argue to the contrary that medicine is in fact an art using examples to illustrate your answer. To what extent, if any, is medicine a science?

I will explain the following statement "Medicine is a science, not an art" and Argue. to that medicine is in fact an art with supports and to what extent is medicine a science.

I will talk about medicine and art in my opinion why, I think medicine is in fact an art and argue with the above statement. I think medicine is an art because of the human body its like a piece of artwork with creations and it is fascinating even more than a artwork of Picccasso or Ven Gough's painting. It's like the artries and vessels ressemble the brushstroke of a painting and the heart is the meaning of the painting. To study about that and become a Doctor is like studying art to become and artist. Both Medicine and Art depend on passion if you don't have the passion you will not enjoy saving lives and will not create beautiful paintings. Medicine and Art are the most fascinating majors. They are completely different but at the sane time completely the same. Emotionally the same.

Now I will talk about the what extent is medicine a science. It depends on what course you are choosing in medicine For e.g. Biomedical it all counts as science it includes chemistry and maths which makes you a Biochemist or Phisyology, these are some interesting courses. Medicine is science because it depends on knowledge the years to study to become a doctor and save lives which is not an easy opprotunity to get.

In my essay I wrote about why I think that medicine is in face not all about sciene but about art too and argued with the above essay. I think Medicine is as fascinating and breathtaking as Art is with all the colours and bueatiful creations made my artists and saved by doctors.

Examiner's Comments:

Introduction: Although it is sometimes useful to outline what you are going to discuss when writing academic essays – you simply do not have enough space to do this in the BMAT. The introduction should be a clear and concise explanation of the statement, which isn't really done in this essay. Repeating the statement in the essay should also be avoided.

Main Body: The student doesn't really have a good grasp of what the question is asking and as a result, the argument is off topic and slightly incoherent. The question requires the student to discuss things like medicine is a science because doctors put into practice medical principles that have an empirical factual basis. Whilst the third paragraph does this to a certain extent – the message is diluted somewhat because of a lack of focus. Medicine is also an 'art' because doctors also need to be able to communicate well with patients, to interpret clinical signs etc. The student seems have interpreted the question to literally mean "medicine is art" vs. "medicine is an art".

Conclusion: When writing a conclusion it is good practice to just make your point, as opposed to telling the reader you are making it. Thus, meta-writing is again not necessary in the conclusion. The final sentence, although interesting is again, off-topic.

Language: There are frequent spelling mistakes e.g. "sane time", "ressemble" and "*bueatiful*". *The phrasing and grammatical errors are more serious and significantly affect the essay's fluency e.g. "talk about the what extent".*

Score: D1

Example Essay 5

"Medicine is a science; not an art."

Explain what this statement means. Argue to the contrary that medicine is in fact an art using examples to illustrate your answer. To what extent, if any, is medicine a science?

Medicine. Arguably one of the most advancing fields in today's society. As a result, many of us have often thought about what medicine actually encompasses. The statement, "medicine is a science; not an art." is one that is constantly the subject of debated today. It questions to what extent that medicine may be considered an art, and to what a science. I feel that the statement does not belove that medicine is an art form but instead, is well and truly a science, and is well within the definition of one.

An art form is usually something which is viewed as being expressive and emotional, as well as also being delicate. One can argue that the notion of caring for patients can be viewed as the non-scientific aspect of medicine, and therefore could be considered art as it requires one to be emotional and expressive. In order for a patient's rehabilitation process to be complete and succesfull, the care directed at the patient should be tailored for them as the recovery of the psychological side of the human body is just as important as the phsiological aspect. In order to be truly effective, the doctor should be able to be empathetic and try and understand the patient's pain when comforting them. This aspect of medicine does not involve the science of the human body or the knowledge of the intricate metabolic reactors which allow the human body to function so effectively.

However, another side of the debate could be that medicine is very much a science. This is due to the fact that medicine involves the analysis of a human body, for example, when diagnosing a patient or maybe understanding the effects a drug could bring to specific situations in the human body, something that is viewed with the utmost importance when administering a drug. The fact that in order to succesfully become a medical practitioner, one has to be aware of the physiology of the human body and also the immense and thorough knowledge of the anatomy of the human body, is the reason that medicine is associated with mainly being a science. This stems back to the days when we used to learn Biology and Chemistry back in school, and because Medicine is largely based on those two core subjects, medicine, as a result, is widely regarded as solely being a science.

Examiner's Comments:

Introduction: The opening is catchy although unnecessarily long-winded. Thus, whilst the first sentence grabs the attention, the rest of it does little to keep it the next few sentences are very wordy and don't actually say very much. This is a prime example of just rephrasing the statement rather than explaining it.

Main Body: There are a good range of examples in the second paragraph- especially those about the rehabilitation process and empathy. Whilst the pro-science arguments are also well made, they are a bit one-dimensional. It would be better to discuss how trials are done to ensure safety rather than just concentrating on the human anatomy and physiology. The last sentence also doesn't really add anything and if anything detracts from the final paragraph.

Conclusion: The essay is badly let down by a lack of a conclusion. This title required a critical analysis of the strengths of the two sides of the arguments in order to produce a well-constructed conclusion that answered the question.

Language: There are some very elegant turns of phrase that sometimes result in a loss of focus. This doesn't affect the essay's readability (and therefore the language score) but indirectly affects the strength of argument quite substantially. Nevertheless, as all parts of the question are answered to a sufficient level, it still scores a solid 3.

Score: A3

Example Essay 6

"Medicine is a science; not an art."

Explain what this statement means. Argue to the contrary that medicine is in fact an art using examples to illustrate your answer. To what extent, if any, is medicine a science?

This statement argues that medicine is more deeply rooted with the facts and set observations associated with scientific principles, and that no aspect of medicine is in itself open to interpretation; or art.

However many of the facets of Medicine could very well be regarded as art. The manual dexterity and presision required by surgeons; particularly the visually aesthetic finish reconstructive or plastic surgery aims towards has a deep basis in artistic ability. Medicine as a career has a hugely important social aspect too; healthcare proffessionals are expected to be involved with communication and, when it comes to patients, even dealing with emotions has an interpretative aspect, and as such could be viewed as art. There is not one set approach to these situations; rather the outcome is reliant on a doctor's own personal judgement and choices as to the best course of action. Theoretical medicine, too, in terms of research may find success in new, recently discovered techniques; the development of which requires thinking 'outside of the box'. The clinical aspect of diagnostic medicine too is subject to unique approached, particularly when introducing extremely complex cases.

Although to the same extent, medicine of course has a heavy involvement with biological structures, chemical processes and even principles of physics- generally all empirical; based on evidence and set in stone. In many cases there is a clear distinction between the right interpretation and thus course of action And the wrong one; for example when prescribing- for many patients (such as when allergies are involved) there are a whole host of drugs and courses of action that are unnacceptable. Therefore, the understanding of the human body and it's inner workings that is so crucial for appropriate and successful medicine could well be argued to be science. Yet it's application; it's uses by doctors and other healthcare proffessionals is less impirical, more open to interpretation, and therefore more so an art.

I feel that despite the fact medicine involves understanding and knowledge of the physiology and anatomy of the human body, it also involves the integral of caring for others, which is definitely more of an art form than a science, showing us that despite all the debates, medicine manages to combine art and science together resulting in the formation of a wondrous profession.

Examiner's Comments:

Introduction: An efficient introduction that explains the statement well. It could be improved by setting up the counter-argument.

Main Body: This is a good effort at a tricky essay – there is good breadth of argument with lots of examples like surgical precision and communication. There is also good consideration of the counter-arguments for why medicine is a science with good depth of argument e.g. drug prescriptions.

Conclusion: A strong conclusion that addresses the question well and summarises arguments from both sides concisely. It uses unnecessarily romantic language "wondrous profession" but nevertheless is an effective closing paragraph.

Language: Although there are a noticeable number of spelling mistakes (*"proffessionals"* and *"impirical"*), they do not detract from the essay's flow.

Score: B4.5

Example Essay 7

"The primary duty of a doctor is to prolong life as much as possible"

What does this statement mean? Argue to the contrary, that the primary duty of a doctor is not to prolong life. To what extent do you agree with this statement?

As a doctor, the main aim is patient benifiscence always. This involves performing all possible tests, treatments and any procedure that would result in preserving the health of the patient and so increasing their life-span.

It is however in not all cases that patient benefiscence would apply to pro-longing life but rather allowing the patient to die, as it is to their benefit, or poses more advantages to them and their families as well as NHS. Cases like this include terminally ill cancer patients whom the doctors have found palliative care to be the best option for them rather than continuous chemotherapy which will discomfort them further, and hence violate the principle of benifiscence. As much as a doctor is obligated to look after the health of individuals, it is the individuals themselves that decide if to follow advices of the doctor, for example, antiretroviral patients who do not take their medication which would prolong their lives cannot be forced to take them, but the doctor will surely have done their part in being a carer and an advicer and therefore if the patients die before the expected time, it would have been the patient's autonomous decicion. Considering the increasing costs of treatments and healthcare nowadays, it is most essential that doctors use available sources wisely. If a patient requires treatment that cannot be afforded by the region or nation they are in, doctor's role in that situation is to provide as much comfort and pain relief treatment possible within the means of his surroundings, and therefore cannot be made accountable to prolonging that patient's life by a treatment which is inaccessible.

In conclusion I agree that a Doctor must do the best he can for his patients however in cases of limitations a doctor's responsibility is to provide relief in that moment.

Examiner's Comments:

Introduction: This is a classic case of answering a topic rather than the question. This title requires an analysis of the differences between quality of life vs. quantity of life. Instead, the student starts to ramble about beneficence which although related, is only part of the essay.

The introduction also contains broad sweeping generalisations like performing 'all possible tests, treatment and any procedures'. In the current economic climate, it is not feasible or necessary to do this. If this student were to be interviewed, these apparently minor points could easily give the impression that the student doesn't know much about the NHS or hasn't learned much from their work experience.

Main Body: Whilst there are good and relevant examples used throughout the main body, they are not applied correctly to form any serious argument. The essay would benefit from a clearer discussion of the balance between simply prolonging life and improving a patient's quality of life even if this means taking medication that could hasten death e.g. Morphine in the 'doctrine of double effect'. The section on patient autonomy again is not as relevant for this essay nor is the discussion about patients being in charge of their own health.

Conclusion: The conclusion discusses the limitations of a doctor's responsibility which again isn't necessary for this essay- reinforcing the overall impression that the student does not understand the key issues.

Language: The lack of a structure reduces the flow of the essay. This isn't helped by the spelling mistakes "advicer" and "*decicion*" which along with the rambling nature of the main body seriously reduce the essay's readability.

Score: D1

Example Essay 8

"The primary duty of a doctor is to prolong life as much as possible"

What does this statement mean? Argue to the contrary, that the primary duty of a doctor is not to prolong life. To what extent do you agree with this statement?

The most important responsibility of doctor is to cure diseases and extend a life of patients at his most ability acquired. The statement also states that doctors should try their best to prolong life of the sufferers as the first principle to consider. However, some might argue with this.

It is true to say that doctors are responsible for improving the conditions of diseases and alleviate the symptoms. This does not necessarily mean that is a major factor to tackle with each disease. Preventive care should be introduced at an early stage, and therefore the primary duty of medical professions, especially doctors should adopt this principle to be their main concern. For example, doctors should be aware of other health conditions of his or her patients that might be developed in the future regarding to patient's lifestyle or eating habit. To only address the present problems, relating to particular disease is not enough. Hence, prolonging life of patients is not the primary concern of doctors but to improve quality of life of the sufferers. By preventing the possible disease and acknowledging the patients are a proper most important role of a doctor.

Some people might argue with the statement as there have been a very controversial issue raised in recent years, euthanasia. Nowadays it is evidently seen that some patients in Switzerland and some other countries have their right to urge a doctor to help end their lives peacefully. Doctor may put an emphasis on methods or alternative ways to help prolong life of patient. Their prime concern is also finding the best beneficial treatment in order to fight with the disease unless there is a possible way. Therefore, putting patients at ease by ending their lives is also a primary concern to a doctor in some countries.

To some extent, I agree and support this statement as doctors have to delegate roles as healer to those who are in pain. Although it is illegal in some regions of the world to allow doctors taking life of a patient with their consent, it does mean that this method apart from prolonging life is one of the main duty for doctors to be well aware.

Examiner's Comments:

Introduction: This is a concise introduction that effectively just rephrases the statement rather than developing on it much – effectively not advancing an argument and thus wasting valuable space. A discussion of what a doctor's <u>primary</u> duty actually is would have been more appropriate here and would have set up the main body far better.

Main Body: This is a rather confusing and muddled account. The second paragraph is difficult to follow and strays from the real topic at hand. The student correctly identifies that a doctor's job is to improve quality of life and not duration. However, this isn't expressed with any degree of clarity or any examples. The third paragraph regarding euthanasia is better but again it is difficult to assess what point the student is trying to make.

Conclusion: Whilst it is perfectly fine to present a one-sided argument, you need to at least consider the counter-arguments. Thus, it was necessary here to consider that both quality of life <u>and</u> are important. In addition, the euthanasia part is somewhat misguided – not all doctors who don't put duration of life as their top priority are in favour of euthanasia.

Language: There are frequent grammatical errors e.g. "as there have been a very" which reduce the essay's fluency and. The sentence phrasing also impacts the essay's overall readability to lead to a poor language score.

Score: C2

Example Essay 9

"The primary duty of a doctor is to prolong life as much as possible"

What does this statement mean? Argue to the contrary, that the primary duty of a doctor is not to prolong life. To what extent do you agree with this statement?

A doctors' job is to cure disease through medical treatment to extend the life of the patient as much as possible. However, there is a certain limit to which doctors can go in order to prolong life as often quality of life is equally (if not more) important as quantity of life.

Doctors provide treatments to patients to help them overcome their disease so that they can live longer. This is also what the patients want. For example, for patients with kidney diseases, doctors will suggest them to have dialysis in order to remove the toxic substance in their body, which will kill them. Through dialysis, the patient's life will be extended and as this is the patient's will, a doctor's primary duty is prolong life. People take preventative method, such as endoscopy of large intestine for symptoms of cancer, to avoid late discovery of disease, which will lead to a high chance of death. Therefore as a doctor has the skills to help people to extend their, they should do as much as they can to fulfil the patient's wish, which is prolonging life.

However, doctors should also respect the patient's autonomy if a patient doesn't want a treatment, even the treatment is effective, doctors should not carry the treatment out, as everyone have the right to control their own life, even doctors want to help patient, doctors should not over-ride the will of the patients.

Although one of a doctor's duties is to prolong life – this shouldn't be at the expense of quality of life. A doctors primary duty is to offer the best possible medical advice and minimise suffering. Although the impact of this is usually to prolong life, in some cases, it may result in maximising quality of life.

Examiner's Comments:

Introduction: An excellent introduction that sets the scene very nicely for the main body and immediately conveys to the examiner that the student understands the essay of the essay.

Main Body: There are good points made throughout e.g. dialysis and the inclusion of preventative treatment shows a good insight into medicine. However, the student is not able to put together a substantial enough argument against prolonging life as they spend too much space discussing the reasons for prolonging life (which are less important). This is a perfect example of an unbalanced essay. In general, there is limited focus on the question and as a result, weak depth of argument.

Conclusion: A satisfactory conclusion that expresses the sentiments of the conclusion nicely and addresses the question well.

Language: The introduction and conclusion rescue this essay – as they convey a high degree of understanding in only a couple of sentences. The essay itself reads well and there are no obvious errors that reduce its fluency.

Score: A3.5

Example Essay 10

Animal euthanasia should be made illegal.

Explain what this statement means. Argue to the contrary that animal euthanasia should remain legal. To what extent do you agree with the statement?

'Animal euthanasia should be made illegal'. In other words this means aided death. For example choosing someone to help end your life. There are many on going debates that euthanasia should remane legal, and one of these reazons could be because it could be seen as 'inhumane' to watch others suffer. If someone can see an animal obviously dying it may not be seen as just to let them die (when treatment/cure is not possible. However the average person may not be 100% sure that the animal is sufering e.g if they are watching a bird therefore if they committed euthanasia they may not be completely certain it was not murder. Therefore in the case of animals (with the exception of humans) should only be done by animal experts, in that field, with the aim to avoid murder.

Another reason for as to why euthanasia should remain legal could be in the example of elderly humans with dementia and Parkinsons disease. These elderly people cannot remember much and can do very little for themselves, they mayaby find communication extremely difficult. In this case a question could be raised – is life worth living if you cannot do or think for yourself anymore- maybe the purpose in life was to have fun – in which case they may want nothing more than to end their life, however due to their circumstances they cannot end their life without help. However on the contrare people may be brainwashed into euthanasia- for a number of reasons- one including that the person could be very wealthy and someone may want that money.

Overall I think euthanasia should remain legal however everybody should make a signed statement regarding their own personal views when they are still young, fit and healthy to make their own decisions. This could be updated every five to ten years.

Examiner's Comments:

Introduction: In general, there is no need to repeat the question word-for-word as this just wastes space. The introduction set off alarm bells as the student is discussing human euthanasia instead of animal euthanasia.

Main Body: It is difficult to separate the introduction from the main body of the essay. The second paragraph is difficult to follow and make sense of. In particular, the part about 'animal experts' committing euthanasia is especially confusing as it is unclear if they student is arguing for or against animal euthanasia. The third paragraph about dementia and Parkinson's is not relevant to this essay. This means that the student has missed the point of the essay.

Conclusion: The conclusion does little to address the statement. Conclusions should use the arguments made throughout the essay to provide a succinct summary e.g. "in light of the human duty to end animal suffering I believe animal euthanasia should be legal. Although this has the potential to be abused, the animals' quality of life is more important."

Language: Avoid double negatives and colloquialisms such as brainwashed. There are a large number of mistakes in the essay ranging from spelling ("contrare" and "mayaby") to colloquial language ("brainwashed"). However, the biggest difficulty derives from the phrasing that aversely impacts the readability of the essay leading to a poor language score.

Score: C1

Example Essay 11

Animal euthanasia should be made illegal.

Explain what this statement means. Argue to the contrary that animal euthanasia should remain legal. To what extent do you agree with the statement?

The statement refers to the ethical dilemma of euthanasia. Euthanasia, synonymous of mercy killing, is the ending of someone's life because of a particular situation in which this living creature's future will be painful, sometimes short or it will ultimately be better to end it soon. The first argument for this statement is the fact that we as humans are generally kind hearted and benevolent: we see pain as a thing to be eradicated if not suppressed, and hence euthanasia could be seen as merciful, given this nature of ours. However, the natural argument against this is the undeniable fact that in the eyes of many, euthanasia is glorified murder, which goes against most people's morals since killing is seen as a negative thing in most societies nowadays. another argument in favour of this process could be the fact that killing is not only condemned but also morally wrong since it involves us "removing" an otherwise healthy living being. The counter-argument illustrated by this statement is the fact that most people would look upon this as a grateful act of mercy, where although the consequences are taken into account, it is, morally, for some, the best thing to do, particularly if an animal, a source of fondness for some, is involved. The last argument to put forth is that animals are intelligent creatures capable of feeling pain like us and should hence receive the same mercy as is sometimes shown to humans. Naturally, people would say that in some cases this would be murder rather than mercy killing, eg the killing of old horses for glue rather than because of old age. I conclude this should remain legal since animals cannot voice their own opinion and hence give more weight to a decision.

Examiner's Comments:

Introduction: This is a good albeit somewhat long introduction. The student has defined euthanasia well and then established that there is an ethical dilemma surrounding it. However, the very long sentences make it needlessly difficult to follow.

Main Body: Whilst the writing style is excellent, there is a limited amount of content here. The student presents arguments for both sides simultaneously which sometimes makes it difficult to follow. This is made more confusing by the lack of paragraphs which means that the essay doesn't flow as well.

There also some long and rambling sentences which detract from the clarity of argument. The essay would benefit from a more focussed approach in which the student gets to the point. The point about killing horses for glue is also not as relevant to euthanasia outside a slippery slope argument (which isn't expanded upon).

Conclusion: The conclusion does not really build upon any of the arguments from the main body. This gives the impression that it was rushed with little planning.

Language: There are no obvious spelling errors but colloquialisms like 'nowadays' should be avoided. Overall, the student clearly understands the topic – but the essay is let down by a limited focus on the question and poor structure due to very long sentences and a lack of paragraphs.

Score: A3

Example Essay 12

Animal euthanasia should be made illegal.

Explain what this statement means. Argue to the contrary that animal euthanasia should remain legal. To what extent do you agree with the statement?

This statement means that the purposeful act of killing animals, carried out by veterinary practitioners should be made against the law. Currently, human euthanasia is illegal and the introduction of legal euthanasia brings with it many potentially harmful implications such as the 'putting down' of healthy animals.

An ethical pillar of medicine is non-maleficence. By making animal euthanasia illegal we uphold this pillar and avoiding causing harm to potentially healthy animals. If animal euthanasia were to be legalised then some people may think it justified to slaughter animal for less than noble purposes.

However, there are many cases in which euthanasia may be the best way of progression in the medical treatment of animals. For example: if an injured or terminally ill animal has no chance of recovery and is suffering then euthanasia may be the most kind and compassionate thing to do e.g. if a horse has broken its leg and will never be able to walk again. In addition, if the quality of life of an animal is very low e.g. they have no home, are starving and there is nowhere for them to live, then euthanasia may also be the most compassionate course of action. This may be especially the case where an area is overpopulated with stray cats and dogs.

Another case where euthanasia seems the most beneficial course of action is if an animal has become infected with a disease that could spread to other animals and humans potentially causing widespread and significant harm e.g. if a dog becomes infected with rabies or a cow becomes infected with foot and mouth disease.

To conclude, I disagree with the statement as I think animal euthanasia remain legal. It should however, only be carried out by a veterinary professional and only when the animal is undergoing significant suffering.

Examiner's Comments:

Introduction: A concise and focussed introduction that answers the first part of the question well and sets up the main body nicely.

Main Body: The student presents a sophisticated argument that addresses all the aspects of the question and uses good examples to back up their points. The arguments are well thought out and naturally follow on from each other. It would be better to argue why euthanasia should remain legal **before** giving reasons for it to be made illegal. This would help improve the flow.

Conclusion: A succinct and well-supported conclusion that ties together the major arguments in the main body. It also introduces a new idea –only vets should be allowed to perform euthanasia. This is a good point but should have been developed somewhat more.

Language: The student clearly understands the essay and puts together a strong essay. There are no glaring spelling or grammatical errors.

Score: A4.5

Summary

Intro
- Does it explain or just repeat?
- Does it set up the main body?
- Does it get to the point?

Main Body
- Are enough points being made? *[Breadth]*
- Are the points explained sufficiently? *[Depth]*
- Does the argument make sense? *[Strength]*

Conclusion
- Does it follow naturally from the main body?
- Does it consider both sides of the argument?
- Does it answer the original question?

General Advice

✓ Always answer the question clearly – this is the key thing examiner look for in an essay.

✓ Analyse each argument made, justifying or dismissing with logical reasoning.

✓ Keep an eye on the time/space available – an incomplete essay may be taken as a sign of a candidate with poor organisational skills.

✓ Use pre-existing knowledge when possible – examples and real world data can be a great way to strengthen an argument- but don't make up statistics!

✓ Present ideas in a neat, logical fashion (easier for an examiner to absorb).

✓ Complete some practice papers in advance, in order to best establish your personal approach to the paper (particularly timings, how you plan etc.).

✗ Attempt to answer a question that you don't fully understand, or ignore part of a question.

✗ Rush or attempt to use too many arguments – it is much better to have fewer, more substantial points.

✗ Attempt to be too clever, or present false knowledge to support an argument – a tutor may call out incorrect facts etc.

✗ Panic if you don't know the answer the examiner wants – there is no right answer, the essay is not a test of knowledge but a chance to display reasoning skill.

✗ Leave an essay unfinished – if time/space is short, wrap up the essay early in order to provide a conclusive response to the question.

Mock Paper A

Section 1

Question 1:

A square sheet of paper is 20cms long. How many times must it be folded in half before it covers an area of 12.5cm^2?

A. 3　　　　　B. 4　　　　　C. 5　　　　　D. 6　　　　　E. 7

Question 2:

Mountain climbing is viewed by some as an extreme sport, while for others it is simply an exhilarating pastime that offers the ultimate challenge of strength, endurance, and sacrifice. It can be highly dangerous, even fatal, especially when the climber is out of his or her depth, or simply gets overwhelmed by weather, terrain, ice, or other dangers of the mountain. Inexperience, poor planning, and inadequate equipment can all contribute to injury or death, so knowing what to do right matters.

Despite all the negatives, when done right, mountain climbing is an exciting, exhilarating, and rewarding experience. This article is an overview beginner's guide and outlines the initial basics to learn; in reality, each step is deserving of an article in its own right, and entire tomes have been written on climbing mountains, so you're advised to spend a good deal of your beginner's learning immersed in reading widely. This basic overview will give you an idea of what is involved in a climb.

Which statement best summarises this paragraph?
A. Mountain climbing is an extreme sport fraught with dangers.
B. Without extensive experience embarking on a mountain climb is fatal.
C. A comprehensive literature search is the key to enjoying mountain climbing.
D. Mountain climbing is difficult and is a skill that matures with age if pursued.
E. The terrain is the biggest unknown when climbing a mountain and therefore presents the biggest danger.

Question 3:

50% of an isolated population contract a new strain of resistant Malaria. Only 20% are symptomatic of which 10% are female. What percentage of the total population do symptomatic males represent?

A) 1%　　　　　B) 9%　　　　　C) 10%　　　　　D) 80%

Question 4:

John is a UK citizen yet is looking to buy a holiday home in the South of France. He is purchasing his new home through an agency: unlike a normal estate agent as they offer monthly discount sales of up to 30%. As a French company, the agency sells in Euros. John decides to hold off on his purchase until the sale, in the interest of saving money. What is the major assumption made in doing this?

A) The house he likes will not be bought in the meantime
B) The agency will not be declared bankrupt
C) The value of the pound will fall more than 30%
D) The value of the pound will fall less than 30%
E) The value of the euro may increase by up to 35% in the coming weeks

Question 5:

In childcare professions, by law, there must be an adult to child ratio of no more than 1:4. Child minders are hired on a salary of £8.50 an hour. What is the maximum number of children that can be continually supervised for a period of 24 hours on a budget of £1,000?

A. 1　　　　　B. 8　　　　　C. 12　　　　　D. 16　　　　　E. 468

Question 6:

A table of admission prices for the local cinema is shown below:

	Peak	Off-peak
Adult	£11	£9.50
Child	£7	£5.50
Concession	£7	£5.50
Student	£5	£5

How much would a group of 3 adults, 5 children, a concession and 4 students save by visiting at an off-peak time rather than a peak time?

A. £11.50   B. £13.50   C. £15.50   D. £17.50   E. £18.50

Question 7:

Which frame comes next in the following sequence?

   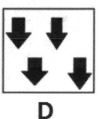

    A   **B**   **C**   **D**

Question 8:

Flow mediated dilation is a method used to assess vascular function within the body. It essentially adopts the use of an ultrasound scan to measure the percentage increase in the width of an artery before and after occlusion with a blood pressure cuff. Ultrasound scans are taken by one sonographer, and the average lumen diameter is then measured by an analyst. What is a potential flaw in the methodology of this technique?

A) Results will not be comparable within an individual if different arteries start at different diameters
B) Results will not be comparable between individuals if they have different baseline arterial diameters
C) Ultrasound is an outdated technique with no use in modern medicine
D) This methodology is subject to human error
E) This methodology is not repeatable

Question 9:

If it takes 20 minutes to board an aeroplane, 15 minutes to disembark and the flight lasts two and a half hours. In the event of a delay it is not uncommon to add 20 minutes to the flight time. Megan is catching the flight in question as she needs to attend a meeting at 5pm. The location of the meeting is 15 minutes from the airport without traffic; 25 minutes with. Which of the following statements is valid considering this information?

A. If Megan wants to be on time for her meeting, given all possibilities described, the latest she can begin boarding at the departure airport is 1.30pm.
B. If Megan starts boarding at 1.40pm she will certainly be late.
C. If Megan aims to start boarding at 1.10pm she will arrive in time whether the plane is delayed or not.
D. If Megan wishes to be on time she doesn't have to worry about the plane being delayed as she can make up the time during the transport time from the arrival airport to the meeting.
E. None of the above are correct.

Question 10:

A cask of whiskey holds a total volume of 500L. Every two and a half minutes half of the total volume is collected and discarded. How many minutes will it take for the entire cask to be emptied?

A) 80   B) 160   C) 200   D) 240   E) ∞

Question 11:

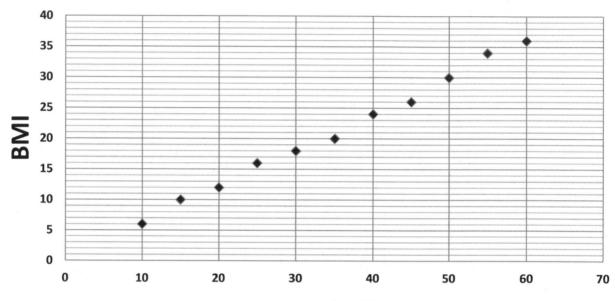

Scatter plot of Waist size vs BMI for some people

What can be concluded from the graph above?

A)   Having a larger waist size causes an increase in BMI
B)   Having a larger BMI causes an increase in waist size
C)   Waist size is reciprocal to BMI
D)   No conclusions can be drawn from this graph
E)   None of the above are correct

Question 12:

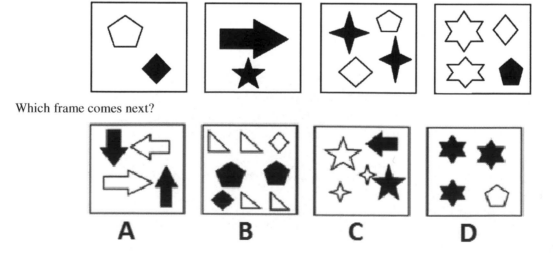

Which frame comes next?

Question 13:
Car A has a fuel tank capacity of 30 gallons and achieves 40mpg. Car B on the other hand has a fuel tank capacity of 50 gallons but only achieves 30mpg. Both cars drive until they run out of fuel. If car A starts with a full tank of petrol and travels 200 miles further than car B; how full was car B's fuel tank?

A) 1/5   B) 1/4   C) 1/3   D) 1/2   E) 2/3

The information below relates to questions 14 and 15:

The art of change ringing adopts the use of 6 bells, numbered 1 to 6 in order of weight (1 being the lightest). Initially the bells are rung in this order: 1, 2, 3, 4, 5, 6 however the aim is to ultimately ring all the possible orders of a 6 number sequence. The rules for doing this are very simple: each bell can only move a maximum of one place in the sequence every time it rings.

Question 14:
What is the total possible number of permutations of 6 bells?

A) 160   B) 220   C) 660   D) 720   E) 1160

Question 15:
Based on the information provided which of the following could be a possible series of bell sequences?

A. 1 2 3 4 5   B. 1 2 3 4 5   C. 1 2 3 4 5   D. 1 2 3 4 5   E. 1 2 3 4 5
    2 1 4 3 5   2 1 4 3 5   4 2 1 3 5   1 4 3 2 5   4 1 3 2 5
    2 3 1 5 4   2 4 1 5 3   4 2 3 1 5   1 2 3 4 5   5 3 1 2 4

Question 16:
The keypad to a safe comprises the digits 1 - 9. The code itself can be of indeterminate length. The code is therefore set by choosing a reference number so that when a code is entered the average of all the numbers entered must equal the chosen reference number.

Which of the following is true?

A)   If the reference number was set greater than 9, the safe would be locked forever
B)   This safe is extremely insecure as if random digits were pressed for long enough it would average out at the correct reference number
C)   More than one number is always required to achieve the reference number
D)   All of the above are true
E)   None of the above are true

Question 17:
The use of antibiotics is one of the major paradoxes in modern medicine. Antibiotics themselves provide a selection pressure to drive the evolution of antibiotic resistant strains of bacteria. This is largely due to the rapid growth rate of bacterial colonies and asexual cell division. As such a widespread initiative is in place to limit the prescription of antibiotics.
Which of the following is a fair assumption?

A)   Antibiotic resistance is impossible to avoid as it is driven by evolution
B)   If bacteria reproduced at a slower rate antibiotic resistance would not be such an issue
C)   Medicine always creates more problems than it solves
D)   In the past antibiotics were used frivolously
E)   All of the above could be possible

The information below relates to questions 18 – 22:

The Spaghetti Bolognese recipe below serves 10 people and each portion contains 300 kcal.

➢ 1kg mince	➢ 1kg tinned tomatoes	➢ 200g grated cheese
➢ 220g pancetta, diced	➢ 300g diced onions	
➢ 30g crushed garlic	➢ 300g sliced mushrooms	

Question 18:
What quantity of cheese is required to prepare a meal for 350 people?

A) 0.7kg   B) 7kg   C) 70kg   D) 700kg   E) 7000k

Question 19:
If 12 portions represent 120% of an individuals recommended calorific intake, what is that individuals recommended calorific intake?

A) 2,600kcal   B) 2,800kcal   C) 3,000kcal   D) 3,200kcal   E) 3,400kcal

Question 20:
The recommended ratio of pasta to Bolognese is 4:1. If cooking for 30 people how much pasta should be used?
A) 30.3kg   B) 36.6kg   C) 42.9kg   D) 49.2kg   E) 55.5kg

Question 21:
What is the ratio of onions to the rest of the ingredients if garlic and pancetta are ignored?
A) 1/2.05   B) 1/3.9   C) 1/6.7   D) 1/9.3   E) 1/10

Question 22:
It takes 4 minutes to prepare the ingredients per portion, and a further 8 minutes per portion to cook. Simon has ample preparation space but is limited to cooking 8 portions at a time. What is the shortest period of time it would take him to turn all the ingredients into a meal for 25 people, assuming he didn't start cooking until all the ingredients were prepared?

A) 3 hours   B) 3 hours 40   C) 4 hours   D) 4 hours 40   E) 5 hours

Question 23:
A company sells custom design t-shirts. A breakdown of their costs is shown below:

| Number of Items | Cost per Item | |
	Black and white	Colour
0 – 99	£3.00	£5.00
100 - 499	£2.50	£4.50
500 - 999	£2.00	£4.00
1000+	£1.00	£3.00

Customers with an ever before printed design must also pay a surcharge of £50 to cover the cost of building a jig. What is the total cost for an order of unique stag do t-shirts; 50 in colour, 200 in black and white?

A) £650   B) £700   C) £750   D) £800   E) £850

Question 24:

The Scouts is a movement for young people first established by Lord Baden Powell. As the founder he was the first chief scout of the association. Since his initial appointment there have been a number of notable chief scouts including Peter Duncan and Bear Grylls. Some of the first camping trips conducted by Lord Powell's scout troop were on Brown Sea Island.

Now the Scout movement is a worldwide global phenomenon giving children from all backgrounds the opportunity not only to embark upon adventure but also to engage in the understanding and teaching of foreign culture. Traditionally religion formed the back bone of the scouting movement which was reflected in the scouts promise: "I promise to do my duty to god and to the queen".

Which of the following applies to the scout movement?
A)   Scouts work for the Queen
B)   The scout network is aimed at adventurous individuals
C)   Chief scout is appointed by the queen
D)   You have to be religious to be a scout
E)   None of the above

Question 25:

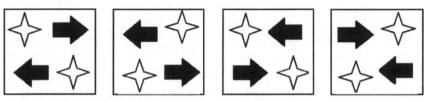

Which frame comes next in the sequence above?

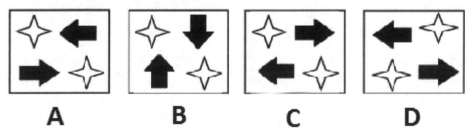

A   B   C   D

Question 26:

The use of human cadavers in the teaching of anatomy is hotly debated. Whilst many argue that it is an invaluable teaching resource, demonstrating far more than a text book can. Others describe how it is an outdated method which puts unfair stress on an already bereaved family. One of the biggest pros for using human tissue in anatomical teaching is the variation that it displays. Whilst textbooks demonstrate a standard model averaged over many 100s of specimens, many argue that it is the variation between cadavers that really reinforces anatomical knowledge.

The opposition argues that it is a cruel process that damages the grieving process of the effected family. For the use of the cadaver often occupies a period of up to 12 months. As such the relative in question is returned to the bereaved family for burial around the time it would be expected that they were recovering as described in the grieving model.

Does the article support or reject the use of cadavers in anatomical teaching?
A)   Supports the use   C)   Impartial   E)   None of the above
B)   Rejects the use   D)   Can't tell

Question 27:

A ferry is carrying its full capacity. At the time of departure (7am) the travel time to the nearest hour is announced as 13 hours. What is the latest that the ferry could arrive at its destination?
A)   08.00   B)   20.00   C)   20.29   D)   20.30   E)   20.50

Question 28:

A game is played using a circle of 55 stepping stones. A die is rolled showing the numbers 1 -6. The number on the die tells you how many steps you may take during your go. The only rule is that during your go you must take your steps in the routine two steps forward, 1 step back.

What is the minimum number or rolls required to win?

A) 28   B) 55   C) 110   D) 165   E) 200

Question 29:

On a race track there are 3 cars recording average lap times of 40 seconds, 60 seconds and 70 seconds. They all started simultaneously 4 minutes ago. How much longer will the race need to continue for them to all cross the start line again at the same time?

A. 23.33 hours   B. 46.67 hours   C. 60.00 hours   D. 83.33 hours   E. 106.67 hours

Question 30:

A class of 60 2nd year medical students are conducting an experiment to measure the velocity of nerve conduction along their radial arteries. This work builds on a previous result obtained demonstrating the effects of how right handed men have faster nerve conduction velocities than gender matched left handed individuals. 60% of the class are female of which 3% were unable to take part due to underlying heart conditions. 2 of the male members of the class were also unable to take part. On average the female cohort had faster nerve conduction velocities than men in their dominant arm.

Right handed women have the fastest nerve conduction velocities.

A) True   B) False   C) Can't tell

Question 31:

Mark is making a double tetrahedron dice by joining two square based pyramids together at their bases. Each square based pyramid is 5cm wide and 8cm tall. What are of card would have been required to produce the nets for the whole die?

A) $150cm^2$ B) $180\,cm^2$ C) $210\,cm^2$ D) $240\,cm^2$ E) $270\,cm^2$

Question 32:

A serial dilution is performed by lining up 10 wells and filling each one with 9ml of distilled water. 1 ml of a concentrated solvent is then added to the first well and mixed. 1 ml of this new solution is drawn from the first well and added to the second and mixed. The process is repeated until all 10 wells have been used.

If the solvent starts off at concentration x, what will its final concentration be after 10 wells of serial dilution?

A. $x/10^9$ B. $x/10^{10}$ C. $x/10^{11}$ D. $x/10^{12}$ E. $x/10^{13}$

Question 33:

A student decides to measure the volume of all the blood in his body. He does this by injecting a known quantity of substrate into his arm, waiting a period of 20 minutes, then drawing a blood sample and measuring the concentration of the substrate in his blood.

What assumption has he made here?

A) The substrate is only soluble in blood
B) The substrate is not bioavailable
C) The substrate is not excreted
D) The substrate is not degraded
E) All of the above

Question 34:

Jason is ordering a buffet for a party. The buffet company can provide a basic spread at £10 a head. However more luxurious items carry a surcharge. Jason is particularly interested in cup-cakes and shell fish. With these items included the buffet company provides a new quote of £10 a head. In addition to simply ordering the food Jason must also purchase cutlery and plates. Plates come in packs of 20 for £8 whilst cutlery is sold in bundles of 60 sets for £10.

With a budget of £2,300 (to the nearest 10 people) what is the maximum number of people Jason can provide food on a plate for?

A)   180   B)   190   C)   209   D)   210   E)   220

Question 35:

What were once methods of hunting have now become popular sports. Examples include archery, the javelin throw, the discuss through and even throwing a boomerang. Why such dangerous hobbies have begun to thrive is now being looked into by social scientists.

One such explanation is that it is because they are dangerous we find them appealing in the first place. Others argue that it is a throwback to our ancestral heritage, where as a hunter gatherer being a proficient hunter was something to show off and flaunt. Whilst this may be the case it is well observed that many find the chase of a hunt exciting if not controversial.

Sports like archery provide excitement analogous to that of the chase during a hunter gatherer hunt.

A)   True   B)   False   C)   Can't tell

END OF SECTION

Section 2

Question 1:
A crocodile's tail weighs 30kg. Its head weighs as much as the tail and one half of the body and legs. The body and legs together weigh as much as the tail and head combined.

What is the total weight of the crocodile?
A) 220kg   B) 240kg   C) 260kg   D) 280kg   E) 300kg

Question 2:
A body is travelling at x ms^{-1} with y J of kinetic energy. After a period of retardation the kinetic energy of the body is $1/16y$. Assuming that the mass of the body has remained constant what is its new velocity?

A) $1/196x$ B) $1/16x$ C) $1/8x$ D) $1/4x$ E) $4x$

Question 3:
Which of the following cannot be classified as an organ?
1. Blood   3. Larynx   5. Prostate   7. Skin
2. Bone   4. Pituitary Gland   6. Skeletal Muscle

A) 1 and 6   B) 2 and 3   C) 5 and 7   D) 1 and 5   E) 1,4, 5 and 6

Question 4:
An increase in aerobic respiratory rate could be associated with which of the following physiological changes?
1. A larger percentage of water vapour in expired air   4. Perspiration
2. Increased expired CO2   5. Vasodilation
3. Increased inspired O2

A) 3 only   C) 1, 2 and 3 only   E) All of the above
B) 1 and 2 only   D) 2, 3 and 5

Question 5:
The nephron is to the kidney, as the ? is to striated muscle:

A) Actin filament   D) Sarcomere
B) Artery   E) Vein
C) Myofibril

Question 6:
A diabetic patient's glucagon and insulin levels are measured over 4 hours. During this time the patient is given two large boluses of glucose. A graphical representation of this is shown to the right.

At which times would you expect the patients' blood glucose to be greatest?

A) 05:00 and 12:00
B) 07:00 and 14.00
C) 08:00 and 15:00
D) 10:00 and 13:00
E) 06:00, 10:00 and 16:00

Question 7:
In addition to the A, B or O classification, blood groups can also be distinguished by the presence of Rhesus antigen (Rh). Care must be taken in blood transfusion as once blood types are mixed a Rh -ve individual will mount an immune response against Rh +ve blood. This is particular well exemplified in haemolytic disease of the newborn – where a Rh-ve mother carries a Rh+ve foetus.

Applying what is written here and your knowledge of the human immune system, explain why the mother's first child would be relatively safe and unaffected, yet further offspring would be at high risk.

A)   The first pregnancy is always such a shock to the body it compromises the immune system
B)   Antibodies take longer than 9 months to produce and mature to an active state
C)   First born children are immunologically privileged
D)   There is a high risk of haemorrhage to both mother and child during birth
E)   Plasma T cells require time to multiply to lethal levels

Question 8:
The pH of a solution has the greatest effect on which type of interaction?
A)   Van der Waals
B)   Induced dipole
C)   Ionic bonding
D)   Metallic interaction
E)   Hydrogen bonding

Question 9:
At present a large effort is being made to produce tailored patient care. One of the ultimate goals of this is to be able to grow personal, genetically identical organs for those with end stage organ failure. This process will first require the harbouring of what cell type?

A)   Cells from the organ that is failing
B)   Haematopoietic stem cells
C)   Embryonic stem cells
D)   Adult stem cells
E)   All of the above

Question 10:
When comparing different isotopes of the same element, which of the following may change?
1.   Atomic number
2.   Mass number
3.   Number of electrons
4.   Chemical reactivity

A)   1 only
B)   1 and 2 only
C)   3 only
D)   2 and 3 only
E)   All of the above

Question 11:
From which of the following elemental groups are you most likely to find a catalyst?

A)   Alkali Metals
B)   d-block elements
C)   Alkaline Earth Metals
D)   Noble Gases
E)   Halogens

Question 12:
1.338kg of francium are mixed in a reaction vessel with an excess of distilled water. What volume will the hydrogen produced occupy at room temperature and pressure?

A) $20.4dm^3$ B) $36dm^3$ C) $40.8dm^3$ D) $60.12dm^3$ E) $72dm^3$

Question 13:
The composition of a compound is Carbon 30%, Hydrogen 40%, Fluorine 20%, and Chlorine 10%.
What is the empirical formula of this compound?

A) CH_2FCl
B) $C_3H_2F_2Cl$
C) C_3H_4FCl
D) $C_3H_4F_2Cl$
E) $C_4H_4F_2Cl$

Question 14:
What is the actual molecular formula of the compound in question 13 if the M_r is 340.5?

A) $C_3H_4F_2Cl$ C) $C_9H_{12}F_6Cl_3$ E) $C_{15}H_{20}F_{10}Cl_5$
B) $C_6H_8F_4Cl_2$ D) $C_{12}H_{16}F_8Cl_4$

Question 15:
1.2×10^{10} kg of sugar is dissolved in 4×10^{12} L of distilled water. What is the concentration?

A) 3×10^{-2} g/dL   C) 3×10^{1} g/dL   E) 3×10^{3} g/dL
B) 3×10^{-1} g/dL   D) 3×10^{2} g/dL

Question 16:
Which of the following is not essential for the progression of an exothermic chemical reaction?

A)   Presence of a catalyst
B)   Increase in entropy
C)   Achieving activation energy
D)   Attaining an electron configuration more closely resembling that of a noble gas
E)   None of the above

Question 17:
What is a common use of cationic surfactants?

A)   Shampoo   C)   Cosmetics   E)   All of the above
B)   Lubricant   D)   Detergents

Question 18:
Which of the following is a unit equivalent to the Volt?
A) $A.\Omega^{-1}$ B) $J.C^{-1}$ C) $W.s^{-1}$ D) $C.s$ E) $W.C.\Omega$

Question 19:
Complete the sentence below:
A voltmeter is connected in _____ and therefore has _____ resistance; whereas an ammeter is connected in _____ and has _____ resistance.

A) Parallel, zero, parallel, infinite
B) Parallel, zero, series, infinite
C) Parallel, infinite, series, zero
D) Series, zero, parallel, infinite
E) Series, infinite, parallel, zero

Question 20:
A body "A" of mass 12kg travelling at 15m/s undergoes inelastic collision with a fixed, stationary object "B" of mass 20kg over a period of 0.5 seconds.

After the collision body A has a new velocity of 3m/s. What force must have been dissipated during the collision?
A)   288N   B)   298N   C)   308N   D)   318N   E)   328N

Question 21:
What process is illustrated here: $^{14}_{6}C \rightarrow\ ^{14}_{7}N + x$
A)   Thermal decomposition   C)   Beta decay
B)   Alpha decay   D)   Gamma decay

Question 22:

A radio dish is broadcasting messages into deep space on a 20 Hz radio frequency of wavelength 3km. With every hour how much further does the signal travel into deep space?

A) 200,000 km   C) 232,000 km   E) 264,000 km
B) 216,000 km   D) 248,000 km

Question 23:

A formula: $\sqrt[3]{\dfrac{z(x+y)(l+m-n)}{3}}$ is given. Would you expect this formula to calculate:

A) A length   C) A volume   E) A geometric average
B) An area   D) A volume of rotation

Question 24:

Evaluate the following: $\dfrac{4.2 \times 10^{10} - 4.2 \times 10^{6}}{2 \times 10^{3}}$

A) 2.09979×10^{6} C) 2.09979×10^{8} E) 2.09979×10^{10}
B) 2.09979×10^{7} D) 2.09979×10^{9}

Question 25:

Calculate a – b

A) 0°
B) 5°
C) 10°
D) 15°
E) 20°

Question 26:

Jack has a bag with a complete set of snooker balls (15 red, 1 yellow, 1 green, 1 brown, 1 blue , 1 pink and 1 black ball) within it. Blindfolded Jack draws two balls from the bag.

What is the probability that he draws a blue and a black ball in any order?
A) 2/41   B) 2/210   C) 1/210   D) 1/105   E) 2/441

Question 27:

An experiment is repeated using an identical methodology and upon further review it is proven to demonstrate identical scientific practice. If the result obtained is different to the first, this would be due to:

A) Calibration Bias   D) Serial dilution
B) Systematic Bias   E) Inaccuracies in the methodology
C) Random Chance

END OF SECTION

Section 3

1) *Doctors should be wearing white coats as it helps produce a placebo effect making the treatment more effective.*

Explain what is meant by this statement. Argue to the contrary. To what extend do you agree with the statement? What points can you see that contradict this statement?

2) *"Medicine is a science of uncertainty and an art of probability."*

William Osler

Explain what this statement means. Argue to the contrary. To what extent do you agree with the statement?

3) *"The New England Journal of Medicine reports that 9 out of 10 doctors agree that 1 out of 10 doctors is an idiot."*

Jay Leno

What do you understand by this statement? Explain why the assumption above may be inaccurate and argue to the contrary.

4) *"My father was a research scientist in tropical medicine, so I always assumed I would be a scientist, too. I felt that medicine was too vague and inexact, so I chose physics."*

Stephen Hawking

Explain what this statement means. Argue to the contrary. To what extent do you agree with the statement?

END OF PAPER

Mock Paper B

Section 1

Question 1:

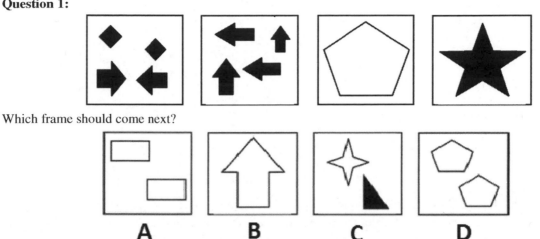

Which frame should come next?

A   B   C   D

Question 2:

Josh is painting the outside walls of his house. The paint he has chosen is sold only in 10L tins. Each tin costs £4.99. Assuming a litre of paint covers an area of $5m^2$, and the total surface area of Josh's outside walls is $1050m^2$; what is the total cost of the paint required if Josh wants to apply 3 coats?

A)   £104.79   B)   £209.58   C)   £314.37   D)   £419.16   E)   £523.95

Question 3:

The stars of the night sky have remained unchanged for many hundreds of years, which allows sailors to navigate using the North Star still to this day. However this only applies within the northern hemisphere as the populations of the southern hemisphere are subject to an alternative night sky.

An asterism can be used to locate the North Star, it comes by many names including the plough, the saucepan and the big dipper. Whilst the North Star's position remains fixed in the sky (allowing it to reliably always point north) the rest of the stars traverse around the North Star in a singular motion. In a very long time, the North Star will one day move from its location due to the movement of the Earth.

Which of the following is **NOT** an assumption made in this argument?
A)   The Earth is rotating on its axis
B)   Sailors still have need to navigate using the stars
C)   An analogous southern star is used to navigate in the Southern hemisphere
D)   The plough is not the only method of locating the North Star
E)   None of the above

Question 4:

John wishes to deposit a cheque. The bank's opening times are 9am until 5pm Monday to Friday, 10am until 4pm on Saturdays and the bank is closed on Sundays. It takes on average 42 bank hours for the money from a cheque to become available.

If John needs the money by 8pm Tuesday, what is the latest he can cash the cheque?

A) 5pm the Saturday before
B) 5pm the Friday before
C) 1pm the Thursday before
D) 1pm the Wednesday before
E) 9am the Tuesday before

Question 5:

How many different diamonds are there in the image shown to the right?

A) 25
B) 32
C) 48
D) 58
E) 63

Question 6:

In 4 years time I will be one third the age that my brother will be next year. In 20 years time he will be double my age. How old am I?

A) 4   B) 9   C) 15   D) 17   E) 23

Question 7:

Aneurysmal disease has been proven to induce systemic inflammatory effects, reaching far beyond the site of the aneurysm. The inflammatory mediator responsible for these processes remains unknown, however the effects of systemic inflammation have been well categorised and observed experimentally in pig models.

In particular this inflammation induces an aberration of endothelial function within the inner most layer of blood vessel walls. The endothelium not only represents the lining of blood vessels but also acts as a transducer converting the haemodynamic forces of blood into a biological response. An example of this is the NO pathway, which uses the shear stress induced by increased blood flow to drive the formation of NO. NO diffuses from the endothelium into the smooth muscle surrounding blood vessels to promote vasodilation and therefore acts to reduce blood flow.

Failure of this process induces high risk of vascular damage and therefore cardiovascular diseases such as thrombosis and atherosclerosis.

What is a valid implication from the text above?

A) Aneurysmal disease does not affect the NO pathway
B) Aneurysms directly increase the likelihood of cardiovascular disease
C) Aneurysms are the opposite of transducers
D) Observations of this kind should be made in humans to see if the results can be replicated
E) Aneurysms induce high blood flow

Question 8:

A traffic surveyor is stood at a T-junction between a main road and a side street; he is only interested in traffic leaving the side street. He logs the class of vehicle, the colour and the direction of travel once on the main road. During an 8 hour period he observes a total of 346 vehicles including bikes. Of which 200 were travelling west whilst the rest travelled east. The over whelming majority of vehicles seen were cars at 90% with bikes, vans and articulated lorries together comprising the remaining 10%. Red was the most common colour observed whilst green was the least. Black and white vehicles were seen in equal quantities.

Which of the following is an accurate inference based on his survey?

A) Global sales are highest for those vehicles which are coloured red
B) Cars are the most popular vehicle on all roads
C) Green vehicle sales are down in the area that the surveyor was based
D) The daily average rate of traffic out of a T junction in Britain is 346 vehicles over 8 hours
E) To the east of the junction is a dead end

Question 9:

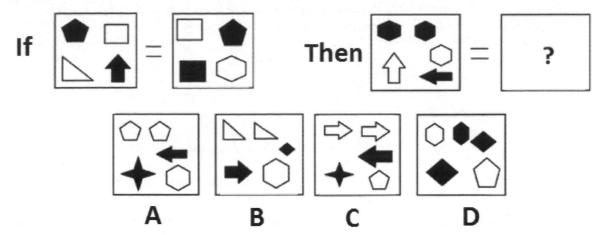

Question 10:

A television is delivered in a box that has volume 60% larger than that of the television. The television is 150cm x 100cm x 10m. How much surplus volume is there?

A) 0.09m^2 B) 0.9 m^2 C) 9 m^2 D) 90 m^2 E) 900 m^2

Question 11:

Matthew and David are deciding where they would like to go camping Friday to Sunday. Upon completing their research they discover the following:

➢ Whitmore Bay charges £5.50 a night and does not require a booking. The site provides showers, washing up facilities and easy access to a beach

➢ Port Eynon charges £5 a night and a booking is compulsory. However the site does not provide showers but does have 240V sockets free of charge

➢ Jackson Bay charges £7 a night and is billed as a luxury site with compulsory booking, private showers, toilets, mobile phone charging facilities and kitchens.

David present the following suggestion:

As Port Eynon is the farthest distance to travel the benefit of its cheap nightly rate is negated by the cost of petrol. Instead he recommends they visit Jackson Bay as it is the shortest distance to travel and will therefore be the cheapest.

Which of the following best illustrates a flaw in this argument?
A) Whitmore bay may be only a few miles further which means the total cost would be less than visiting Jackson Bay
B) With kitchen facilities available they will be tempted to buy more food increasing the cost
C) The campsite may be fully booked
D) There may be a booking fee driving the cost up above that of the other campsites
E) All of the above

Question 12:

The manufacture of any new pharmaceutical is not permitted without scrupulous testing and analysis. This has led to the widespread, and controversial use of animal models in science.

Whilst it is possible to test cyto-toxicity on simple cell cultures, to truly predict the effect of a drug within a physiological system it must be trialled in a whole organism. With animals cheap to maintain, readily available, rapidly reproducing and not subject to the same strict ethical laws they have become an invaluable component of modern scientific practice.

Which of the following best illustrates the main conclusion of this argument?

A) New pharmaceuticals cannot be approved without animal experimentation
B) Cell culture experiments are unhelpful
C) Modern medicine would not have achieved its current standard without animal experimentation
D) Logistically animals are easier to keep than humans for mandatory experiments
E) All of the above

The information below relates to questions 13 – 17:

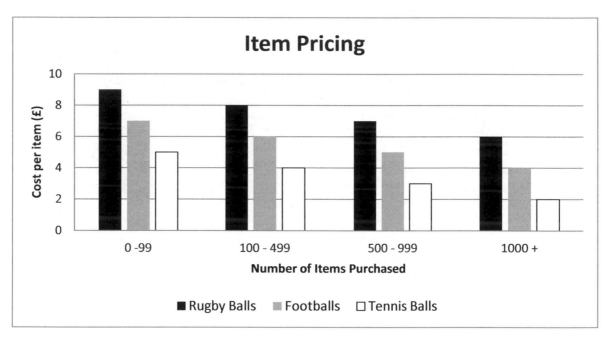

The graph above shows item pricing from a wholesaler. The wholesaler is happy to deliver for a cost of £35 to companies or £5 to individuals. Any order over the cost of £100 qualify for free delivery. Items are defined as how they come to the wholesaler therefore 1 item = 2 rugby balls or 1 football or 5 tennis balls.

Question 13:
What is the total cost to an individual purchasing 12 rugby balls and 120 tennis balls?

A) £174   B) £179   C) £208   D) £534   E) £588

Question 14:
A private gym wishes to purchase 10 of everything, how short are they of the free delivery boundary?

A) £5.00   D) £10.01
B) £5.01   E) They are already over the boundary
C) £10.00

Question 15:

What is the most number of balls that can be bought by an individual with £1,000 pounds.
Who is sitting in the front right seat?

A. 200   B. 250   C. 500   D. 1,000   E. 1,250

Question 16:

The wholesaler sells all his products for a profit of 120%. If he sells £1,320 worth of goods at his prices, what did he actually spend on acquiring them himself?

A) £400   B) £600   C) £800   D) £1,100   E) £1,120

Question 17:

If the wholesaler pays 25% tax on the amount over £12,000 pounds; how much tax does he pay when receiving an order of 2000 of each item?

A) £2,000   B) £3,000   C) £4,000   D) £5,000   E) £6,000

Question 18:

Which frame best fits the algorithm observed in the sequence of diagrams above?

A   **B**   **C**   **D**

Question 19:

A train driver runs a service between Cardiff and Merthyr. On average a one way trip takes 40 minutes to drive but he requires 5 minutes to unload passengers and a further 5 minutes to pick up new ones. As the crow flies the distance between Cardiff and Merthyr is 22 miles.

Assuming he works an 8 hour shift with two 20 minute breaks, and when he arrives to work the first train is already loaded with passengers how far does he travel?

A) 132   B) 143   C) 154   D) 176   E) 198

Question 20:

The massive volume of traffic that travels down the M4 corridor regularly leads to congestion at times of commute morning and evening. A case is being made by local councils in congestion areas to introduce relief lanes thus widening the motorway in an attempt to relieve the congestion. This would involve introducing either a new 2 or 4 lanes to the motorway on average costing 1 million pound per lane per 10 miles.

Many conservationist groups are concerned as this will involve the destruction of large areas of countryside either side of the motorway. They argue that the side of a motorway is a unique habitat with many rare species residing there.

The local councils argue that with many hundreds if not thousands of cars siding idle on the motorway pumping pollutants out into the surrounding areas, it is better for the wildlife if the congestion is eased and traffic can flow through. The councils have also remarked that if congestion is eased there would be less money needed to repair the roads from car incidents with could in theory be given to the conservationist groups as a grant.
Which of the following is assumed in this passage?

A) Wildlife living on the side of the motorway cannot be re-homed
B) Congestion causes car incidents
C) Relief lanes have been proven to improve traffic jams
D) A and B
E) B and C
F) All of the above
G) None of the above

Question 21:

Apples and oranges are sold in packs of 5 for the price of £1 and £1.25 respectively. Alternatively apples can be purchased individually for 30p and oranges can be purchased individually for 50p.
Helen is making a fruit salad, she remarks that order would have cost her an extra £6.25 if she had purchased the fruit individually. Which of the following could have been her order?

A) 15 apples 10 oranges
B) 15 apples 15 oranges
C) 25 apples 10 oranges
D) 25 apples, 15 oranges
E) 30 apples, 30 oranges

Question 22:

Janet is conducting an experiment to assess the sensitivity of a bacterial culture to a range of antibiotics. She grows the bacteria so they cover an entire petri dish and then pipettes a single drop of antibiotic at different locations. A schematic of her results are shown below where black represents growth of bacteria.

Which of the following best describes Janet's results?
A) This strain of bacteria is susceptible to all antibiotics used
B) This strain of bacteria is susceptible to none of the antibiotics used
C) E was the most effective antibiotic
D) C was the most ineffective
E) D is the most likely to be used in further testing

Question 23:

Laura is blowing up balloons for a birthday party. The average volume of a balloon is 300cm^3 and Laura's maximum forced expiratory rate in a single breathe is 4.5l/min. What is the fastest Laura could inflate 25 balloons assuming it takes her 0.5 secs to breathe in per balloon in and somebody else ties the balloons for her?

A. 112.5 seconds
B. 122.5 seconds

C. 132.5 seconds
D. 142.5 seconds

E. 152.5 seconds

Question 24:

George reasons that A is equal to B which is not equal to C. In which case C is equal to D which is equal to E. Which of the following, if true, would most *weaken* George's argument?

A) A does not equal D
B) B is equal to E

C) A and B are not not equal
D) C is equal to 0

E) None of the above

Question 25:

In a single day how many times do the hour, minute and second hands of analogue clock all point to the same number?

A) 12

B) 24

C) 36

D) 48

E) 72

Question 26:

A game of noughts and crosses is illustrated below. James is noughts and it is his turn to play; he is thinking about the outcome of the game and trying to devise a winning strategy. If James plays perfectly can he win?

A) Cannot win
B) Possible to win
C) Certain to win

Question 27:

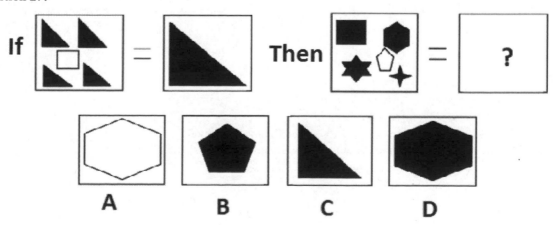

Question 28:
The statement "The human race is not dependent on electricity" assumes what?

A) We have no other energy resource
B) Electricity is cheap
C) Electrical appliances dominate our lives
D) Electricity is now the accepted energy source and is therefore the only one available
E) All of the above

Question 29:
Wine is sold in cases of 6 bottles. A bottle of wine holds 70cl of fluid whereas a wine glass holds 175ml. Cases of wine are currently on offer £42 a case but by one get one free.

If Elin is hosting a 3 course dinner party for 27 of her friends, and she would like to provide everyone with a glass of wine per course, how much will the wine cost her?

A. £42   B. £84   C. £126   D. £168   E. £210

Question 30:
Hannah buys a television series in boxset. It contains a full 7 series with each series comprising 12 episodes. Rounded to the nearest 10 each episode lasts 40 minutes.

What is the shortest amount of time it could possible take to watch all the episodes back to back?

A) 49 hours   B) 51 hours   C) 53 hours   D) 56 hours   E) 60 hours

Question 31:
Many are familiar with the story that aided in the discovery of "germ". Semmelweis worked in a hospital where maternal death rates during labour were astronomically high. He noticed that medical students often went straight from dissection of cadavers to the maternity wards. As an experiment Semmelweis split the student cohort in half. Half did their maternity rotation instead before dissection whereas the other half maintained their traditional routine. In the new routine, maternity ward before dissection, Semmelweis recorded an enormous reduction in maternal deaths and thus the concept of the pathogen was born.

What is best exemplified in this passage?
A) Science is a process of trial and error
B) Great discoveries come from pattern recognition
C) Provision of healthcare is closely associated with technological advancements
D) Experiments always require a control
E) All of the above

Question 32:
Jack sits at a table opposite a stranger. The stranger says here I have 3 precious jewels: a diamond, a sapphire and an emerald. He tells Jack that if he makes a truthful statement Jack will get one of the stones, if he lies he will get nothing.

What must Jack say to ensure he gets the sapphire?
A. Tell the stranger his name
B. Tell the stranger he must give him the sapphire
C. Tell the stranger he wants the emerald
D. Tell the stranger he does not want the emerald or the diamond
E. Tell the stranger he will not give him the emerald or the diamond

Question 33:

Simon invests 100 pounds in a saver account that awards compound interest on a 6 monthly basis at 50%. Simon's current account awards compound interest on a yearly basis at 90%.

After 2 years will Simon's investment in the saver account yield more money than it would have in the current account?

A) Yes   B) No   C) Can't tell

Question 34:

My mobile phone has a 4 number pin code using the values 1 – 9. To determine this I use a standard algorithm of multiplying the first two numbers, subtracting the third and then dividing by the fourth. I change the code by changing the answer to this algorithm – I call this the key. What is the largest possible key?

A) 42   B) 55   C) 70   D) 80   E) 81

Question 35:

Which frame comes next in the sequence above?

A   B   C   D

END OF SECTION

Section 2

Question 1:
GLUT2 is an essential, ATP independent, mediator in the liver's uptake of plasma glucose. This is an example of:

A. Active transport
B. Diffusion
C. Exocytosis

D. Facilitated Diffusion
E. Osmosis

Question 2:
The molecular weight of glucose is 180 g/mol. 5.76Kg of glucose is split evenly between two cell cultures under anaerobic conditions. One cell culture is taken from human cardiac muscle, whilst the other is a yeast culture. What will be the difference (in moles) between the amount of CO_2 produced between the two cultures.

A) 0 mol
B) 4 mol
C) 8 mol
D) 12 mol
E) 16 mol

Question 3:
Which of the following cell types will have the greatest flux along endocytotic pathways?

A) Kidney cells
B) Liver cells
C) Nerve cells

D) Red blood cells
E) White blood cell

Question 4:
Compared to the Krebs cycle, the Calvin cycle demonstrates which of the following differences?

A) CO_2 as a substrate rather than a product
B) Photon dependent
C) Utiliation of different electron transporters

D) Net loss of ATP
E) All of the above

Question 5:
Pepsin and trypsin are both digestive enzymes. Pepsin acts in the stomach whereas trypsin is secreted by the pancreas. Which graph below (trypsin in black and pepsin in grey) would most accurately demonstrate their relative activity against pH?

Question 6:
MRSA is an example of:

A) Natural selection
B) Genetic engineering
C) Sexual reproduction

D) Lamarckism
E) Co-dominance

Question 7:
What is the electron configuration of magnesium in $MgCl_2$?

A) 2,8
B) 2,8,2
C) 2,8,4

D) 2,8,8
E) None of the above

Question 8:
A calcium sample is run in a mass spectrometer. It is later discovered that the sample was contaminated with the most abundant isotope of chromium. A section of the trace is shown below. What was the actual abundance of the most common calcium isotope?

A) 1/9   B) 6/17   C) 1/2   D) 11/19   E) 17/19

Question 9:
A warehouse receives 15 tonnes of arsenic in bulk. Assuming that the sample is at least 80% pure, what is the minimum amount, in moles, of arsenic that they have obtained?

A) 1.6×10^5 B) 2×10^5 C) 1.6×10^6 D) 2×10^6 E) 1.6×10^7

Question 10:
A sample of silicon is run in a mass spectrometer. The resultant trace shows m/z peaks at 26 and 30 with relative abundance 60% and 30% respectively. What other isotope of silicon must have been in the sample to give an average atomic mass of 28?

A) 28   B) 30   C) 32   D) 34   E) 36

Question 11:
72.9g of pure magnesium ribbon is mixed in a reaction vessel with the equivalent of 54g of steam. The ensuing reaction produces $72dm^3$ of hydrogen. Which of the following statements is true?

A) This is a complete reaction
B) This is a partial reaction
C) There is an excess of steam

D) There is an excess of magnesium
E) Magnesium hydroxide is a product

Question 12:

Which species is the reducing agent in: $3Cu^{2+} + 3S^{2-} + 8H^+ + 8NO_3^- \rightarrow 3Cu^{2+} + 3SO_4^{2-} + 8NO + 4H_2O$

A) Cu^{2+} B) S^{2-} C) H^+ D) NO_3^- E) H_2O

Question 13:

Which of the following is not true of alkanes?

A) CnH2n+2
B) Saturated
C) Reactive
D) Produce only CO_2 and water when burnt in an excess of oxygen
E) None of the above

Question 14:

A rubber balloon is inflated and rubbed against a sample of animal fur for a period of 15 seconds. At the end of this process the balloon is carrying a charge of -5 coulombs. What magnitude of current must have been induced during the process of rubbing the balloon against the animal fur; and in which direction was it flowing?

A) 0.33A into the balloon   D) 75A into the balloon
B) 0.33A into the fur   E) 75A into the fur
C) 0.33A in no net direction

Question 15:

Which of the following is a unit equivalent to the Amp?

A) $V.\Omega$ B) $(W.V)/s$ C) $C.\Omega$ D) $(J.s^{-1})/V$ E) $C.s$

Question 16:

The output of a step down transformer is measured at 24V and 10A. Given that the transformer is 80% efficient what must the initial power input have been?

A) 240W   B) 260W   C) 280W   D) 300W   E) 320W

Question 17:

An electric winch system hoists a mass of 20kg 30 metres into the air over a period of 20 seconds. What is the power output of the winch assuming the system is 100% efficient?

A) 100W   B) 200W   C) 300W   D) 400W   E) 500W

Question 18:

6×10^{10} atoms of a radioactive substance remain, the activity of the substance is quantified as 3.6×10^9. What is the decay constant of this material?

A) 0.00006   B) 0.0006   C) 0.006   D) 0.06   E) 0.6

Question 19:

An 80W filament bulb draws 0.5A of household electricity. What is the efficiency of the bulb?

A) 25%   B) 33%   C) 50%   D) 66%   E) 75%

Question 20 :

Rearrange the following equation in terms of t: $x = \frac{\sqrt{b^3-9st}}{13j} + \int_{-z}^{z} 9a - 7$

A) $t = \frac{(13jx - \int_{-z}^{z} 9a-7)^2 - b^3}{9s}$

B) $t = \frac{13jx^2}{b^3-9s} - \int_{-z}^{z} 9a - 7$

C) $t = x - \frac{\sqrt{b^3-9s}}{13j} - \int_{-z}^{z} 9a - 7$

D) $t = \frac{x^2}{\frac{b^3-9s}{13j} + \int_{-z}^{z} 9a-7}$

E) $t = \frac{[13j(x - \int_{-z}^{z} 9a-7)]^2 - b^3}{-9s}$

Question 21:

An investment of £500 is made in a compound interest account. At the end of 3 years the balance reads £1687.50. What is the interest rate?

A) 20%   B) 35%   C) 50%   D) 65%   E) 80%

Question 22:

What is the equation of the line of best fit for the scatter graph below?

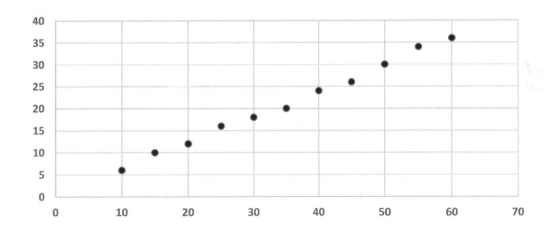

A) y = 0.2x + 0.35   D) y = 0.4x – 0.35
B) y = 0.2x – 0.35   E) y = 0.6x + 0.35
C) y = 0.4x + 0.35

Question 23 :

Simplify: $m = \sqrt{\frac{9xy^3z^5}{3x^9yz^4}} - m$

A) $m = \sqrt{\frac{3y^2z}{x^8}} - m$

B) $m^2 = \frac{3y^2z}{x^8} - m$

C) $2m = \sqrt{\frac{3y^2z}{x^8}}$

D) $2m^2 = 3x^{-8}y^2z$

E) $4m^2 = 3x^{-8}y^2z$

Question 24:
Which of the following is a suitable descriptive statistic for non-normally distributed data?

A) Mean

B) Normal range

C) Confidence interval

D) Interquartile range

E) Mode

Question 25:
Which best describes the purpose of statistics?

A) Evaluate acceptable scientific practice

B) Reduce the ability of others to criticise the data

C) To quickly analyse data

D) Calculate values representative of the population from a subset sample

E) To allow for universal comparison of scientific methods

Question 26:
A rotating disc has two wells, in which bacteria are cultured. The first well is 10 cm from the centre whereas the second well is 20 cm from the centre. If the inner well completes a revolution in 1 second, how much faster is the outer well travelling?

A) 0.314m/s   B) 0.628m/s   C) 0.942m/s   D) 1.256m/s   E) 1.590m/s

Question 27:

Which is the equivalent function to: $y = 9x^{-\frac{1}{3}}$?

A) $y = \frac{1}{x}$

B) $y = \sqrt[3]{9x}$

C) $y = \frac{1}{\sqrt[3]{9x}}$

D) $y = \frac{9}{\sqrt[3]{x}}$

E) $y = \frac{3}{\sqrt[3]{x}}$

END OF SECTION

Section 3

1) *"Progress is made by trial and failure; the failures are generally a hundred times more numerous than the successes; yet they are usually left unchronicled."*

Williams Ramsey

Explain what this statement means. Argue to the contrary. To what extent do you agree with the statement?

2) *"He who studies medicine without books sails an uncharted sea, but he who studies medicine without patients does not go to sea at all."*

William Osler

Explain what this statement means. Argue to the contrary. To what extent do you agree with the statement?

3) *'"Medicine is the restoration of discordant elements; sickness is the discord of the elements infused into the living body"*

Leonardo da Vinci

Explain what this statement means. Argue to the contrary. To what extent do you think this simplification holds true within modern medicine?

4) *"Modern medicine is a negation of health. It isn't organized to serve human health, but only itself, as an institution. It makes more people sick than it heals."*

Ivan Illich

What does this statement mean? Argue to the contrary, that the primary duty of a doctor is not to prolong life. To what extent do you agree with this statement?

END OF PAPER

Mock Paper C

Section 1

Question 1:

Adam, Beth and Charlie are going on holiday together. A single room costs £60 per night, a double room costs £105 per night and a four person room costs £215 per night. It is possible to opt out from the cleaning service and to pay £12 less each night per room.

What is the minimum amount the three friends could pay for their holiday for a three night stay at the hotel?

A. £122   B. £144   C. £203   D. £423   E. £432

Question 2:

I have two 96ml glasses of squash. The first is comprised of $\frac{1}{6}$ squash and $\frac{5}{6}$ water. The second is comprised of $\frac{1}{4}$ water and $\frac{3}{4}$ squash. I take 48ml from the first glass and add it to glass two. I then take 72ml from glass two and add it to glass one. How much squash is now in each glass?

A. 16ml squash in glass one and 72ml squash in glass two
B. 40ml squash in glass one and 32ml squash in glass two
C. 48ml squash in glass one and 32ml squash in glass two
D. 48ml squash in glass one and 40ml squash in glass two
E. 80ml squash in glass one and 40ml squash in glass two

Question 3:

It may amount to millions of pounds each year of taxpayers' money; however it is strongly advisable for the HPV vaccination in schools to remain. The vaccine, given to teenage girls, has the potential to significantly reduce cervical cancer deaths and furthermore, the vaccines will decrease the requirement for biopsies and invasive procedures related to the follow-up tests. Extensive clinical trials and continued monitoring suggest that both Gardasil and Cervarix are safe and tolerated well by recipients. Moreover, studies demonstrate that a large majority of teenage girls and their parents are in support of the vaccine.

1.

Which of the following is the conclusion of the above argument?

A. HPV vaccines are safe and well tolerated
B. It is strongly advisable for the HPV vaccination in schools to remain
C. The HPV vaccine amounts to millions of pounds each year of taxpayers' money
D. The vaccine has the potential to significantly reduce cervical cancer deaths
E. Vaccinations are vital to disease prevention across the population

Question 4:

Anna cycles to school, which takes 30 minutes. James takes the bus, which leaves from the same place as Anna, but 6 minutes later and gets to school at the same time as Anna. It takes the bus 12 minutes to get to the post office, which is 3km away. The speed of the bus is $\frac{5}{4}$ the speed of the bike. One day Anna leaves 4 minutes late. How far does she get before she is overtaken by the bus?

A. 1.5km   B. 2km   C. 3km   D. 4km   E. 6km

Question 5:

The set two maths teacher is trying to work out who needs to be moved up to set one and who to award a certificate at the end of term. The students must fulfil certain criteria:

Move to set one	**Attendance over 95%**
	Average test mark over 92
	Less than 5% homework handed in late
Awarded a Certificate	**Absences below 4%**
	Average test mark over 89
	At least 98% homework handed in on time

	Terry	Alex	Bahara	Lucy	Shiv
Attendance %	97	92	97	100	98
Average test mark %	89	93	94	95	86
Homework handed in on time %	96	92	100	96	98

Who would move up a set and who would receive a certificate?

A. Bahara would move up a set and receive a certificate
B. Bahara and Lucy would move up a set and Bahara would receive a certificate
C. Bahara, Terry and Lucy would move up a set and Bahara and Shiv would receive a certificate
D. Lucy would move up a set and Bahara would receive a certificate
E. Lucy would move up a set and Bahara and Terry would receive a certificate

Question 6:

18 years ago A was 25 years younger than B is now. In 21 years time, A will be 28 years older than B was 14 years ago. How old is A now if A is $\frac{5}{6}$B?

A. 27   B. 28   C. 35   D. 42   E. 46

Question 7:

The time now is 10.45am. I am preparing a meal for 16 guests who will arrive tomorrow for afternoon tea. I want to make 3 scones for each guest, which can be baked in batches of 6. Each batch takes 35 minutes to prepare and 25 minutes to cook in the oven and I can start the next batch while the previous batch is in the oven. I also want to make 2 cupcakes for each guest, which can be baked in batches of 8. It takes 15 minutes to prepare the mixture for each batch and 20 minutes to cook them in the oven. I will also make 3 cucumber sandwiches for each guest. 6 cucumber sandwiches take 5 minutes to prepare.

What will the time be when I finish making all the food for tomorrow?
A. 4:35pm   B. 5.55pm   C. 6:00pm   D. 6:05pm   E. 7:20pm

Question 8:

Pyramid	Base edge (m)	Volume (m³)
1	3	33
2	4	64
3	2	8
4	6	120
5	2	8
6	6	120
7	4	64

What is the difference between the height of the smallest and tallest pyramids?
A. 1m   B. 5m   C. 4m   D. 6m   E. 8m

Question 9:

The wage of Employees at Star Bakery is calculated as: £210 + (Age x 1.2) – 0.8 (100 - % attendance)

Jessica is 35 and her attendance is 96%   --- Samira is 65 and her attendance is 89%

What is the difference between their wages?

A. £30.4   B. £60.5   C. £248.8   D. £263.2   E. £279.2

Question 10:

It is important that research universities demonstrate convincing support of teaching. Undergraduates comprise an overwhelming proportion of all students and universities should make an effort to cater to the requirements of the majority of their student body. After all, many of these students may choose to pursue a path involving research and a strong education would provide students with skills equipped towards a career in research.

What is the conclusion of the above argument?

A. Undergraduates comprise an overwhelming proportion of all students
B. A strong education would provide a strong foundation and skills equipped towards a career in research
C. Research universities should strongly support teaching
D. Institutions should provide undergraduates with a high quality learning experience
E. Research has a greater impact than teaching and limited universities funds should mainly be invested in research

Question 11:

American football has reached a level of violence that puts its players at too high a level of risk. It has been suggested that the NFL, the governing body for American football should get rid of the iconic helmets. The hard plastic helmets all have to meet minimum impact-resistance standards intended to enhance safety, however in reality they gave players a false sense of security that only resulted in harder collisions. Some players now suffer from early onset dementia, mood swings and depression. The proposal to ban helmets for good should be supported. Moreover, it would prevent costly legal settlements involving the NFL and ex-players suffering from head trauma.

What is the conclusion of the above argument?

A. Sports players should not be exposed to unnecessary danger
B. Helmets give players a false sense of security
C. Players can suffer from early onset dementia, mood swings and depression
D. The proposal to ban helmets should be supported
E. American football is too violent and puts its players at risk

Question 12:

At the final stop (stop 6), 10 people get off the tube. At the previous stop (stop 5) $\frac{1}{2}$ of passengers got off. At stop 4, $\frac{3}{5}$ of passengers got off. At stop 3, $\frac{1}{3}$ of passengers got off and at stops 1 and 2, $\frac{1}{6}$ of passengers got off.

How many passengers got on at the first stop?

A. 10   B. 36   C. 90   D. 108   E. 3600

Question 13:

Everyone likes English. Some students born in spring like Maths and some like Biology. All students born in winter like Music and some like Art. Of those born in autumn, no one likes Biology and everyone likes Art.

Which of the following is true?

A. Some students born in spring like both Biology and Maths
B. Students born in spring, winter and autumn all like Art
C. No one born in winter or autumn likes Biology
D. No one who likes Biology also likes Art
E. Some students born in winter like 3 subjects

Question 14:

Until the twentieth century, the whole purpose of art was to create beautiful, flawless works. Artists attained a level of skill and craft that took decades to perfect and could not be mirrored by those who had not taken great pains to master it. The serenity and beauty produced from movements such as impressionism has however culminated in repulsive and horrific displays of rotting carcasses designed to provoke an emotional response rather than admiration. These works cannot be described as beautiful by either the public or art critics. While these works may be engaging on an intellectual or academic level, they no longer constitute art.

Which of the following is an assumption of the above argument?

A. Beauty is a defining property of art
B. All modern art is ugly
C. Twenty first century artists do not study for decades
D. The impressionist movement created beautiful works of art
E. Some modern art provokes an emotional response

Question 15:

The cost of sunglasses is reduced over the bank holiday weekend. On Saturday, the price of the sunglasses on Friday is reduced by 10%. On Sunday the price of the sunglasses on Saturday is reduced by 10%. On Monday, the price of the sunglasses on Sunday is reduced by a further 10%. What percentage of the price on Friday is the price of the sunglasses on Monday?

A. 55.12%   B. 59.10%   C. 63.80%   D. 70.34%   E. 72.9%

Question 16:

Putting the digit 7 on the right hand side of a two digit number causes the number to increase by 565. What is the value of the two digit number?

A. 27   B. 52   C. 62   D. 66   E. 627

Question 17:

When folded, which box can be made from the net shown below?

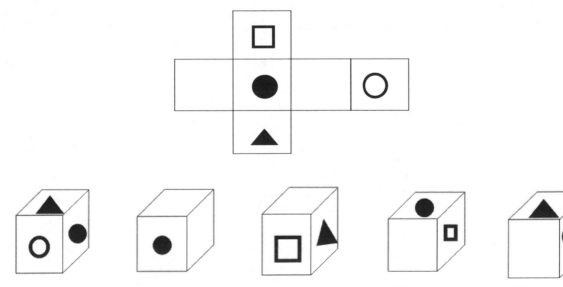

Question 18:

The grid is comprised of 49 squares. The shape's area is 588cm². What is its perimeter in cm?

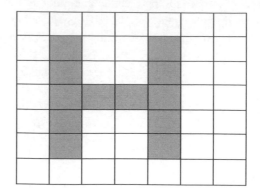

A. 26   B. 49   C. 84   D. 126   E. 182

Questions 19-21 refer to the following information:

$$BMI = weight\ (kg)\ \div\ height^2\ (m^2)$$

Men	**BMR= (10 x weight in kg) + (6.25 x height in cm) – (5 x age in years) + 5**
Women	BMR= (10 x weight in kg) + (6.25 x height in cm) – (5 x age in years) -161

Recommended Intake:

Amount of Exercise	Daily Kilocalories required
Little to no exercise	BMR x 1.2
Light exercise 1-3 days per week	BMR x 1.375
Moderate exercise 3-5 days per week	BMR x 1.55
Heavy exercise 6-7 days per week	BMR x 1.725
Very heavy exercise twice per day	BMR x 1.9

Question 19:

A child weighs 35kg and is 120cm tall. What is the BMI of the child to the nearest 2 d.p?

A. 0.0024   B. 24.28   C. 24.31   D. 42.01   E. 42.33

Question 20:

What is the BMR of a 32 year old woman weighing 80kg and measuring 1.7m in height?

A. 643.7 kcal   B. 1537 kcal   C. 1541.5 kcal   D. 1707.5 kcal   E. 2707.5 kcal

Question 21:

What is the recommended intake of a 45 year old man weighing 80kg and measuring 1.7m in height who does little to no exercise each week?

A. 1642.5 kcal   B. 1771.8 kcal   C. 1851 kcal   D. 1971 kcal   E. 2712.5 kcal

Questions 22 and 23 relate to the following passage:

The achievement levels of teenagers could be higher if school started later. Teenagers are getting too little sleep because they attend schools that start at 8:30am or earlier. A low level of sleep disrupts the body's circadian rhythms and can contribute to health problems such as obesity and depression. Some doctors are now urging schools to start later in order for teenagers to get sufficient sleep; ideally 8.5 to 9.5 hours each night. During adolescence, the hormone melatonin is released comparatively later in the day and the secretion levels climb at night. Consequently, teenagers can have trouble getting to sleep earlier in the night before sufficient melatonin is present. A school in America tested this idea by starting one hour later and the percentage of GCSEs at grades A*-C increased by 16%. Schools in the UK should follow by example and shift start times later.

Question 22:
Which of the following is a flaw in the above argument?

A. Slippery slope
B. Hasty generalisation
C. It confuses correlation with cause
D. Circular argument
E. Schools should not prioritise academic achievement

Question 23:
Which of the following, if true, would most strengthen the above argument?

A. Teenagers who are more alert will disrupt the class more
B. Getting more sleep at night is proven to increase activity levels
C. American schools and British schools teach the same curriculum
D. The school in America did not alter any other aspects of the school during the trial for example curriculum, teachers, and number of students in each class
E. Teachers get tired towards the end of the school day and are less effective

Question 24:
The UK energy market is highly competitive. In an effort to attract more business and increase revenue, the company EnergyFirst has divested significant funds into its publicity sector. Last month, they doubled their advertising expenditures, becoming the energy company to invest the greatest proportion of investment into advertising. As a result it is expected that EnergyFirst will expand its customer base at a rate exceeding its competitors in the ensuing months. Other energy companies are likely to follow by example.

Which of the following, if true, is most likely to weaken the above argument?
A. Other companies invest more money into good customer service
B. Research into the energy industry demonstrates a low correlation between advertising investment and new customers
C. The UK energy market is not highly competitive
D. EnergyFirst currently has the smallest customer base
E. Customers are heavily influenced by visual advertising

Question 25:
The consumption of large quantities of red meat is suggested to have negative health ramifications. Carnitine is a compound present in red meat and a link has been discovered between carnitine and the development of atherosclerosis, involving the hardening and narrowing of arteries. Intestinal bacteria convert carnitine to trimethylamine-N-oxide, which has properties that are damaging to the heart. Moreover, red meat consumption has been associated with a reduced life expectancy. It may be that charring meat generates toxins that elevate the chance of developing stomach cancer. If people want to be healthy, a vegetarian diet is preferable to a diet including meat. Vegetarians often have lower cholesterol and blood pressure and a reduced risk of heart disease.

Which of the following is an assumption of the above argument?
A. Diet is essential to health and we should all want to be healthy
B. Vegetarians do the same amount of exercise as meat eaters
C. Meat has no health benefits
D. People who eat red meat die earlier
E. Red meat is the best source of iron

Question 26:
Auckland is 11 hours ahead of London. Calgary is 7 hours behind London. Boston is 5 hours behind London. The flight from Auckland to London is 22 hours, but the plane must stop for 2 hours in Hong Kong. The flight from London to Calgary is 8 hours 30 minutes. The flight from Calgary to Boston is 6 hours 30 minutes. Sam leaves Auckland at 10am for London. On arrival to London, he waits 3 hours then gets the plane to Calgary. Once in Calgary, he waits 1.5 hours and gets the plane to Boston. What time is it when Sam arrives in Boston?

A. 13:30pm   B. 22.30pm   C. 01:00am   D. 01:30am   E. 03:30am

Question 27:
Light A flashes every 18 seconds, light B flashes every 33 seconds and light C flashes every 27 seconds. The three lights all flashed at the same time 5 minutes ago. How long will it be until they next all flash simultaneously?

A. 33 seconds   B. 294 seconds   C. 300 seconds   D. 333 seconds   E. 594 seconds

Question 28:
There are 30 students in a class. They must all play at least 1 instrument, but no more than 3 instruments. 70% play the piano, 40% play the violin, 20% play the guitar and 10% play the saxophone. Which of the following statements must be true?

1. 3 or more students play piano and violin
2. 12 students or less play the piano and the violin
3. 9 or more students do not play piano or violin

A. 1 only   B. 1 and 2   C. 2 only   D. 2 and 3   E. 3 only

Question 29:
Neil, Simon and Lucy are playing a game to see who can role the highest number with two dice. They start with £50 each. The losers have to half their money and give it to the winner of each game. If it is a draw, the two winners share the loser's money. If all three tie, then they keep their money. Neil wins game 1, Simon and Lucy win game 2 and 5 and Lucy wins games 3 and 4. How much money does Lucy gain?

A. £15.63   B. £75   C. £75.16   D. £78.13   E. £128.1

Question 30:
Drivers in the age group 17-19 comprise 1.5% of all drivers; however 12% of all collisions involve young drivers in this age category. The RAC Foundation wants a graduated licensing system with a 1 year probationary period with restrictions on what new drivers can do on roads. Additionally, driving instructors need to emphasise the dangers of driving too fast and driving tests should be designed to make new drivers more focused on noticing potential hazards. These changes are essential and could stop 4,500 injuries on an annual basis.

What is the assumption of the above argument?
A. Young drivers are more likely to have more passengers than other age groups
B. Young drivers spend more hours driving than older drivers
C. Young drivers are responsible for the collisions
D. The cars that young people drive are unsafe
E. Most young drivers involved in accidents are male

Question 31:
The mean weight of 6 apples is 180g. The lightest apple weighs 167g. What is the highest possible weight of the heaviest apple?

A. 193g   B. 225g   C. 235g   D. 245g   E. 255g

Question 32:
Which option represents the mirror image of the image shown to the right?

A   **B**   **C**   **D**   **E**

Question 33:
The farmer had 184 sheep to sell. He intended to sell each for £112. However, he sold less than one quarter on day 1. As a result he reduced the price by $\frac{1}{8}$. On the second day he sold twice as many and made £3528 more than on day 1, leaving him with less than $\frac{1}{3}$ of original. How many sheep did he sell altogether?

A. 42   B. 84   C. 98   D. 112   E. 126

Question 34:
There is no empirical evidence that human activities directly result in global warming and this is used as a reason against decreasing carbon emissions. However, many scientists believe that human activity is highly likely to cause global warming since higher levels of greenhouse gases cause the atmosphere to thicken, retaining heat. It therefore seems sensible that we should not wait for proof considering the catastrophic effects of climate change, regardless of subsequent findings. Similarly, if a tree branch had a significant chance of falling on you, it would be sensible to move away immediately.
What is the main conclusion?

A. Many scientists believe that human activity is highly likely to cause global warming
B. We should not wait for proof of climate change
C. If a tree branch had a significant chance of falling on you, it would be sensible to move away immediately
D. The effects of climate change are catastrophic
E. There is no empirical evidence that human activities directly result in global warming so we should not reduce carbon emissions

Question 35:
The average of 8 numbers is y. If 13 and 31 are added, the mean of the 10 numbers is also y. What is y?

A. 11   B. 22   C. 25   D. 27   E. 44

END OF SECTION

Section 2

Question 1:
Which of the following are correct regarding polymers?

1. Sucrose is formed by the condensation of hundreds of monosaccharides
2. Lactose is found in milk and is formed by condensation of two glucose molecules
3. Glucose has two isomers
4. Glycogen, starch and cellulose are all polysaccharides formed by condensation of multiple glucose molecules
5. People with lactose intolerance lack lactase and can experience diarrhoea after drinking milk

A. 1 only
B. 1, 2 and 3
C. 1 and 3 only

D. 3, 4 and 5
E. 4 and 5 only

Question 2:
Which of the following statements regarding enzymes are correct?

1. Enzymes are denatured at high temperatures or extreme pH values
2. Amylase is produced in the salivary glands only and converts starch to sugars
3. Lipases catalyse the breakdown of oils and fats into glycerol and fatty acids. This takes place in the small intestine
4. Bile is stored in the pancreas and travels down the bile duct to neutralise stomach acid
5. Isomerase can be used to convert glucose into fructose for use in slimming products

A. 1 and 3 only
B. 1, 3 and 4 only
C. 1, 3 and 5

D. 2 and 4 only
E. 3 and 5 only

Question 3:
Which of the following describes the role of the colon?

A. Food is combined with bile and digestive enzymes
B. Storage of faeces
C. Reabsorption of water
D. Faeces leave the alimentary canal
E. Any digested food is absorbed into the lymph and blood

Question 4:
Which of the following are true?

1. A nerve impulse is transmitted along the nerve axon as an electrical impulse and across the synapse by diffusion of chemical neurotransmitters
2. drugs that block synaptic transmission can cause complete paralysis
3. the fatty sheath around the axon slows the speed at which nerve impulses are transmitted
4. the peripheral nervous system includes the brain and spinal cord
5. a reflex arc bypasses the brain and enables a fast, autonomic response

A. 1 and 2
B. 1, 2 and 3
C. 1, 2 and 5

D. 2, 4 and 5
E. 3, 4 and 5

Question 5:

Which of the following statements are true regarding the transition elements?

1. Iron (II) compounds are light green
2. Transition elements are neither malleable nor ductile
3. Transition metal carbonates may undergo thermal decomposition
4. Transition metal hydroxides are soluble in water
5. When Cu^{2+} ions are mixed with sodium hydroxide solution, a blue precipitate is formed

A. 1 and 2   B. 1 and 3   C. 1, 3 and 5   D. 3 and 5   E. 5 only

Question 6:

What is the value of C when the equation is balanced?

$$\underline{5}\ PhCH_3 + \underline{A}\ KMnO_4 + \underline{9}\ H_2SO_4 = \underline{5}\ PhCOOH + \underline{B}\ K_2SO_4 + \underline{C}\ MnSO_4 + \underline{14}\ H_2O$$

A. 3   B. 4   C. 5   D. 7   E. 9

Question 7:

Tongue-rolling is controlled by the dominant allele T, while non-rolling is controlled by the recessive allele, t. Red-green colour blindness is controlled by a sex-linked gene on the X chromosome. Normal colour vision is controlled by dominant allele B, while red-green colour blindness is controlled by the recessive allele, b.
The mother of a family is colour blind and heterozygous for tongue-rolling, while the father has normal colour vision and is a non-roller.

Which of the following statements are correct?

1. More males than females in a population are red-green colour blind
2. 50% of children will be non-rollers
3. All the male children will be colour-blind

A. 1 and 2 only   D. 2 and 3 only
B. 1, 2 and 3   E. 3 only
C. 2 only

Question 8:

Make y the subject of the formula: $\frac{y+x}{x} = \frac{x}{a} + \frac{a}{x}$

A. $y = \frac{x^2}{a} + a$

B. $y = \frac{x^2 + a^2 - ax}{a}$

C. $y = \frac{-ax}{x^2 + a^2}$

D. $y = \frac{x^2}{ax} + a - x$

E. $y = a^2 - ax$

Question 9:

What is the mass in grams of calcium chloride, $CaCl_2$ in $25cm^3$ of a solution with a concentration of 0.1 mol l^{-1}? (Ar of Ca is 40 and Ar of Cl is 35)

A. 0.28g   B. 0.46g   C. 0.48g   D. 0.72g   E. 1.28g

Question 10:

Consider the equations: A: y = 3x and B: $y = \frac{6}{x} - 7$. At what values of x do the two equations intersect?

A. x=2 and x=9   D. x=6
B. x=3 and x=6   E. x=18
C. x=6 and x=27

Question 11:
Which of the following statements regarding the circulatory system are correct?

1. The pulmonary artery carries oxygenated blood from the right ventricle to the lungs
2. The aorta has a high content of elastic tissue and carries oxygenated blood from the left ventricle around the body
3. The mitral valve is between the pulmonary vein and the left atrium
4. The vena cava carries deoxygenated blood from the body to the right atrium

A. 1 and 3   B. 1 and 2   C. 2 only   D. 2 and 4   E. 3 only

Question 12:
A compound with a molar mass of 120 gmol^{-1} contains 12 g of carbon, 2 g of hydrogen and 16 g oxygen. What is the molecular formula of the compound?

A. CH_2O B. $C_2H_4O_2$ C. C_4H_2O D. $C_4H_8O_4$ E. $C_8H_{16}O_8$

Question 13:
Rupert plays one game of tennis and one game of squash.

The probability that he will win the tennis game is $\frac{3}{4}$

The probability that he will win the squash game is $\frac{1}{3}$

What is the probability that he will win one game only?

A. $\frac{3}{12}$ B. $\frac{7}{12}$ C. $\frac{4}{5}$ D. $\frac{13}{12}$ E. $\frac{7}{6}$

Question 14:
What is the median of the following numbers: $\frac{7}{36}$; $0.\dot{3}$; $\frac{11}{18}$; 0.25; 0.75; $\frac{62}{72}$; $\frac{7}{7}$

A. $\frac{7}{36}$

B. $0.\dot{3}$

C. $\frac{11}{18}$

D. $\frac{62}{72}$

E. 0.75

Question 15:
16.4g of nitrobenzene is produced from 13g of benzene in excess nitric acid: $C_6H_6 + HNO_3 -> C_6H_5NO_2 + H_2O$

What is the percentage yield of nitrobenzene ($C_6H_5NO_2$)?
A. 65%   B. 67%   C. 72%   D. 78%   E. 80%

Question 16:
Which of the following points regarding electromagnetic waves are correct?

1. Radiowaves have the longest wavelength and the lowest frequency
2. Infrared has a shorter wavelength than visible light and is used in optical fibre communication, heater and night vision equipment
3. All of the waves from gamma to radio waves travel at the speed of light (about 300,000,000 m/s)
4. Infrared radiation is used to sterilise food and to kill cancer cells
5. Darker skins absorb more UV light, so less ultraviolet radiation reaches the deeper tissues

A. 1 and 2   B. 1 and 3   C. 1, 3 and 5   D. 2 and 3   E. 2 and 4

Question 17:

Two carriages of a train collide and then start moving together in the same direction. Carriage 1 has mass 12,000 kg and moves at 5ms^{-1} before the collision. Carriage 2 has mass 8,000 kg and is stationary before the collision. What is the velocity of the two carriages after the collision?

A. 2 ms^{-1} B. 3 ms^{-1} C. 4 ms^{-1} D. 4.5 ms^{-1} E. 5 ms^{-1}

Question 18:

Which of the following statements are true?

1. Control rods are used to absorb electrons in a nuclear reactor to control the chain reaction
2. Nuclear fusion is commonly used as an energy source
3. An alpha particle is comprised of two protons and two neutrons and is the same as a helium nucleus
4. When $^{14}_{6}C$ undergoes beta decay, an electron and $^{14}_{7}N$ are produced
5. Beta particles are less ionising than gamma rays and more ionising than alpha particles

A. 1 and 2   D. 3, 4 and 5
B. 1 and 3   E. None of the statements are true
C. 3 and 4

Question 19:

Simplify fully: $\dfrac{(3x^{1/2})^3}{3x^2}$

A. $\dfrac{3x}{\sqrt{x}}$ B. $\dfrac{9}{x}$ C. $3x^{1/2}$ D. $3x\sqrt{x}$ E. $\dfrac{9}{\sqrt{x}}$

Question 20:

Which of the following are true?

1. Lightning, as well as nitrogen-fixing bacteria, converts nitrogen gas to nitrate compounds
2. Decomposers return nitrogen to the soil as ammonia
3. The shells of marine animals contain calcium carbonate, which is derived from dietary carbon
4. Nitrogen is used to make the amino acids found in proteins

A. 1 only   D. 2, 3 and 4
B. 1 and 2   E. They are all true
C. 2 and 3

Question 21:

Write $\dfrac{\sqrt{20}-2}{\sqrt{5}+3}$ in the form: $p\sqrt{5} + q$

A. $2\sqrt{5} - 4$ B. $3\sqrt{5} - 4$ C. $3\sqrt{5} - 5$ D. $4\sqrt{5} - 6$ E. $5\sqrt{5} + 4$

Question 22:

Which of the following statements are false?
1. Simple molecules do not conduct electricity because there are no free electrons and there is no overall charge
2. The carbon and silicon atoms in silica are arranged in a giant lattice structure and it has a very high melting point
3. Ionic compounds do not conduct electricity when dissolved in water or when melted because the ions are too far apart
4. Alloys are harder than pure metals

A. 1 and 2   B. 1, 2 and 4   C. 1, 2, 3 and 4   D. 2 and 4   E. 3 only

Question 23:
The graph below shows a circle with radius 5 and centre (0,0).

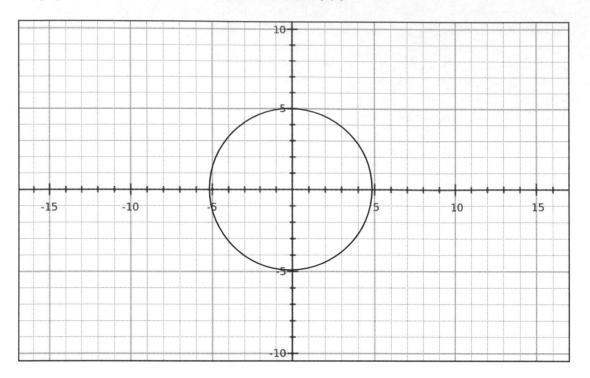

What are the values of x when the line y=3x-5 meets the circle?

A. x=0 or x=3
B. x=0 or x=3.5
C. x=1 or x=3.5
D. x=1.5 or x=-3
E. x=1.5 or x=-2

Question 24:
Which if the following statements regarding heat transfer are correct?

1. Heat energy is transferred from hotter to colder places by conduction because particles in liquid and gases move more quickly when heated
2. Liquid and gas particles in hot areas are less dense than in cold areas
3. Radiation does not need particles to travel
4. Dull surfaces are good at absorbing and poor at reflecting infrared radiation, whereas shiny surfaces are poor at absorbing, but good at reflecting infrared radiation

A. 1 and 2   B. 1, 2 and 4   C. 2 and 3   D. 2 and 4   E. 4 only

Question 25:
The following points refer to the halogens:

1. Iodine is a grey solid and can be used to sterilise wounds. It forms a purple vapour when warmed
2. The melting and boiling points increase as you go up the group
3. Fluorine is very dangerous and reacts instantly with iron wool, whereas iodine has to be strongly heated as well as the iron wool for a reaction to occur and the reaction is slow
4. When bromine is added to sodium chloride, the bromine displaces chlorine from sodium chloride
5. The hydrogen atom and chlorine atom in hydrogen chloride are joined by a covalent bond

Which of the above statements are false?

A. 1, 3 and 5   B. 1, 2 and 3   C. 2 and 4   D. 3 only   E. 3, 4 and 5

Question 26:

Consider the triangle below where BE=4cm, EC=2cm and AC=9cm.
What is the length of side DE?

A. 4cm

B. 5.5cm

C. 6cm

D. 7.5cm

E. 8cm

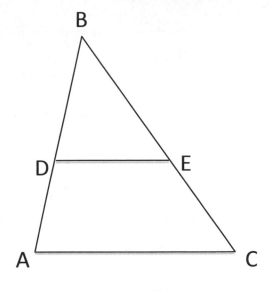

Question 27:

A ball is projected vertically upwards with an initial speed of 40 ms^{-1}. What is the maximum height reached? (Take gravity to be 10 ms^{-2} and assume negligible air resistance).

A. 25m

B. 45m

C. 60m

D. 75m

E. 80m

END OF SECTION

Section 3

1) 'The NHS should not treat obese patients'

Explain what this statement means. Argue to the contrary, that we **should** treat obese patients. To what extent do you agree with this statement?

2) 'We should all become vegetarian'

Explain what this statement means. Argue to the contrary, that we **should not** all become vegetarian. To what extent do you agree with this statement?

3) 'Certain vaccines should be mandatory'

Explain what this statement means. Argue to the contrary, that vaccines **should not** be mandatory. To what extent do you agree with this statement?

4) 'Compassion is the most important quality of a healthcare professional'

Explain what this statement means. Argue to the contrary, that there are more important qualities than compassion for health professionals. To what extent do you agree with this statement?

END OF PAPER

ANSWERS

Answer Key

Question	Answer	Question	Answer	Question	Answer	Question	Answer
1	A	51	A	101	C	151	B
2	C	52	B	102	D	152	C
3	A	53	D	103	C	153	B
4	A	54	A	104	E&F	154	C
5	C	55	C	105	D	155	D
6	D	56	D	106	C	156	D
7	D	57	C	107	B	157	C
8	A	58	A	108	A	158	C
9	A	59	D	109	C	159	C
10	B	60	D	110	B	160	A
11	D	61	D	111	C	161	C
12	C	62	B	112	D	162	A
13	D	63	C	113	B & C	163	E
14	A	64	B	114	B	164	C
15	D	65	B	115	B & D	165	B
16	A	66	D	116	D	166	B
17	B	67	E	117	F	167	C
18	B	68	C	118	D	168	B
19	A	69	D	119	D	169	C
20	B	70	D	120	B & D	170	E
21	A	71	F	121	B	171	D
22	C	72	B	122	C	172	C
23	C	73	A	123	C	173	B
24	A	74	C	124	D	174	E
25	B	75	D	125	B	175	D
26	A	76	A	126	C	176	A
27	D	77	B	127	B	177	C
28	A	78	D	128	E	178	A
29	A	79	A	129	B	179	B
30	B	80	B	130	D	180	C
31	A	81	E	131	D	181	A
32	C & E	82	B	132	C	182	B
33	B	83	C	133	C	183	F
34	B	84	C	134	B	184	C
35	D	85	D	135	C	185	E
36	A	86	C	136	C	186	B
37	A	87	C	137	C	187	B
38	B	88	A	138	D	188	C
39	D	89	C	139	C	189	C
40	A	90	C	140	E	190	C
41	B	91	A	141	D	191	F
42	B	92	A	142	C	192	C
43	E	93	D	143	A	193	A
44	B	94	B	144	A	194	C
45	D	95	E	145	C & E	195	A
46	E	96	E	146	D	196	B
47	B	97	D	147	D	197	B
48	D	98	E	148	B	198	E
49	B	99	E	149	D	199	E
50	D	100	A	150	A	200	C

Question	Answer	Question	Answer	Question	Answer	Question	Answer
201	B	251	C	301	A	351	D
202	C	252	B	302	F	352	A
203	D	253	C	303	F	353	B
204	C	254	D	304	A	354	C
205	B	255	A	305	C	355	C
206	D	256	D	306	C	356	A
207	C	257	B	307	D	357	B
208	C	258	D	308	B	358	C
209	A	259	D	309	A	359	B
210	C	260	C	310	D	360	F
211	B	261	C	311	D	361	E
212	E	262	C	312	A	362	F
213	D	263	A	313	C	363	A
214	C	264	B	314	A	364	A
215	B	265	D	315	E	365	A
216	E	266	B	316	D	366	C
217	C	267	A	317	A	367	A
218	C	268	D	318	D	368	A
219	E	269	B	319	D	369	F
220	B	270	C	320	B	370	E
221	D	271	B	321	A	371	D
222	C	272	D	322	E	372	B
223	D	273	F	323	D	373	D
224	E	274	C	324	F	374	A
225	B	275	B	325	F	375	F
226	C	276	A	326	F	376	D
227	C	277	B	327	D	377	F
228	D	278	A	328	C	378	A
229	B	279	C	329	E	379	A
230	E	280	C	330	E	380	D
231	C	281	C	331	C	381	C
232	A	282	C	332	C	382	B
233	C	283	C	333	A	383	F
234	C	284	D	334	E	384	A
235	D	285	C	335	A	385	C
236	A	286	D	336	A	386	C
237	D	287	C	337	C	387	E
238	D	288	C	338	A	388	F
239	C	289	C	339	F	389	G
240	C	290	C	340	H	390	F
241	C	291	E	341	C	391	A
242	E	292	C	342	H	392	C
243	D	293	C	343	B	393	B
244	C	294	D & E	344	F	394	D
245	B	295	C	345	E	395	B
246	E	296	C	346	B	396	E
247	C	297	C	347	A	397	B
248	B	298	C	348	I	398	ANSWERS
249	E	299	D	349	C	399	D
250	D	300	C	350	B	400	D

Question	Answer	Question	Answer	Question	Answer	Question	Answer
401	D	451	F	501	D	551	D
402	E	452	A	502	B	552	A
403	E	453	D	503	G	553	F
404	B	454	E	504	D	554	D
405	B	455	G	505	A	555	A
406	G	456	C	506	E	556	D
407	A	457	D	507	C	557	D
408	B	458	E	508	D	558	F
409	E	459	D	509	D	559	D
410	B	460	C	510	C	560	C
411	D	461	F	511	D	561	B
412	A	462	B	512	F	562	C
413	A	463	C	513	B	563	A
414	B	464	G	514	A	564	A
415	C	465	D	515	C	565	C
416	B	466	E	516	C	566	B
417	A	467	A	517	G	567	D
418	F	468	E	518	C	568	C
419	A	469	G	519	B	569	A
420	E	470	E	520	B	570	C
421	F	471	H	521	E	571	C
422	H	472	E	522	C	572	C
423	B	473	G	523	E	573	B
424	E	474	D	524	E	574	D
425	D	475	E	525	D	575	E
426	A	476	D	526	B	576	D
427	D	477	G	527	C	577	D
428	D	478	F	528	C	578	B
429	C	479	B	529	C	579	E
430	G	480	A	530	E	580	E
431	E	481	C	531	A	581	B
432	D	482	G	532	C	582	C
433	D	483	D	533	E	583	A
434	F	484	D	534	E	584	C
435	C	485	E	535	C	585	B
436	A	486	B	536	E	586	B
437	B	487	A	537	E	587	B
438	E	488	E	538	E	588	C
439	C	489	D	539	B	589	C
440	D	490	F	540	C	590	A
441	C	491	E	541	B	591	C
442	C	492	F	542	B	592	D
443	A	493	B	543	C	593	C
444	C	494	C	544	D	594	D
445	B	495	D	545	C	595	A
446	B	496	F	546	B	596	C
447	B	497	E	547	A	597	B
448	E	498	C	548	F	598	B
449	D	499	C	549	D	599	A
450	C	500	B	550	A	600	C

Mock Paper Answer Key

	Paper A				Paper B				Paper C		
	Section 1		**Section 2**		**Section 1**		**Section 2**		**Section 1**		**Section 2**
1	C	1	B	1	B	1	D	1	D	1	D
2	D	2	D	2	C	2	E	2	D	2	C
3	B	3	A	3	C	3	E	3	B	3	C
4	D	4	E	4	E	4	E	4	B	4	C
5	D	5	D	5	D	5	D	5	B	5	C
6	B	6	B	6	B	6	A	6	C	6	E
7	B	7	D	7	D	7	A	7	D	7	B
8	D	8	E	8	C	8	D	8	D	8	B
9	C	9	D	9	A	9	A	9	A	9	A
10	E	10	D	10	A	10	D	10	C	10	C
11	E	11	B	11	E	11	A	11	D	11	D
12	D	12	E	12	D	12	B	12	D	12	D
13	E	13	D	13	A	13	C	13	E	13	B
14	D	14	C	14	D	14	A	14	A	14	C
15	E	15	B	15	E	15	D	15	E	15	E
16	A	16	A	16	B	16	B	16	C	16	C
17	D	17	E	17	A	17	C	17	E	17	B
18	B	18	B	18	A	18	D	18	E	18	C
19	C	19	C	19	E	19	D	19	C	19	E
20	B	20	A	20	E	20	E	20	C	20	E
21	D	21	C	21	D	21	C	21	D	21	A
22	E	22	B	22	E	22	E	22	B	22	E
23	D	23	C	23	A	23	E	23	D	23	A
24	E	24	B	24	B	24	D	24	B	24	D
25	C	25	A	25	B	25	D	25	A	25	C
26	C	26	B	26	B	26	B	26	A	26	C
27	C	27	C	27	D	27	C	27	B	27	E
28	B			28	C			28	B		
29	B			29	B			29	D		
30	C			30	E			30	C		
31	C			31	E			31	D		
32	B			32	C			32	B		
33	E			33	A			33	E		
34	D			34	D			34	B		
35	A			35	C			35	B		
								36	E		

Mock Paper: Raw to Scaled Scores

	Section 1									Section 2					
1	1	11	2.8	21	5.4	31	8.3		1	1	11	3.5	21	6.6
2	1	12	3.0	22	5.7	32	8.5		2	1	12	3.7	22	6.9
3	1	13	3.2	23	6.0	33	8.7		3	1.3	13	4	23	7.3
4	1	14	3.5	24	6.3	34	9		4	1.6	14	4.3	24	7.6
5	1.2	15	3.7	25	6.6	35	9		5	1.9	15	4.6	25	8
6	1.5	16	4.0	26	6.9				6	2.2	16	5	26	8.5
7	1.8	17	4.2	27	7.1				7	2.5	17	5.3	27	9
8	2.0	18	4.5	28	7.4				8	2.8	18	5.6		
9	2.3	19	4.8	29	7.7				9	3.0	19	5.9		
10	2.5	20	5.1	30	8.0				10	3.2	20	6.2		

Worked Answers

Question 1: A
Whilst **B**, **C** and **D** may be true, they are not completely stated, **A** is clearly stated and so is the correct answer.

Question 2: C
The main argument of the first paragraph is to propose the point that it is more society that controls gender behaviour not genetics. **A** and **D** do not indicate either as they only allude to the end result of gender behaviour and so are incorrect. Hormonal effects are not mentioned in the first paragraph and so **B** is incorrect. **C** would undermine the argument that society *predominately* controls gender, and so is correct.

Question 3: A
B, **C** and **D** are not stated and so are incorrect. **A** is directly stated and so is correct.

Question 4: A
B and **D** are contraindicated by the statement and so are incorrect. **C** could be true but implies children always like the same thing as their same-gendered parent irrelevant of how they are treated as a child, which is contrary to the statement and so is not correct. **A** is correct as is the overall message.

Question 5: C
D may help prevent problems with sexual identity but does not prevent stereotyping and so is incorrect. **A** is not stated, and **B** is implied but not stated and so are incorrect. **C** is the end message of how to prevent gender stereotyping and so is correct.

Question 6: D
A, **B** and **C** may be true but are not mentioned in the statement and so are incorrect. The statement implies that children born with different external organs to those that their sex chromosomes would match may find it difficult to accept this difference and be uncomfortable.

Question 7: D
The text states that 'Those who regularly took 30-minute naps were more than twice as likely to remember simple words such as those of new toys.' Which means those who napped were twice as likely to remember teddy's name than the 5% who did not, 5% x 2 = 10%, which would be twice as likely, ruling out **A** and **B**. But being 'more than twice' the only possible answer is **D**.

Question 8: A
The answer is to work out 10% (the percentage of napping toddlers more likely to suffer night disturbances) of 75% (the percentage of toddlers who regularly nap). Hence 10 % of 75% is 7.5%.

Question 9: A
B, **C** and **D** may be true but there is nothing in the text to support them. **A** is suggested, as the passage states 'non-napping counterparts, who also had higher incidences of memory impairment, behavioural problems and learning difficulties'. If the impaired memory were the cause, as opposed to the result, of irregular sleeping then it would offer an alternative reason why those who nap less remember less.

Question 10: B
A and **C** are possible implications but not stated and so are incorrect. It is said that parents cite napping having 'the benefits of their child having a regular routine' so hence **B** is more correct than **D** as it refers to the benefit to the toddlers' rather than the parents.

Question 11: D
B, if true would counteract the conclusion, as it would imply that, the study is skewed. The same is true of **C**, which if true would imply unreliable results as the toddler sample are all the same age within a year, but not within a few weeks. **A**, if true, would not provide any additional support to the conclusion and so is incorrect. **D** if true would provide the most support for the conclusion as it proposes using groups with a higher incidence of napping in comparison to those with a lower incidence.

Question 12: C

Although it can be argued that **A, B, D** and **E** are true they are not the best answer to demonstrate a flaw in Tom's father's argument. **C** is the best because it accounts for other factors determining success for the Geography A-level exam such as aptitude for the subject.

Question 13: D

A is never stated and is incorrect. **B** and **C** are referred to being 'many people's' beliefs, and are cited as others' opinions not an argument supported by evidence in the passage, and so are not valid conclusions. It is implied that the NHS may have to reduce its services in the future, some of which could be fertility treatments hence **D** is the most correct answer.

Question 14: A

C does not severely affect the strength of the argument, as it is only relevant to the length of the time taken for the effects of the argument to come into place.

D is incorrect, as people breaking speed limits already would not negate the argument that speed limits should be removed, but could even be seen as supporting it. These people may count as the 'dangerous drivers' who would be ultimately weeded out of the population.

B may affect part of the argument's logic (as it undermines the idea that dangerous drivers are born to dangerous drivers), but the final conclusion that dangerous drivers will end up killing only themselves still stands, and so the ultimate population of only safe drivers may be obtained. The fact that one dead dangerous driver could have produced a safe one does not necessarily challenge the main point of this argument.

A if true would most weaken the argument as it states that fast driver is more likely to harm others and not the driver itself, which would negate the whole argument.

Question 15: D

Whilst is it stated that the Government assesses risk it is not described as an obligation, hence **A** is incorrect. The overall conclusion of the statement is that on balance the Government was justified in not spending money on flooding preparation, as it was unlikely to occur, so **C, B** and **E** are incorrect and **D** is correct.

Question 16: A

C is incorrect and **D** is a possible course of action rather than a conclusion. **B** and **E** are possible inferences but not the conclusion of the statement. The overall conclusion of the statement is that the way that children interact has changed to the solitary act of playing computer games.

Question 17: B

The passage does state that in this case the £473 million could have been put to better use, however, there is no mention that no drug should ever be stockpiled for a similar possible pandemic. The passage discusses the lack of evidence behind Tamiflu and therefore is stating that in a situation where there is a lack of evidence, there may not be justification for stockpiling millions of pounds worth of the drug. Stockpiling in the case of drugs with high effectiveness is not discussed so we should not assume this is a generic argument against preparation for any pandemic and stockpiling of any drug.

Question 18: B

The passage discusses the fact that unhealthy eating is associated with other aspects of an unhealthy lifestyle so the argument that tackling only the unhealthy eating aspect does not logically follow. The other statements are all possible reasons why the solution given may not be optimal, but are not directly referred to in the passage.

Question 19: A

This is a tricky question in which **A, B, C** and **D** are all true. However, the question asks for the conclusion of the passage, which is best represented by **A**.

B is a premise that gives justification for why the elderly should take care of themselves and **C** provides a justification for why they may not.

D is implied in the text but statement **A** is explicitly stated.

E is incorrect as the passage implies that people should spend the money that they have in old age, not stop saving altogether.

Question 20: B

The passage states stem cell research is an area where there are possible high financial and personal gains, however there is no mention of these being the main driving factors in either this area of research or others.

Although rivalry between groups may be a reason driving publishing, this is not mentioned in the passage.

The image discrepancies were in only one paper but the passage implies the protocol and replication problems were in both papers.

Question 21: A

D actually weakens the argument, and is therefore not a conclusion. C is simply a fact stated to introduce the argument, and is not a conclusion. B is a reason given in the passage to support the main conclusion. If we accept B as being true, it helps support the statement in A. E is not discussed in the passage. A is the main conclusion of this passage

Question 22: C

The passage describes improved safety features and better brakes in cars, and concludes that this means the road limit could be increased to 80mph without causing more road fatalities. However, if C is not true, this conclusion no longer follows on from this reasoning. At no point is it stated that C is true, so C is therefore the assumption in the passage. The statements in B and D are not *required* to be true for the argument's conclusion to lead on from its reasoning. A is a statement which is strengthened by this passage, and is not an assumption from the passage. E is not relevant to the conclusion or mentioned in the passage.

Question 23: C

Answers A and D are both reasons given to explain fingerprints under the theory of evolution, and contribute towards the notion given in C, that they do not offer support to intelligent design. Thus, A and D are reasons given in the passage, and C is the main conclusion. B is simply a fact stated to introduce the passage, whilst E actually contradicts something mentioned in the argument (namely that Intelligent Design is religious-based, and scientifically discredited). Neither of these options are conclusions.

Question 24: A

Answers C, D and E obviously present ways in which the conclusions drawn from the study could be wrong, without any mistakes being made by those carrying out the study, and thus are potential reasons. B is also a potential reason, because those with a low alcohol consumption could have many other risk factors for cancer, and end up with a higher *overall* risk. If the study does not take account of these, it could produce erroneous conclusions. A cannot be a valid reason because the passage *states* that it is *'proven'* that alcohol increases the risk of cancer. Thus, we must accept this as true, so A is not a potential reason.

Question 25: B

The passage states that the average speed *including* time spent stood still at stations was 115mph. Thus, A is incorrect, as the stopping points have already been included in the calculations of journey time. Similarly, the passage states that the train completes its journey at Kings cross, so D is incorrect. C is not correct because we have been given the total length of the journey. Whether it took the most direct route is irrelevant. E is completely irrelevant and does not affect the answer. B is an assumption, because we have only been given the *scheduled* time of departure. If the train was delayed in leaving, it would not have left at 3:30, and so would have arrived *after* 5:30.

Question 26: A

The argument discusses healthcare spending in England and Scotland, and whether this means the population in Scotland will be healthier. It says nothing about whether this system is fair, and does not mention the expenditure in Wales. Thus, C and D are incorrect. Similarly, the argument makes no reference to whether healthcare spending should be increased, so B is incorrect. E is true but not the main message of the passage. The passage does suggest that the higher healthcare expenditure per person in Scotland does not necessarily mean that the Scottish population will be healthier, so A is a conclusion from this passage.

Question 27: D

C is an incorrect statement, as the passage says that Polio *hasn't* been eradicated yet. A and B are reasons given to support the conclusion, which is that given in D. E, meanwhile, is an opinion given in the passage, and is not relevant to the passage's conclusion.

Question 28: A

This passage provides various positive points of the Y chromosome, before describing how all of this means it is a fantastic tool for genetic analysis. Thus, the conclusion is clearly that given in **A**. The statement in **B** is a further point given to provide evidence of its utility, as stated in the passage. Thus **B** is not a conclusion in itself, but further evidence to support the main conclusion, given in **A**. **C** is also a reason given to support the conclusion in **A**, whilst **D** is simply a fact stated to introduce the passage. As for **E,** there is no mention of Genghis Khan's children (only his descendants).

Question 29: A

Answers **C** and **E** are not valid assumptions because the argument has *stated* that a patient *must* be treated with antibiotics for a bacterial infection to clear. B is not a flaw, because this does not affect whether the antibiotics would clear the infection if it were bacterial. D is an irrelevant statement, and also disagrees with a stated phrase in the passage (that antibiotics are required to clear a bacterial infection). A is a valid flaw, because the passage does not say that antibiotics are *sufficient* or *guaranteed* to clear a bacterial infection, simply that they are *necessary*. Thus, it is possible that the infection *is* bacterial but the antibiotics failed to clear it.

Question 30: B

A, C and D, if accepted as true, all contribute towards supporting the statement given in **B**, which is a valid conclusion given in this passage. Thus, **A**, **C** and **D** are all reasons given to support the main conclusion, which is the statement given in **B**. **E** is not a valid conclusion, as the passage makes no reference to action that should be taken relating to smoking, it simply discusses its position as the main risk factor for lung cancer.

Question 31: A

D is only given as a method, with no mention of its effectiveness. We do not know if **C** is true because it is not stated. **B** is not discussed in the passage. Whilst statement **E** is true, it is supporting evidence for the conclusion, not the conclusion itself.

Question 32: C & E

Whilst **A** and **B** may be true, cost is not mentioned as a deterring factor and we are only concerned with use in the UK, so they are irrelevant. Whether cannabis was the only class C drug is not important to the argument so **D** is not correct. **C** and **E** are the correct answers because the statement concerns the use of cannabis in the UK, directly stating use will decrease from people knowing it has been upgraded to a more dangerous category and from fearing longer prison sentences from higher-class drugs.

Question 33: B

Whilst **A** and **C** may be true, they are not part of the argument. **D** is a possible, but cannot be logically proposed from the information above. **E** would be a flaw if the argument were 'all levels of sports teams reduce bullying' but the passage explicitly states 'well-performing' teams. Hence **B** is correct as it undermines the whole argument, reversing the cause and effect.

Question 34: B

Options **A, C** and **D** do not directly weaken the argument as if any 16 year olds were buying/drinking alcohol (whether the minority or majority) – police would still be spending time catching them. The suggested benefit to reduce police time spent catching underage drinkers would be negated if **B** were true, hence it is the correct answer.

Question 35: D

A is an interpretation of the last sentence and doesn't accurately summarise the argument in the passage. **B** is untrue as there is no mention of if the government can afford to give grants or not. **C** and **E** are incorrect as the passage only talks about small businesses. **D** is correct as it best summarises the change in government policy regarding small businesses.

Question 36: A

The statement discusses a case that was reported, but aims to argue that there may be important errors occurring everyday in medicine that go unreported. Option A if true, would significantly weaken this argument as would negate it being a possibility. **B, C, D** and **E** may be true, but they do not negate the argument – if doctors are trained, accidents like the above may still occur. Operations that are successful do not affect those that are not, nor do unavoidable errors have any relation to avoidable ones. That the patient may have died without these errors similarly does not mean that errors, when they do occur, should not be considered errors.

Question 37: A

The main point of the statement is to highlight that although there are numerous safety precautions in place to protect patients, when the weaknesses in these precautions align big errors can occur. So **A** is correct. While **E**, **C, B** and **D** may well be true, they are not the overall conclusion of the statement.

Question 38: B

Though not the first to be cited, the original error is cited as being the incorrect copying of the sidedness of the kidney to be removed, hence **B** is the correct option. The other options represent errors that in the 'Swiss cheese model' would have not been allowed to occur if the original had not taken place.

Question 39: D

In this instance the 'tip of the iceberg' refers to the number of medical errors reported, implying there may be a significantly larger proportion that go unreported, hence the correct option is **D**, and not **B**.

Question 40: A

The description given about the consultant's performance versus emotional arousal, is described as initially increasing then eventually decreasing over time, which is best represented by graph **A.**

Question 41: B

The consultant says that the 'public perception is that medical knowledge increases steadily over time' which is best represented by graph **B.** The consultant says the regarding the acquisition of medical knowledge, 'many doctors [reach] their peak in the middle of their careers', which is best described by the graph **D.**

Question 42: B

Obesity is not mentioned in the passage, so **E** is incorrect. There is no mention exercise specifically as it relates to old age, so **A** and **D** are also wrong. The diseases associated with lack of exercise are not specifically stated to cause early death, only that they are associated with older people, so **C** is also incorrect. The passage does, however, argue that lack of exercise is associated with illness, and so exercise would be linked to a lack of illness, or good health, so **B** is correct.

Question 43: E

The preference of women to have their babies at hospital versus home is not commented upon so **B** is incorrect. **F** is never inferred, only that midwives are capable of assisting in normal births and assessing when women need to be transferred to be to hospital, so it is wrong. **A** and **D** are possible inferences at certain points but not conclusions of the statement. **C** is never implied, only that normal home births are no more risky than those in hospital. The overall conclusion of the statement is that the home births should be encouraged where possible as they are not more risky in the cases of normal births, and hospital births are an unsustainable cost in cash-strapped NHS.

Question 44: B

While **A, C** and **D** would, if true, make the practicalities of increasing home births more difficult they would not weaken the argument as **B** would. Where the statement's whole argument rests on home births being as safe as hospital **B**, if true, would negate this.

Question 45: D

The statement says 'With the increase in availability of health resources we now, too often, use services such as a full medical team for a process that women have been completing single-handedly for thousands of years.' Thus implying **D**, 'excessive availability of health resources' is the cause of 'medicalisation of childbirth'.

Question 46: E

1 and **3** identify weaknesses in the argument. If campaigns are what help keep deaths by fire low, they can be seen as 'necessary', and their necessity may be proven by the promisingly low fire-related mortalities. If there are more people with hernias than in fires, more people can possibly die from hernias, but this does not mean the fires are less dangerous to the (fewer) individuals involved in them. **2** is irrelevant, as the argument is about how dangerous fires are in their entirety, not in relation to their constituent parts. Therefore **E**, '1 and 3 only', is correct.

Question 47: B

Since 'some footballers' that like Maths are not necessarily the same 'some' who like History we can exclude **A** and **D**. Equally, while **C** may or may not be true, we are not given any information about rugby players' preference for History, so it is incorrect. We know that all basketball players like English and Chemistry, and that none of them like History, but as we do not know about a third subject they may like **E** is incorrect. We know all of the rugby players like English and Geography and some of them Chemistry, hence there must be a section of rugby players that like all three subjects so **B** is correct.

Question 48: D

The passage discusses the problems surrounding controlling drugs, and focuses on the rapid manufacture of new 'legal highs': it is therefore implied that this is the current major problem. The passage also suggests that as the authorities cannot keep up with drugs manufacture, the legality of drugs doesn't reflect their risks.

1 is incorrect as the passage says health professionals feel legality is less relevant now, but it doesn't say that it is not still important. **3** is incorrect as the last sentence says a potential problem of legal highs is that the risks are not as clear, which contradicts the statement that the public are not concerned about any risks.

Question 49: B

The passage is discussing how banning those with the mentioned medical conditions from mountain climbing are *essential* to ensuring safety. It does not claim that this is *sufficient* to ensure safety, simply that it is *necessary*. Thus **C** is irrelevant, as risks from other activities do not affect the risk from mountain climbing. **D** is also irrelevant, because the argument discusses how it is essential to ensure safety of people on WilderTravel holidays, so those using other companies are irrelevant. **A** is an irrelevant statement because the passage is discussing what should be done *to ensure safety*, not whether this is the morally correct course of action. Thus, a discussion of whether people should choose to accept the risks is not relevant. However, **B** *is* a flaw, because the guidelines only mention those with *severe* allergies, so thinking those with less severe allergies are in danger is a false assumption that has been made by the directors.

Question 50: D

The hospital director's comments make it abundantly clear that the most important aspect of the new candidate is good surgery skills, because the hospital's surgery success record requires improvement. If we accept his reasoning as being true, then it is clear that the candidate who is most proficient at surgery should be hired, and patient interaction should not be the deciding factor. Thus, Candidate 3 should be hired, as suggested by **D**.

Question 51: A

Answers **B** and **D** are irrelevant to the argument's conclusion, since the argument only talks about how medical complications could be avoided *if* winter tyres were fitted. Whether this is possible (as in **B**) or whether there are other options (as in **D**) are irrelevant to this conclusion. C is not an assumption because the passage states that delays cause many complications, which could be avoided with quicker treatment. However, the argument does not state that winter tyres would allow ambulances to reach patients more quickly, so **A** is an assumption.

Question 52: B

The passage discusses how anti-vaccine campaigns cause deaths by spreading misinformation and reducing vaccination rates. It claims that therefore *in order to protect* people, we should block the campaigners from spreading such misinformation freely. Thus it is made clear that this action should be taken *because the campaigners cause deaths*, not simply because they are spreading misinformation. Thus, **B** is the principle embodied in the passage, and **C** is incorrect. **A** actually demonstrates an opposite principle, whilst **D** is a somewhat irrelevant statement, as the passage makes no reference to whether we should promote successful public health programmes.

Question 53: D

The passage states that the tumour has established its own blood supply (it says this was shown during the testing), and that a blood supply is *necessary* for the tumour to grow beyond a few centimetres. Thus **A** and **B** are not assumptions. **C** is not an assumption, as it actually disagrees with something the passage has implied. The passage has actually said that action *must* be taken, implying that something *can* be done to stop the tumour. However, at no point has it been said that a blood supply is *sufficient* for a tumour to grow larger than a few centimetres. If this is not true, then the argument's conclusion that we should expect the tumour to grow larger than a few centimetres, and that action must be taken, no longer readily follows on from its reasoning. It is possible the tumour will still fail to grow larger than a few centimetres. Thus, **D** is an assumption in the passage, and a flaw in its reasoning.

Question 54: A

D is incorrect, as the passage has stated the runners are people running to raise money for the GNAA. **B** and **C**, meanwhile, are incorrect as the passage is only talking about whether the GNAA *will be able to* get a new helicopter. Thus, references to whether it wishes to, or whether this is the best use of money, are irrelevant. **A**, however, is an assumption on the part of the passage's writer. The passage says that the GNAA will be able to get a helicopter if £500,000 is raised, but this does *not* mean that it won't be able to if the £500,000 is not raised by the runners. It could well be that they secure funding from elsewhere, or that prices drop. The money being *sufficient* to get a new helicopter does not mean it is *necessary* to get one.

Question 55: C

B and **D** somewhat strengthen this argument, suggesting that more people going on courses leads to better growth, and that people who have gone on these courses are more attractive to employers. **A** does not really affect the strength of the argument, as the current rate of growth does not affect whether government subsidies would lead to increased growth. **C**, however, weakens the argument significantly by suggesting that people would not be more likely to attend the courses if the government were to subsidise them, as the cost has little effect on the numbers of people attending.

Question 56: D

B is simply a fact stated in the passage. It does not draw upon any other reasons given in the passage, so it is not a conclusion. **C** is not a conclusion because it does not follow on from the passage's reasoning. The passage discusses what should be done *if* Pluto is to be classified as a planet, it does not make any mention of whether this *should* happen. **A** and **D** are both valid conclusions from the passage. However, on closer examination we can see that if we accept **A** as being true, it gives us good reason to believe the statement in **D**. Thus, **D** is the *main* conclusion in the passage, whilst **A** is an *intermediate* conclusion, which goes on to support this main conclusion.

Question 57: C

A, **B** and **D** would all affect whether the calculation of the Glasgow train's arrival time is correct, but none are assumptions because all of these things have been stated in the passage. However, the passage has *not* stated that the trains will travel at the same speed, and if this is not true, then the conclusion that the Glasgow train will arrive at 8:30pm is no longer valid. Thus, **C** is an assumption.

Question 58: A

C can actually be seen to be probably untrue, as the passage mentions a need to escape immune responses, suggesting that the immune system *can* tackle these cells. **E** is true but not representative of the main argument made in the passage. **B** and **D** are not *definitely* true. The passage mentions several *essential* steps that *must* occur, but this does not mean that they are *sufficient* for carcinogenesis to occur, or guaranteed to allow it. Equally, the passage makes no reference to multiple mechanisms by which carcinogenesis can occur. It could be there is only one pattern in which these steps can occur. **A**, however, can be reliably concluded, because the passage does mention several steps that are *essential* for carcinogenesis to occur.

Question 59: D

Answers **A** and **C** are stated in the passage (the passage states 'deservedly known'), so these can be reliably concluded. **B** can also be concluded, as it is stated that in over 50% of cancers, a loss of functional P53 is identified. **D** however, cannot be concluded, as the passage simply states that any cell that has a mutation in P53 *is at risk* of developing dangerous mutations. Thus, it cannot be concluded that a given cell *will* develop such a mutation.

Question 60: D

D is not an assumption because Sam's calculations are based on the *cost per 1000 miles*, not on a given amount of fuel being used up. Thus, he has *not* assumed anything about whether the fuel usage is the same for each car. All of the others are assumptions, which have not been considered. Each of these will affect the total saving he will make if they are not true. For example, if the Diesel car costs £100 more than the Petrol car, the total saving will be £1700, *not* £1800 as calculated.

Question 61: D

The passage discusses how alcohol is more dangerous than cannabis, and states that this highlights the gross inconsistencies in UK drugs policy. Thus, **D** is the main conclusion of the passage, whilst **A** is a reason given to support this conclusion. The passage simply highlights that the policy is grossly inconsistent, and does not mention whether it should be changed, or how (whether alcohol should be banned or cannabis allowed).

Thus, **B** and **C** are not valid conclusions from this passage. The fact alcohol is freely advertised only mentioned briefly in the passage to add strength to the argument that alcohol is more accessible than cannabis, but no judgment is made on whether this should not be so, so **E** is also not a valid conclusion from this passage.

Question 62: B

The passage discusses how if first aid supplies were available, many accidents could be avoided. B correctly points out that this is a flaw – first aid supplies may help treat accidents and reduce the prevalence of *injuries and deaths*, but there is no reason why first aid supplies should reduce the incidence of *accidents*. Answers **C** and **D** are irrelevant, since the argument is talking about how first aid supplies could reduce *accidents*, not *injuries* or deaths. Thus, discussing cases in which they could not treat the injuries, or whether they need other components to do so is irrelevant. Equally A is irrelevant, as the argument is simply talking about what could happen *if* first aid supplies were stocked in homes, and makes no reference to whether this is financially viable.

Question 63: C

Answers **A** and **D** are not flaws because the passage does not conclude the things mentioned in these. No mention is made to the safety of the drug, and the argument only states that it is thought the compound *may* be of use in combating cancer. No premature conclusions are drawn, only suggestions are made. B is not a flaw because we can see that the experiments *may* produce misleading results if the wrong solutions are used, suggesting that DNA replication is inhibited even if it is not. C, however, is a valid flaw because the argument erroneously concludes that the wrong solutions must have been used when it says the experiments *do not reflect what is actually happening*. This clearly indicates a conviction that the wrong solutions were used, which does not follow on from the experiments being old.

Question 64: B

The passage has not said anything about who scored the winning goal, so **A** is not an assumption. **C** is also incorrect, because the passage states that South Shields won the game. B correctly identifies that whilst beating South Shields was *sufficient* to win the league, it was *not* necessary. If Rotherham wins their other 2 games, they will still win the league, so **B** demonstrates an assumption in the passage. **D** is not relevant, as it does not affect the erroneous nature of the claim that Rotherham *will not* win the league having lost the match to South Shields.

Question 65: B

C and D actually strengthen or reinforce the CEO's reasoning, with C suggesting as time progresses Middlesbrough will have more and more people compared to Warrington, whilst D suggests that the market share in Warrington may not be as high as suggested, adding further reasons to build in Middlesbrough. A somewhat weakens the CEO's argument, but it is not a flaw in the reasoning, because the CEO is simply talking about how Middlesbrough will bring them within the range of more people, so the market share comment is a counterargument, not a flaw in his reasoning. B, however, is a valid flaw in this argument. Just because Warrington's population is falling, and Middlesbrough's is rising, does not necessarily mean that Middlesbrough's will be higher.

Question 66: D

1 and 2 are assumptions. The information given does *not* necessarily lead on to the conclusion that these extinction events will continue without further conservation efforts. Equally, there is nothing in the passage that says conservation efforts cannot be stepped up without increased funding. However, 3 is not an assumption, because the passage *states* that global warming has caused changed weather patterns, which have caused destruction of many habitats, which have led to many extinction events. Thus, it is given that global warming has indirectly caused these extinctions, and so the answer is **D**.

Question 67: E

The argument is suggesting that in Austria, the rail service's high passenger numbers and approval ratings are accounted for by the fact that road travel is difficult in much of Austria. It then concludes that the public subsidies have no effect. We can see that **1** instantly weakens this argument by providing evidence to the contrary, (in France, difficult road travel is not prevalent and so cannot account for the high passenger numbers/approval ratings the country possesses). 3 also weakens this conclusion by suggesting multiple factors affect the situation. This makes the conclusion based on the evidence from Austria less strong. Thus, the answer is **E**. 2 actually strengthens the argument that the public subsidies do not cause high passenger numbers/approval ratings, as Italy has high subsidies but low passenger numbers/approval ratings.

Question 68: C

A is incorrect, in 2011 24% of men and 26% of women were obese (one should not confuse this with the rates of combined obese and overweight). B is also incorrect, as what it states is true for adults; however, the figures for children aged 2-15 have changed little over the past year. D is not stated or implied by the passage. C is implied in the last two sentences of the article, and so the correct answer.

Question 69: D

Whilst the text suggests that smokers tend to have high-risk life-styles, the text does not claim that all smokers drink excessively. Some smokers might, but others might not. This differentiation is important to make.

Question 70: D

Be careful of using your own knowledge here! Whilst A and B may be true, they are not the main message of the passage. C may be true but is not discussed in the passage. E is speculative, as the passage does not say if the transplant would be a 'good alternative'. D is correct as it echoes the main message of the passage.

Question 71: F

Smoking and Diabetes are risk factors for vascular disease (not a cause). Vascular disease does not always lead to infarction. The passage does not give sufficient detail about necrotic tissue to conclude C or D.

Question 72: B

A is irrelevant to the argument's conclusion. Meanwhile E does nothing to alter the conclusion, as the fact that schools receive similar funds does not affect the fact that more funding could provide better resources, and thus improve educational attainment. C actually weakens the argument; by implying that banning the richer from using the state school system would not raise many funds, as most do not use it anyway. D does not strengthen the conclusion as stating that a gap exists does not do anything to suggest that more funding will help close it. B clearly supports the conclusion that more funding, and better resources, would help close the gap in educational attainment.

Question 73: A

D and E are irrelevant to the argument's conclusion. C is actually contradicting the argument. B is stated in the passage, so is not an assumption of the passage. A describes an assumption: the increase of DVDs does not, necessarily, cause the loss of cinema customers.

Question 74: C

The question refers to aeroplanes being the fastest form of transport, and states that this means that travelling by air will allow John to arrive as soon as possible. C correctly points out that the argument has neglected to take into account other delays induced by travelling by aeroplane. Cost and legality are irrelevant to the question, so B and E are incorrect. Meanwhile, D actually reinforces the argument, and A refers to future possible developments that will not affect John's current journey.

Question 75: D

The argument states that people should not seek to prevent spiders from entering their homes. It does not say anything about whether people should like spiders being in their home, so A is incorrect. The argument also makes no allusion to the notion of people preventing flies from entering their homes, so B is incorrect. The argument also does not mention or implies that any efforts should be made to encourage spiders to enter homes, or that they should be cultivated, so C and E are also incorrect.

Question 76: A

A correctly identifies an assumption in the argument. At no point is it stated that bacterial infections in hospitals are resulting in deaths. B, C, D and E are all valid points but they do not affect the notion that pressure for more antibiotic research would save lives. Therefore, none of these statements affect the conclusion of the argument and as such they are not assumptions in this context.

Question 77: B

The passage does not state that John disregards arguments because of the gender of the speaker, so D is incorrect. A and C are also wrong, as John states he finds women with armpit hair necessarily unattractive, so a different face or the knowledge of concealed hair would not make him find the female in question more appealing to his aesthetic. John does not state Katherine wants other women to stop shaving, so E is incorrect.

B is the correct answer, as Katherine was simply speaking about societal norms, and at no point is it said she was trying to convince John to find her, with armpit hair, attractive.

Question 78: D

A is irrelevant to the argument, which says nothing about what will happen to Medicine in the future. The argument is describing how Sunita is incorrect, and how better medicine is not responsible for a high death rate from infectious disease in third world countries, and how better medicine will actually decrease this rate. **C** is a direct contradiction to this conclusion, so is incorrect. **E** is a fact stated in the argument to explain some of its reasoning, and is not a conclusion, therefore **E** is incorrect.

Both **B** and **D** are valid conclusions from the argument. However, **B** is not the main conclusion, because the fact that 'Better medicine is not responsible for a high death rate from infectious disease in third world countries' actually supports the statement in **D**, 'Better medicine will lead to a decrease in the death rate from infectious disease in third world countries'. Therefore, **B** is an example of an intermediate conclusion in this argument, which contributes to supporting the main conclusion, which is that given in D.

Question 79: A

The statement in A, that housing prices will be higher if demand for housing is higher, is not stated in this argument. However, it is implied to be true, and if it is not true, then the argument's conclusion is not valid from the reasoning given. Therefore **A** correctly identifies an assumption in the argument. The other statements do not affect how the reasons given in the argument lead to the conclusion of the argument, and are therefore not assumptions in the argument.

Question 80: B

A and **E** are both contradictory to the argument, which concludes that because of the new research, Jellicoe motors should hire a candidate with good team-working skills. **C** refers to an irrelevant scenario, as the argument is referring to only one candidate being hired, and at no point does it state or imply that several should be hired.

B correctly identifies the conclusion of the argument that Jellicoe motors should hire a new candidate with good team-working skills in order to boost their productivity and profits. **D** meanwhile exaggerates the consequences of not following this course of action. The argument does not make any reference to the notion that Jellicoe motors will struggle to be profitable if they do not hire a candidate with good team-working skills.

Question 81: E

D is in direct contradiction to the argument, so is not the main conclusion. Meanwhile, **B** is a reason stated in the argument to explain some of the situations described. It is not a conclusion, as it does not follow on from the reasons given in the argument.

A and **E** are both valid conclusions from the argument. However, only **E** is the *main* conclusion. This is because both **A** goes on to support the statement in **E**. If bacterial resistance to current antibiotics could result in thousands of deaths, this supports the notion that the UK government must provide incentives for pharmaceutical firms to research new antibiotics if it does not wish to risk thousands of deaths.

Meanwhile, **C** appears to be another intermediate conclusion in the argument that also supports the main conclusion. However, on close inspection this is not the case. **C** refers to the UK government directly investing in new antibiotic research, whilst the argument refers to the government providing incentives for pharmaceutical firms to do so. Therefore, **C** is not a valid conclusion from the argument.

Question 82: B

E is completely irrelevant because the question is referring to an unsustainable solution *if* the UN's development targets are met, so the likelihood of them being met is irrelevant. **C** is irrelevant because they do not affect the fact that the situation would be unsustainable if everybody used the amount of water used by those in developed countries, as stated in the question. **A** is also irrelevant, as the passage does not mention price as a factor to be considered within the argument.

Meanwhile, **D** would actually strengthen the argument's conclusion.

Therefore, the answer is **B**. **B** correctly identifies that if those in developed countries use less water, it may be possible for everyone to use the same amount as these people and still be in a sustainable situation.

Question 83: C

There is no mention of treatment, so **A** is incorrect. A need to travel abroad for the post is not stated either, so **B** is incorrect. The need for a cool head is stated explicitly, but not necessarily that this be a leader, so **D** is also wrong. Other qualities are irrelevant to the argument, so **E** is also incorrect. **C** would only be relevant if there was indeed a link between 'a specific phobia' and 'a general tendency to panic'. Thus, **C** highlights the flaw: if a fear of flying does not necessitate a general disposition of panic, the argument for not hiring this employee crumbles.

Question 84: C

The passage does not suggest there are no more university places, nor does it make a distinction between the qualities of different universities, so **A** is incorrect and **D** is irrelevant. The argument does not deny the fact that people can be successful without a university education, so **B** is also wrong. **C** is correct, as the passage specifically states 'many more graduates', but not all, are equipped with better skills and better earning potential. This suggests not all degrees produce these skill-sets in their graduates, and so not all university places will create high-earning employees.

Question 85: D

B is unrelated to the argument, as other contributing factors would not negate the damaging potential of TV. Watching sport on television would not be akin to actually playing sport, so **A** is also incorrect. The possibility of eye damage is stated as caused by TV, so **C** is incorrect. However, if people watch television *and* partake in sport, which the passage seems to imply cannot happen, they may not suffer the negative effects of obesity and social exclusion. For example, they may play sport during the day and watch television in the evening, thus experiencing the benefits of exercise and also enjoying the sedentary activity. Therefore, various potential threats supposedly posed by watching excessive television are undermined, and **D** is correct.

Question 86: C

D directly counters the above argument, and so is incorrect. Though **A**, **B** and **D** are all suggested or stated by the passage, they each act as evidence for the main conclusion, **C**, describing the 'multiple reasons to legalise cannabis'.

Question 87: C

C is not an assumption as it has been explicitly stated in the question that the salary is fixed, and therefore it will not change. The rest of the statements are all assumptions that Mohan has made. At no point has it been stated that any of the other statements are true, but they are all required to be true for Mohan's reasoning to be correct. Therefore, they are all assumptions Mohan has made.

Question 88: A

The answer is not **B** because, although the Holocaust was a tragedy, this is not explicitly stated in the passage. It cannot be **C** or **E**, as these are also not directly stated above. **D** provides an intermediary conclusion that leads to the main conclusion of **A**: we should not let terrible things happen again, and through teaching we can achieve this, so therefore 'we should teach about the Holocaust in schools'.

Question 89: C

DVDs are irrelevant – though one could access disturbing material through a DVD, this does not mean the material to be seen on TV is less disturbing. The argument also is not concerned with adults, and the suggestion is that violence in any quantity may have a detrimental effect, even if a show is not entirely made up of it. **A**, **B** and **D** are thus not the correct answers. **C** contradicts the argument, as it suggests there is no link between witnessing and re-enacting what one has witnessed. Children may watch the scenes of rape and recognise the horror of the action, and so be sworn off ever committing that crime.

Question 90: C

A is irrelevant, as the passage states it *could* teach children, not that it necessarily would. **B** and **C** are also irrelevant, as the entertainment quality of the show or the likeability of its protagonist would not undermine the logic of the argument. **C** is the correct answer, as it shows how the question uses one model of success and projects it onto all other models, which is illogical: just because Frank succeeds without morality, does not mean all others must reject morality to succeed.

Question 91: A

B, **C**, **D** and **E** are all irrelevant to Freddy's argument that he cannot say a sexist thing because he is a feminist. The woman's discomfort, Neil's feminist stance, the appropriateness of making comments about men, or lewd comments in general do not affect his claim. The presumed link between the two (inability to say something sexist, and feminist self-description) is the flaw in Freddy's argument: someone may believe in equal rights for the genders, and still say a sexist thing.

Question 92: A

At no point is it stated or implied that car companies should prioritise profits over the environment, so C) is incorrect. Neither is it stated that the public do not care about helping the environment, so E) is incorrect.

B) is a reason given in the argument, whilst D) is impossible if we accept the argument's reasons as true, so neither of these are conclusions.

Question 93: D

The easiest thing to do is draw the relative positions. We know Harrington is north of Westside and Pilbury. We know that Twotown is between Pilbury and Westside. Crewville is south of Twotown, Westside and Harrington but we do not know but its location relative to Pilbury.

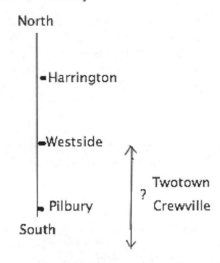

Question 94: B

By making a grid and filling in the relevant information the days Dr James works can be deduced:

	Sunday	Monday	Tuesday	Wednesday	Thursday	Friday	Saturday
Dr Evans	X	√	X	X	√	√	√
Dr James	X	√	√	√	√	X	√
Dr Luca	X	X	√	√	X	√	√

➢ No one works Sunday.
➢ All work Saturday.
➢ Dr Evans works Mondays and Fridays.
➢ Dr Luca cannot work Monday or Thursday.
➢ So, Dr James works Monday.
➢ And, Dr Evans and Dr James must work Thursday.
➢ Dr Evans cannot work 4 days consecutively so he cannot work Wednesday.
➢ Which means Dr James and Luca must work Wednesday.
➢ (mentioned earlier in the question) Dr Evans only works 4 days, so cannot work Tuesday.
➢ Which means Dr James and Luca work Tuesday.
➢ Dr James cannot work 5 days consecutively so cannot work Friday.
➢ Which means Dr Luca must work Friday.

Question 95: E
Working algebraically, using the call out rate as C, and rate per mile as M.
So,   C + 4m = 11
C + 5m = 13
Hence; (C + 5m) – (C + 4m) = £13 - £11
M = £2
Substituting this back into C + 4m = 11
C + (4 x 2) = 11
Hence, C = £3
Thus a ride of 9 mile will cost £3 + (9 x £2) = £21.

Question 96: E
Use the information to create a Venn diagram.
We don't know the exact position of both Trolls and Elves, so **A** and **D** are true. Goblins are mythical but not magical, so **C** is true. Gnomes are neither so **B** is true. But **E** is not true.

Question 97: D
The best method may be work backwards from 7pm. The packing (15 minutes) of all 100 tiles must have started by 6:45pm, hence the cooling (20 minutes) of the last 50 tiles started by 6:25pm, and the heating (45 minutes) by 5:40pm. The first 50 heating (45 minutes) must have started by 4:35pm, and cooling (20 minutes) by 5:20pm. The decoration (50 minutes) of the second 50 can occur anytime during 4:35pm- 5:40pm as this is when the first 50 are heating and cooling in the kiln, and so does not add time. The first 50 take 50 minutes to decorate and so must be started by 3:45pm.

Question 98: E
Speed = distance/time. Hence for the faster, pain impulse the speed is 1m/ 0.001 seconds. Hence the speed of the pain impulse is 1000 metres per second. The normal touch impulse is half this speed and so is 500 metres per second.

Question 99: E
Using the months of the year, Melissa could be born in March or May, Jack in June or July and Alina in April or August. With the information that Melissa and Jack's birthdays are 3 months apart the only possible combination is March and June. Hence Alina must be born in August, which means it is another 7 months until Melissa's birthday in March.

Question 100: A
PC Bryan cannot work with PC Adams because they have already worked together for 7 days in a row, so **C** is incorrect. **B** is incorrect because if PC Dirk worked with PC Bryan that would leave PC Adams with PC Carter who does not want to work with him. PC Carter can work with PC Bryan.

Question 101: C
Paying for my next 5 appointments will cost £50 per appointment before accounting for the 10% reduction, hence the cost counting the deduction is £45 per appointment. So the total for 4 appointments = 5 x £45 = £225 for the hair. Then add £15 for the first manicure and £10 x 2 for the subsequent manicures using the same bottle of polish bringing an overall total of £260.

Question 102: D
Elena is married to Alex or David, but we are told that Bertha is married to David and so Alex must be married to Elena. Hence David, Bertha, Elena and Alex are the four adults. Bertha and David's child is Gemma. So Charlie and Frankie must be Alex and Elena's two children. Leaving only options **A** or **D** as possibilities. Only Frankie and Gemma are girls so Charlie must be a boy.

Question 103: C

Using, x (minutes) as the, unknown amount of time, the second student took to examine, we can plot the time taken with the information provided thus:

	1st student		2nd student		3rd student
1st examination:	4x	1	2x	1	2x
			Break: 8 minutes		
1st examination:	x	1	x	1	x

Hence the total time taken, 45minutes (14:30-15:15)

Is represented by,   4x + 2x + 2x + x+ x+ x+ 1+1+ 8+1+1

$$45 \text{ minutes} = 11x \text{ (minutes)} + 12 \text{ minutes}$$
$$33 \text{ minutes} = 11x \text{ (minutes)}$$

Hence, x = 3 minutes, so the amount of time the second student took the first time, 2x, is 6 minutes.

Question 104: E & F

To work out the amount of change is the sum £5 - (2 x £1.65), which = £3.30. Logically we can then work out that the 3 coins in the change that are the same must be 1p as no other 3 coin combination can yield £1.70 when made up with 5 more coins. Thus we know that 3 of the coins are 1p, 1p & 1p. We can then deduce that there must also have been 2p and 5p coins in the change as £1.70 is divisible by ten. The only way then to make up the remaining £1.60 in 3 different coins is to have £1, 50p and 10p, Hence the change in coins is 1p, 1p, 1p, 2p, 5p, 10p, 50p and £1. So the two coins not given in change are £2 and 20p.

Question 105: D

If we express the speed of each train as W ms^{-1}. Then the relative speed of the two trains is 2W ms^{-1}.

Using Speed=distance/time: 2W = (140 + 140)/ 14.

Thus, 2W = 20, and W = 10. Thus, the speed of each train is 10 ms^{-1}.

To convert from metres to kilometres, divide by 1,000. To convert from seconds to hours, divide by 3,600.

Therefore, the conversion factor is to divide by 1,000/3,600 = 10/36 = 5/18

Thus, to convert from ms^{-1} to kmph, multiply by 18/5. Therefore, the final speed of the train is 18/5 x 10 = 36km/hr.

Question 106: C

Taking the day to be 24 hours long, this means the first tap fills 1/6 of the pool in an hour, the second 1/48, the third $\frac{1}{72}$ and the fourth $\frac{1}{96}$.

Taking 288 as the lowest common denominator, this gives: $\frac{48}{288} + \frac{6}{288} + \frac{4}{288} + \frac{3}{288}$ which $= \frac{61}{288}$ full in one hour.

Hence the pool will be $\frac{244}{288}$ full in 4 hours.

The pool fills by approximately $\frac{15}{288}$ every 15 minutes.

Thus, in 4 Hours 15: $\frac{244 + 15}{288} = \frac{249}{288}$

Thus, in 4 Hours 30: $\frac{244 + 30}{288} = \frac{274}{288}$

Thus, in 4 Hours 45: $\frac{244 + 45}{288} = \frac{289}{288}$

Question 107: B

Every day up until day 28 the ant gains a net distance of 1cm, so at the end of day 27 the ant is at 27cm height and therefore only 1cm below the top. On day 28 the 3cm the ant climbs in the day is enough to take it to the top of the ditch and so it is able to climb out.

Question 108: A

To solve this question three different sums are needed to use the information given to deduce the costs of the various items. With the information that 30 oranges cost £12, £12/30 = 40p per orange with the 20% discount, hence oranges must cost 50p at full price. With the information that 5 sausages and 10 oranges cost £8.50, we know that the oranges at a 10% discount account for 10 x 45p = £4.50 so 5 undiscounted sausages cost £4 so each full price sausage is £4/5 = 80p. Finally we know that 10 sausages and 10 apples cost £9, at 10% discount the sausages cost 72p each thus accounting for 10 x 72p = £7.20 of the £9, hence the 10 apples at a 10% discount must cost £1.80, so each apple costs 18p at 10% discount. So an apple is 20p full price. Now to add up the final total: 2 oranges + 13 sausages + 2 apples = (2 x 50p) + (13 x 72p) + (12 x 18p) = <u>£12.52.</u>

Question 109: C

If we take the number of haircuts per year to be x, the information we have can be shown:

Membership	Annual Fee	Cost per cut	Total Yearly cost
None	None	£60	60x
VIP	£125	£50	£125 + 50x
Executive VIP	£200	£45	£200 + 45x

As we know that changing to either membership option would cost the same for the year, we can express the cost for the year, y as;

VIP: y = £125 + 50x

Executive VIP: y = £200 + 45x

Therefore: £125 + 50x = £200 + 45x

Simplified   5x = £75, therefore the number of haircuts a year, x is 15.

Substituting in x, we can therefore work out:

Membership	Annual Fee	Cost per cut	Total Yearly cost
None	None	£60	£900
VIP	£125	£50	£875
Executive VIP	£200	£45	£875

Hence the amount saved by buying membership is £25.

Question 110: B

All thieves are criminals. So the circle must be fully inside the square, we are told judges cannot be criminals so the star must be completely separate from the other two.

Question 111: C

We are told that March and May have the same last number, which must be either 3 or 13. Taking the information from the question that one of the factors is related to the letters of the month names, we can interpret that 13 represents the M which starts both March and May. Therefore we know the rule is that the last number is the position of the starting letter. Knowing that there is another factor about the letters of the month that controls the code we can work out that one of the number may code for the number of letters. Which in March would be 5, which is the second letter, so we have the rule of the 2nd number. Finally through observation we may note that the first number codes for the months' relative position in the year. Hence the code of April will be 4, (for its position), 5 (for the number of letters in the name) and 1 for the position of the starting letter 'A') and so 451 is the code.

Question 112: D

If *b* is the number of years older than 5, and *a* the number of A*s, the money given to the children can be expressed:

£5 + £3b + £10a

Hence for Josie £5 + (£3 x 11) + (£10 x 9) = £128

We know that Carson receives £44 less yearly, and his b value is 13, so his amount can be expressed:

£5 + (£3 x 13) + (£10a) = £84

Simplified: £44 + £10a = £84

I.e. £10a = £40,

So Carson's 'a' value, i.e. his number of A*s is 4, so the difference between Josie and Carson is 5.

Question 113: B & C

Using the information to make a diagram:

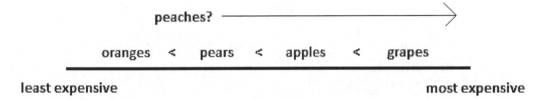

Hence **A** is incorrect. **D** and **E** may be true but we do not have enough information to say for sure. **B** is correct as we know peaches are more expensive than oranges but not about their price relative to pears. Equally we know **C** to be true as grapes are more expensive than apples so they must be more expensive than pears.

Question 114: B

It's easy to assume all the cuts should be in the vertical plane as a cake is usually sliced, however there is a way to achieve this with fewer cuts. Only three cutting motions are needed. **Start by cutting in the horizontal plane** through the centre of the cake to divide the top half from the bottom half. Then slice in the vertical plane into quarters to give 8 equally sized pieces with just three cuts.

Question 115: B & D

After the changes have been made, at 12 PM (GMT +1):

– Russell thinks it is 11 AM

– Tom thinks it is 12 PM

– Mark thinks it is 1 PM

Thus, in current GMT+1 time zone, Mark will arrive an hour early at 11 AM, Russell an hour late at 1 PM and Tom on time at 12 PM. There is therefore a two hour difference between the first and last arrival. For options E and F, be careful: the time zone listed is **NOT** GMT +1 that everyone else is working in. 1PM in GMT +3 = 11am GMT +1 (the summer time zone just entered) so that is Mark's actual arrival time; 12pm GMT +0 is the old time zone that Russell didn't change out of so that is Russell's correct arrival time.

Question 116: D

Using Bella's statements, as she must contradicted herself with her two statements, as one of them must be true, we know that it was definitely either Charlotte or Edward. Looking to the other statements, e.g. Darcy's we know that it was either Charlotte or Bella, as only one of the two statements saying it was both of them can have been a lie. Hence it must have been Charlotte.

Question 117: F

The only way to measure 0.1 litres or 100ml, is to fill the 300ml beaker, pour into the half litre/ 500 ml beaker, fill the 300ml again and pour (200ml) into the 500ml, which will make it full, leaving 100ml left in the 300ml beaker. The process requires 600ml of solution to fill the 300ml beaker twice.

Question 118: D

If you know how many houses there are on the street it is possible to work out the average, which then you can round up and down and to find the sequence of number, e.g. if you know there are 6 houses in the street 870/ 6 = 145. Which is not a house number because they are even so going up and down one even number consequentially one discovers that the numbers are 146, 144, 148, 150, 142 and 140. But it is not possible to determine Francis' house number without knowing its relative position i.e. highest, 3rd highest, lowest etc.

Question 119: D

Expressed through time:

Event	People Present
There were 20 people exercising in the cardio room	20
Four people were about to leave	20
A doctor was on the machine beside him (one of the original 20)	20
Emerging from his office one of the personal trainers called an ambulance.	21
Half of the people who were leaving, left (-2)	19
Eight people came into the room to hear the man being pronounced dead. (+8)	27
the two paramedics arrived, (+2)	29
the man was pronounced dead (-1)	28

Question 120: B & D

Blood loss can be described as 0.2 L/min.

For the man:

8 litres – 40% (3.2 L) = 4.8 L When he collapses, taking 16 minutes (3.2 / 0.2 = 16)

For the woman:

7 litres – 40% (2.8L) = 4.2: when she collapses, taking 14 minutes (2.8 / 0.2 = 14)

Hence the woman collapses 2 minutes before the man so **B** is correct, and **A** is incorrect. The total blood loss is 3.2L + 2.8L which = 6L so **C** is incorrect. The man's blood loss is 3.2L when he collapses so **E** is incorrect. The woman has a remaining blood volume of 4.2L when she collapses so **D** is correct. Blood loss is 0.2 L/min, which equates to 5 minutes per litre, which is 10 minutes per 2 litres not 12 L, so **F** is incorrect.

Question 121: B

Work out the times taken by each girl – (distance/pace) x 60 (converts to minutes) + lag time to start

Jenny: (13/8) x 60 = 97.5 minutes

Helen: (13/10) x 60 + 15 = 93 minutes

Rachel (13/11) x 60 + 25 = 95.9 minutes

Question 122: C

Work through each statement and the true figures.

A. Overlap of pain and flu-like symptoms must be at least 4% (56+48-100). 4% of 150: 0.04 x 150=6
B. 30% high blood pressure and 20% diabetes, so max percentage with both must be 20%. 20% of 150: 0.2*150 = 30
C. Total number of patients – patients with flu-like symptoms – patients with high blood pressure. Assume different populations to get min number without either. 150 – (0.56 x 150) – (0.3 x 150) = 21
D. This is an obvious trap that you might fall into if you added up the percentages and noted that the total was >100%. However, this isn't a problem as patients can discussed two problems.

Question 123: C

This is easiest to work out if you give all products an original price, I have used £100. You can then work out the higher price, and the subsequent sale price, and thus the discount from the original £100 price. As the price increases and decreases are in percentages, they will be the same for all items regardless of the price so it does not matter what the initial figure you start with is.

Marked up price: 100 x 1.15 = £115

Sale price: 115 x 0.75 = £86.25

Percentage reduction from initial price is 100 – 86.25 = 13.75%

Question 124: D

The recipe states 2 eggs makes 12 pancakes, therefore each egg makes 6 pancakes, so the number Steve must make should be a multiple of 6 to ensure he uses a whole egg.

Steve requires a minimum of 15 x 3 = 45 pancakes. To ensure use of whole eggs, this should be increased to 48 pancakes.

The original recipe is for 12 pancakes, therefore to make 48 pancakes, require 4x recipe (48/12).

Therefore quantities: 8 eggs, 400g plain flour and 1200 ml milk.

Question 125: B

Work through the question backwards.

In 6 litres of diluted bleach, there are 4.8 litres of water and 1.2 litres of partially diluted bleach.

In the 1.2 litres of partially diluted bleach, there is 9 parts water to one part original warehouse bleach. Remember that a ratio of 1:9 means 1/10 bleach and 9/10 water. Therefore working through, there is 120ml of warehouse bleach needed.

Question 126: C

We know that Charles is born in 2002, therefore in 2010 he must be 8. There are 3 years between Charles and Adam, and Charles is the middle grandchild. As Bertie is older than Adam, Adam must be younger than Charles so Adam must be 5 in 2010. In 2010, if Adam is 5, Bertie must be 10 (states he is double the age of Adam).

The question asks for ages in 2015: Adam = 10, Bertie = 15, Charles = 13

Question 127: B

Make the statements into algebraic equations and then solve them as you would simultaneous equations. Let a denote the flat fixed rate for hire, and b the price per half hour.

Cost = a + b(time in mins/30)

Peter: a + 6b (6 half hours) = 14.50 (equation 1)

Kevin: 2a + 18b = 41, or this can be simplified to give cost per kayak, a + 9b = 20.5 (equation 2)

If you subtract equation 1 from equation 2:

3b = 6, therefore b = 2

Substitute b into either equation to calculate a, using equation 1, a + 12 = 14.50, therefore a = 2.50

Finally use these values to work out the cost for 2 hours:

2.50 (flat fee) + 4 x 2 (4half hours x cost/half hour) = £10.50

Question 128: E

It is most helpful to write out all the numbers from 0 – 9 in digital format to most easily see which light elements are used for each number. You can then cross out any numbers which don't use all the lights from the digit 7.

Go through the digits methodically and you can cross out: 1, 2, 4, 5, and 6. These numbers don't contain all three

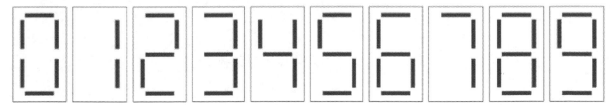

bars from the digit 7.

Question 129: B

In this question it is worth remembering it will take more people a shorter amount of time.

Work out how many man hours it takes to build the house. Days x hours x builders

12 x 7 x 4 = 336 hours

Work out how many hours it will take the 7man workforce: 336/7 = 48 hours

Convert to 8 hour days: 48/8 = 6 days

Question 130: D

By far the easiest way to do these type of questions is to draw a Venn diagram (use question marks if you are unsure about the exact position):

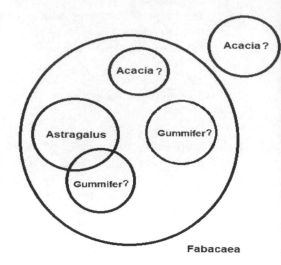

Now, it is a case of going through each statement:

A. Incorrect - Acacia may be fabacaea. Acacia are not astragalus, but does not logically follow that they therefore can't be fabacaea.
B. Incorrect – astragalus and gummifer are not necessarily separate within fabacaea.
C. Incorrect – the statement is not reversible so the fact that all astragalus and gummifer are fabacaea does not mean all facacaea are gummifer and/or astragalus. E.g. Fabacaea could be acacia.
D. Correct
E. Incorrect – Whilst some acacia could be gummifer, there is no certainty that they are.

Question 131: D

Area of a trapezium = (a+b)/2 x h
Area of cushion = (50+30)/2 x 50 = 2000cm^2
Since each width of fabric is 1m wide, both sides of one cushion can fit into one width. The required length is therefore 75cm x 4 = 3m with a cost of 3 x £10 = £30.
Cost of seamstress = £25 x 4 = £100
Total cost is £130

Question 132: C

There are 30 days in September, so Lisa will buy 30 coffees.
In Milk, every 10th coffee is free, so Lisa will pay for 27 coffees at 2.40 = £64.80
In Beans, Lisa gets 20 points each day and needs 220 points to get a free coffee, which is 11 days, with 5 points left over. Therefore, in 30 days she will get 2 free coffees. The cost for 28 coffees at 2.15 is £60.20
Beans is cheaper, and the difference is £64.80 - £60.20 = £4.60.

Question 133: C

Work backwards and take note of how often each bus comes.
Must get off 220 bus at 10.57 latest. Can get 10.40 bus therefore (arrive at 10.54).
Latest can get on 283 bus is 10.15 as to make the 220 bus connection. 283 comes every 10mins (question doesn't state at what points past the hour), so Paula should be at the bus stop at 10.06 to ensure a bus comes by 10.15 at the latest. If the bus comes every 10mins, even if a bus comes at 10.05 which Paula will miss, the next bus will come at 10.15 and therefore she will still be on time.
Therefore Paula must leave at 10.01

Question 134: B

You are working out the time taken to reach the same distance (D). Make sure to take into account changing speeds of train A, and that train B leaves 20 minutes earlier.

$Speed = \frac{distance}{time}$

Make sure you keep the answers consistent in the time units you are using, the worked answer is all in minutes (hence the need to multiply by 60).

Train A: time for first $20km = \frac{20}{100} \ x \ 60 \ = \ 12 \ minutes$

So the distance where it equals B is $12 \ + (\frac{D-20}{150}) \ x \ 60$

You need to use D-20 to account for the fact you have already calculated the time at the slower speed for the first 20km

Train B: $(\frac{D}{90}) \ x \ 60 - 20$

Make the equations equal each other as they describe the same time and distance, and solve.

Simplifies to $32 + \frac{2D}{5} - 8 \ = \ \frac{2D}{3}$ so $D \ = \ 90km$

Train B will take 60 minutes to travel 90 km and train A will take 40 minutes (but as it leaves 20 minutes later, this will be point at which it passes).

Question 135: C

Work out the annual cost of local gym: 12 x 15 = £180

Upfront cost + class costs of university gym must therefore be >£180.

Subtract upfront cost to find number of classes: 180 – 35 = £145

Divide by cost per class (£3) to find number of classes: 145/3 = 48 1/3

48 1/3 classes would make the two gyms the same price, so for the local gym to be cheaper, you would need to attend 49 classes.

Question 136: C

A is definitely true, since the question states that all herbal drugs are not medicines. **B** is also definitely true as all antibiotics are medicines which are all drugs. **C** is definitely false, because all antibiotics are medicine, yet no herbal drugs are medicines. **D** is true as all antibiotics are medicines.

Question 137: C

Answer **A** cannot be reliably concluded, because from the information given a non-"Fast" train could stop at Newark, but not at Northallerton or Durham. We have no information on whether *all* trains stopping at Newark also stop at Northallerton.

Answer **B** is not correct because 8 is the *average* number of trains that stop at Northallerton. It is possible that on some days more than 16 trains run, and more than 8 will thus stop at Northallerton. Answer **D** is incorrect because it is mentioned that *all* trains stopping at Northallerton also stop at Durham, giving a total 6 stops as a minimum for a train stopping at Northallerton (the others being the 4 stops which *all* trains stop at).

Answer **E** is incorrect for a similar reason to **A**. We have no information on whether all trains stopping at Newark also stop at Northallerton, so cannot determine that they must also stop at Durham.

Answer **C** is correct because "Fast" trains make less than 5 stops. Since all trains already stop at 4 stops (Peterborough, York, Darlington and Newcastle), they cannot then stop at Durham, as this would give 5 stops.

Question 138: D

From the information we are given, we can compose the following image of how these towns are located (not to scale, but shows the direction of each town with respect to the others):

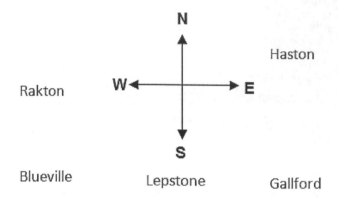

From this "map", we can see that all statements apart from **D** are true. Statement **D** is definitely *not true*, since Blueville is south west of Haston it cannot be East of Haston.

Question 139: C

We are told that in order to form a government, a party (or coalition) must have *over* 50% of seats. Thus, they must have at least 50% of the total seats plus 1, which is 301 seats.

We are told that we are looking for the *minimum* number of seats the greens can have in order to form a coalition with red and orange. Thus, we are seeking for Red and Orange to have the *maximum* number of seats possible, under the criteria given.

Thus we can calculate as follows:

- No party has over 45% of seats, so the maximum that the Red party can have is 45%, which is 270 seats.
- No party except for red and blue has won more than 4% of seats. We are told that the green party won the 4th highest number of seats, so it is possible that the Orange party won the 3rd highest.
- Thus, the maximum number of seats the orange party can have won is 4% of the total, which is 24 seats.
- Thus, the maximum possible combined total of the Red and Orange party's seats won is 294.

Thus, in order to achieve a total of 301 seats in a Red-Orange-Green coalition, the Green party have to have won at least 7 seats.

Question 140: E

Expressing the amount each child receives:

Youngest	M
2nd youngest	$M + D$
3rd youngest/ 3rd oldest	$M + 2D$
4th youngest/ 2nd oldest	$M + 3D$
Oldest	$M + 4D$

Question 141: D

The total amount of money received;
£100, = $M + M + D + M + 2D + M + 3D + M + 4D$
Simplified, thus is:
£100 = $5M + 10D$

Question 142: C

The two youngest are expressed as M and $M + D$. Simplified as $2M + D$.
The three oldest are expressed as $M + 2D$, $M + 3D$ and $M + 4D$, Simplified as $3M + 9D$
Hence 7 times the two youngest together is expressed $7(2M + D)$, so altogether the Answer is $7(2M + D) = 3M + 9D$.

Question 143: A

To work this out, simplify the two equations:

$7(2M + D) = 3M + 9D$

$14M + 7D = 3M + 9D$

$11M = 2D$

$M = \frac{2D}{11}$

Question 144: A

Substitute M into the equation £ $100 = 5M + 10D$

$5\left(\frac{2D}{11}\right) + 10D = £100$

$\frac{10D}{11} + 10D = \frac{10D}{11} + \frac{110D}{11} = \frac{120D}{11}$

Question 145: C & E

The easiest way to work this out is using a table. With the information we know:

1st		Madeira
2nd		
3rd	Jaya	
4th		

Ellen made carrot cake and it was not last. It now cannot be 1st or 3rd as these places are taken so it must be second:

1st		Madeira
2nd	Ellen	Carrot cake
3rd	Jaya	
4th		

Aleena's was better than the tiramisu, so she can't have come last, therefore Aleena must have placed first

1st	Aleena	Madeira
2nd	Ellen	Carrot cake
3rd	Jaya	
4th		

And the girl who made the Victoria sponge was better than Veronica:

1st	Aleena	Madeira
2nd	Ellen	Carrot cake
3rd	Jaya	Victoria Sponge
4th	Veronica	Tiramisu

Question 146: D

The information given can be expressed to show the results that the teams must have had to make their points total.

Team	Points	Game Results			
Celtic Changers	2	L	L	D	D
Eire Lions	?	?	?	?	?
Nordic Nesters	8	W	W	D	D
Sorten Swipers	5	W	D	D	L
Whistling Winners	1	D	L	L	L

The results so far total 3 wins, 6 losses and 7 draws. Since, the number of draws must be even, there must have been another draw. So we know one of the Eire Lions results is a draw.

The difference between wins (3) and losses (6) is 3. Thus, there must be another 3 wins to account for this difference. So the Eire Lions results must be 3 wins and 1 draw. Thus, they scored 3 x 3 + 1 = 10.

Question 147: D

Remember to consider the gender of each person. Then draw a quick diagram to show the given information you can see that only D is correct.

Question 148: B

After the first round; he knocks off 8 bottles to leave 8 left on the shelf. He then puts back 4 bottles. There are therefore 12 left on the shelf. After the second round, he has hit 3 bottles and damages 6 bottles in total, and an additional 2 at the end. He then puts up 2 new bottles to leave $12 - 8 + 2 = 6$ bottles left on the shelf. After the final round, John knocks off 3 bottles from the shelf to leave 3 bottles standing.

Question 149: D

Based on the information we have we can plot the travel times below. Change over times are in a smaller font.

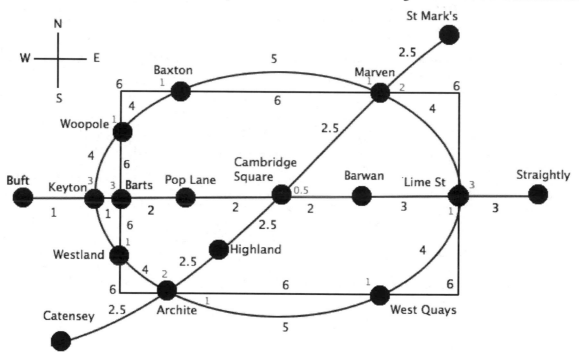

Hence on the St Mark's line, St Mark's to Archite takes 4 x 2.5 minutes = 10 minutes.

Question 150: A

Going from stop to stop on the Straightly line end Buft to Straightly would take 14 minutes, but we are told earlier on there is an express train that goes end to end and only takes 6.

Question 151: B

The quickest route from Baxton to Pop Lane is via Marven and Cambridge Square, which takes $5 + 2 + 2.5 + 0.5 + 2 = 12$ minutes. Baxton to Pop Lane via Barts would take $4 + 1 + 6 + 3 + 2 = 16$ minutes, which is longer so **E** is incorrect. Other options include times failing to take account of, or incorrectly adding changeover times, and so are incorrect.

Question 152: C

From Cambridge Square:
➤ Catensey is (2.5 x 3 =) 7.5 minutes away.
➤ Woopole, is (4 + 3 + 1 +2 + 2 =) 12 minutes.
➤ Buft is (1 + 1 + 2 + 2 =) 6 minutes.
➤ Westland is (4 + 2 + 2.5 + 2.5 =) 11 minutes.

Question 153: B

With the new delay information we can plot the travel times as before, adjusted for the delays. Plus a 5 minute delay on the platforms when waiting on any platform for a train.

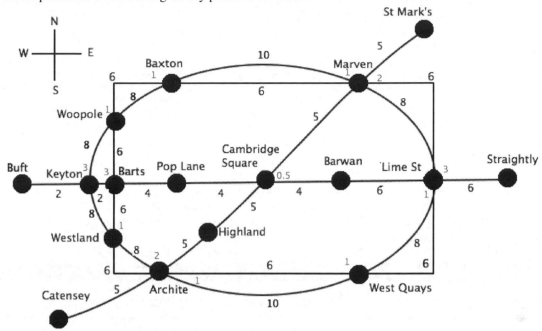

The quickest way from Westland to Marven now uses the non delayed reliable rectangle line. Four stops on the rectangle line take 6 mins each so 24 minutes in total on the train. Add to this the additional 5 minutes platform waiting time to give a total journey time of 29 minutes.

Question 154: C

- Baxton to Archite via Barts using only the Rectangle line takes (5 + 6 +6+ 6 +6=) 29 minutes.
- Baxton to Woopole on the Rectangle line, then Oval to Archite via Keyton takes (5 + 6 + 1 + 5 + 8 + 8 + 8 =) 41 minutes
- Baxton to Archite on the Oval line only takes (5 + (8 x 4) =) 37 minutes
- Baxton to Woopole on the Oval line, then Rectangle to Archite via Barts takes (5 + 8 + 1 + 5 + 6 + 6 + 6 =) 37 minutes
- As the bus takes 27-31 minutes, it is not possible to tell from between the options which will be slower/quicker so option **C** is the right answer.

Question 155: D

Remember the 5-minute platform wait. We are not told that the St Mark's express train from end to end is no longer running so we must assume that it is, which takes 5 minutes (plus the wait at St Mark's to go to Catensey).

Then, there is a 5 minute wait at Catensey to Archite, and a 2 + 5 minute changeover at Archite onto the Rectangle line which then takes 6 minutes to West Quays. 5 + 5 + 5 + 5 + 2 + 5 + 6 = 33 minutes. Via Lime St the journey takes 5 + 5 + 5+ 2 + 5 + 6+ 6 = 29 minutes.

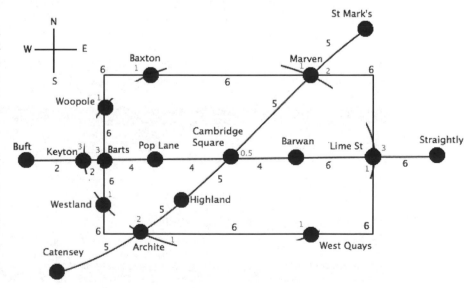

Question 156: D

From the information:

- "Simon's horse wore number 1."
- "...the horse that wore 3, which was wearing red..."
- "the horse wearing blue wore number 4."

We can plot the information below:

Place	Owner	Number	Colours
	Simon	1	
		2	
		3	Red
		4	Blue

In addition: "The horse wearing green; Celia's, came second"

Which means Celia's horse must have worn number two because it cannot have worn number 1 because that is Simon's horse. Also it cannot have worn number three or four because they wore red and blue respectively. So we can plot this further deduction:

Place	Owner	Number	Colours
	Simon	1	
2nd	Celia	2	Green
		3	Red
		4	Blue

We also know that

- "Arthur's horse beat Simon's horse"
- "Celia's horse beat the horse that wore number 1." i.e. Simon's

We know Celia's horse came second, and that both Celia's and Arthur's horses beat Simon's. This means that Simon's horse must have come last. So;

Place	Owner	Number	Colours
4th	Simon	1	
2nd	Celia	2	Green
		3	Red
		4	Blue

And knowing that:

- "Only one horse wore the same number as the position it finished in."

The horses wearing numbers 3 and 4 must have placed 1st and 3rd respectively. Hence:

Place	Owner	Number	Colours
4th	Simon	1	
2nd	Celia	2	Green
1st		3	Red
3rd		4	Blue

"Lila's horse wasn't painted yellow nor blue"

So Lila's must have been red, and Simon's yellow. Leaving the only option for Arthur's to be blue. So we now know:

Place	Owner	Number	Colours
4th	Simon	1	Yellow
2nd	Celia	2	Green
1st	Lila	3	Red
3rd	Arthur	4	Blue

Question 157: C
Year 1 – 40 x 1.2 = 48
Year 2 – 48 x 1.2= 57.6
Year 3 – 57.6 x 1.1= 63.36
Year 4 – 63.36 x 1.1 = 69.696.

Question 158: C
To minimise the total cost to the company, they want the wage bills for each site to be less than £200,000. Working this out involves some trial and error; you can speed this up by splitting employees who earn similar amounts between the sites e.g. Nicola and John as they are the top two earners.
Nicola + Daniel + Luke = £ 198,500 and John + Emma + Victoria = £ 199,150

Question 159: C
Remember that pick up and drop off stops may be the same stop, therefore the minimum number of stops the bus had to make was 7. This would take 7 x 1.5 = 10.5 minutes.
Therefore the total journey time = 24 + 10.5 = 34.5 minutes.

Question 160: A
The best method here is to work backwards. We know the potatoes have to be served immediately, so they should be finished roasting at 4pm, so they should start roasting 50 minutes prior to that, at 3:10. We also know they have to be roasted immediately after boiling, so they should be prepared by 3:05, in order to boil in time. She should therefore start preparing them no later than 2:47, though she could prepare them earlier.
The chicken needs to be cooked by 3:55 to give it time to stand, so it should begin roasting at 2:40, and Sally should begin to prepare it no later than 2:25.
You can construct a rough timeline:

We can see from this timeline that from 2:40 onwards, there will be no long enough period of time in which there is a free space in the cooker for the vegetables to be boiled. They therefore must be finished cooking at 3:05. The latest time prior to this that Sally has time to prepare them (5 minutes) is at 2:40, between preparing the chicken and the potatoes. She should therefore begin preparing the vegetables at 2:42, then begin boiling at 2:47, so they can be finished cooking by 2:55, in time for the potatoes to boil at 3:05.
Chicken: 2:25
Potatoes: 2:47
Vegetables: 2:42

Question 161: C

The quickest way to do this is via trial and error. However, for the sake of completion: let each child's age be denoted by the letter of their name, and form an equation for their total age:

$$P + J + A + R = 80$$

The age of each child can be written in terms of Paul's age.

$P = 2J$, therefore $J = \frac{P}{2}$

$$A = \frac{P+J}{2}$$

Now substitute in $J = \frac{P}{2}$ to get in terms of P only: $A = \frac{P+\frac{P}{2}}{2} = \frac{P}{2} + \frac{P}{4} = \frac{3P}{4}$

$$R = P + 2$$

Thus: $P + \frac{P}{2} + \frac{3P}{4} + P(+2) = 80$

Simplify to give: $\frac{13P}{4} = 78$

$13P = 312$. Thus, $P = 24$

Substitute P = 24 into the equations for the other children to get: J = 12, A = 18, R = 26

Question 162: A

The total number of buttons is 71 + 86 + 83 = 240. The total number of suitable buttons is 22 + 8 = 30. Thus, she will have to remove a maximum of 210 buttons in order to guarantee picking a suitable button on the next attempt.

Question 163: E

This question requires you to calculate the adjusted score for Ben for each segment. If Ben has a 50% chance of hitting the segment he is aiming for, we can assume he hits each adjacent segment 25% of the time. Thus:

$$Adjusted\ Score = \frac{Segment\ aimed\ at}{2} + \frac{First\ Adjacent\ Segment}{4} + \frac{Second\ Adjacent\ Segment}{4}$$

$$Adjusted\ Score = \frac{Segment\ aimed\ at}{2} + \frac{Sum\ of\ Adjacent\ Segments}{4}$$

E.g. if he aims at segment 1: He will score $\frac{1}{2} + \frac{18+20}{4} = 10$

Now it is a simple case of trying the given options to see which segment gives the highest score. In this case, it is segment 19: $\frac{19}{2} + \frac{7+3}{4} = 12$

Question 164: C

The total cost is £8.75, and Victoria uses a £5.00 note, leaving a total cost of £3.65 to be paid using change.
Up to 20p can be paid using 1p and 2p pieces, so she could use 20 1p coins to make up this amount.
Up to 50p can be paid using 5p and 10p pieces, so she could use 10 5p pieces to make up this amount. This gives a total of 30 coins, and a total payment of £0.70.
Up to £1.00 can be paid using 20p pieces and 50p pieces. Thus, she could use up to 5 20p pieces, giving a total of 35 coins used, and a total payment of £1.70.

The smallest denomination of coin that can now be used is a £1.00 coin. Hence Victoria must use 2 £1.00 coins, giving a total of 37 coins, and a total payment of £3.70. However, we know that the total cost to pay in change was £3.65, and that Victoria paid the exact amount, receiving no change. Thus, we must take away coins to the value of 5p, removing the smallest number of coins possible. This is achieved by taking away 1 5p piece, giving a grand total of 36 coins.

Question 165: B

The time could be 21:25, if first 2 digits were reversed by the glass of water (21 would be reversed to give 15). **A** cannot be the answer, because this would involve altering the last 2 digits, and we can see that 25 on a digital clock, when reversed simply gives 25 (the 2 on the left becomes a 5 on the right, and the 5 on the right becomes a 2 on the left). **C** cannot be the answer, as this involves reversing the middle 2 digits. As with the right two digits, the middle 2 digits of 2:5 would simply reverse to give itself, 2:5. **D** could be the time if the 2nd and 4th digits were reversed, as they would both become 2's. However, the question says that 2 *adjacent* digits are reversed, meaning that the 2nd and 4th digits cannot be reversed as required here. **E** is not possible as it would require all four numbers to be reversed.

Thus, the answer is **B**.

Question 166: B

We can see from the question that Lorkdon is a democracy and therefore cannot have been invaded by a democracy because of the treaty (we are assuming this treaty is upheld, as said in the question). Thus, Nordic (which has invaded Lorkdon) *must* be a dictatorship. Now, we can see that Worsid has been invaded by a dictatorship, *and* has invaded a dictatorship. The question states that no dictatorship has undergone both of these events. Thus, we know that Worsid cannot be a dictatorship. We also know from the question that each of these countries is *either* a dictatorship or a democracy. Thus, Worsid must be a democracy.

Question 167: C

The total price of all of these items would usually be £17. However, with the DVD offer, the customer saves £1, giving a total cost of £16. Thus, the customer will need to receive £34 in change.

Question 168: B

To answer this, we simply calculate how much total room in the pan will be taken up by the food for each guest:
- 2 rashers of bacon, giving a total of 14% of the available space.
- 4 sausages, taking up a total of 12% of the available space.
- 1 egg takes up 12% of the available space.

Adding these figures together, we see that each guest's food takes up a total of 38% of the available space.

Thus, Ryan can only cook for 2 guests at once, since 38% multiplied by 3 is 114%, and we cannot use up more than 100% of the available space in the pan.

Question 169: C

To calculate this, let the total number of employees be termed "Y".

We can see that £60 is the total cost for providing cakes for 40% of "Y".

We know that £2 is required for each cake. Thus, we can work out that 30 must be 40% of Y.

0.4Y = 60/2
0.4Y = 30
Y = 75

Thus, we can calculate that the total number of employees must be 75.

Question 170: E

The normal waiting time for treatment is 3 weeks. However, the higher demand in Bob's local district mean this waiting time is extended by 50%, giving a total of 4.5 weeks.

Then, we must consider the delay induced because Bob is a lower risk case, which extends the waiting time by another 20%. 20% of 4.5 is 0.9, so there is a delay of another 0.9 weeks for treatment.

Thus, Bob can expect to wait 5.4 weeks for specialist treatment on his tumour.

Question 171: D

In the class of 30, 40% drink alcohol at least once a month, which is 12. Of these, 75% drink alcohol once a week, which is 9. Of these, 1 in 3 smoke marijuana, which is 3.

In the class of 30, 60% drink alcohol less than once a month, which is 18. Of these, 1 in 3 smoke marijuana, which is 6.

Therefore the total number of students who smoke marijuana is 3+6, which is 9.

Question 172: C

The sequence can either be thought of as doubling the previous number then adding 2, or adding 1 then doubling. Double 46 is 92, plus 2 is 94.

Question 173: B

If the mode of 5 numbers of 3, it must feature at least two threes. If the median is 8, we know that the 3rd largest number is an 8. Hence we know that the 3 smallest numbers are 3, 3, and 8. Because the mean is 7, we know that the 5 numbers must add up to 35. The three smallest numbers add up to 14. Hence the two largest must add up to 21.

Question 174: E

The biggest difference in the weight of potatoes will be if the bag with only 5 potatoes in weighs the maximum, 1100g, and the bag with 10 potatoes weighs the minimum, 900g. If there are 5 equally heavy potatoes in a bag weighing 1100g, each weighs 220g. If there are 10 equally heavy potatoes in a 900g bag, each weighs 90g. The difference between these is 130g.

Question 175: D

There are 60 teams, and 4 teams in each group, so there are 15 groups. In each group, if each team plays each other once, there will be 6 matches in each group, making a total of 90 matches in the group stage. There are then 16 teams in the knockout stages, so 8 matches in the first round knockout, then 4, then 2, then 1 final match when only two teams are left. Hence there are 105 matches altogether ($90 + 8 + 4 + 2 + 1 = 105$).

Question 176: A

We know the husband's PIN number must be divisible by 8 because it has been multiplied by 2 3 times and had a multiple of 8 added to it. The largest 4 digit number which is divisible by 8 is 9992. Minus 200 is 9792. Divide by 2 is 4896. Hence the largest the husband's last 4 card digits can be is 4896. Minus 200 is 4696. Divide by 2 is 2348. Hence the largest my last 4 card digits can be is 2348. Minus 200 is 2148. Divide by 2 is 1074. Hence the largest my PIN number can be is 1074.

Question 177: C

If the first invitation is sent as early as possible, it will be sent on the 50th birthday. It will be accepted after 2 reminders and hence conducted at 50 years 11 months. The time between each screening will be 3 years 11 months. Hence, the second screening will be at 54 years 10 months. The third screening will be at 58 years 9 months. Hence, the fourth screening will be at 62 years 8 months.

Question 178: A

Ellie has worked for the company for more than five but less than six whole years. At the end of each whole year she receives a pay rise in thousands equal to the number of years of her tenure. Therefore at the end of the first year the raise is £1,000, then at the end of the second year it is £2,000 and so on to year 5. Thus the total amount of her pay comprised by the pay rises is £15,000, so the basic pay before accounting for these rises was £40,000 - £15,000 = £25,000.

Question 179: B

The trains come into the station together every 40 minutes, as the lowest common multiple of 2, 5 and 8 is 40. Hence, if the last time trains came together was 15 minutes ago, the next time will be in 25 minutes.

Question 180: C

If you smoke, your risk of getting Disease X is 1 in 24. If you drink alcohol, your risk of getting Disease X is 1 in 6. Each tablet of the drug halves your risk. Therefore a drinker taking 1 tablet means their risk is 1 in 12, and taking 2 tablets means their risk is 1 in 24, the same as someone who smokes.

Question 181: A

There are 10 red and 8 green balls. Clearly the most likely combination involves these colours only. Since there are more red balls than green, the probability of red-red is greater than green-green. However, there are **two** possible ways to draw a combination, either the red first followed by green or green first followed by red. The probability of red-red = $\left(\frac{10}{20} x \frac{9}{19}\right) = \frac{9}{38}$.

The probability of red and green = $\left(\frac{8}{20} x \frac{10}{19}\right) + \left(\frac{10}{20} x \frac{8}{19}\right) = \frac{8}{38} + \frac{8}{38} = \frac{16}{38}$. Therefore the combination of red and green is more likely.

Question 182: B

The least likely combination of balls to draw is blue and yellow. You are much more likely to draw a green ball than either a blue or yellow one because there are many more in the bag. Since the draw is taken without replacement, yellow and yellow is impossible because there is only one yellow ball.

Question 183: F

Since there is only 1 blue and 1 yellow ball, it is possible to take 18 balls which are red or green. You would need to take 19 of the 20 balls to be certain of getting either the blue ball or the yellow ball.

Question 184: C

The smallest number of parties required would theoretically be 3 – Namely Labour, the Liberal Democrats and UKIP, giving a total of 355 seats. However, the Liberal Democrats will not form a coalition with UKIP, so this will not be possible. Thus, there are 2 options:

➢ Labour can form a coalition with the Greens and UKIP, which is not contradictory to anything mentioned in the question. This would give a total of 325 seats, and would thus need the next 2 largest parties (The Scottish National Party and Plaid Cymru) in order to get more than 350 seats, meaning 5 parties would need to be involved.

➢ Alternatively, Labour can form a coalition with the Liberal Democrats and the Green Party. This would give a total of 340 seats. Only one more party (e.g. the Scottish National Party) would be required to exceed 350 seats, giving a grand total of 4 parties.

Thus, the smallest number of parties needed to form a coalition would be 4.

Question 185: E

360 appointments are attended and only 90% of those booked are attended, meaning there were originally 400 appointments booked in and 40 have been missed. 1 in 2 of the booked appointments were for male patients, so 200 appointments were for male patients. Male patients are three times as likely to miss booked appointments, so of the 40 that were missed, 30 were missed by men. Given that of 200 booked appointments, 30 were missed, this means 170 were attended.

Question 186: B

If every one of 60 students studies 3 subjects, this is 180 subject choices altogether. 60 of these are Maths, because everyone takes Maths. 60% of 60 is 36, so 36 are Biology. 50% of 60 is 30, so 30 are Economics and 30 are Chemistry. 60+36+30+30=156, so there are 24 subject choices left which must be Physics.

Question 187: B

If 100,000 people are diagnosed with chlamydia and 0.6 partners are informed each, this is 60,000 people, of which 80% (so 48,000) have tests. 12,000 of the partners who are informed, as well as 240,000 who are not (300,000 – 60,000) do not have tests. This makes 252,000 who are not tested. We can assume that half of these people would have tested positive for chlamydia, which is 126,000. So the answer is 126,000.

Question 188: C

Tiles can be added at either end of the 3 lines of 2 tiles horizontally or at either end of the 2 lines of 2 tiles vertically. This is a total of 10, but in two cases these positions are the same (at the bottom of the left hand vertical line and the top of the right hand vertical line). So the answer is 10 – 2 = 8.

Question 189: C

Harry needs a total of 4000ml + 1200ml = 5200ml of squash. He has 1040ml of concentrated squash, which is a fifth of the total dilute squash he needs. So he will need 4 parts water to every 1 part concentrated squash, therefore the resulting liquid is 1/5 squash and 4/5 water.

Question 190: C

There are 24 different possible arrangements (4 x 3 x 2 x 1), which means that there are 23 other possible arrangements than Alex, Beth, Cathy, Daniel.

Question 191: F

A is incorrect because the distance travelled is only 10 miles. **B** is incorrect because the distance travelled is 19 miles. **C** is incorrect because no town is visited twice. **D** is incorrect because Hondale and Baleford are both visited twice. **E** is incorrect because no town is visited twice. Therefore **F** is the correct answer.

Question 192: C

Georgia is shorter than her Mum and Dad, and each of her siblings is at least as tall as Mum (and we know Mum is shorter than Dad because Ellie is between the two), so we know Georgia is the shortest. We know that Ellie, Tom and Dad are all taller than Mum, so Mum is second shortest. Ellie is shorter than Dad and Tom is taller than Dad, so we can work out that Ellie must be third shortest.

Question 193: A

Danielle must be sat next to Caitlin. Bella must be sat next to the teaching assistant. Hence these two pairs must sit in different rows. One pair must be sat at the front with Ashley, and the other must be sat at the back with Emily. Since the teaching assistant has to sit on the left, this must mean that Bella is sat in the middle seat and either Ashley or Emily (depending on which row they are in) is sat in the right hand seat. However, Bella cannot sit next to Emily, so this means Bella and the teaching assistant must be in the front row. So Ashley must be sat in the front right seat.

Question 194: C

The dishwasher is run 2+p times a week, where p is the number of people in the house. Let the number of people in the house when the son is not home be s, and when the son is home it is s+1. In 30 weeks when the son is home, she would buy 6 packs of dishwasher tablets. In 30 weeks when the son is not home, she would buy 5 packs of dishwasher tablets. So 1.2 times as many packs of dishwasher tablets are bought when he is home. So 2+s+1 is 1.2 time 2+s.

i.e. $2.4 + 1.2s = 2 + s + 1$

Therefore 0.2s = 0.6

s = 3

When her son is home, there are s + 1 = 4 people in the house.

Question 195: A

No remaining days in the year obey the rule. The next date that does is 01/01/2015 (integers are 0, 1, 2, 5). This is 6 days later than the specified date.

Question 196: B

If each town is due North, South, East or West of at least 2 other towns and we know that one is east and one is north of a third, then they must be arranged in a square. So Yellowtown is 4 miles east of Bluetown to make a square, which means it must be 5 miles north of Redtown. So Redtown is 5 miles south of Yellowtown.

Question 197: B

Jenna pours 4/5 of 250 ml into each glass, which is 200 ml. Since she has 1500 ml of wine, she pours 100 ml into the last glass, which is 2/5 of the 250 ml full capacity.

Question 198: E

The maximum number of girls in Miss Ellis's class with brown eyes and brown hair is 10, because the two thirds of the girls with brown eyes could also all have brown hair. The minimum number is 0 because it could be that all the boys, and the third of the girls without brown eyes, all had brown hair, which would be 2/3 of the class.

Question 199: E

A negative "score" results from any combination of throws which includes a 1 but from no other combination. Given that a negative score has a 0.75 probability, a positive or zero score has a 0.25 probability. Therefore throwing two numbers that are not 1 twice in a row has a probability of 0.25. Hence, the probability of throwing a non-1 number on each throw is $\sqrt{0.25} = 0.5$. So the probability of throwing a 1 on an individual throw is $1 - 0.5 = 0.5$.

Question 200: C
We can work out from the information given the adult flat rate and the charge per stop. Let the charge per stop be s and the flat rate be f. Therefore: 15s + f = 1.70
8s + f = 1.14
We can hence work out that: 7s = 0.56, so s = 0.08. Hence, f = 0.50
Megan is an adult so she pays this rate. For 30 stops, the rate will be 0.08 x 30 + 0.50 = 2.90.

Question 201: B
We found in the previous question that the flat rate for adults is £0.50 and the rate per stop is £0.08. We know that the child rate is half the flat rate and a quarter of the "per stop" rate, so the child flat rate is £0.25 and the rate per stop is 2p. So for 25 stops, Alice pays:
0.02 x 25 + 0.25 = 0.75

Question 202: C
We should first work out how many stops James can travel. For £2, he can afford to travel as many stops as £1.50 will take him once the flat rate is taken into account. The per stop rate is 8p per stop, so he can travel 18 stops, so he will need to go to the 18th stop from town. So he will need to walk past 7 stops to get to the stop he can afford to travel from.

Question 203: D
The picture will need a 12 inch by 16 inch mount, which will cost £8. It will need a 13 inch by 17 inch frame, which will cost £26. So the cost of mounting and framing the picture will be £8 + £26 = £34.

Question 204: C
Mounting and framing an 8 by 8 inch painting will cost £5 for the mount and £22 for the frame, which is £27. Mounting and framing a 10 by 10 inch painting will cost £6 for the mount and £26 for the frame, which is £32. The difference is £32 - £27 = £5.

Question 205: B
We found in the last question that mounting and framing a 10 by 10 inch painting will cost £6 for the mount and £26 for the frame, which is £32 total. We can calculate that each additional inch of mount and frame for a square painting costs £2.50; £2 for the frame and £0.50 for the mount. So an 11 inch painting will cost £34.50 to frame and mount, a 12 inch £37, a 13 inch £39.50, a 14 inch £42. The biggest painting that can be mounted and framed for £40 is a 13 inch painting.

Question 206: D
Recognise that the pattern is *"consonants move forward by two consonants; vowel stay the same"*. This allows coding of the word MAGICAL to PAJIFAN to RALIHAQ.

Forward two			Forward two	
M	$\Rightarrow$	O (skips to) P	$\Rightarrow$ R
A	$\Rightarrow$	Stays the same	$\Rightarrow$ A
G	$\Rightarrow$	I (skips to) J	$\Rightarrow$ L
I	$\Rightarrow$	Stays the same	$\Rightarrow$ I
C	$\Rightarrow$	E (skips to) F	$\Rightarrow$ H
A	$\Rightarrow$	Stays the same	$\Rightarrow$ A
L	$\Rightarrow$	N	$\Rightarrow$ Q

Question 207: C
If f donates the flat rate, and k denotes the rate per km, we can form simultaneous equations:
f + 5k = £6 AND f + 3k = £4.20
Subtract equation two from equation one:
(f + 5k) - (f + 3k) = £6 - £4.20
Thus, 2k = £1.80 and k = £0.90
Therefore, f + (5 x 0.90) = £6
So, f + £4.50 = £6. Thus, f = £1.50
7k will be £1.50 + 7 x £0.90 = £7.80

Question 208: C

The increase from 2001/2 to 2011/12 was 1,019 to 11,736, which equals a linear increase of 10,717 admissions. So, in 20 years, we would expect to see an increase by 10,717 x 2 = 21,434. Add this to the number in 2011 to give 33,170 admissions.

Question 209: A

As the question uses percentages, it does not matter what figure you use. To make calculations easier, use an initial price of £100. When on sale, the dress is 20% off, so using a normal price of £100, the dress would be £80. When the dresses are 20% off, the shop is making a 25% profit. Therefore: £80 = 1.25 x purchase price. Therefore, the purchase price is: $\frac{80}{1.25}$ = £64. Thus, the normal profit is £100 - £64 = £36. I.e. when a dress sells for £100, the shop makes £36 or 36% profit.

Question 210: C

1. Incorrect. There must be 6 general committee clinical students, plus the treasurer, and 2 sabbatical roles, none of whom can be preclinical, so there must be a maximum of 11 preclinical students.
2. Correct. There must two general for each year plus welfare and social officers, totalling to 6.
3. Incorrect. The committee is made up of 20 students, 2 roles are sabbatical, so there are 18 studying students, and therefore there can be 3 from each year.
4. Correct. There are 18 studying students on the committee, and there must be 6 general committee members from pre-clinical, plus welfare and social, therefore there must be a minimum of 8 pre-clinical students, so there must be 10 clinical students.
5. Incorrect. You need to count up the number of specific roles on the committee, which is 5, and there must be 2 students from each year, which is 12. This leaves 3 more positions, which the question doesn't state can't be first years. Therefore there could be up to 5 first years.
6. Incorrect. There must be at least 2 general committee members from each year. However, the worked answer to 5 shows there are 15 general committee members which are split across the 6 years, and so there must be an uneven distribution.

Question 211: B

Remember 2012 was a leap year. Work through each month, adding the correct number of days, to work out what day each 13th would be on.

If a month was 28 days, the 13th would be the same day each month, therefore to work this out quickly, you only need to count on the number of days over 28. For example, in a month with 31 days, the 13th will be 3 weekdays (31-28) later.

Thus if 13th January is a Friday, 13th February is a Monday, (February has 29 days in 2012), 13th March is a Tuesday and 13th April is a Friday.

Question 212: E

There are 18 sheep in total. The question states there are 8 male sheep, which means there are 10 female sheep before some die. 5 female sheep die, so there are 5 female sheep alive to give birth to lambs. Each delivers 2 lambs, making 10 lambs in total. There are 4 male sheep and 5 mothers so the total is 10 + 4 + 5 = 19 sheep.

Question 213: D

We can see from the fact that all the possible answers end "AME" that the letters "AME" must be translated to the last 3 letters of the coded word, "JVN", under the code. J is the 10th letter of the alphabet so it is 9 letters on from A (V is the 21st letter of the alphabet and M is the 13th, and N is the 14th letter of the alphabet and E is the 5th, therefore these pairs are also 9 letters apart). Therefore P is the code for the letter 9 letters before it in the alphabet. P is the 16th letter of the alphabet, therefore it is the code for the 7th letter of the alphabet, G. Therefore from these solutions the only possibility for the original word is GAME.

Question 214: C

Let x be the number of people who get on the bus at the station.

It is easiest to work backwards. After the 4th stop, there are 5 people on the bus. At the 4th stop, half the people who were on the bus got off (and therefore half stayed on) and 2 people got on. Therefore, 5 is equal to 2 plus half the number of people who were on the bus after the 3rd stop. So half the number of people who were on the bus after the 3rd stop must be 3. Therefore, after the 3rd stop, there must have been 6 people on the bus.

We can then say that 6 is equal to 2 plus half the number of people who were on the bus after the 2nd stop. Therefore there were 8 people on the bus after the 2nd stop.

We can then say that 8 is equal to 2 plus half the number of people who were on the bus after the 1st stop. Therefore there were 12 people on the bus after the 1st stop.

We can then say that 12 is equal to 2 plus half the number of people who got on the bus at the station. Therefore the number of people who got on the bus at the station is 20.

Question 215: B

We know from the question that I have purchased small cans of blue and white paint, and that blue paint accounted for 50% of the total cost. Since a can of blue paint is 4 X the price of a can of white paint, we know I must have purchased 4 cans of white paint for each can of blue paint.

Each can of small paint covers a total of $10m^2$, and I have painted a total of $100m^2$, in doing so using up all the paint. Therefore, I must have purchased 10 cans of paint. Therefore, I must have purchased 2 cans of blue paint and 8 cans of white paint. So I must have painted $20m^2$ of wall space blue.

Question 216: E

The cost for x cakes under this offer can be expressed as: $x(42-x^2)$

Following this formula, we can see that 2 cakes would cost 76p, 3 cakes would cost 99p, and 4 cakes would cost 104p. As the number of cakes increases beyond 4, we see that the overall price actually drops, as 5 cakes would cost 85p and 6 cakes would cost 36p. This confirms Isobel's prediction that the offer is a bad deal for the baker, as it ends up cheaper for the customer to purchase more cakes. It is clear that 6 cakes is the smallest number for which the price will be under 40p, and the price will continue to drop as more cakes are purchased.

Question 217: C

Adding up the percentages of students in University A who do "Science" subjects gives:
$23.50 + 6.25 + 30.25 = 60\%$.
60% of 800 students is 480, so 480 students in University A do "Science" subjects.
Adding up the percentages of students in University B who do "Science subjects" gives:
$13.25 + 14.75 + 7.00 = 35\%$. 35% of 1200 students is 420, so 420 students in University B do "Science" subjects. Therefore:
$480 - 420 = 60$
60 more students in University A than University B take a "Science" subject.

Question 218: C

Let the number of miles Sonia is travelling be x. Because she is crossing 1 international border, travelling by Traveleasy Coaches will cost Sonia: £(5 + 0.5x)
Travelling by Europremier coaches will cost Sonia: £(15 + 0.1x).

Because we know the cost is the same for both companies, the number of miles she is travelling can be found by setting these two expressions equal to each other: $5 + 0.5x = 15 + 0.1x$.
This equation can be rearranged to give: $0.4x = 10$
Therefore: $x = 10/0.4 = 25$

Question 219: E

To find out whether many of these statements are true it is necessary to work out the departure and arrival times, and journey time, for each girl.

Lauren departs at 2:30pm and arrives at 4pm, therefore her journey takes 1.5 hours
Chloe departs at 1:30pm and her journey takes 1 hour longer than 1.5 hours (Lauren's journey), therefore her journey takes 2.5 hours and she arrives at 4pm
Amy arrives at 4:15pm and her journey takes 2 times 1.5 hours (Lauren's journey), therefore her journey takes 3 hours and she departs at 1:15pm.
Looking at each statement, the only one which is definitely true is **E**: Amy departs at 1:15pm and Chloe departs at 1:30pm therefore Amy departed before Chloe.

D *may* be true, but nothing in the question shows it is *definitely* true, so it can be safely ignored.

Question 220: B

First consider how many items of clothing she can take by weight. The weight allowance is 20kg. Take off 2kg for the weight of the empty suitcase, then take off another 3kg (3 X 1000g) for the books she wishes to take. Therefore she can fit 15kg of clothes in her suitcase. To find out how many items of clothing this is, we can divide 15kg=15000g by 400g: 15000/400 = 150/4 = 37.5

So she can pack up to 37 items of clothing by weight.

Now consider the volume of clothes she can fit in. The total volume of the suitcase is:

50cm x 50cm x 20cm = 50000cm^3

The volume of each book is: 0.2m x 0.1m x 0.05m = 1000cm^3

So the volume of space available for clothes is: 50000 – (3 x 1000) = 47000cm^3

To find out how many items of clothing she can fit in this space, we can divide 47000 by 1500:

47000/1500 = 470/15 = 31 1/3

So she can pack up to 31 items of clothing by volume.

Although she can fit 37 items by weight, they will not fit in the volume of the suitcase, so the maximum number of items of clothing she can pack is 31.

Question 221: D

We can work out the Answer by considering each option:

Bed Shop A: £120 + £70 = £190

Bed Shop B: £90 + £90 = £180

Bed Shop C: £140 + (1/2 x £60) = £170

Bed Shop D: (2/3) x (£140+£100) = (2/3) x (£240) = £160

Bed Shop E: £175

Therefore the cheapest is Bed Shop **D**.

Question 222: C

The numbers of socks of each colour is irrelevant, so long as there is more than one of each (which there is). There are only 4 colours of socks, so if Joseph takes 5 socks, it is guaranteed that at least 2 of them will be the same colour.

Question 223: D

Paper comes in packs of 500, and with each pack 20 magazines can be printed. Each pack costs £3.

Card comes in packs of 60, and with each pack 60 magazines can be printed. Each pack costs £3 x 2 = £6.

Each ink cartridge prints 130 sheets, which is 130/26 = 5 magazines. Each cartridge costs £5.

The lowest common multiple of 20, 60 and 5 is 60, so it is possible to work out the total cost for printing 60 magazines. Printing 60 magazines will require 3 packs of paper at £3, 1 pack of card at £6 and 12 ink cartridges at £5. So the total cost of printing 60 magazines is: (3 x 3) + 6 + (12 x 5) = £75.

The total budget is £300.

£300/£75 = 4

So we can print 4x60 magazines in this budget, which is 240 magazines.

Question 224: E

We can express the information we have as: $\frac{1}{4} - \frac{1}{5} = \frac{1}{20}$

So the six additional lengths make up 1/20 of Rebecca's intended distance. So the number of lengths she intended to complete was: 20 x 6 = 120.

Question 225: B

Sammy has a choice of 3 flavours for the first sweet that he eats. Each of the other sweets he eats cannot be the same flavour as the sweet he has just eaten. So he has a choice of 2 flavours for each of these four sweets. So the total number of ways that he can make his choices is:

$3 \times 2 \times 2 \times 2 \times 2 = 48$

Question 226: C

Suppose that today Gill is x years old. It follows that Granny is 15x years old. In 4 years' time, Gill will be (x+4) years old and Granny will be 15x+4 years old. We know that in 4 years' time, Granny's age is equal to Gill's age squared, so: $15x + 4 = (x + 4)^2$

Expanding and rearranging, we get: $x^2 - 7x + 12 = 0$

We can factorise this to get: $(x - 3)(x - 4)$

So x is either 3 or 4. Gill's age today is either 3 or 4 so Granny is either 45 or 60. We know Granny's age is an even number, so she must be 60 and hence Gill must be 4. So the difference in their ages is 56 years.

Question 227: C

If Pierre is telling the truth, everyone else is not telling the truth. But, also in this case, what Qadr said is not true, and hence Ratna is telling the truth. So we have a contradiction. So we deduce that Pierre is not telling the truth. Therefore, Qadr is telling the truth, and so Ratna is not telling the truth. So Sven is also telling the truth, and hence Tanya is not telling the truth. So Qadr and Sven are telling the truth and the other three are not telling the truth.

Question 228: D

Angus walks for 20 minutes at 3 mph and runs for 20 minutes at 6 mph. 20 minutes is one-third of an hour. So the number of miles that Angus covers is: $3 \times 13 + 6 \times 13 = 6$

Bruce covers the same distance. So Bruce walks 12×3 miles at 3 mph which takes him 30 minutes and runs the same distance at 6 mph which takes him 15 minutes. So altogether it takes Bruce 45 minutes to finish the course.

Question 229: B

Although you could do this quickly by forming simultaneous equations, it is even quicker to note that 72 x 4 = 288. Since Species 24601 each have 4 legs; it leaves a single member of species 8472 to account for the other 2 legs.

Question 230: E

None of the options can be concluded for certain. We are not told whether any chicken dishes are spicy, only that they are all creamy. Whilst all vegetable dishes are spicy, some non-vegetable dishes could also be spicy. There is no information on whether dishes can be both creamy and spicy, nor on which, if any, dishes contain tomatoes. Remember, if you're really stuck, draw a Venn diagram for these types of questions.

Question 231: C

At 10mph, we can express the time it takes Lucy to get home as: $60 \times 8/10 = 48$

Since Simon sets off 20 minutes later, his time taken to get home, in order to arrive at the same time, must be:

$48 - 20 = 28$

Therefore his cycling speed must be: $48/28 \times 10 = 17$mph

Question 232: A

The total profit from the first transaction can be expressed as: 2000 x 8 = 16,000p

The total profit from the second transaction is: 1000 x 6 = 6,000p

Therefore the total profit is 22,000p or £220 before charges. There are four transactions at a cost of £20 each, therefore the overall profit is: £220 – (20 x 4) = £140

Question 233: C

For the total score to be odd, there must be either three odd or one odd and two even scores obtained. Since the solitary odd score could be either the first, second or third throw there are four possible outcomes that result in an odd total score. Additionally, there are the same number of possibilities giving an even score (either all three even or two odd and one even scores obtained), and the chance of throwing odd or even with any given dart is equal. Therefore, there is an equal probability of three darts totalling to an odd score as to an even score, and so the chance of an odd score is ½.

Question 234 C

This is a compound interest question. £5,000 must be increased by 5%, and then the answer needs to be increased by 5% for four more iterations. After one year: £5,000 x 1.05 = £5,250

Increasing sequentially gives 5512, 5788, 6077 and 6381 after five years. Therefore the answer is £6,381.

Question 235: D

If in 5 years' time the sum of their ages is 62, the sum of their ages today will be: 62 – (5 x 2) = 52

Therefore if they were the same age they would both be 26, but with a 12 year age gap they are 20 and 32 today. Michael is the older brother, so 2 years ago he would have been aged 30.

Question 236: A

Tearing out every page which is a multiple of 3 removes 166 pages. All multiples of 6 are multiples of 3, so no more pages are torn out with that instruction. Finally, half of the remaining pages are removed, which equates to an additional 167 pages. Therefore 333 pages are removed in total. The total surface area of these pages is 15 x 30 x 333 = 149,850 cm^2 = 14.9m^2. At 110 gm^2, 14.9 m^2 weighs 14.9 x 110 = 1,650g (1,648g unrounded)

Question 237: D

The cost of fertiliser is 80p/kg = 8p/100g. At 200g the incremental increase in yield is 65 pence/m. At each additional 100g it will be reduced by 30%, therefore at 300g/m it is 45.5p, at 400g/m it is 31.8p, at 500g/m it is 22.3p, at 600g/m it is 15.6p, at 700g/m it is 10.9p, and at 800g it is 7.6p. So at 800g the gain in yield is less than the cost of the fertiliser to produce the gain, and so it is no longer cost effective to fertilise more.

Question 238: D

Statements **A**, **C** and **E** are all definitely true. Meanwhile, statement **B** may be not true but is not definitely untrue, as this depends on the number of cats and rabbit owned.

Only statement **D** is definitely untrue. The type of animal requiring the most food is a dog, and as can be seen from the tables, Furry Friends actually sells the most expensive dog food, not the cheapest.

Question 239: C

The largest decrease in bank balance occurs between January 1st and February 1st, totalling £171, reflecting the amount spent during the month of January, £1171. However, because there is a pay rise beginning on March 10th, we need to consider that from April onwards, the bank balance will have increased by £1100, not £1000. This means that the same decrease in bank balance reflects £100 more spending if it occurs after March. This means that 2 months now have seen more spending than February. Between March 1st and April 1st, the bank balance has decreased by £139. With the salary increase, the salary is now £1100, so the total spending for the month of March is £1239. This is greater than the total spending during the month of January.

Similarly, the month of April has also seen more spending than January once the pay rise is considered, a total of £1225 of spending. However, this is still less than the month of March.

Question 240: C

If Amy gets a taxi, she can set off 100 minutes before 1700, which is 1520.

If Amy gets a train, she must get the 1500 train as the later train arrives after 1700, so she must set off at 1500.

Since Northtown airport is 30 minutes from Northtown station, there is no way Amy can get the flight and still arrive at Northtown station by 1700. Therefore Amy should get a taxi and should leave at 1520.

Question 241: C

We can decompose the elements of the multiplication grid into their prime factors, thus:

	C	D
A	2 x 2 x 2 x 3 x 7	2 x 2 x 2 x 2 x 3 x 3 x 5
B	7 x 17	2 x 3 x 5 x 17

bc = 7 x 17, so one of b and c must be 7 and the other must be 17. b must be 17 because bd is a multiple of 17 and not of 7, and c must be 7 because ac is a multiple of 7 and not of 17. ac is 168, so a must be 168 divided by 7, which is 24. ad is 720 so d must be 720 divided by 24, which is 30. Hence the answer is 30.

Alternatively approach the question by eliminating all answers which are not factors of both 720 and 510.

Question 242: E

48% of the students are girls, which is 720 students. Hence 80 is 1/9 of the girls, so 1/9 of boys are mixed race. The remaining 780 students are boys, so 87 boys are mixed race to the nearest person. There is a shortcut to this question. Notice that 80 girls are mixed race, and the proportion is the same for boys. As there are more boys than girls we know the answer is greater than 80. Option **E** 90 is the only option for which this holds true.

Question 243: D

Don't be fooled – this is surprisingly easy. We can see that between Monday and Thursday, Christine has worked a total of 30 hours. We can also calculate how long her shift on Friday was supposed to be. She is able to make up the hours by working 3 extra hours next week, and 5 hours on Sunday. Thus, the Friday shift must have been planned to be 8 hours long. Adding this to the other 30 hours, we see that Christine was supposed to work 38 hours this week.

Question 244: C

130°. Each hour is 1/12 of a complete turn, equalling 30°. The smaller angle between 8 and 12 on the clock face is 4 gaps, therefore 120°. In addition, there is 1/3 of the distance between 3 and 4 still to turn, so an additional 10° must be added on to account for that.

Question 245: B

The total price of all of these items would usually be £17. However, with the DVD offer, the customer saves £1, giving a total cost of £16. Thus, the customer will need to receive £34 in change.

Question 246: E

A. Incorrect. UCL study found eating more portions of fruit and vegetables was beneficial.
B. Incorrect. This is a possible reason but has yet to be fully investigated.
C. Incorrect. Fruit and vegetables are more protective against cardiovascular disease, and were shown to have little effect on cancer rates.
D. Incorrect. Inconclusive – people who ate more vegetables generally had a lower mortality but unknown if this is due to eating more vegetables or other associated factors.
E. Correct. Although this has previously been the case, this study did not find so. 'they recorded no additional decline for people who ate over 5 portions'.
F. Incorrect. The 5% decline per portion was only up to 5 portions and no additional reduction in mortality for 7 than 5 portions.
G. Incorrect. Study only looks at cancers in general and states need to look into specific cancers.

Question 247: C

Deaths in meta-analysis = 56423/800000 = 0.07 or 7%
1% lower in UCL study so 6%
6% of 65,000 = 65000 x 0.06 = 3,900

Question 248: B
A. Eating more fruit and vegetables doesn't particularly lower overall risk but need research into specific cancer risk.
B. The UCL research alone found that increasing the number of fruit and vegetable portions had a beneficial effect, even though this wasn't the overall conclusion when combined with results from the meta-analysis.
C. The results were not exactly the same but showed similar overall trends.
D. Although this may be true, there is no mention of this in the passage.
E. Fruit and vegetables are protective against cardiovascular disease, but not exclusively. They also reduce the rates of death from all causes.
F. The UCL study is in England only and the meta-analysis a combination of studies from around the world.
G. Suggested by the UCL research, but not the meta-analysis, so not an overall conclusion of the article.

Question 249: E
Remember that you don't need to calculate exact values for question 249 – 251. Thus, you should round numbers frequently to make this more manageable. Work out percentage of beer and wine consumption and then the actual value using the total alcohol consumption figure:

Belarus: $17.3 + 5.2 = 22.5\%$;
$0.225 \times 17.5 = 3.94$

Lithuania: Missing figure $100 - 7.8 - 34.1 - 11.6 = 46.5$
$46.5 + 7.8 = 54.3\%$
$0.543 \times 15.4 = 8.36$

France: $18.8 + 56.4 = 75.2\%$
$0.752 \times 12.2 = 9.17$

Ireland: $48.1 + 26.1 = 74.2$
$0.742 \times 11.9 = 8.83$

Andorra: missing figure $100 - 34.6 - 20.1 = 45.3$
$34.6 + 45.3 = 79.9\%$
$0.799 \times 13.8 = 11.0$

Question 250: D

Russia:
2010 – Total $= 11.5 + 3.6 = 15.1$. Spirits $= 0.51 \times 15.1 = 7.7$
2020 – Total $= 14.5$. Spirits $= 0.51 \times 14.5 = 7.4$
Difference $= 0.3$ L

Belarus:
2010 – Total $= 14.4 + 3.2 = 17.6$. Spirits $= 0.466 \times 17.6 = 8.2$
2020 – Total $= 17.1$. Spirits $= 0.466 \times 17.1 = 8.0$
Difference $= 0.2$ L

Lithuania:
2010 – Total $= 15.4$. Spirits $= 0.341 \times 15.4 = 5.3$
2020 – Total $= 16.2$. Spirits $= 0.341 \times 16.2 = 5.5$
Difference $= 0.2$ L

Grenada:
2010 – Total $= 12.5$. Spirits $\% = 100 - 29.3 - 4.3 - 0.2 = 66.2\%$. Spirits $= 0.662 \times 12.5 = 8.3$
2020 – Total $= 10.4$. Spirits $= 0.662 \times 10.4 = 6.8$
Difference $= 1.5$ L

Ireland:
2010 – Total $= 11.9$. Spirits $= 0.187 \times 11.9 = 2.2$
2020 – Total $= 10.9$. Spirits $= 0.187 \times 10.9 = 2$
Difference $= 0.2$ L

Question 251: C
Work out 4.9 as a percentage of total beer consumption in Czech Republic and search other rows for similar percentage.

4.9/13 = 0.38, approx. 38% which is very similar to percentage consumption in Russia (37.6).

Question 252: B
We can add up the total incidence of the 6 cancers in men, which is 94,000. Then we can add up the total incidence in women, which is 101,000. As a percentage of 10 million, this is 0.94% of men and 1.01% of women. Therefore the difference is 0.07%.

Question 253: C
Given there are 1.15 times as many men as women, the incidence of each cancer amongst men needs to be greater than 1.15 times the incidence amongst women in order for a man to be more likely to develop it. The incidence is at least 1.15 higher in men for 3 cancers (prostate, lung and bladder).

Question 254: D
If 10% of cancer patients are in Sydney, there are 10,300 prostate/bladder/breast cancer patients and 9,200 lung/bowel/uterus cancer patients in Sydney. Hence the total number of hospital visits is 10,300 + 18,400, which is 28,700.

Question 255: A
The proportion of men with bladder cancer is 2/3 and women 1/3.

Question 256: D
First we work out the size of each standard drink. 50 standard drinks of vodka is equivalent to 1250ml, so one drink is 25ml or 0.025 litres. 11.4 standard drinks of beer is 10 pints of 5700ml, so one standard drink is 500ml or 0.5 litres. 3 standard drinks of cocktail is 750ml so one is 250ml or 0.25 litres. 3.75 standard drinks of wine is 750ml, so one is 200ml or 0.2 litres.
We can then work out the number of units in each drink. Vodka has 0.025 x 40 = 1 unit, Beer has 0.5 x 3 = 1.5 units, Cocktail has 0.25 x 8 = 2 units and Wine has 0.2 x 12.5 = 2.5 units. Since the drink with the most units is wine, the answer is D.

Question 257: B
We found in the last question that vodka has 1 unit, beer has 1.5, cocktail has 2 and wine has 2.5. Hence in the week, Hannah drinks 23.5 units and Mark drinks 29 units. Hence Hannah exceeds the recommended amount by 9.5 units and Mark by 9 units.

Question 258: D
We found that vodka has 1 unit, beer has 1.5, cocktail has 2 and wine has 2.5. Hence it is possible to make 5 combinations of drinks that are 4 units: 4 vodkas, 2 cocktails, 2 vodkas and a cocktail, 1 vodka and 2 beers, or a wine and a beer.

Question 259: D
The total number of males in Greentown is 12,890. Adding up the rest of the age categories, we can see that 10,140 of these are in the older age categories. Hence there are 2750 males under 20.

Question 260: C
Given that in the first question we found the number of males under 20 is 2,750, we can then add up the totals in the age categories (apart from 40-59) in order to find that 15,000 of the residents of Greentown are in other age categories. Hence 9,320 of the population are aged 40-59. We know that 4,130 of these are male, therefore 5,190 must be female.

Question 261: C
The age group with the highest ratio of males:females is 20-39, with approximately 1.9 males per females (approximately 3800:2000). As a ratio of females to males, this is 1:1.9.

Question 262: C
There are 4 instances where the line for Newcastle is flat from one month to the next per year, hence in 2008-2012 (5 years) there are 20 occasions when the average temperature is the same from month to month. During 2007, there are 2 occasions, and during 2013 there are 3.

Question 263: A
The average temperature is lower than the previous month in London for all months from August to December, which is 5 months. However, in August and November in Newcastle, the average temperature remains the same as the previous month. Hence there are only 3 months where the average temperature is lower in both cities. Hence from 2007 to 2012, there are 18 months where the average temperature is lower than the previous month. During 2013, the only included month where the temperature is lower in both cities than the previous month is September. Hence there are 19 months in total when the temperature is lower in both cities than the previous month.

Question 264: B
Firstly, work out the difference between average temperatures for each month (2, 3, 1, 2, 1, 3, 3, 2, 2, 5, 1, 0). Then sum them to give 25. Divide by the number of months (12) to give $2^1/_{12}$, which is 2°C to the nearest 0.5°C.

Question 265: D
There is not enough information to tell which month the highest sales are in. We know it increases up to a point and decreases after it, but as we don't know by how much we cannot project where the maximum sales will be.

Question 266: B
Given that by observation, Q2 and Q3 both account for 1/3 of the sales and Q4 accounts for 1/4, this leaves that Q1 accounts for 1/12 of sales. 1/12 of £354,720 is £29,560.

Question 267: A
Quarter 2 accounts for 1/3 of the sales, which is £60,000 in sales revenue. If a tub of ice cream is sold for £2 and costs the manufacturer £1.50, this means profit is 1/4 of sales revenue. Hence £15,000 profit is made during Q2. Hence the answer is A.

Question 268: D
A. and B – Incorrect. Both *could* be true but neither is *definitely* true as it is dependent on the relative number of families with each number of children, which is not given in the question. Therefore we cannot know for certain whether these statements are true.
C – Incorrect. C is definitely *untrue* as half of the families spend £400 a month on food, which totals £4800 a year.
D – Correct. This option is true as 1/6 of families with 1 child and 1/6 of families with 3 children spent £100 a month on food.
E – Incorrect. This option is definitely untrue as the average expenditure for families with 2 children is actually £400 a month.

Question 269: B
2210 out of 2500 filled in responses, meaning that 290 did not. 290 as a percentage of 2500 is roughly 12% (11.6%) of the school that did not respond.

Question 270: C
The percentage of students that saw bullying and reported it was 35%, so 65% of those who saw it did not which is equivalent to 725 students. Of this 725, 146 which roughly equals 20%, gave the reason that they did not think it was important.

Question 271: B
Of the students who told a teacher, 286 did not witness any action. Of those who did notice action, i.e. 110, only 40% noticed any direct action with the bully involved. 40% of 110 is 44, so the correct answer is B.

Question 272: D
"427 cited fears of being found out" which means about 59% out of the 725 students that did not tell about the bullying, cited that it was because they worried about others finding out.

Question 273: F

North-east: 56 per 100,000 on average. This means that there must be a higher proportion of women than this and a lower proportion of men, such that the average is 56/100,000

We must make the reasonable assumption that there are the same number of men and women in the population as the question asks us to approximate.

Therefore there are 18.6/50,000 men and 37.3/50,000 women

This scales to 74.4/100,000 women which is roughly 74/100,000.

Question 274: C

8 million children – question tells to approximate to 4 million girls and 4 million boys.

Girls: 20% eat 5 portions fruit and vegetables a day. 20% of 4 million: 4 x 0.2 = 0.8 million

Boys: 16% eat 5 portions of fruit and vegetables a day. 16% of 4 million: 4 x 0.16 = 0.64 million

Number of more girls: 800,000 – 640,000 = 160,000.

Question 275: B

A. Incorrect. Women: 13619+10144+6569 = 30332. Men: 16818 + 9726 + 7669 + 6311 = 40524
B. Correct. Flu + pneumonia, lung cancer and chronic lower respiratory diseases = 15361 + 13619 + 14927 = 43907
C. Incorrect. More common cause of death but no information surrounding prevalence.
D. Incorrect. Colon cancer ranking 8 for both.

Question 276: A

The government has claimed a 20% reduction, so we are looking for an assessment criterion which has reduced 20% from 2013 to 2014. We can see that only "Number of people waiting for over 4 hours in A&E" has reduced by 20%, so this must be the criterion the government has used to describe "waiting times in A&E". Thus, the answer is A.

Question 277: B

Rovers must have played 10 games overall as they played each other's team twice. They lost 9 games scoring no points and so must have won 1 game, which scores 3 points.

Question 278: A

To have finished between City and United, Athletic must have got between 23 and 25 points. Hence they must have got 24 points because no team got the same number of points as another. Athletic won 7 games which is 21 points, so they must have also got 3 points from drawing 3 games. This accounts for all 10 games they played, so they did not lose any games.

Question 279: C

United won 8 games and drew 1, which is 25 points. Rangers drew 2 games and won none, which is 2 points. Therefore the difference in points is 23.

Question 280: C

Type 1 departments reached the new target of 95% at least three times since it was introduced. All the other statements are correct.

Question 281: C

Total attendances in Q1 08-9: 5.0 million
Total attendances in Q1 04-5: 4.5 million
The difference = 0.5 million
0.5/5 x 100 = 10% increase

Question 282: C

There are 16 quarters in total since the new target came into effect.
4/16 = 0.25, so the target has been hit 25% of the time i.e. missed 75% of the time.

Question 283: C
Ranjna must leave Singapore by 20:00 to get to Bali by 22:00. The latest flight she can therefore get is the 19:00. Thus, she must arrive in Singapore by 17:00 (accounting 2 hours for the stopover). The flight from Manchester to Singapore takes 14 hours. Manchester is 8 hours behind Singapore so she must leave Manchester 22 hours before 17:00 on Wednesday i.e. by 19:00 on Wednesday. Thus, the latest flight she can get is the 18:00 on Wednesday.

Question 284: D
The 08:00 flight will arrive at Singapore for 22:00 on Monday (GMT) or 06:00 Tuesday Singapore time. She then needs a 2 hour stopover, so earliest connecting flight she can get is 08:30 on Tuesday. The flight lands in Bali at 10:30. She then spends 1 hour and 45 minutes getting to her destination – arriving at 12:15 Tuesday.

Question 285: C
A. Incorrect. The graph is about level, and certainly not the steepest gradient post 2007.
B. Incorrect. Although there has been a general decline, there are some blips of increased smoking.
C. Correct.
D. Incorrect. The smoking rate in men decreased from 51% in 1974 to 21% in 2010. Thus, it decreased by more than a half.
E. Incorrect. The percentage difference between men and women smokers has been minimal in the 21st century.

Question 286: D
For this type of question you will have to use trial and error after you've analysed the data pattern to find the correct answer. The quickest way to do this is to examine outliers to try and match them to data in the table e.g. the left-most point is an outlier for the X-axis but average for the y-axis. Also look for any duplicated results in the table and if they are present on the graph, e.g. Hannah and Alice weigh 68 kg but this can't be found on the graph.

Question 287: C
This is pretty straightforward; the point is at approximately 172-174 cm in height and 164 -166 cm in arm span. Matthew is the only student who fits these dimensions.

Question 288: C
This is straightforward – just label the diagram using the information in the text and it becomes obvious that C is the correct answer.

Question 289: C
Since we do not know whether they went to university or not, we must add the number of women with children who work and those who went to university, 2, to the number of women with children who work but did not go to university, 1 (2 + 1 = 3).

Question 290: C
To work this out we must add up all the numbers within the rectangle, 4 + 6 + 1 + 2 + 11 + 12 + 7 + 15 = 58

Question 291: E
Calculate the number of men + women who have children and work i.e. 11 + 5 + 2 = 18

Question 292: C
To solve this we must work out the total number of people who had children i.e. 3 + 6 + 5 + 11 + 1 + 2 =28. Then we work out the total number of people who went to university, but that do not also have children so that these are not counted twice: 13 + 12 = 25. Then we add these two numbers together, 28 + 25 = 53 and subtract the number of people who fell into both categories i.e. 53 - (5 + 11 + 2) = 35

Question 293: C
To work this out we must add up all the numbers outside the rectangle that also fall within both the circle and the square, which is 5.

Question 294: D & E

This question asks for identification of the blank space, which is the space within the triangle, the rectangle and the square i.e. indicating working women who went to university but did not have children. This also reveals non-working men who did not have children and did not go to university.

Question 295: C

The normal price of these items would be £18.50 (£8 + £7 + £3.50). However, with the 50% discount on meat products, the price in the sale for these items will be £9.25. Thus, Alfred would receive £10.75 of change from a £20 note.

Question 296: C

The number of games played and points scored is a red herring in this question. The important data is 'Goals For' and 'Goals Against'. As this is a defined league and the teams have only played each other, the 'Goals For' column must equal the 'Goals Against' column.

Total Goals For = 16 + 11 + 8 + 7 + 8 + 4 = 54

Total Goals Against = 2 + Wilmslow + 7 + 9 + 12 + 14 = 44 + Wilmslow

For both columns to be equal, Wilmslow must have a total of 54 – 44 = 10 Goals Against.

Question 297: C

Working with the table it is possible to work out that the BMIs of Julie and Lydia must be 21 and 23, and hence their weights 100 and 115 lbs. Thus Emma's weight is 120 lbs, and her BMI must be 22, making her height equivalent to 160 cm.

Question 298: C

Working through the results, starting with the highest and lowest values, it is possible to plot all values and decipher which point is marked.

Question 299: D

This is a question of estimation. The average production across the year is at least 7 million barrels per day. Multiplying this by 365 gives around 2,550 million barrels per year. All other options require less than 7 million barrels daily production to be produced, and it is clear there is at least 7 million barrels per day. Therefore the answer is 2,700 million.

Alternatively we can estimate using 30 days per month, and multiplying the amount of barrels produced per day in each month by 30 (this is more accurate but more time consuming). 6+7+7+7.5+7.5+7+7.5+8+8.5+8.5+8+9 = 91.5, multiplying by 30 gives just over 2,700 million barrels.

Question 300: C

Use both graphs. For July, multiply the oil price by the amount sold in the month, and multiply by the number of days in the month. Thus, July = 7.5 million barrels x $75 per barrel x 31 days = $17,400 million = $17.4 billion

Question 301: A

DNA consists of 4 bases: adenine, guanine, thymine and cysteine. The sugar backbone consists of deoxyribose, hence the name DNA. DNA is found in the cytoplasm of prokaryotes.

Question 302: F

Mitochondria are responsible for energy production by ATP synthesis. Animal cells do not have a cell wall, only a cell membrane. The endoplasmic reticulum is important in protein synthesis, as this is where the proteins are assembled.

Question 303: F

If you aren't studying A-level biology, this question may stretch you. However, it is possible to reach an answer by process of elimination. Mitochondria are the 'powerhouse' of the cell in aerobic respiration, responsible for cell energy production rather than DNA replication or protein synthesis. As energy producers they are required in muscle cells in large numbers, and in sperm cells to drive the tail responsible for movement. They are enveloped by a double membrane, possibly because they started out as independent prokaryotes engulfed by eukaryotic cells.

Question 304: A

The majority of bacteria are commensals and don't lead to disease.

Question 305: C

Bacteria carry genetic information on plasmids and not in nuclei like animal cells. They don't need meiosis for replication, as they do not require gametes. Bacterial genomes consist of DNA, just like animal cells.

Question 306: C

Active transport requires a transport protein and ATP, as work is being done against an electrochemical gradient. Unlike diffusion, the relative concentrations of the materials being transported aren't important.

Question 307: D

Meiosis produces haploid gametes. This allows for fusion of 2 gametes to reach a full diploid set of chromosomes again in the zygote.

Question 308: B

Mendelian inheritance separates traits into dominant or recessive. It applies to all sexually reproducing organisms. Don't get confused by statement C – the offspring of 2 heterozygotes has a 25% chance of expressing a recessive trait, but it will be homozygous recessive.

Question 309: A

Hormones are released into the bloodstream and act on receptors in different organs in order to cause relatively slow changes to the body's physiology. Hormones frequently interact with the nervous system, e.g. Adrenaline and Insulin, however, they don't directly cause muscles to contract. Almost all hormones are synthesised.

Question 310: D

Neuronal signalling can happen via direct electrical stimulation of nerves or via chemical stimulation of synapses which produces a current that travels along the nerves. Electrical synapses are very rare in mammals, the majority of mammalian synapses are chemical.

Question 311: D

Remember that pH changes cause changes in electrical charge on proteins (= polypeptides) that could interfere with protein – protein interactions. Whilst the other statements are all correct to a certain extent, they are the downstream effects of what would happen if enzymes (which are also proteins) didn't work.

Question 312: A

The bacterial cell wall is made up of murein and protects the bacterium from the external environment, in particular from osmotic stresses, and is important in most bacteria.

Question 313: C

Sexual reproduction relies on formation of gametes during **meiosis**. Mitosis doesn't produce genetically distinct cells. Mitosis is, however, the basis for tissue growth.

Question 314: A

A mutation is a permanent change in the nucleotide sequence of DNA. Whilst mutations may lead to changes in organelles and chromosomes, or even be harmful, they are strictly defined as permanent changes to the DNA or RNA sequence.

Question 315: E

Mutations are fairly common, but in the vast majority of cases do not have any impact on phenotype due to the redundancy of the genome. Sometimes they can confer selective advantages and allow organisms to survive better (i.e. evolve by natural selection), or they can lead to cancers as cells start dividing uncontrollably.

Question 316: D

Antibodies represent a pivotal molecule of the immune system. They provide very pointed and selective targeting of pathogens and toxins without causing damage to the body's own cells.

Question 317: A

Kidneys are not involved in digestion, but do filter the blood of waste products. Glucose is found in high concentrations in the urine of diabetics, who cannot absorb it without working insulin.

Question 318: D

Hormones are slower acting than nerves and act for a longer time. Hormones also act in a more general way. Adrenaline is also a hormone released into the body causing the fight-or-flight response. Although it is quick acting, it still lasts for a longer time than a nervous response, as you can still feel its effects for a time after the response, e.g. shaking hands.

Question 319: D

Homeostasis is about minimising changes to the internal environment by modulating both input and output.

Question 320: B

There is less energy and biomass each time you move up a trophic level. Only 10% of consumed energy is transferred to the next trophic level, so only one tenth of the previous biomass can be sustained in the next trophic level up.

Question 321: A

In asexual reproduction, there is no fusion of gametes as the single parent cell divides. There is therefore no mixing of chromosomes and, as a result, no genetic variation.

Question 322: E

The image is first formed on the retina which conveys it to the brain via a sensory nerve. The brain then sends an impulse to the muscle via a motor neuron.

Question 323: D

Blood from the kidney returns to the heart via the renal (kidney-related) vein, which drains into the inferior vena cava. The blood then passes through the pulmonary vasculature (veins carry blood to the heart, arteries away from the heart) before going into the aorta and eventually the hepatic (liver-related) artery.

Question 324: F

Clones are genetically identical by definition, and a large number of them could conceivably reduce the gene pool of a population. In adult cell cloning, the genetic material of an egg is replaced with the genetic material of an adult cell. Cloning is possible for all DNA based life forms, including plants and other types of animals.

Question 325: F

Gene varieties cause intraspecies variation, e.g. different eye colours. If mutations confer a selective advantage, those individuals with the mutation will survive to reproduce and grow in numbers. Genetic variation is caused by mixing of parent genomes and mutations. Species with similar characteristics often do have similar genes.

Question 326: F

Alleles are different versions of the same gene. If you are a homozygous for a trait, you have two identical alleles for that particular gene, and if you are heterozygous you have two different alleles of that gene. Recessive traits only appear in the phenotype when there are no dominant alleles for that trait, i.e. two recessive alleles are carried.

Question 327: D

Remember that red blood cells don't have a nucleus and therefore have no DNA. In meiosis, a diploid cell divides in such a way so as to produce four haploid cells. Any type of cell division will require energy.

Question 328: C

The hypothalamus detects too little water in the blood, so the pituary gland releases ADH. The kidney maintains the blood water level, and allows less water to be lost in the urine until the blood water level returns to normal.

Question 329: E

Venous blood has a higher level of carbon dioxide and lower oxygen. Carbon dioxide forms carbonic acid in aqueous solution, thus making the pH of venous blood slightly more acidic than arterial blood. This leaves only E and F as possibilities, but releasing pH levels cannot fluctuate significantly gives pH 7.4.

Question 330: E

The cytoplasm is 80% water, but also contains, among other things, electrolytes and proteins. The cytoplasm doesn't contain everything, e.g. DNA is found in the nucleus.

Question 331: C

ATP is produced in mitochondria in aerobic respiration and in the cytoplasm during anaerobic respiration only.

Question 332: C

The cell membrane allows both active transport and passive transport by diffusion of certain ions and molecules, and is found in eukaryotes and prokaryotes like bacteria. It is a phospholipid bilayer.

Question 333: A

1 and 2 only: 223 PAIRS = 446 chromosomes; meiosis produces 4 daughter cells with half of the original number of chromosomes each, while mitosis produces two daughter cells with the original number of chromosomes each.

Question 334: E

If Bob is homozygous dominant (RR) the probability of having a child with red hair is 0%. However, if Bob is heterozygous (Rr), there is a 50% chance of having a child with red hair, since Mary must be homozygous recessive (rr) to have red hair. As we do not know Bob's genotype, both possibilities must be considered.

Question 335: A

If an offspring is born with red hair, it confirms Bob is heterozygous (Rr). He cannot have a red-haired child if he is homozygous dominant (RR), and would himself have red hair were he homozygous recessive (rr).

Question 336: A

Monohybrid cross rr and Rr results in 50% Rr and 50% rr offspring. 50% of offspring will have black hair, but they will be heterozygous for the hair allele.

Question 337: C

When the chest walls expand, the intra-thoracic pressure decreases. This causes the atmospheric pressure outside the chest to be greater than pressure inside the chest, resulting in a flow of air into the chest.

Question 338: A

Producers are found at the bottom of food chains and always have the largest biomass.

Question 339: F

All the statements are true; the carbon and nitrogen cycles are examinable in Section 2, so make sure you understand them! The atmosphere is 79% inert N_2 gas, which must be 'fixed' to useable forms by high-energy lightning strikes or by bacterial mediation. Humans also manually fix nitrogen for fertilisers with the Haber process.

Question 340: H

None of the above statements are correct. Mutations can be silent, cause a loss of function, or even a gain in function, depending on the exact location in the gene and the base affected. Mutations only cause a change in protein structure if the amino acids expressed by the gene affected are changed. This is normally due to a shift in reading frame. Whilst cancer arises as a result of a series of mutations, very few mutations actually lead to cancer.

Question 341: C

Remember that heart rate is controlled via the autonomic nervous system, which isn't a part of the central nervous system.

Question 342: H
None of the above are correct. There is no voluntary input to the heart in the form of a neuronal connection. Parasympathetic neurones slow the heart and sympathetic nervous input accelerates heart rate.

Question 343: B
If lipase is not working, fat from the diet will not be broken down, and will build up in the stool. Lactase, for instance, is responsible for breaking down lactose, and its malfunctioning causes lactose-intolerance.

Question 344: F
Oxygenated blood flows from the lungs to the heart via the pulmonary vein. The pulmonary artery carries deoxygenated blood from the heart to the lungs. Animals like fish have single circulatory systems. Deoxygenated blood is found in the superior vena cava, returning to the heart from the body. Veins in the arms and hands frequently don't have valves.

Question 345: E
Enzymatic digestion takes place throughout the GI tract, including in the mouth (e.g. amylase), stomach (e.g. pepsin), and small intestine (e.g. trypsin). The large intestine is primarily responsible for water absorption, whilst the rectum acts as a temporary store for faecal matter (i.e. digestion has finished by the rectum).

Question 346: B
This is an example of the monosynaptic stretch reflex; these reflexes are performed at the spinal level and therefore don't involve the brain.

Question 347: A
Statement 2 describes diffusion, as CO_2 is moving with the concentration gradient. Statement 3 describes active transport, as amino acids are moving against the concentration gradient.

Question 348: I
3 is the correct equation for animals, and 4 is correct for plants.

Question 349: C
The mitochondria are only the site for aerobic respiration, as anaerobic respiration occurs in the cytoplasm. Aerobic respiration produces more ATP per substrate than anaerobic respiration, and therefore is also more efficient. The chemical equation for glucose being respired aerobically is: $C_6H_{12}O_6 + 6O_2 \rightarrow 6CO_2 + 6H_2O$. Thus, the molar ratio is 1:6 (i.e. each mole glucose produces 6 moles of CO_2).

Question 350: B
The nucleus contains the DNA and chromosomes of the cell. The cytoplasm contains enzymes, salts and amino acids in addition to water. The plasma membrane is a bilayer. Lastly, the cell wall is indeed responsible for protecting vs. increased osmotic pressures.

Question 351: D
When a medium is hypertonic relative to the cell cytoplasm, it is more concentrated than the cytoplasm, and when it is hypotonic, it is less concentrated. So, when a medium is hypotonic relative to the cell cytoplasm, the cell will gain water through osmosis. When the medium is isotonic, there will be no net movement of water across the cell membrane. Lastly, when the medium is hypertonic relative to the cell cytoplasm, the cell will lose water by osmosis.

Question 352: A
Stem cells have the ability to differentiate and produce other kinds of cells. However, they also have the ability to generate cells of their own kind and stem cells are able to maintain their undifferentiated state. The two types of stem cells are embryonic stem cells and adult stem cells. The adult stem cells are present in both children and adults.

Question 353: B
All of the following statements are examples of natural selection, except for the breeding of horses. Breeding and animal husbandry are notable methods of artificial selection, which are brought about by humans.

Question 354: C

Enzymes create a stable environment to stabilise the transition state. Enzymes do not distort substrates. Enzymes generally have little effect on temperature directly. Lastly, they are able to provide alternative pathways for reactions to occur.

Question 355: C

A negative feedback system seeks to minimise changes in a system by modulating the response in accordance with the error that's generated. Salivating before a meal is an example of a feed-forward system (i.e. salivating is an anticipatory response). Throwing a dart does not involve any feedback (during the action). pH and blood pressure are both important homeostatic variables that are controlled via powerful negative feedback mechanisms, e.g. massive haemorrhage leads to compensatory tachycardia.

Question 356: A

One of the major functions of white blood cells is to defend the body against bacterial and fungal infections. They can kill pathogens by engulfing them and also use antibodies to help them recognise pathogens. Antibodies are produced by white blood cells.

Question 357: B

The CV system does indeed transport nutrients and hormones. It also increases blood flow to exercising muscles (via differential vasodilatation) and also helps with thermoregulation (e.g. vasoconstriction in response to cold). The respiratory system is responsible for oxygenating blood.

Question 358: C

Adrenaline always increases heart rate and is almost always released during sympathetic responses. It travels primarily in the blood and affects multiple organ systems. It is also a potent vasoconstrictor.

Question 359: B

Protein synthesis occurs in the cytoplasm. Proteins are usually coded by several amino acids. Red blood cells lack a nucleus and, therefore, the DNA to create new proteins. Protein synthesis is a key part of mitosis, as it allows the parent cell to grow prior to division.

Question 360: F

Remember that most enzymes work better in neutral environments (amylase works even better at slightly alkaline pH). Thus, adding sodium bicarbonate will increase the pH and hence increase the rate of activity. Adding carbohydrate will have no effect, as the enzyme is already saturated. Adding amylase will increase the amount of carbohydrate that can be converted per unit time. Increasing the temperature to 100° C will denature the enzyme and reduce the rate.

Question 361: E

Taking the normal allele to be C and the diseased allele to be c, one can model the scenario with the following Punnett square:

		Carrier Mother	
		C	c
Diseased Father	c	Cc	cc
	c	Cc	cc

The gender of the children is irrelevant as the inheritance is autosomal recessive, but we see that all children produced would inherit at least one diseased allele.

Question 362: F

All of the organs listed have endocrine functions. The thyroid produces thyroid hormone. The ovary produces oestrogen. The pancreas secretes glucagon and insulin. The adrenal gland secretes adrenaline. The testes produce testosterone.

Question 363: A
Insulin works to decrease blood glucose levels. Glucagon causes blood glucose levels to increase; glycogen is a carbohydrate. Adrenaline works to increase heart rate.

Question 364: A
The left side of the heart contains oxygenated blood from the lungs which will be pumped to the body. The right side of the heart contains deoxygenated blood from the body to be pumped to the lungs.

Question 365: A
Since Individual 1 is homozygous normal, and individual 5 is heterozygous and affected, the disease must be dominant. Since males only have one X-chromosome, they cannot be carriers for X-linked conditions. If Nafram syndrome was X-linked, then parents 5 and 6 would produce sons who always have no disease and daughters that always do. As this is not the case shown in individuals 7-10, the disease must be autosomal dominant.

Question 366: C
We know that the inheritance of Nafram syndrome is autosomal dominant, so using N to mean a diseased allele and n to mean a normal allele, 5, 7 and 8 must be Nn because they have an unaffected parent. 2 is also Nn, as if it was NN all its progeny would be Nn and so affected by the disease, which is not the case, as 3 and 4 are unaffected.

Question 367: A
Since 6 is disease free, his genotype must be nn. Thus, neither of 6's parents could be NN, as otherwise 6 would have at least one diseased allele.

Question 368: A
Urine passes from the kidney into the ureter and is then stored in the bladder. It is finally released through the urethra.

Question 369: F
Deoxygenated blood from the body flows through the inferior vena cava to the right atrium where it flows to the right ventricle to be pumped via the pulmonary artery to the lungs where it is oxygenated. It then returns to the heart via the pulmonary vein into the left atrium into the left ventricle where it is pumped to the body via the aorta.

Question 370: E
During inspiration, the pressure in the lungs decreases as the diaphragm contracts, increasing the volume of the lungs. The intercostal muscles contract in inspiration, lifting the rib cage.

Question 371: D
Whilst A, B, C and E are true of the DNA code, they do not represent the property described, which is that more than one combination of codons can encode the same amino acid, e.g. Serine is coded by the sequences: TCT, TCC, TCA, TCG.

Question 372: B
The degenerate nature of the code can help to reduce the deleterious effects of point mutations. The several 3-nucleotide combinations that code for each amino acid are usually similar such that a point mutation, i.e. a substitution of one nucleotide for another, can still result in the same amino acid as the one coded for by the original sequence.

The degenerate nature of the code does little to protect against deletions/insertions/duplications, which will cause the bases to be read in incorrect triplets, i.e. result in a frame shift.

Question 373: D
The hypothalamus is the site of central thermoreceptors. A decrease in environmental temperature decreases sweat secretion and causes cutaneous vasoconstriction to minimise heat loss from the blood.

Question 374: A
The movement of carbon dioxide in the lungs and neurotransmitters in a synapse are both examples of diffusion. Glucose reabsorption is an active process, as it requires work to be done against a concentration gradient.

Question 375: F

Some enzymes contain other molecules besides protein, e.g. metal ions. Enzymes can increase rates of reaction that may result in heat gain/loss, depending on if the reaction is exothermic or endothermic. They are prone to variations in pH and are highly specific to their individual substrate.

Question 376: D

Different isotopes are differentiated by the number of neutrons in the core. This gives them different molecular weights and different chemical properties with regards to stability. The number of protons defines each element, and the number of electrons its charge.

Question 377: E

A displacement reaction occurs when a more reactive element displaces a less reactive element in its compound. All 4 reactions are examples of displacement reactions as a less reactive element is being replaced by a more reactive one.

Question 378: A

There needs to be 3Ca, 12H, 14O and 2P on each side. Only option A satisfies this.

Question 379: A

To balance the equation there needs to be 9Ag, 9N, $9O_3$, 9K, 3P on each side. Only option A satisfies this.

Question 380: D

A more reactive halogen can displace a less reactive halogen. Thus, chlorine can displace bromine and iodine from an aqueous solution of its salts, and fluorine can replace chlorine. The trend is the opposite for alkali metals, where reactivity increases down the group as electrons are further from the core and easier to lose.

Question 381: C

$2Mg + O_2 = 2MgO$
so, $2 \times 24 = 48$ and $2 \times (24 + 16) = 80$
so, 48 g of magnesium produces 80g of magnesium oxide
so 1g of magnesium produces 1g x 80g/48g = 1.666g oxide
so 75g x 1.666 = 125g

Question 382: B

$H_2 + 2OH^- \rightarrow 2H_2O + e^-$
Thus, the hydrogen loses electrons i.e. is oxidised.

Question 383: F

Ammonia is 1 nitrogen and 3 hydrogen atoms bonded covalently. N = 14g and H = 1g per mole, so percentage of N in NH_3 = 14g/17g = 82%. It can be produced from N_2 through fixation or the industrial Haber process for use in fertiliser, and may break down to its components.

Question 384: A

Milk is weakly acidic, pH 6.5-7.0, and contains fat. This is broken down by lipase to form fatty acids - turning the solution slightly more acidic.

Question 385: C

Glucose loses four hydrogen atoms; one definition of an oxidation reaction is a reaction in which there is loss of hydrogen.

Question 386: C

Isotopes have the same number of protons and electrons, but a different number of neutrons. The number of neutrons has no impact on the rate of reactions.

Question 387: E

$Mg + H_2SO_4 \rightarrow MgSO_4 + H_2$

Number of moles of Mg $= \frac{6}{24} = 0.25$ moles.

1 mole of Mg reacts with 1 mole H_2SO_4 to produce 1 mole of magnesium sulphate. Therefore, 0.25 moles H_2SO_4 will react to produce 0.25 moles of $MgSO_4$.

M_r of $H_2SO_4 = 2 + 32 + 64 = 98$g per mole

The mass of H_2SO_4 used = 0.25 moles x 98g per mole = 24.5g.

Since 30g of H_2SO_4 is present, H_2SO_4 is in excess and the magnesium is the limiting reagent.

M_r of $MgSO_4 = 24 + 32 + 64 = 120$g per mole

The mass of $MgSO_4$ produced = 0.25 moles x 120g per mole = 30g which is the same mass as that of sulphuric acid in the original reaction.

Question 388: F

Reactivity series of metals:

Cu is more reactive than Ag and will displace it.

Ca is more reactive than H and will displace it.

2 and 4 are incorrect because Fe is higher in the reactivity series than Cu and Fe is lower in the reactivity series than Ca, so no displacement will occur.

Question 389: G

Moving left to right is the equivalent of moving down the metal reactivity series (i.e. Na is most reactive and Zn is least reactive). Therefore, moving from left to right, the reactivity of the metals decreases, likelihood of corrosion decreases, less energy is required to separate metals from their ores and metals lose electrons less readily to form positive ions.

Question 390: F

Halogens become less reactive as you progress down group 17. Thus in order of increasing reactivity from left to right: I$\rightarrow$ Br$\rightarrow$ Cl. Therefore, I will not displace Br, Cl will displace Br and Br will displace I.

Question 391: A

Wires are made out of copper because it is a good conductor of electricity. Copper is also used in coins (not aluminium). Aluminium is resistant to corrosion but because of a layer of aluminium oxide (not hydroxide).

Question 392: C

$2Li + 2H_2O \rightarrow 2LiOH + H_2$

Therefore, 2 moles of Li react to produce 1 mole of H_2 gas (24 dm^3).

The number of moles of Li $= \frac{21}{7} = 3$ moles.

Thus, 1.5 moles of H_2 gas are produced = 36 dm^3.

Question 393: B

$MgCl_2$ contains stronger bonds than NaCl because Mg ions have a 2+ charge, thus having a stronger electrostatic pull for negative chloride ions. The smaller atomic radius also means that the nucleus has less distance between it and incoming electrons. Transition metals are able to form multiple stable ions e.g. Fe^{2+} and Fe^{3+}.

Covalently bonded structures do tend to have lower MPs than ionically bonded, but the giant covalent structures (diamond and graphite for example) have very high melting points. Graphite is an example of a covalently bonded structure which conducts electricity.

Question 394: D

Energy is released from reaction **A**, as shown by a negative enthalpy. The reaction is therefore exothermic. Since energy is released, the product CO_2 has less energy than the reactants did. Therefore, CO_2 is more stable. Reaction **B** has a positive enthalpy, which means energy must be put into the reaction for it to occur i.e. it's an endothermic reaction. That means that the products (CaO and CO_2) have more energy and are less stable than the reactants ($CaCO_3$).

Question 395: B
Solid oxides are unable to conduct electricity because the ions are immobile. Metals are extracted from their molten ores by electrolysis. Fractional distillation is used to separate miscible liquids with similar boiling points. Mg^{2+} ions have a greater positive charge and a smaller ionic radius than Na^+ ions, and therefore have stronger bonds.

Question 396: E
Li^+ (2) and Na^+ (2, 8)
Mg^{2+} (2, 8) and Ne (2, 8)
Na^{2+} (2, 7) and Ne (2, 8)
O^{2-} (2, 4) and a Carbon atom (2, 4)

Question 397: B
Reactivity of both group 1 and 2 increases as you go down the groups because the valence electrons that react are further away from the positively charged nucleus (which means the electrostatic attraction between them is weaker). Group 1 metals are usually more reactive because they only need to donate one electron, whilst group 2 metals must donate two electrons.

Question 398: D
This is a straightforward question that tests basic understanding of kinetics. Catalysts help overcome energy barriers by reducing the activation energy necessary for a reaction.

Question 399: D
H^1 contains 1 proton and no neutrons. Isotopes have the same numbers of protons, but different numbers of neutrons. Thus, H^3 contains two more neutrons than H^1.

Question 400: D
Oxidation is the loss of electrons and reduction is the gain of electrons (therefore increasing electron density). Halogens tend to act as electron recipients in reactions and are therefore good oxidising agents.

Question 401: D
These statements all come from the Kinetic Theory of Gases, an idealised model of gases that allows for the derivation of the ideal gas law. The angle at which gas molecules move is not related to temperature; movement is random. Gas molecules lose no energy when they collide with each other, collisions are assumed elastic. The average kinetic energy of gas molecules is the same for all gases at the same temperature as they are assumed to be point masses. Momentum = mass x velocity. Therefore, the momentum of gas molecules increases with pressure as a greater force is exerted on each molecule.

Question 402: E
An exothermic reaction is defined as a chemical reaction that releases energy. Thus, aerobic respiration producing life energy, the burning of magnesium, and the reacting of acids/bases are almost always exothermic processes. Similarly, the combustion of most things (including hydrogen) is exothermic. Evaporation of water is a physical process in which no chemical reaction is taking place.

Question 403: E
$2 C_3H_6 + 9 O_2 \rightarrow 6 H_2O + 6 CO_2$
Assign the oxidation numbers for each element:
For C_3H_6: C = -2; H = +1
For O_2: O = 0
For H_2O: H = +1; O = -2
For CO_2: C = +4; O = -2
Look for the changes in the oxidation numbers:
H remained at +1
C changed from -2 to +4. Thus, it was oxidized
O changed from 0 to -2. Thus, it was reduced.

Question 404: B

The equation for the reaction is: $Zn + CuSO_4 \rightarrow ZnSO_4 + Cu$

Assign oxidation numbers for each element:

For Zn: $Zn = 0$

For $CuSO_4$: $Cu = +2$; $S = +6$; $O = -2$

For $ZnSO_4$: $Zn = +2$; $S = +6$; $O = -2$

For Cu: $Cu = 0$

With these oxidation numbers, we can see that Zn was oxidized and Cu in $CuSO_4$ was reduced. Thus, Zn acted as the reducing agent and Cu in $CuSO_4$ is the oxidizing agent.

Question 405: B

Acids are proton donors which only exist in aqueous solution, which is a liquid state. Strong acids are fully ionised in solution and the reaction between an acid and a base $\rightarrow$ salt + water.

The pH of weak acids is usually between 4 and 6.

Question 406: G

Let x be the relative abundance of Z^6 and y the relative abundance of Z^8.

The average atomic mass takes the abundances of all 3 isotopes into account.

Thus, (Abundance of Z^5)(Mass Z^5) + (Abundance of Z^6)(Mass Z^6) + (Abundance of Z^8)(Mass Z^8) = 7

Therefore: $(5 \times 0.2) + 6x + 8y = 7$

So: $6x + 8y = 6$

Divide by two to give: $3x + 4y = 3$

The abundances of all isotopes $= 100\% = 1$

This gives: $0.2 + x + y = 1$

Solve the two equations simultaneously:

$y = 0.8 - x$

$3x + 4(0.8 - x) = 3$

$3x + 3.2 - 4x = 3$

Therefore, $x = 0.2$

$y = 0.8 - 0.2 = 0.6$

Thus, the overall abundances are $Z^5 = 20\%$, $Z^6 = 20\%$ and $Z^8 = 60\%$. Therefore, all the statements are correct.

Question 407: A

If a metal is more reactive than hydrogen, a displacement reaction will occur resulting in the formation of a salt with the metal cation and hydrogen.

Question 408: B

$6\ FeSO_4 + K_2Cr_2O_7 + 7\ H_2SO_4 \rightarrow 3\ (Fe)_2(SO_4)_3 + Cr_2(SO_4)_3 + K_2SO_4 + 7\ H_2O$

In order to save time, you have to quickly eliminate options (rather than try every combination out).

The quickest way is to do this is algebraically:

For Potassium:

$2b = 2e = 2f$

Therefore, $b = f$.

Option F does not fulfil $b = e = f$.

For Iron:

$a = 2d$

Options C, D and E don't fulfil $a = 2d$.

For Hydrogen:

$2c = 2g$

Therefore, $c = g$.

Option A does not fulfil $c = g$.

This leaves option B as the answer.

Question 409: E

Atoms are electrically neutral. Ions have different numbers of electrons when compared to atoms of the same element. Protons provide just under 50% of an atom's mass, the other 50% is provided by neutrons. Isotopes don't exhibit significantly different kinetics. Protons do indeed repel each other in the nucleus (which is one reason why neutrons are needed: to reduce the electrical charge density).

Question 410: B

The noble gasses are extremely useful, e.g. helium in blimps, neon signs, argon in bulbs. They are colourless and odourless and have no valence electrons. As with the rest of the periodic table, boiling point increases as you progress down the group (because of increased Van der Waals forces). Helium is the most abundant noble gas (and indeed the 2nd most abundant element in the universe).

Question 411: D

Alkenes can be hydrogenated (i.e. reduced) to alkanes. Aromatic compounds are commonly written as cyclic alkenes, but their properties differ from those of alkenes. Therefore alkenes and aromatic compounds do not belong to the same chemical class.

Question 412: A

The average atomic mass takes the abundances of both isotopes into account:

(Abundance of Cl^{35})(Mass Cl^{35}) + (Abundance of Cl^{37})(Mass Cl^{37}) = 35.453

34.969(Abundance of Cl^{35}) + 36.966(Abundance of Cl^{37}) = 35.453

The abundances of both isotopes = 100% = 1

I.e. abundance of Cl^{35} + abundance of Cl^{37} = 1

Therefore: $x + y = 1$ which can be rearranged to give: $y = 1-x$

Therefore: $x + (1 - x) = 1$.

$34.969x + 36.966(1-x) = 35.453$

$x = 0.758$

$1 - x = 0.242$

Therefore, Cl^{35} is 3 times more abundant than Cl^{37}.

Note that you could approximate the values here to arrive at the solution even quicker, e.g. 34.969 → 35, 36.966 → 37 and 35.453 → 35.5

Question 413: A

Transition metals form multiple stable ions which may have many different colours (e.g. green Fe^{2+} and brown Fe^{3+}). They usually form ionic bonds and are commonly used as catalysts (e.g. iron in the Haber process, Nickel in alkene hydrogenation). They are excellent conductors of electricity and are known as the d-block elements.

Question 414: B

$2Na + 2H_2O$ → $2NaOH + H_2$

$8000 \ cm^3 = 8 \ dm^3 = $ ⅓ moles of H_2

2 moles of Na react completely to form 1 mole of H_2.

Therefore, ⅔ moles of Na must have reacted to produce ⅓ moles of Hydrogen. ⅔ x 23g per mole = 15.3g.

% Purity of sample = $\frac{15.3}{20}$ x 100 = 76.5%

Question 415: C

Assume total mass of molecule is 100g. Therefore, it contains 70.6g carbon, 5.9g hydrogen and 23.5g oxygen.

Now, calculate the number of moles of each element using $Moles = \frac{Mass}{Molar \ Mass}$

$Moles \ of \ Carbon = \frac{70.6}{12} \approx 6$

$Moles \ of \ Hydrogen = \frac{5.9}{1} \approx 6$

$Moles \ of \ Oxygen = \frac{23.5}{16} \approx 1.5$

Therefore, the molar ratios give an empirical formula of $C_6H_6O_{1.5} = C_4H_4O$.

Molar mass of the empirical formula = (4 x 12) + (4 x 1) + 16 = 68.

Molar mass of chemical formula = 136. Therefore, the chemical formula = $C_8H_8O_2$.

Question 416: B

$S + 6\,HNO_3 \rightarrow H_2SO_4 + 6\,NO_2 + 2\,H_2O$

In order to save time, you have to quickly eliminate options (rather than try every combination out).

The quickest way to do this is algebraically:

For Hydrogen:

$b = 2c + 2e$

Options A, C, D, E and F don't fulfil $b = 2c + 2e$.

This leaves options B as the only possible answer.

Note how quickly we were able to get the correct answer here by choosing an element that appears in 3 molecules (as opposed to Sulphur or Nitrogen which only appear in 2).

Question 417: A

Alkenes undergo addition reactions, such as that with hydrogen, when catalysed by nickel, whilst alkanes do not as they are already fully saturated. The C=C bond is stronger than the C-C bond, but it is not exactly twice as strong, so will not require twice the energy to break it. Both molecules are organic and will dissolve in organic solvents.

Question 418: F

Diamond is unable to conduct electricity because all the electrons are involved in covalent bonds. Graphite is insoluble in water + organic solvents. Graphite is also able to conduct electricity because there are free electrons that are not involved in covalent bonds.

Methane and Ammonia both have low melting points. Methane is not a polar molecule, so cannot conduct electricity or dissolve in water. Ammonia is polar and will dissolve in water. It can conduct electricity in aqueous form, but not as a gas.

Question 419: A

Catalysts increase the rate of reaction by providing an alternative reaction path with a lower activation energy, which means that less energy is required and so costs are reduced. The point of equilibrium, the nature of the products, and the overall energy change are unaffected by catalysts.

Question 420: E

The 5 carbon atoms in this hydrocarbon make it a "pent" stem. The C=C bond makes it an alkene, and the location of this bond is the 2nd position, making the molecule pent-2-ene.

Question 421: F

Group 1 elements form positively charged ions in most reactions and therefore lose electrons. Thus, the oxidation number must increase. Their reactivity increases as the valence electrons are further away from the positively charged nucleus down group. Although they all react **spontaneously** with oxygen only the latter half of Group 1 elements react **instantaenously** with oxygen.

Question 422: H

The cathode attracts positively charged ions. The cathode reduces ions and the anode oxidises ions. Electrolysis can be used to separate compounds but not mixtures (i.e. substances that are not chemically joined).

Question 423: B

Pentane, C_5H_{12}, has a total of 3 isomers. A, C and D are correctly configured. However, the 4th Carbon atom in option B has more than 4 bonds which wouldn't be possible. If you're stuck on this – draw them out!

Question 424: E

$3\,Cu + 8\,HNO_3 \rightarrow 3\,Cu(NO_3)_2 + 2\,NO + 4\,H_2O$

In order to save time, you have to quickly eliminate options (rather than try every combination out).

The quickest way to do this is algebraically, by first assigning coefficients to the equation:

$\mathbf{a}Cu + \mathbf{b}HNO_3 \rightarrow \mathbf{c}Cu(NO_3)_2 + \mathbf{d}NO + \mathbf{e}H_2O$

For Nitrogen: $b = 2c + d$.

In this case, only option E satisfies $b = 2c + d$.

Note that using copper wouldn't be as useful, as all the options satisfy $a = c$.

Question 425: D

Alkenes are an organic series and have twice as many hydrogen atoms as carbon atoms. Bromine water is decolourised in their presence and they take part in addition reactions. Alkenes are more reactive than alkanes because they contain a C=C bond.

Question 426: A

Group 17 elements are missing one valence electron, so form negative ions. Bromine is a liquid at room temperature, and is also coloured brown. Reactivity decreases as you progress down Group 17, so fluorine reacts more vigorously than iodine. All Group 17 elements are found bound to each other, e.g. F_2 and Cl_2.

Question 427: D

CO poisoning and spontaneous combustion do not occur in the electrolysis of brine. The products of cathode and anode in the electrolysis of brine are Cl_2 and H_2. If these two gases react with each other they can form HCl, which is extremely corrosive.

Question 428: D

The hydrogen produced is positively charged and therefore needs to be reduced by the addition of an electron before being released. This happens at the cathode. The chlorine produced is negatively charged and therefore needs to lose electrons. This happens at the anode. NaOH is formed in this process.

Question 429: C

Alkanes are made of chains of singly bonded carbon and hydrogen atoms. C-H bonds are very strong and confer alkanes a great deal of stability. An alkane with 14 hydrogen atoms is called Hexane, as it has 6 carbon atoms. Alkanes burn in excess oxygen to produce carbon dioxide and water. Bromine water is decolourised in the presence of alkenes.

Question 430: G

You've probably got a lot of experience of organic chemistry by now, so this should be fairly straightforward. Alcohols by definition contain an R-OH functional group and because of this polar group are highly soluble in water. Ethanol is a common biofuel.

Question 431: E

Alkanes are saturated (and therefore non-reducible), have the general formula C_nH_{2n+2} and have no effect on Bromine solution. Alkenes are unsaturated (and therefore reducible), have the general formula C_nH_{2n} and turn bromine water colourless because they can undergo an addition reaction with bromine.

Question 432: D

The balanced equation for the reaction between magnesium oxide and hydrochloric acid is:

$MgO + 2HCl \rightarrow MgCl_2 + H_2$

The relative molecular mass of MgO is 24 + 16 = 40g per mole.

Therefore 10g of MgO represents 10/40 = 0.25 moles.

As the ratio of MgO to $MgCl_2$ is 1:1, we know that the amount of $MgCl_2$ produced will also be 0.25 moles. One mole of $MgCl_2$ has a molecular mass of 24 + (2 x 35.5) = 95g per mole.

Therefore the reaction will produce 0.25 x 95 = 23.75g of $MgCl_2$.

Question 433: D

Moving up the alkane series, as size and mass of the molecule increases (and thus the Van der Waals forces increase), the boiling point and viscosity increase and the flammability and volatility decrease. Therefore pentadecane will be more viscous than pentane.

Question 434: F

All of the factors mentioned will affect the rate of a reaction. The temperature affects the movement rate of particles, which if moving faster in higher temperatures will collide more often, thus increasing the rate of reaction. Collision rate is also increased with a higher concentration of reactants, and with a higher concentration of a catalyst or one with larger surface area, which will provide more active sites, thus increasing the rate of reaction.

Question 435: C

The total atomic mass of the end product is $C[12 + (2 \times 16)] + D[(2 \times 1) + 16] = 44C + 18D$

We know that $176 = 44C$. Therefore $C = 4$, and that $108 = 18D$ so $D = 6$.

Thus, the equation becomes: $C_aH_b + O_2 \rightarrow 4CO_2 + 6H_2O$.

This gives a ratio of 4C to 12H, which is a ratio of 1:3 carbon to hydrogen. This means the unknown hydrocarbon must be a multiple of this ratio. By balancing the equation we can see that the unknown hydrocarbon must be ethane, C_2H_6: $2C_2H_6 + 7O_2 \rightarrow 4CO_2 + 6H_2O$.

Question 436: A

$C_2H_5OH \rightarrow C_2H_4O$. Thus, ethanol has lost two hydrogen atoms, i.e. has been oxidised. Note that although another substrate may be reduced (therefore making it a redox reaction), ethanol has only been oxidised.

Question 437: B

This is fairly straightforward but you can save time by doing it algebraically:

For Barium: $3a = b$

For Nitrogen: $2a = c$

Let $a = 1$, thus, $b = 3$ and $c = 2$

Question 438: E

There are 14 oxygen atoms on the left side. Thus: $3b + 2c = 14$.

Note also that for Sulphur: $a = c$, and for Iron: $a = 2b$.

This sets up an easy trio of simultaneous equations:

Substitute a into the first equation to give: $1.5a + 2a = 14$. Thus: $a = 14/3.5 = 4$.

Therefore, $a = c = 4$ and $b = 2$

Question 439: C

The average atomic mass takes the abundances of all isotopes into account:

Mass = (Abundance of Mg^{23})(Mass Mg^{23}) + (Abundance of Mg^{25})(Mass Mg^{25}) + (Abundance of Mg^{26})(Mass Mg^{26})

$Mass = 23 \times 0.80 + 25 \times 0.10 + 26 \times 0.10$

$= 18.4 + 2.5 + 2.6 = 23.5$

Question 440: D

Cl_2 and Fe_2O_3 are reduced in their reactions and are therefore oxidising agents. Similarly, CO and Cu^{2+} are oxidised in their reactions and are therefore reducing agents. Cl is a stronger oxidising agent than Br as it is higher up in the reactivity series, and will displace negative Br ions from its compounds to form the oxidised Br_2. Mg is a stronger reducing agent than Cu, as it is higher up in the reactivity series. Thus, Mg would displace a positive copper ion from its compound to form copper atoms. Therefore Mg reduces Cu.

Question 441: C

NaCl is an ionic compound and therefore has a high melting point. It is highly soluble in water but only conducts electricity in solution/as a liquid.

Question 442: C

The equation for the reaction is: $2NaOH + Zn(NO_3)_2 \rightarrow 2NaNO_3 + Zn(OH)_2$

Therefore, the molar ratio between NaOH and $Zn(OH)_2$ is 2:1.

Molecular Mass of NaOH = 23 + 16 + 1 = 40

Molecular Mass of $Zn(OH)_2$ = 65 + 17 x 2 = 99

Thus, the number of moles of NaOH that react = 80/40 = 2 moles.

Therefore, 1 mole of $Zn(OH)_2$ is produced. Mass = 99g per mole x 1 mole = 99g

Question 443: A

Metal + Water $\rightarrow$ Hydroxide + Hydrogen gas; the reaction is always exothermic. Reactivity increases down the group, so potassium reacts more vigorously with water than sodium.

Question 444: C

Electrolysis separates NaCl into sodium and chloride ions but not CO_2 (which is a covalently bound gas). Sieves cannot separate ionically bound compounds like NaCl. Dyes are miscible liquids and can be separated by chromatography. Oil and water are immiscible liquids, so a separating funnel is necessary to separate the mixtures. Methane and diesel are separated from each other during fractional distillation, as they have different boiling points.

Question 445: B

The reaction between water and caesium can cause spontaneous combustion and therefore doesn't make the reaction safer. The reaction between caesium and fluoride is highly exothermic and does not require a catalyst. The reaction produces CsF which is a salt.

Question 446: B

The nucleus of larger elements contain more neutrons than protons to reduce the charge density, e.g. Br^{80} contains 35 protons but 45 neutrons. Stable isotopes very rarely undergo radioactive decay.

Question 447: B

The vast majority of salts contain ionic bonds that require a significant amount of heat energy to break.

Question 448: E

306ml of water is 306g, which is the equivalent of 306g/18g per mole of H_2O = 17 moles. 17 times Avogadro's constant gives the number of molecules present, which is 1.02×10^{25}. There are 10 protons and 10 electrons in each water molecule. Hence there are 1.02×10^{26} protons.

Question 449: D

The number of moles of each element = Mass/Molar Mass. Let the % represent the mass in grams: Hydrogen: 3.45g/1g per mole = 3.45 moles
Oxygen: 55.2g/16g per mole = 3.45 moles
Carbon: 41.4g/12g per mole = 3.45 moles
Thus, the molar ratio is 1:1:1. The only option that satisfies this is option D.

Question 450: C

Group 17 elements are non-metals, whilst group 2 elements are metals. Thus, the Group 17 element must gain electrons when it reacts with the Group 2 element, i.e. B is reduced. The easy way to calculate the formula is to swap the valences of both elements: A is +2 and B is -1. Thus, the compound is AB_2.

Question 451: F

That the amplitude of a wave determines its mass is false. Waves are not objects and do not have mass.

Question 452: A

We know that displacement s = 30 m, initial speed u = 0 ms^{-1}, acceleration a = 5.4 ms^{-2}, final speed v = ?, time t = ?
And that $v^2 = u^2 + 2as$
$v^2 = 0 + 2 \times 5.4 \times 30$
$v^2 = 324$ so v = 18 ms^{-1}
and $s = ut + 1/2\ at^2$ so $30 = 1/2 \times 5.4 \times t^2$
$t^2 = 30/2.7$ so t = 3.3 s

Question 453: D

The wavelength is given by: velocity $v = \lambda f$ and frequency f = 1/T so $v = \lambda/T$ giving wavelength $\lambda = vT$
The period T = 49 s/7 so λ = 5 ms^{-1} x 7 s = 35 m

Question 454: E

This is a straightforward question as you only have to put the numbers into the equation (made harder by the numbers being hard to work with).
$$Power = \frac{Force\ x\ Distance}{Time} = \frac{375\ N\ x\ 1.3\ m}{5\ s}$$
$= 75\ x\ 1.3 = 97.5\ W$

Question 455: G

$v = u + at$

$v = 0 + 5.6 \times 8 = 44.8$ ms^{-1}

And $s = ut + \frac{at^2}{2} = 0 + 5.6 \times \frac{8^2}{2} = 179.2$

Question 456: C

The sky diver leaves the plane and will accelerate until the air resistance equals their weight – this is their terminal velocity. The sky diver will accelerate under the force of gravity. If the air resistance force exceeded the force of gravity the sky diver would accelerate away from the ground, and if it was less than the force of gravity they would continue to accelerate toward the ground.

Question 457: D

$s = 20$ m, $u = 0$ ms^{-1}, $a = 10$ ms^{-2}

and $v^2 = u^2 + 2as$

$v^2 = 0 + 2 \times 10 \times 20$

$v^2 = 400$; $v = 20$ ms^{-1}

Momentum = Mass x velocity = $20 \times 0.1 = 2$ kgms^{-1}

Question 458: E

Electromagnetic waves have varying wavelengths and frequencies and their energy is proportional to their frequency.

Question 459: D

The total resistance = R + r = 0.8 + 1 = 1.8 Ω

and $I = \frac{e.m.f}{total\ resistance} = \frac{36}{1.8} = 20\ A$

Question 460: C

Use Newton's second law and remember to work in SI units:

So $Force = mass \times accelaration = mass \times \frac{\Delta velocity}{time}$

$= 20 \times 10^{-3} \times \dfrac{100 - 0}{10 \times 10^{-3}}$

$= 200\ N$

Question 461: F

In this case, the work being done is moving the bag 0.7 m

i.e. $Work\ Done = Bag's\ Weight \times Distance = 50 \times 10 \times 0.7 = 350\ N$

$Power = \frac{Work}{Time} = \frac{350}{3} = 116.7$ W

$= 117$ W to 3 significant figures

Question 462: B

Firstly, use P = Fv to calculate the power [Ignore the frictional force as we are not concerned with the resultant force here].

So P = 300 x 30 = 9000 W

Then, use P = IV to calculate the current.

I = P/V = 9000/200 = 45 A

Question 463: C

Work is defined as W = F x s. Work can also be defined as work = force x distance moved in the direction of force. Work is measured in joules and 1 Joule = 1 Newton x 1 Metre, and 1 Newton = 1 Kg x ms^{-2} [F = ma]. Thus, 1 Joule = Kgm^{2}s^{-2}

Question 464: G

Joules are the unit of energy (and also Work = Force x Distance). Thus, 1 Joule = 1 N x 1 m.

Pa is the unit of Pressure (= Force/Area). Thus, Pa = N x m^{-2}. So J = Nm^{-2} x m^3 = Pa x m^3. Newton's third law describes that every action produces an equal and opposite reaction. For this reason, the energy required to decelerate a body is equal to the amount of energy it possess during movement, i.e. its kinetic energy, which is defined as in statement 1.

Question 465: D

Alpha radiation is of the lower energy, as it represents the movement of a fairly large particle consisting of 2 neutrons and 2 protons. Beta radiation consists of high-energy, high-speed electrons or positrons.

Question 466: E

The half-life does depend on atom type and isotope, as these parameters significantly impact on the physical properties of the atom in general, so statement 1 is false. Statement 2 is the correct definition of half-life. Statement 3 is also correct: half-life in exponential decay will always have the same duration, independent of the quantity of the matter in question; in non-exponential decay, half-life is dependent on the quantity of matter in question.

Question 467: A

In contrast to nuclear fission, where neutrons are shot at unstable atoms, nuclear fusion is based on the high speed, high-temperature collision of molecules, most commonly hydrogen, to form a new, stable atom while releasing energy.

Question 468: E

Nuclear fission releases a significant amount of energy, which is the basis of many nuclear weapons. Shooting neutrons at unstable atoms destabilises the nuclei which in turn leads to a chain reaction and fission. Nuclear fission can lead to the release of ionizing gamma radiation.

Question 469: G

The total resistance of the circuit would be twice the resistance of one resistor and proportional to the voltage, as given by Ohm's Law. Since it is a series circuit, the same current flows through each resistor and since they are identical the potential difference across each resistor will be the same.

Question 470: E

The distance between Earth and Sun = Time x Speed = 60 x 8 seconds x 3 x 10^8 ms^{-1} = 480 x 3 x 10^8 m
Approximately = 1500 x 10^8 = 1.5 x 10^{11} m.
The circumference of Earth's orbit around the sun is given by $2\pi r$ = 2 x 3 x 1.5 x 10^{11}
= 9 x 10^{11} = 10^{12} m

Question 471: H

Speed is a scalar quantity whilst velocity is a vector describing both magnitude and direction. Speed describes the distance a moving object covers over time (i.e. speed = distance/time), whereas velocity describes the rate of change of the displacement of an object (i.e. velocity = displacement/time). The internationally standardised unit for speed is meters per second (ms^{-1}), while ms^{-2} is the unit of acceleration.

Question 472: E

Ohm's Law only applies to conductors and can be mathematically expressed as $V \alpha I$. The easiest way to do this is to write down the equations for statements c, d and e. C: $I \alpha \frac{1}{V}$; D: $I \alpha V^2$; E: $I \alpha V$. Thus, statement E is correct.

Question 473: G

Any object at rest is not accelerating and therefore has no resultant force. Strictly speaking, Newton's second law is actually: Force = rate of change of momentum, which can be mathematically manipulated to give statement 2:

$$Force = \frac{momentum}{time} = \frac{mass \times velocity}{time} = mass \times accelaration$$

Question 474: D

Statement 3 is incorrect, as *Charge = Current x time*. Statement 1 substitutes $I = \frac{V}{R}$ and statement 2 substitutes $I = \frac{P}{V}$.

Question 475: E

Weight of elevator + people = mg = 10 x (1600 + 200) = 18,000 N

Applying Newton's second law of motion on the car gives:

Thus, the resultant force is given by:

F_M = Motor Force – [Frictional Force + Weight]

F_M = M – 4,000 – 18,000

Use Newton's second law to give: F_M = M – 22,000 N = ma

Thus, M – 22,000 N = 1,800a

Since the lift must accelerate at 1ms^{-2}: M = 1,800 kg x 1 ms^{-2} + 22,000 N

M = 23,800 N

Question 476: D

Total Distance = Distance during acceleration phase + Distance during braking phase

Distance during <u>acceleration phase</u> is given by:

$$s = ut + \frac{at^2}{2} = 0 + \frac{5 \times 10^2}{2} = 250 \, m$$

$$v = u + at = 0 + 5 \times 10 = 50 \, ms^{-1}$$

And use $a = \frac{v-u}{t}$ to calculate the deceleration: $a = \frac{0-50}{20} = -2.5 \text{ ms}^{-2}$

Distance during the <u>deceleration phase</u> is given by:

$$s = ut + \frac{at^2}{2} = 50 \times 20 + \frac{-2.5 \times 20^2}{2} = 1000 - \frac{2.5 \times 400}{2}$$

$$s = 1000 - 500 = 500 \, m$$

Thus, $Total \; Distance \; = \; 250 \; + \; 500 \; = \; 750 \, m$

Question 477: G

It is not possible to calculate the power of the heater as we don't know the current that flows through it or its internal resistance. The 8 ohms refers to the external copper wire and not the heater. Whilst it's important that you know how to use equations like P = IV, it's more important that you know when you *can't* use them!

Question 478: F

This question has a lot of numbers but not any information on time, which is necessary to calculate power. You cannot calculate power by using P= IV as you don't know how many electrons are accelerated through the potential difference per unit time. Thus, more information is required to calculate the power.

Question 479: B

When an object is in equilibrium with its surroundings, it radiates and absorbs energy at the same rate and so its temperature remains constant i.e. there is no *net* energy transfer. Radiation is slower than conduction and convection.

Question 480: A

The work done by the force is given by: $Work \; Done \; = \; Force \; x \; Distance \; = \; 12 \, N \times 3 \, m \; = \; 36 \, J$

Since the surface is frictionless, $Work \; Done \; = \; Kinetic \; Energy$.

$$E_k = \frac{mv^2}{2} = \frac{6v^2}{2}$$

Thus, $36 = 3v^2$

$$v = \sqrt{12} = \sqrt{4}\sqrt{3} = 2\sqrt{3} \, ms^{-1}$$

Question 481: C

$Total\ energy\ supplied\ to\ water\ =\ Change\ in\ temperature \times Mass\ of\ water \times 4,000\ J$
$=\ 40 \times 1.5 \times 4,000\ =\ 240,000\ J$

$Power\ of\ the\ heater\ = \dfrac{Work\ Done}{time} = \dfrac{240,000}{50 \times 60} = \dfrac{240,000}{3,000} = 80\ W$

Using $P\ =\ IV\ = \dfrac{V^2}{R}$:

$R\ = \dfrac{V^2}{P} = \dfrac{100^2}{80} = \dfrac{10,000}{80} = 125\ ohms$

Question 482: G

The large amount of energy released during atomic fission is the basis underlying nuclear power plants. Splitting an atom into two or more parts will by definition produce molecules of different sizes than the original atom; therefore it produces two new atoms. The free neutrons and photons produced by the splitting of atoms form the basis of the energy release.

Question 483: D

Gravitational potential energy is just an extension of the equation work done = force x distance (force is the weight of the object, *mg*, and distance is the height, *h*). The reservoir in statement 3 would have a potential energy of 10^{10} Joules i.e. 10 Giga Joules ($E_p= 10^6$ kg x 10 N x 10^3 m).

Question 484: D

Statement 1 is the common formulation of Newton's third law. Statement 2 presents a consequence of the application of Newton's third law.

Statement 3 is false: rockets can still accelerate because the products of burning fuel are ejected in the opposite direction from which the rocket needs to accelerate.

Question 485: E

Positively charged objects have lost electrons. $Charge\ =\ Current \times Time\ = \dfrac{Voltage}{Resistance} \times Time$.
Objects can become charged by friction as electrons are transferred from one object to the other.

Question 486: B

Each body of mass exerts a gravitational force on another body with mass. This is true for all planets as well. Gravitational force is dependent on the mass of both objects. Satellites stay in orbit due to centripetal force that acts tangentially to gravity (not because of the thrust from their engines). Two objects will only land at the same time if they also have the same shape or they are in a vaccum (as otherwise air resistance would result in different terminal velocities).

Question 487: A

Metals conduct electrical charge easily and provide little resistance to the flow of electrons. Charge can also flow in several directions. However, all conductors have an internal resistance and therefore provide *some* resistance to electrical charge.

Question 488: E

First, calculate the rate of petrol consumption:

$\dfrac{Speed}{Consumption} = \dfrac{60\ miles/hour}{30\ miles/gallon} = 2\ gallons/hour$

Therefore, the total power is:

$2\ gallons\ =\ 2 \times 9 \times 10^8 = 18 \times 10^8 J$

$1\ hour\ =\ 60 \times 60\ =\ 3600\ s$

Power $= \dfrac{Energy}{Time} = \dfrac{18 \times 10^8}{3600}$

$P = \dfrac{18}{36} \times 10^6 = 5 \times 10^5\ W$

Since efficiency is 20%, the power delivered to the wheels = $5 \times 10^5 \times 0.2 = 10^5\ W = 100\ kW$

Question 489: D
Beta radiation is stopped by a few millimetres of aluminium, but not by paper. In β⁻ radiation, a neutron changes into a proton plus an emitted electron. This means the atomic mass number remains unchanged.

Question 490: F
Firstly, calculate the mass of the car $= \frac{Weight}{g} = \frac{15,000}{10} = 1,500\ kg$

Then using $v = u + at$ where v = 0 ms⁻¹ and u = 15 ms⁻¹ and t = 10 x 10⁻³ s
$a = \frac{0-15}{0.01} = 1500ms^{-2}$
$F = ma = 1500\ x\ 1500 = 2\ 250\ 000\ N$

Question 491: E
Electrical insulators offer high resistance to the flow of charge. Insulators are usually non-metals; metals conduct charge very easily. Since charge does not flow easily to even out, they can be charged with friction.

Question 492: F
The car accelerates for the first 10 seconds at a constant rate and then decelerates after t=30 seconds. It does not reverse, as the velocity is not negative.

Question 493: B
The distance travelled by the car is represented by the area under the curve (integral of velocity) which is given by the area of two triangles and a rectangle:
$$Area = \left(\frac{1}{2}\ x\ 10\ x\ 10\right) + (20\ x\ 10) + \left(\frac{1}{2}\ x\ 10\ x\ 10\right)$$
$$Area = 50 + 200 + 50 = 300\ m$$

Question 494: C
Using the equation force = mass x acceleration, where the unknown acceleration = change in velocity over change in time.

Hence: $\frac{F}{m} = \frac{change\ in\ velocity}{change\ in\ time}$

We know that F = 10,000 N, mass = 1,000 kg and change in time is 5 seconds.

So, $\frac{10,000}{1,000} = \frac{change\ in\ velocity}{5}$

So change in velocity = 10 x 5 = 50 m/s

Question 495: D
This question tests both your ability to convert unusual units into SI units and to select the relevant values (e.g. the crane's mass is not important here).

0.01 tonnes = 10 kg; 100 cm = 1 m; 5,000 ms = 5 s
$$Power = \frac{Work\ Done}{Time} = \frac{Force\ x\ Distance}{Time}$$

In this case the force is the weight of the wardrobe $= 10\ x\ g = 10\ x\ 10 = 100N$

Thus, $Power = \frac{100\ x\ 1}{5} = 20\ W$

Question 496: F
Remember that the resistance of a parallel circuit (R_T) is given by: $\frac{1}{R_T} = \frac{1}{R_1} + \frac{1}{R_2} + \ ...$

Thus, $\frac{1}{R_T} = \frac{1}{1} + \frac{1}{2} = \frac{3}{2}$ and therefore $R = \frac{2}{3}\ \Omega$
Using Ohm's Law: I $= \frac{20\ V}{\frac{2}{3}\Omega} = 20\ x\ \frac{3}{2} = 30\ A$

Question 497: E
Water is denser than air. Therefore, the speed of light decreases when it enters water and increases when it leaves water. The direction of light also changes when light enters/leaves water. This phenomenon is known as refraction and is governed by Snell's Law.

Question 498: C
The voltage in a parallel circuit is the same across each branch, i.e. branch A Voltage = branch B Voltage.
The resistance of Branch A = 6 x 5 = 30 Ω; the resistance of Branch B = 10 x 2 = 20 Ω.
Using Ohm's Law: I= V/R. Thus, $I_A = \frac{60}{30} = 2\ A$; $I_B = \frac{60}{20} = 3\ A$

Question 499: C
This is a very straightforward question made harder by the awkward units you have to work with. Ensure you are able to work comfortably with prefixes of 10^9 and 10^{-9} and convert without difficulty.
50,000,000,000 nano Watts = 50 W and 0.000000004 Giga Amperes = 4 A.
Using $P = IV$: $V = \frac{P}{I} = \frac{50}{4} = 12.5\ V = 0.0125\ kV$

Question 500: B
Radioactive decay is highly random and unpredictable. Only gamma decay releases gamma rays and few types of decay release X-rays. The electrical charge of an atom's nucleus decreases after alpha decay as two protons are lost.

Question 501: D
Using $P = IV$: $I = \frac{P}{V} = \frac{60}{15} = 4\ A$
Now using Ohm's Law: $R = \frac{V}{I} = \frac{15}{4} = 3.75\ \Omega$
So, each resistor has a resistance of $\frac{3.75}{3} = 1.25\ \Omega$.
If two more resistors are added, the overall resistance = 1.25 x 5 = 6.25 Ω

Question 502: B
$Total\ Work\ Done\ by\ Engine = Force\ \text{x}\ Distance = Weight\ of\ Tractor\ \text{x}\ Distance$
Thus, $Work\ Done = 5{,}000 \times 10 \times 100 = 5 \times 10^6 J$
$If\ 1\ ml\ contains\ 20{,}000\ J\ then\ 1{,}000\ ml\ has\ 20{,}000 \times 1{,}000\ J = 2 \times 10^7 J$
$Efficiency = \frac{Useful\ work\ done}{Total\ energy\ used} = \frac{5\ \text{x}\ 10^6}{2\ \text{x}\ 10^7} = 2.5 \times 10^{-1} = 0.25 = 25\%$

Question 503: G
Electromagnetic induction is defined by statements 1 and 2. An electrical current is generated when a coil moves in a magnetic field.

Question 504: D
An ammeter will always give the same reading in a series circuit, not in a parallel circuit where current splits at each branch in accordance with Ohm's Law.

Question 505: D
Electrons move in the opposite direction to current (i.e. they move from negative to positive).

Question 506: A
For a fixed resistor, the current is directly proportional to the potential difference. For a filament lamp, as current increases, the metal filament becomes hotter. This causes the metal atoms to vibrate and move more, resulting in more collisions with the flow of electrons. This makes it harder for the electrons to move through the lamp and results in increased resistance. Therefore, the graph's gradient decreases as current increases.

Question 507: E
Vector quantities consist of both direction and magnitude, e.g. velocity, displacement, etc., and can be added by taking account of direction in the sum.

Question 508: C

The gravity on the moon is 6 times less than 10 ms^{-2}. Thus, $g_{moon} = \frac{10}{6} = \frac{5}{3}$ ms^{-2}.

Since weight = mass x gravity, the mass of the rock = $\frac{250}{\frac{5}{3}} = \frac{750}{5} = 150\ kg$

Therefore, the density = $\frac{mass}{volume} = \frac{150}{250} = 0.6\ kg/cm^3$

Question 509: D

An alpha particle consists of a helium nucleus. Thus, alpha decay causes the mass number to decrease by 4 and the atomic number to decrease by 2. Five iterations of this would decrease the mass number by 20 and the atomic number by 10.

Question 510: C

Using Ohm's Law: The potential difference entering the transformer (V_1) = 10 x 20 = 200 V

Now use $\frac{N1}{N2} = \frac{V1}{V2}$ to give: $\frac{5}{10} = \frac{200}{V2}$

Thus, $V_2 = \frac{2,000}{5} = 400$ V

Question 511: D

For objects in free fall that have reached terminal velocity, acceleration = 0.
Thus, the sphere's weight = resistive forces.
Using Work Done = Force x Distance: Force = 10,000 J/100 m = 100 N.
Therefore, the sphere's weight = 100 N and since $g = 10ms^{-2}$, the sphere's mass = 10 kg

Question 512: F

The wave length of ultraviolet waves is longer than that of x-rays. Wavelength is inversely proportional to frequency. Most electromagnetic waves are not stopped with aluminium (and require thick lead to stop them), and they travel at the speed of light. Humans can only see a very small part of the spectrum.

Question 513: B

If an object moves towards the sensor, the wavelength will appear to decrease and the frequency increase. The faster this happens, the faster the increase in frequency and decrease in wavelength.

Question 514: A

$Acceleration = \frac{Change\ in\ Velocity}{Time} = \frac{1,000}{0.1} = 10,000\ ms^{-2}$

Using Newton's second law: The Braking Force = Mass x Acceleration.

Thus, Braking Force = 10,000 x 0.005 = 50 N

Question 515: C

Polonium has undergone alpha decay. Thus, Y is a helium nucleus and contains 2 protons and 2 neutrons.
Therefore, 10 moles of Y contain 2 x 10 x 6 x 10^{23} protons = 120 x 10^{23} = 1.2 x 10^{25} protons.

Question 516: C

The rod's activity is less than 1,000 Bq after 300 days. In order to calculate the longest possible half-life, we must assume that the activity is just below 1,000 Bq after 300 days. Thus, the half-life has decreased activity from 16,0 00 Bq to 1,000 Bq in 300 days.
After one half-life: Activity = 8,000 Bq
After two half-lives: Activity = 4,000 Bq
After three half-lives: Activity = 2,000 Bq
After four half-lives: Activity = 1,000 Bq
Thus, the rod has halved its activity a minimum of 4 times in 300 days. 300/4 = 75 days

Question 517: G

There is no change in the atomic mass or proton numbers in gamma radiation. In β decay, a neutron is transformed into a proton (and an electron is released). This results in an increase in proton number by 1 but no overall change in atomic mass. Thus, after 5 rounds of beta decay, the proton number will be $89 + 5 = 94$ and the mass number will remain at 200. Therefore, there are 94 protons and $200-94 = 106$ neutrons.

NB: You are not expected to know about β^+ decay.

Question 518: C

Calculate the speed of the sound $= \frac{distance}{time} = \frac{500}{1.5} = 333 \, ms^{-1}$

Thus, the $Wavelength = \frac{Speed}{Frequency} = \frac{333}{440}$

Approximate 333 to 330 to give: $\frac{330}{440} = \frac{3}{4} = 0.75 \, m$

Question 519: B

Firstly, note the all the answer options are a magnitude of 10 apart. Thus, you don't have to worry about getting the correct numbers as long as you get the correct power of 10. You can therefore make your life easier by rounding, e.g. approximate π to 3, etc.

The area of the shell $= \pi r^2$.

$= \pi \times (50 \times 10^{-3})^2 = \pi \times (5 \times 10^{-2})^2$

$= \pi \times 25 \times 10^{-4} = 7.5 \times 10^{-3} \, m^2$

The deceleration of the shell $= \frac{u-v}{t} = \frac{200}{500 \times 10^{-6}} = 0.4 \times 10^6 \, ms^{-2}$

Then, using Newton's Second Law: $Braking \; force = mass \times acceleration = 1 \times 0.4 \times 10^6 = 4 \times 10^5 N$

Finally: $Pressure = \frac{Force}{Area} = \frac{4 \times 10^5}{7.5 \times 10^{-3}} = \frac{8}{15} \times 10^8 \, Pa \approx 5 \times 10^7 Pa$

Question 520: B

The fountain transfers 10% of 1,000 J of energy per second into 120 litres of water per minute. Thus, it transfers 100 J into 2 litres of water per second.

Therefore the Total Gravitational Potential Energy, $E_p = mg\Delta h$

Thus, $100 \, J = 2 \times 10 \times h$

Hence, $h = \frac{100}{20} = 5 \, m$

Question 521: E

In step down transformers, the number of turns of the primary coil is larger than that of the secondary coil to decrease the voltage. If a transformer is 100% efficient, the electrical power input = electrical power output (P=IV).

Question 522: C

The percentage of C^{14} in the bone halves every 5,730 years. Since it has decreased from 100% to 6.25%, it has undergone 4 half-lives. Thus, the bone is $4 \times 5,730$ years old $= 22,920$ years

Question 523: E

This is a straightforward question in principle, as it just requires you to plug the values into the equation: $Velocity = Wavelength \times Frequency$ – Just ensure you work in SI units to get the correct answer.

$Frequency = \frac{2 \, m/s}{2.5 \, m} = 0.8 \, Hz = 0.8 \times 10^{-6} MHz = 8 \times 10^{-7} \, MHz$

Question 524: E

If an element has a half-life of 25 days, its BQ value will be halved every 25 days.

A total of $350/25 = 14$ half-lives have elapsed. Thus, the count rate has halved 14 times. Therefore, to calculate the original rate, the final count rate must be doubled 14 times $= 50 \times 2^{14}$.

$2^{14} = 2^5 \times 2^5 \times 2^4 = 32 \times 32 \times 16 = 16,384$.

Therefore, the original count rate $= 16,384 \times 50 = 819,200$

Question 525: D

Remember that $V = IR = \frac{P}{I}$ and $Power = \frac{Work\ Done}{Time} = \frac{Force\ x\ Distance}{Time} = Force\ x\ Velocity$;

Thus, A is derived from: $V = IR$,

B is derived from: $= \frac{P}{I}$,

C is derived from: $Voltage = \frac{Power}{Current} = \frac{Force\ x\ Velocity}{Current}$,

Since $Charge = Current\ x\ Time$, E and F are derived from: $Voltage = \frac{Power}{Current} = \frac{Force\ x\ Distance}{Time\ x\ Current} = \frac{J}{As} = \frac{J}{C}$,

D is incorrect as Nm = J. Thus the correct variant would be NmC^{-1}

Question 526: B

Each three-block combination is mutually exclusive to any other combination, so the probabilities are added. Each block pick is independent of all other picks, so the probabilities can be multiplied. For this scenario there are three possible combinations:

P(2 red blocks and 1 yellow block) = P(red then red then yellow) + P(red then yellow then red) + P(yellow then red then red) =

$(\frac{12}{20} \times \frac{11}{19} \times \frac{8}{18}) + (\frac{12}{20} \times \frac{8}{19} \times \frac{11}{18}) + (\frac{8}{20} \times \frac{12}{19} \times \frac{11}{18}) =$

$\frac{3\ x\ 12\ x\ 11\ x\ 8}{20\ x\ 19\ x\ 18} = \frac{44}{95}$

Question 527: C

Multiply through by 15: $3(3x + 5) + 5(2x - 2) = 18\ x\ 15$

Thus: $9x + 15 + 10x - 10 = 270$

$9x + 10x = 270 - 15 + 10$

$19x = 265$

$x = 13.95$

Question 528: C

This is a rare case where you need to factorise a complex polynomial:

(3x   )(x   ) = 0, possible pairs: 2 x 10, 10 x 2, 4 x 5, 5 x 4

(3x - 4)(x + 5) = 0

3x - 4 = 0, so x = $\frac{4}{3}$

x + 5 = 0, so x = -5

Question 529: C

$\frac{5(x-4)}{(x+2)(x-4)} + \frac{3\ (x+2)}{(x+2)(x-4)}$

$= \frac{5x-20+\ 3x+6}{(x+2)(x-4)}$

$= \frac{8x-14}{(x+2)(x-4)}$

Question 530: E

$p \propto \sqrt[3]{q}$, so $p = k\sqrt[3]{q}$

$p = 12$ when $q = 27$ gives $12 = k\sqrt[3]{27}$, so $12 = 3k$ and $k = 4$

so, $p = 4\sqrt[3]{q}$

Now $p = 24$:

$24 = 4\sqrt[3]{q}$, so $6 = \sqrt[3]{q}$ and $q = 6^3 = 216$

Question 531: A

$8 \times 9 = 72$

$8 = (4 \times 2) = 2 \times 2 \times 2$

$9 = 3 \times 3$

$(2 \times 2 \times 2 \times 3 \times 3)^2 = 2 \times 2 \times 2 \times 2 \times 2 \times 2 \times 3 \times 3 \times 3 \times 3 = 2^6 \times 3^4$

Question 532: C

Note that $1.151 \times 2 = 2.302$.

Thus: $\frac{2 \times 10^5 + 2 \times 10^2}{10^{10}} = 2 \times 10^{-5} + 2 \times 10^{-8}$

$= 0.00002 + 0.00000002 = 0.00002002$

Question 533: E

$y^2 + ay + b$

$= (y+2)^2 - 5 = y^2 + 4y + 4 - 5$

$= y^2 + 4y + 4 - 5 = y^2 + 4y - 1$

So $a = 4$ and $y = -1$

Question 534: E

Take $5(m + 4n)$ as a common factor to give: $\frac{4(m+4n)}{5(m+4n)} + \frac{5(m-2n)}{5(m+4n)}$

Simplify to give: $\frac{4m+16n+5m-10n}{5(m+4n)} = \frac{9m+6n}{5(m+4n)} = \frac{3(3m+2n)}{5(m+4n)}$

Question 535: C

$A \propto \frac{1}{\sqrt{B}}$. Thus, $= \frac{k}{\sqrt{B}}$.

Substitute the values in to give: $4 = \frac{k}{\sqrt{25}}$.

Thus, $k = 20$.

Therefore, $A = \frac{20}{\sqrt{B}}$.

When $B = 16$, $A = \frac{20}{\sqrt{16}} = \frac{20}{4} = 5$

Question 536: E

Angles SVU and STU are opposites and add up to 180°, so STU = 91°

The angle of the centre of a circle is twice the angle at the circumference so

SOU = 2 x 91° = 182°

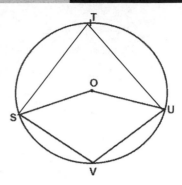

Question 537: E

The surface area of an open cylinder A = $2\pi rh$. Cylinder B is an enlargement of A, so the increases in radius (r)

and height (h) will be proportional: $\frac{r_A}{r_B} = \frac{h_A}{h_B}$. Let us call the proportion coefficient n, where $n = \frac{r_A}{r_B} = \frac{h_A}{h_B}$.

So $\frac{Area\ A}{Area\ B} = \frac{2\pi r_A h_A}{2\pi r_B h_B} = n\ x\ n = n^2$. $\frac{Area\ A}{Area\ B} = \frac{32\pi}{8\pi} = 4$, so, n = 2.

The proportion coefficient n = 2 also applies to their volumes, where the third dimension (also radius, i.e. the r^2

in $V = \pi r^2 h$) is equally subject to this constant of proportionality. The cylinder's volumes are related by $n^3 = 8$.

If the smaller cylinder has volume 2π cm^3, then the larger will have volume 2π x $n^3 = 2\pi$ x 8 = 16π cm^3.

Question 538: E

$= \frac{8}{x(3-x)} - \frac{6(3-x)}{x(3-x)}$

$= \frac{8-18+6x}{x(3-x)}$

$= \frac{6x-10}{x(3-x)}$

Question 539: B

For the black ball to be drawn in the last round, white balls must be drawn every round. Thus the probability is

given by $P = \frac{9}{10}$ x $\frac{8}{9}$ x $\frac{7}{8}$ x $\frac{6}{7}$ x $\frac{5}{6}$ x $\frac{4}{5}$ x $\frac{3}{4}$ x $\frac{2}{3}$ x $\frac{1}{2}$

$= \frac{9\ x\ 8\ x\ 7\ x\ 6\ x\ 5\ x\ 4\ x\ 3\ x\ 2\ x\ 1}{10\ x\ 9\ x\ 8\ x\ 7\ x\ 6\ x\ 5\ x\ 4\ x\ 3\ x\ 2\ x\ 1} = \frac{1}{10}$

Question 540: C

The probability of getting a king the first time is $\frac{4}{52} = \frac{1}{13}$, and the probability of getting a king the second time is

$\frac{3}{51}$. These are independent events, thus, the probability of drawing two kings is $\frac{1}{13}$ x $\frac{3}{51} = \frac{3}{663} = \frac{1}{221}$

Question 541: B

The probabilities of all outcomes must sum to one, so if the probability of rolling a 1 is x, then: $x + x + x + x +$

$2x = 1$. Therefore, $x = \frac{1}{7}$.

The probability of obtaining two sixes $P_{12} = \frac{2}{7}$ x $\frac{2}{7} = \frac{4}{49}$

Question 542: B

There are plenty of ways of counting, however the easiest is as follows: 0 is divisible by both 2 and 3. Half of the numbers from 1 to 36 are even (i.e. 18 of them). 3, 9, 15, 21, 27, 33 are the only numbers divisible by 3 that we've missed. There are 25 outcomes divisible by 2 or 3, out of 37.

Question 543: C

List the six ways of achieving this outcome: HHTT, HTHT, HTTH, and TTHH, THTH, THHT. There are 2^4 possible outcomes for 4 consecutive coin flips, so the probability of two heads and two tails is: $6 \, x \frac{1}{2^4} = \frac{6}{16} = \frac{5}{8}$

Question 544: D

Count the number of ways to get a 5, 6 or 7 (draw the square if helpful). The ways to get a 5 are: 1, 4; 2, 3; 3, 2; 4, 1. The ways to get a 6 are: 1, 5; 2, 4; 3, 3; 4, 2; 5, 1. The ways to get a 7 are: 1, 6; 2, 5; 3, 4; 4, 3; 5, 2; 6, 1. That is 15 out of 36 possible outcomes.

	1	2	3	4	5	6
1	2	3	4	5	6	7
2	3	4	5	6	7	8
3	4	5	6	7	8	9
4	5	6	7	8	9	10
5	6	7	8	9	10	11
6	7	8	9	10	11	12

Question 545: C

There are x+y+z balls in the bag, and the probability of picking a red ball is $\frac{x}{(x+y+z)}$ and the probability of picking a green ball is $\frac{z}{(x+y+z)}$. These are independent events, so the probability of picking red then green is $\frac{xz}{(x+y+z)^2}$ and the probability of picking green then red is the same. These outcomes are mutually exclusive, so are added.

Question 546: B

There are two ways of doing it, pulling out a red ball then a blue ball, or pulling out a blue ball and then a red ball. Let us work out the probability of the first: $\frac{x}{(x+y+z)} \times \frac{y}{x+y+z-1}$, and the probability of the second option will be the same. These are mutually exclusive options, so the probabilities may be summed.

Question 547: A

[x: Player 1 wins point, y: Player 2 wins point]

Player 1 wins in five rounds if we get: yxxxx, xyxxx, xxyxx, xxxyx.

(Note the case of xxxxy would lead to player 1 winning in 4 rounds, which the question forbids.)

Each of these have a probability of $p^4(1-p)$. Thus, the solution is $4p^4(1-p)$.

Question 548: F

$4x + 7 + 18x + 20 = 14$

$22x + 27 = 14$

Thus, $22x = -13$

Giving $x = -\frac{13}{22}$

Question 549: D

$$r^3 = \frac{3V}{4\pi}$$

Thus, $r = \left(\frac{3V}{4\pi}\right)^{1/3}$

Therefore, $S = 4\pi\left[\left(\frac{3V}{4\pi}\right)^{\frac{1}{3}}\right]^2 = 4\pi\left(\frac{3V}{4\pi}\right)^{\frac{2}{3}}$

$$= \frac{4\pi(3V)^{\frac{2}{3}}}{(4\pi)^{\frac{2}{3}}} = (3V)^{\frac{2}{3}} \times \frac{(4\pi)^1}{(4\pi)^{\frac{2}{3}}}$$

$$= (3V)^{\frac{2}{3}}(4\pi)^{1-\frac{2}{3}} = (4\pi)^{\frac{1}{3}}(3V)^{\frac{2}{3}}$$

Question 550: A

Let each unit length be x.

Thus, $S = 6x^2$. Therefore, $x = \left(\frac{S}{6}\right)^{\frac{1}{2}}$

$V = x^3$. Thus, $V = [\left(\frac{S}{6}\right)^{\frac{1}{2}}]^3$ so $V = \left(\frac{S}{6}\right)^{\frac{3}{2}}$

Question 551: B

Multiplying the second equation by 2 we get $4x + 16y = 24$. Subtracting the first equation from this we get $13y = 17$, so $y = \frac{17}{13}$. Then solving for x we get $x = \frac{10}{13}$. You could also try substituting possible solutions one by one, although given that the equations are both linear and contain easy numbers, it is quicker to solve them algebraically.

Question 552: A

Multiply by the denominator to give: $(7x + 10) = (3y^2 + 2)(9x + 5)$

Partially expand brackets on right side: $(7x + 10) = 9x(3y^2 + 2) + 5(3y^2 + 2)$

Take x terms across to left side: $7x - 9x(3y^2 + 2) = 5(3y^2 + 2) - 10$

Take x outside the brackets: $x[7 - 9(3y^2 + 2)] = 5(3y^2 + 2) - 10$

Thus: $x = \frac{5(3y^2 + 2) - 10}{7 - 9(3y^2 + 2)}$

Simplify to give: $x = \frac{(15y^2)}{(7 - 9(3y^2 + 2))}$

Question 553: F

$$3x\left(\frac{3x^7}{x^{\frac{1}{3}}}\right)^3 = 3x\left(\frac{3^3 x^{21}}{x^{\frac{3}{3}}}\right)$$

$$= 3x\frac{27x^{21}}{x} = 81x^{21}$$

Question 554: D

$$2x[2^{\frac{7}{14}} x^{\frac{7}{14}}] = 2x[2^{\frac{1}{2}} x^{\frac{1}{2}}]$$

$$= 2x(\sqrt{2}\sqrt{x}) = 2\left[\sqrt{x}\sqrt{x}\right][\sqrt{2}\sqrt{x}]$$

$$= 2\sqrt{2x^3}$$

Question 555: A

$A = \pi r^2$, therefore $10\pi = \pi r^2$

Thus, $r = \sqrt{10}$

Therefore, the circumference is $2\pi\sqrt{10}$

Question 556: D

$3.4 = 12 + (3 + 4) = 19$

$19.5 = 95 + (19 + 5) = 119$

Question 557: D

$2.3 = \dfrac{2^3}{2} = 4$

$4.2 = \dfrac{4^2}{4} = 4$

Question 558: F

This is a tricky question that requires you to know how to 'complete the square':

$(x + 1.5)(x + 1.5) = x^2 + 3x + 2.25$

Thus, $(x + 1.5)^2 - 7.25 = x^2 + 3x - 5 = 0$

Therefore, $(x + 1.5)^2 = 7.25 = \dfrac{29}{4}$

Thus, $x + 1.5 = \sqrt{\dfrac{29}{4}}$

Thus $x = -\dfrac{3}{2} \pm \sqrt{\dfrac{29}{4}} = -\dfrac{3}{2} \pm \dfrac{\sqrt{29}}{2}$

Question 559: B

Whilst you definitely need to solve this graphically, it is necessary to complete the square for the first equation to allow you to draw it more easily:

$(x + 2)^2 = x^2 + 4x + 4$

Thus, $y = (x + 2)^2 + 10 = x^2 + 4x + 14$

This is now an easy curve to draw ($y = x^2$ that has moved 2 units left and 10 units up). The turning point of this quadratic is to the left and well above anything in x^3, so the only solution is the first intersection of the two curves in the upper right quadrant around (3.4, 39).

Question 560: C

By far the easiest way to solve this is to sketch them (don't waste time solving them algebraically). As soon as you've done this, it'll be very obvious that $y = 2$ and $y = 1-x^2$ don't intersect, since the latter has its turning point at (0, 1) and zero points at $x = -1$ and 1. $y = x$ and $y = x^2$ intersect at the origin and (1, 1), and $y = 2$ runs through both.

Question 561: B

Notice that you're not required to get the actual values – just the number's magnitude. Thus, 897653 can be approximated to 900,000 and 0.009764 to 0.01. Therefore, 900,000 x 0.01 = 9,000

Question 562: C

Multiply through by 70: $7(7x + 3) + 10(3x + 1) = 14 \times 70$

Simplify: $49x + 21 + 30x + 10 = 980$

$79x + 31 = 980$

$x = \dfrac{949}{79}$

Question 563: A

Split the equilateral triangle into 2 right-angled triangles and apply Pythagoras' theorem:

$x^2 = \left(\dfrac{x}{2}\right)^2 + h^2$. Thus $h^2 = \dfrac{3}{4}x^2$

$h = \sqrt{\dfrac{3x^2}{4}} = \dfrac{\sqrt{3x^2}}{2}$

The area of a triangle = ½ x base x height $= \dfrac{1}{2}x\dfrac{\sqrt{3x^2}}{2}$

Simplifying gives: $x\dfrac{\sqrt{3x^2}}{4} = x\dfrac{\sqrt{3}\sqrt{x^2}}{4} = \dfrac{x^2\sqrt{3}}{4}$

Question 564: A

This is a question testing your ability to spot 'the difference between two squares'.

Factorise to give: $3 - \dfrac{7x(5x - 1)(5x+1)}{(7x)^2(5x+1)}$

Cancel out: $3 - \dfrac{(5x - 1)}{7x}$

Question 565: C

The easiest way to do this is to 'complete the square':

$(x - 5)^2 = x^2 - 10x + 25$

Thus, $(x - 5)^2 - 125 = x^2 - 10x - 100 = 0$

Therefore, $(x - 5)^2 = 125$

$x - 5 = \pm\sqrt{125} = \pm\sqrt{25}\sqrt{5} = \pm5\sqrt{5}$

$x = 5 \pm 5\sqrt{5}$

Question 566: B

Factorise by completing the square:

$x^2 - 4x + 7 = (x - 2)^2 + 3$

Simplify: $(x - 2)^2 = y^3 + 2 - 3$

$x - 2 = \pm\sqrt{y^3 - 1}$

$x = 2 \pm \sqrt{y^3 - 1}$

Question 567: D

Square both sides to give: $(3x + 2)^2 = 7x^2 + 2x + y$

Thus: $y = (3x + 2)^2 - 7x^2 - 2x = (9x^2 + 12x + 4) - 7x^2 - 2x$

$y = 2x^2 + 10x + 4$

Question 568: C

This is a fourth order polynomial, which you aren't expected to be able to factorise at GCSE. This is where looking at the options makes your life a lot easier. In all of them, opening the bracket on the right side involves making $(y \pm 1)^4$ on the left side, i.e. the answers are hinting that $(y \pm 1)^4$ is the solution to the fourth order polynomial.

Since there are negative terms in the equations (e.g. $-4y^3$), the solution has to be:

$(y - 1)^4 = y^4 - 4y^3 + 6y^2 - 4y + 1$

Therefore, $(y - 1)^4 + 1 = x^5 + 7$

Thus, $y - 1 = (x^5 + 6)^{\frac{1}{4}}$

$y = 1 + (x^5 + 6)^{1/4}$

Question 569: A

Let the width of the television be 4x and the height of the television be 3x.

Then by Pythagoras: $(4x)^2 + (3x)^2 = 50^2$

Simplify: $25x^2 = 2500$

Thus: $x = 10$. Therefore: the screen is 30 inches by 40 inches, i.e. the area is 1,200 inches^2.

Question 570: C

Square both sides to give: $1 + \frac{3}{x^2} = (y^5 + 1)^2$

Multiply out: $\frac{3}{x^2} = (y^{10} + 2y^5 + 1) - 1$

Thus: $x^2 = \frac{3}{y^{10} + 2y^5}$

Therefore: $x = \sqrt{\frac{3}{y^{10} + 2y^5}}$

Question 571: C

The easiest way is to double the first equation and triple the second to get:

$6x - 10y = 20$ *and* $6x + 6y = 39$.

Subtract the first from the second to give: $16y = 19$,

Therefore, $y = \frac{19}{16}$.

Substitute back into the first equation to give $x = \frac{85}{16}$.

Question 572: C

This is fairly straightforward; the first inequality is the easier one to work with: B and D and E violate it, so we just need to check A and C in the second inequality.

C: $1^3 - 2^2 < 3$, but A: $2^3 - 1^2 > 3$

Question 573: B

Whilst this can be done graphically, it's quicker to do algebraically (because the second equation is not as easy to sketch). Intersections occur where the curves have the same coordinates.

Thus: $x + 4 = 4x^2 + 5x + 5$

Simplify: $4x^2 + 4x + 1 = 0$

Factorise: $(2x + 1)(2x + 1) = 0$

Thus, the two graphs only intersect once at $x = -\frac{1}{2}$

Question 574: D

It's better to do this algebraically as the equations are easy to work with and you would need to sketch very accurately to get the answer. Intersections occur where the curves have the same coordinates. Thus: $x^3 = x$

$x^3 - x = 0$

Thus: $x(x^2 - 1) = 0$

Spot the 'difference between two squares': $x(x + 1)(x - 1) = 0$

Thus there are 3 intersections: at $x = 0, 1 \text{ and} - 1$

Question 575: E

Note that the line is the hypotenuse of a right angled triangle with one side unit length and one side of length ½.

By Pythagoras, $\left(\frac{1}{2}\right)^2 + 1^2 = x^2$

Thus, $x^2 = \frac{1}{4} + 1 = \frac{5}{4}$

$x = \sqrt{\frac{5}{4}} = \frac{\sqrt{5}}{\sqrt{4}} = \frac{\sqrt{5}}{2}$

Question 576: D

We can eliminate z from equation (1) and (2) by multiplying equation (1) by 3 and adding it to equation (2):

3x + 3y – 3z = -3	Equation (1) multiplied by 3
2x – 2y +3z = 8	Equation (2) then add both equations
5x + y = 5	We label this as equation (4)

Now we must eliminate the same variable z from another pair of equations by using equation (1) and (3):

2x + 2y – 2z = -2	Equation (1) multiplied by 2
2x – y + 2z = 9	Equation (3) then add both equations
4x + y = 7	We label this as equation (5)

We now use both equations (4) and (5) to obtain the value of x:

5x + y = 5	Equation (4)
- 4x - y = -7	Equation (5) multiplied by -1
x = -2	

Substitute x back in to calculate y:

4x + y = 7

4(-2) + y = 7

- 8 + y = 7

y = 15

Substitute x and y back in to calculate z:

x + y – z = -1

-2 + 15 – z = -1

13 – z = -1

-z = -14

z = 14

Thus: x = -2, y = 15, z = 14

Question 577: D

This is one of the easier maths questions. Take 3a as a factor to give:

$3a(a^2 – 10a + 25) = 3a(a – 5)(a – 5) = 3a(a – 5)^2$

Question 578: B

Note that 12 is the Lowest Common Multiple of 3 and 4. Thus:

-3 (4x + 3y) = -3 (48)   Multiply each side by -3

 4 (3x + 2y) = 4 (34)   Multiply each side by 4

-12x – 9y = -144

12x + 8y = 136   Add together

$\quad$ -y = -8

$\quad$ y = 8

Substitute y back in:

4x + 3y = 48

4x + 3(8) = 48

4x + 24 = 48

4x = 24

x = 6

Question 579: E

Don't be fooled, this is an easy question, just obey BODMAS and don't skip steps.

$$\frac{-(25-28)^2}{-36+14} = \frac{-(-3)^2}{-22}$$

This gives: $\frac{-(9)}{-22} = \frac{9}{22}$

Question 580: E

Since there are 26 possible letters for each of the 3 letters in the license plate, and there are 10 possible numbers (0-9) for each of the 3 numbers in the same plate, then the number of license plates would be:

$(26) \times (26) \times (26) \times (10) \times (10) \times (10) = 17,576,000$

Question 581: B

Expand the brackets to give: $4x^2 - 12x + 9 = 0$.

Factorise: $(2x - 3)(2x - 3) = 0$.

Thus, only one solution exists, x = 1.5.

Note that you could also use the fact that the discriminant, $b^2 - 4ac = 0$ to get the answer.

Question 582: C

$$= \left(x^{\frac{1}{2}}\right)^{\frac{1}{2}} (y^{-3})^{\frac{1}{2}}$$

$$= x^{\frac{1}{4}} y^{-\frac{3}{2}} = \frac{x^{\frac{1}{4}}}{y^{\frac{3}{2}}}$$

Question 583: A

Let x, y, and z represent the rent for the 1-bedroom, 2-bedroom, and 3-bedroom flats, respectively. We can write 3 different equations: 1 for the rent, 1 for the repairs, and the last one for the statement that the 3-bedroom unit costs twice as much as the 1-bedroom unit.

(1) x + y + z = 1240

(2) 0.1x + 0.2y + 0.3z = 276

(3) z = 2x

Substitute z = 2x in both of the two other equations to eliminate z:

(4) x + y + 2x = 3x + y = 1240

(5) 0.1x + 0.2y + 0.3(2x) = 0.7x + 0.2y = 276

-2(3x + y) = -2(1240)	Multiply each side of (4) by -2
10(0.7x + 0.2y) = 10(276)	Multiply each side of (5) by 10
(6) -6x -2y = -2480	Add these 2 equations
<u>**(7)** 7x + 2y = 2760</u>	
x = 280	
z = 2(280) = 560	Because z = 2x
280 + y + 560 = 1240	Because x + y + z = 1240
y = 400	

Thus the units rent for £ 280, £ 400, £ 560 per week respectively.

Question 584: C

Following BODMAS:

$$= 5 \left[5(6^2 - 5 \times 3) + 400^{\frac{1}{2}}\right]^{1/3} + 7$$

$$= 5 \left[5(36 - 15) + 20\right]^{\frac{1}{3}} + 7$$

$$= 5 \left[5(21) + 20\right]^{\frac{1}{3}} + 7$$

$$= 5 \left(105 + 20\right)^{\frac{1}{3}} + 7$$

$$= 5 \left(125\right)^{\frac{1}{3}} + 7$$

$$= 5 \left(5\right) + 7$$

$$= 25 + 7 = 32$$

Question 585: B

Consider a triangle formed by joining the centre to two adjacent vertices. Six similar triangles can be made around the centre – thus, the central angle is 60 degrees. Since the two lines forming the triangle are of equal length, we have 6 identical equilateral triangles in the hexagon.

Now split the triangle in half and apply Pythagoras' theorem:

$$1^2 = 0.5^2 + h^2$$

Thus, $h = \sqrt{\frac{3}{4}} = \frac{\sqrt{3}}{2}$

Thus, the area of the triangle is: $\frac{1}{2}bh = \frac{1}{2} \times 1 \times \frac{\sqrt{3}}{2} = \frac{\sqrt{3}}{4}$

Therefore, the area of the hexagon is: $\frac{\sqrt{3}}{4} \times 6 = \frac{3\sqrt{3}}{2}$

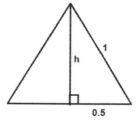

Question 586: B

Let x be the width and x+19 be the length.

Thus, the area of a rectangle is $x(x + 19) = 780$.

Therefore:

$x^2 + 19x - 780 = 0$

$(x - 20)(x + 39) = 0$

$x - 20 = 0$ or $x + 39 = 0$

$x = 20$ or $x = -39$

Since length can never be a negative number, we disregard $x = -39$ and use $x = 20$ instead.

Thus, the width is 20 metres and the length is 39 metres.

Question 587: B

The quickest way to solve is by trial and error, substituting the provided options. However, if you're keen to do this algebraically, you can do the following:

Start by setting up the equations: Perimeter = 2L + 2W = 34

Thus: L + W = 17

Using Pythagoras: $L^2 + W^2 = 13^2$

Since L + W = 17, W = 17 - L

Therefore: $L^2 + (17 - L)^2 = 169$

$L^2 + 289 - 34L + L^2 = 169$

$2L^2 - 34L + 120 = 0$

$L^2 - 17L + 60 = 0$

$(L - 5)(L - 12) = 0$

Thus: L = 5 and L = 12

And: W = 12 and W = 5

Question 588: C

Multiply both sides by 8: $4(3x - 5) + 2(x + 5) = 8(x + 1)$

Remove brackets: $12x - 20 + 2x + 10 = 8x + 8$

Simplify: $14x - 10 = 8x + 8$

Add 10: $14x = 8x + 18$

Subtract 8x: $6x = 18$

Therefore: $x = 3$

Question 589: C

Recognise that 1.742 x 3 is 5.226. Now, the original equation simplifies to: $= \frac{3 \times 10^6 + 3 \times 10^5}{10^{10}}$

$= 3 \times 10^{-4} + 3 \times 10^{-5} = 3.3 \times 10^{-4}$

Question 590: A

$Area = \frac{(2 + \sqrt{2})(4 - \sqrt{2})}{2}$

$= \frac{8 - 2\sqrt{2} + 4\sqrt{2} - 2}{2}$

$= \frac{6 + 2\sqrt{2}}{2}$

$= 3 + \sqrt{2}$

Question 591: C

Square both sides: $\frac{4}{x} + 9 = (y - 2)^2$

$\frac{4}{x} = (y - 2)^2 - 9$

Cross Multiply: $\frac{x}{4} = \frac{1}{(y-2)^2-9}$

$x = \frac{4}{y^2-4y+4-9}$

Factorise: $x = \frac{4}{y^2-4y-5}$

$x = \frac{4}{(y+1)(y-5)}$

Question 592: D

Set up the equation: $5x - 5 = 0.5\,(6x + 2)$

$10x - 10 = 6x + 2$

$4x = 12$

$x = 3$

Question 593: C

Round numbers appropriately: $\frac{55 +(\frac{9}{4})^2}{\sqrt{900}} = \frac{55 +\frac{81}{16}}{30}$

81 rounds to 80 to give: $\frac{55 +5}{30} = \frac{60}{30} = 2$

Question 594: D

There are three outcomes from choosing the type of cheese in the crust. For each of the additional toppings to possibly add, there are 2 outcomes: 1 to include and another not to include a certain topping, for each of the 7 toppings

Thus, the number of different kinds of pizza is: $3 \times 2 \times 2 \times 2 \times 2 \times 2 \times 2 \times 2 = 3 \times 2^7$

$= 3 \times 128 = 384$

Question 595: A

Although it is possible to do this algebraically, by far the easiest way is via trial and error. The clue that you shouldn't attempt it algebraically is the fact that rearranging the first equation to make x or y the subject leaves you with a difficult equation to work with (e.g. $x = \sqrt{1 - y^2}$) when you try to substitute in the second.

An exceptionally good student might notice that the equations are symmetric in x and y, i.e. the solution is when $x = y$. Thus $2x^2 = 1$ and $2x = \sqrt{2}$ which gives $\frac{\sqrt{2}}{2}$ as the answer.

Question 596: C

If two shapes are congruent, then they are the same size and shape. Thus, congruent objects can be rotations and mirror images of each other. The two triangles in E are indeed congruent (SAS). Congruent objects must, by definition, have the same angles.

Question 597: B

Rearrange the equation: $x^2 + x - 6 \geq 0$

Factorise: $(x + 3)(x - 2) \geq 0$

Remember that this is a quadratic inequality so requires a quick sketch to ensure you don't make a silly mistake with which way the sign is.

Thus, $y = 0$ when $x = 2$ and $x = -3$. $y > 0$ when $x > 2$ or $x < -3$.

Thus, the solution is: $x \leq -3 \ and \ x \geq 2$.

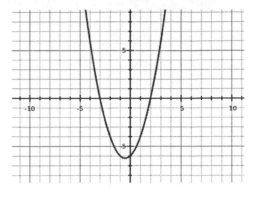

Question 598: B

Using Pythagoras: $a^2 + b^2 = x^2$

Since the triangle is equilateral: $a = b, \ so \ 2a^2 = x^2$

Area $= \frac{1}{2} base \ x \ height = \frac{1}{2}a^2$. From above, $a^2 = \frac{x^2}{2}$

Thus the area $= \frac{1}{2}x\frac{x^2}{2} = \frac{x^2}{4}$

Question 599: A

If X and Y are doubled, the value of Q increases by 4. Halving the value of A reduces this to 2. Finally, tripling the value of B reduces this to ⅔, i.e. the value decreases by ⅓.

Question 600: C

The quickest way to do this is to sketch the curves. This requires you to factorise both equations by completing the square:

$x^2 - 2x + 3 = (x - 1)^2 + 2$

$x^2 - 6x - 10 = (x - 3)^2 - 19$ Thus, the first equation has a turning point at (1, 2) and doesn't cross the x-axis. The second equation has a turning point at (3, -19) and crosses the x-axis twice.

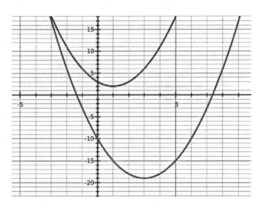

Mock Paper Answers

Mock Paper A: Section 1

Question 1: C
The simplest solution is to calculate the total area at the start as 20 x 20 = 400cm^2. Then recognise that with every fold the area will be reduced by half therefore the area will decrease as follows: 400, 200, 100, 50, 25, 12.5 – requiring a total of 5 folds.

Question 2: D
This is the only correct as it is the only statement that doesn't categorically state a fact that was discussed in conditional tense in the paragraph.

Question 3: B
Off the 50% carrying the parasite 20% are symptomatic. Therefore 0.5 x 0.2 = 10% of the total population are infected and symptomatic. Of which 0.1 x 0.9 = 9% are male.

Question 4: D
The most important part of the question to note is the figure of 30% reduction during sale time. Although A and B are possible the question asks specifically with regard to cost. Therefore it is only worth waiting for the sale period if the sterling to euro exchange rate does not depreciate more than the magnitude of the sale. As such solution D is the only correct answer as it describes anticipating a loss in sterling value less than 30% against the euro.

Question 5: D
Begin by calculating the number of childminders that can be hired for a 24 hour period as 24 x 8.5 = 204. Therefore a total of 4 childminders can be hired continually for 24 hours with £184 left over – as the question states the hire has to be for a whole 24 hour period and therefore the remainder £184 cannot be used. As such D is the correct answer of 4 x 4 = 16.

Question 6: B
The simplest way to approach this question is to recognise that there is a difference of £1.50 between peak and off-peak prices for all individuals except students. The total savings can therefore be calculated as (3 + 5 + 1) x 1.5 = 9 x 1.5 = 13.5.

Question 7: B
Recognise that with each progressive frame the number of black shapes decreases by one whilst the number of white shapes increases by two. Therefore B is the correct answer with 9 white shapes and 0 black shapes.

Question 8: D
Answers A and B are simply incorrect as the measurement taken is a percentage increase (/decrease) which will normalise baseline diameters therefore allowing for comparison over multiple time points. You should be aware from your studies that ultrasound is an invaluable technique in distinguishing between adjacent tissue types. Any methodology is repeatable if it is correctly chronicled and followed therefore leaving the correct answer of D.

Question 9: C
If both the flight and travel from the airport are delayed this will be the longest the journey could possible take – producing a total journey time of 20 + 15 + 150 + 20 + 25 = 230 minutes or 3 hours 50 minutes. Therefore given all possible eventualities, to arrive at 5pm, boarding should begin at 13.10pm. Answer D is incorrect as a delayed plan would add 20 minutes to the journey whilst the transport to the meeting at the other end takes a minimum of 15 minutes – even if Megan could teleport instantaneously from the airport to the meeting she would be 5 minutes later than if there wasn't a plane delay.

Question 10: E

This is almost a trick question and simply an application of exponential decay. Recall that an exponential decay is asymptotic to 0 as no matter how small the volume within the cask becomes, only half of it is ever removed. It could be argued that this process cannot continue once a single molecule of whiskey is left – and when splitting that single molecule in half it is no longer whiskey. However the question does not ask "how long till all the whiskey is gone" but rather "how many minutes will it take for the entire cask to be emptied" and therefore the process can continue infinitely – even if the only thing left in the cask is a collection of quarks … or half that.

Question 11: E

With these questions it is important to only consider information displayed in the graph and not involve any assumptions provided by your prior knowledge. Therefore this question is questioning your ability to consider correlation as opposed to causation. The graph simply shows that waist size and BMI are positively correlated with one another and that is it. The nature of a scatter plot does not allow you to deduce which of the variables (if any) drives the result observed in the dependent variable. However the fact that they are correlated is an important result and therefore D is also incorrect.

Question 12: D

Observe that in the depicted frames the total number of sides increases by 8 each time independent of the colours used. Therefore as the 4th displayed frame has 33 sides, the correct answer is D with 41 sides.

Question 13: E

The question can be expressed as $(40 \times 30) – x(50 \times 30) = 200 = 1,200 – x1,500$. Therefore $x = 2/3$.

Question 14: D

The information given is very much a red herring in this question. This can be solved using your own application of sequence theory. If a sequence is 6 numbers long, the 6 numbers can be re-arranged into a total of 6! possible sequences = $1 \times 2 \times 3 \times 4 \times 5 \times 6 = 720$

Question 15: E

Although this is an extremely abstract question, all the information needed to answer it is provided. The key rule to have isolated from the information is that with each progressive sequence, a bell can only move one position at most. Therefore looking through each in turn – for example we can exclude A as the 3 goes from position 4 to position 2. This leaves the only correct answer of B. Recall that the information states bells can only move a maximum of one place – they can of course move 0 places.

Question 16: A

As the largest digit on the number pad is 9, even if 9 was pressed for an infinitely long time the entered code would still average out at no larger than 9. Therefore it would be impossible to achieve a reference number larger than 9. Indeed this is an extremely insecure safe but not for the reason described in B (for if the same incorrect number was pressed indefinitely it would never average out as the correct one) but rather because the safe could in theory be opened with a single digit.

Question 17: D

A is incorrect as it ignores the section of the text that states the evolution of resistant strains is driven by the presence of antibiotics themselves. The text states that the rate of bacterial reproduction is a large contributing factor and therefore not wholly responsible – hence B is incorrect. Since this is just one example (and only the information in the text should be considered for these questions) for C to make such a general statement is complete unjustified.

Question 18: B

The fastest way to solve this question is to calculate the quantity of cheese per portion as $200/10 = 20$. Which for 350 people would require $350 \times 20 = 7000g$ or 7kg.

Question 19: C
Calculate the calorific content of 12 portions as 12 x 300 = 3,600kcal. As this represents 120%, evaluate what the initial amount would be as (3,600/120) x100 = 3,000kcal.

Question 20: B
Begin by calculating the initial weight of all the ingredients in the Bolognese sauce which comes to a total of 3.05kg. Therefore when cooking for 10 people 3.05 x 4 = 12.2kg of pasta should be used. Which in turn means for 30 people 3 x 12.2 = 36.6kg should be used.

Question 21: D
Calculate the new weight of ingredients in the Bolognese sauce excluding garlic and pancetta which produces a total of 2.8kg. Note that onions represent 0.3kg per 10 people and as such the ratio can be represented as 0.3/2.8 or alternatively dividing top and bottom by 0.3 → 1/9.3

Question 22: E
Begin with calculating total preparation time as 25 x 4 = 100 mins. The fact that Simon can only cook 8 portions at a time is somewhat a red herring as it doesn't impact the calculation. Total cooking time can be calculated as a further 25 x 8 = 200 mins. Producing a total time of 300mins or 5 hours.

Question 23: D
Due to the quantities colour t-shirts are priced at £5 and black and white at £2.50. Therefore the order will incur a total cost of 50 + (50 x 5) + (200 x 2.5) = £800.

Question 24: E
Answers A and B directly conflict with information presented in the text whilst C and D may well be true but there is insufficient information in the text to address these points. This is an important reminder that although you may well have been a scout and be able to comment on options C and D, you may only consider these arguments in terms of the text provided.

Question 25: C
Note that with each progressing frame, although the whole frame is rotated 90 degrees clockwise, the black arrows are rotated 90 degrees anticlockwise. As such after 4 frames the sequence resets back to the initial frame and C is the correct answer.

Question 26: C
The article seen here is a particularly good effort at a discursive text as it is completely impartial. Note that the article simply states the facts from either side in equal measure. Nowhere does the author present their opinion on the matter nor do they insinuate their beliefs in anyway.

Question 27: C
The journey time is rounded to the nearest hour (13). Therefore the longest it could possibly be is 13 hours 29 minutes or it would be round up to 8 hours. Therefore the latest the ferry will arrive, assuming the travel time estimate is accurate, is given as 20.29.

Question 28: B
The correct answer is 28. Assume, although very unlikely, that you roll a 2 every single go – you will never need to take a step back, only your two forward. Therefore rolling a lower number in this case is beneficial.

Question 29: B
The simplest way to calculate this is to find the lowest common multiple of the given laptops which is 40 x 60 x 70 = 168,000 seconds = 2,800 minutes = 46.67 hours – although they will not all be on the same lap number at this time.

Question 30: C

A large amount of subtly different data is described here. Of note is the first experiment which describes how nerve conduction is faster in right handed men than it is in left handed men. This result is not transferable to women until it is proven! The experiment currently being conducted only considers dominant hand in men vs women. That could be either hand or not necessarily the females' right hand. For example all of the females in this experiment could have been left handed and there is no information in the text to say otherwise, therefore we cannot tell.

Question 31: C

Recognise that two square based pyramids will comprise 8 triangles of base width 5 and height 8; plus two 5 x 5 squares. Thus giving at total area of $8(8/2 \times 5) + 2(5 \times 5) = 210 \, cm^2$

Question 32: B

In order to approach this question first realise that in the first well 1ml of solvent is being combined with 9ml of distilled water producing 1eq of solute in 10ml – hence the first well produces a dilution by a factor of 10. With each progressive dilution the concentration is reduced by a further factor of 10 – hence by well 10 the concentration is at $x/10^{10}$

Question 33: E

The compartments of the human body are occupied by numerous fluids, as the student is only interested in measuring the volume of blood, it is essential he chooses a solute that will only dissolve in blood. So as his known quantity of solute remains no, it must be neither removed nor added during its time in the body. Hence all of the written assumptions must be made and many more.

Question 34: D

The fastest way to approach this question is by calculating the total price per head as 10 + (8/20) + (10/60) = 10.567. To make the maths simpler this can be rounded safely to £11 a head at this stage. 2,300/11 is approximately equal to 209 which when rounded to the nearest 10 is 210 people.

Question 35: A

Whilst this passage is attempting to weigh up two sides of an argument, it has a clear one sided approach focussing heavily on the excitement of dangerous sports. It even states that hunting is recognised as exciting by some. Since the previous sentence discussed the link between archery and hunting, the statement is a fair extrapolation to make.

END OF SECTION

Mock Paper A: Section 2

Question 1: B
Let tail = T, body and legs = B and head = H.
As described in the question H = T + 0.5B and B = T + H.
We have already been told that T = 30Kg.
Therefore substitute the second equation into the first as H = 30 + 0.5(30 + H).
Re-arranging reveals that -0.5H = 45Kg and therefore the weight of the head is 90Kg, the body and legs 120Kg and as we were told the tail weighs 30Kg.
Thus giving a total weight of 240Kg

Question 2: D
Recall that kinetic energy can be calculated as $E = 0.5mv^2$. Therefore if mass remains constant it is the v^2 term that must be reduced to a sixteenth. In other words $v^2 = 1/16$ and therefore the correct velocity is $1/4x$.

Question 3: A
An organ is defined as comprising multiple tissue types. As blood and skeletal muscle are themselves tissues they cannot be classified as organs.

Question 4: E
This question is best considered in terms of the aerobic respiration equation. With that in mind it becomes apparent that increased forward drive through the reaction will produce large amounts of water and CO_2 whilst demanding an increased supply of O_2. Further from this equation we realise that aerobic respiration produces large amounts of heat, and as such it is expected – in the interest of thermoregulation – that the body will both perspire and vasodilate in attempt to increase heat loss. Therefore E is the correct answer.

Question 5: D
Recall that the nephron is the smallest functional unit of the kidney. The question therefore is asking you what is the smallest basic functional unit of striated muscle? To which the answer is the sarcomere. Note that a myofibril is a collection of many sarcomeres and is therefore not the correct answer.

Question 6: B
Insulin is a polypeptide hormone released by the pancreas in response to elevated plasma glucose levels. Therefore it can be expected that plasma glucose concentration will be proportional to the concentration of insulin in the blood. Furthermore recall that glucagon also released by the pancreas mobilises glucose stores. Therefore the greatest concentration of plasma glucose would be expected at the time when glucagon is highest during a period of elevated insulin.

Question 7: D
Answers a and c are both nonsense and can be eliminated straight away. You will know from your study of the immune system that it is plasma B cells that produce antibodies and that plasma T cells do not exist. Also recall that an immune response can be mounted as quickly as within a fortnight which leaves the only correct answer d. The passage states that only once blood types are mixed is the immune response initiated, therefore answer d provides an explanation as to how this happens but also why the first born child is unaffected.

Question 8: E
Recall that pH is a logarithmic scale of proton concentration and therefore will have the largest effect on hydrogen bonding.

Question 9: D
An organ consists of many cell types which once differentiated are committed to that single cell line. Therefore a totipotent stem cell is required to produce the multiple cell types required. In order to ensure that the organ is an exact genetic match, stem cells from the individual in question must be used. Unless that individual is an embryo, adult stem cells must be used.

Question 10: D

Isotopes of an element all contain the same number of protons but a different number of neutrons. As atomic number refers solely to the number of protons it will not change. However as mass number is the sum of atomic number and neutron number – it would be expected to change. If an isotope contains one extra proton, then assuming that the charge of that isotope is 0, then it must also contain one extra electron. Chemical properties are the same for all isotopes. Therefore the correct answer is D.

Question 11: B

The transition metals are the most abundant catalysts – presumably due to their ability to achieve a variable number of stable states. Therefore the correct answer is the d-block elements.

Question 12: E

Begin by writing down the balanced equation that describes the reaction of francium with water: $2Fr + 2H_2O \rightarrow 2FrOH + H_2$. Next calculate the moles of francium entering the reaction as $1338/223 = 6$. We therefore know from the stoichiometry of the equation that this reaction will produce 3 moles of hydrogen. Recall that 1 mole of gas at room temperature and pressure occupies $24dm^3$. Therefore the hydrogen produced in this reaction will occupy $3 \times 24 = 72dm^3$.

Question 13: D

The simplest way to approach this type of question is to assume that there are 10 atoms within the compound. In this case that produces the following result: $C_3H_4F_2Cl$. Next look to see if any of the subscript numbers are divisible by a common factor. Also if there are any decimals, multiply up by a common factor until only integers are present. In this case the correct answer is achieved straight away.

Question 14: C

This question requires you to have a correct answer from the previous question, although these questions are unfair in the fact that this current question cannot be answered without success in the first part – there are always one or two of these per paper. Simply calculate the Mr of your empirical formula: 113.5. And then divide 340.5 by this: $340.5/113.5 = 3$. Therefore multiply your empirical formula up by a factor of 3.

Question 15: B

The calculation in this question is simple: concentration = mass/volume, what this question is really testing is the manipulation of unorthodox units. Begin by noting the use of g/dL in the final answers and therefore begin by converting the quantities in the question into these units. 1.2×10^{10} kg = 1.2×10^{13} grams and with 10 decilitres in a litre, 4×10^{12} L = 4×10^{13} dL. $\frac{(1.2 \times 10^{13})}{(4 \times 10^{13})} = 3 \times 10^{-1}$ g/dL.

Question 16: A

A catalyst is not essential for the progression of a chemical reaction, it only acts to lower the activation energy and therefore increase the likelihood and rate of reaction.

Question 17: E

Cationic surfactants represent a class of molecule that demonstrates both hydrophilic and hydrophobic domains. This allows it to act as an emulsifying agent which is particularly useful in the disruption of grease or lipid deposits. Therefore cationic surfactants have applications in all of the products listed.

Question 18: B

Recall that V = E/Q; therefore when substituting SI units into these equation it is discovered that $V = J/C = JC^{-1}$.

Question 19: C

Recall that voltmeters are always connected in parallel – and so that they don't draw any current from the circuit have an infinite resistance. Ammeters on the other hand are connected in series and therefore must not perturb the flow of given, meaning they have zero resistance.

Question 20: A

Much of the information in this question is not needed and is simply put there to distract you. This question can be most quickly solved using the equation F=ma or force = mass x acceleration. As object A is the only things moving in this scenario it is the only source of energy to be considered. Its mass will be the same before and after the collision and so we need only calculate the magnitude of retardation. Given as $(15 - 3)/0.5 = 24ms^{-2}$. Therefore when plugging into the first equation we realise that F = 12 x 24 = 288N of force dissipated. Alternatively this question could be solved by calculating the rate of change of momentum.

Question 21: C

Note the atomic masses and numbers in the equation. Whilst the atomic mass has remained constant the atomic number has increased by one and hence the element has changed. The only explanation for this is that a neutron has turned into a proton (and an electron which is represented by x). Therefore the correct answer is C – beta radioactive decay.

Question 22: B

Begin by calculating the velocity of the wave as speed = wavelength x frequency = 3 x 20 = 60km/s. Which in a time period of one hour (3600s) would equate to a total distance of 60 x 3600 = 216,000km.

Question 23: C

The numerator of the fraction consists of 3 distinct terms or 3 distinct dimensions. As all other functions within the equation are constants one would consider this the volume of a complex 3D shape.

Question 24: B

Expand the larger scientific number so that it reads 10 to the power 6 like so: $4.2 \times 10^{10} = 42000 \times 10^6$. Now that the powers are the same across the numerators, a simple subtraction can be performed $(42000 – 4.2) \times 10^6 = 41995.8 \times 10^6$ which can be simplified to 4.19958×10^{10}. Next consider the division which can be competed in a two-step process, first divide the numerator by 2 like so $(4.19958/2) \times 10^{10} = 2.09979 \times 10^{10}$ and then subtract the powers like so $2.09979 \times 10^{(10-3)} = 2.09979 \times 10^7$.

Question 25: A

Note the triangle formed by the right angle lines and the tangent. Recall that as this is a right angle triangle then the other two angles must be 45°. As angles along a straight line add up to 180° a must equal 180 – 45 = 135°. Angles around the origin must add up to 360° and therefore b = (360 – 90)/2 = 135°. Therefore the correct answer is A.

Question 26: B

The probability of drawing a blue ball (1/21) and then a black ball (1/20) is 1/21 x 1/20 = 1/420. However note that it is also possible that these balls could also be drawn out in the opposite order. Therefore the probability must be multiplied by two like so 1/420 x 2 = 2/420 = 1/210.

Question 27: C

The question states that the repeat experiment is identical to the first in all aspects apart from the result. Therefore although a number of the options may be true like calibration bias, it would have been applied to both experiments and therefore should not affect the result. As such the difference in results is simply due to random chance.

END OF SECTION

Mock Paper A: Section 3

Doctors should be wearing white coats as it helps produce a placebo effect making the treatment more effective.

➢ This statement addresses the role of the patient's personal experience in his/her cure or treatment of their disease. It is an interesting topic since the role of psychological factors in the treatment of disease is largely unexplored. There is a growing body of evidence that supports the effectiveness of placebo treatments for some diseases when it comes to managing patient symptoms, but there is very little that addresses the role of attire and visual appearance of doctors.

➢ It is also important to immediately question the truth of the statement. There is some evidence to suggest that there is such a thing as a "white coat effect" that influences patient's behaviour and the perception of their problems when they are faced with a doctor. Questioning the statement is very important as it demonstrates that you reflect on the issue.

➢ When answering this question, there are several factors to consider. There is the role that clothing plays in the definition of professions. How does the attire of an individual influence the way he or she is perceived by those receiving his/her service? Some examples here are police officers or judges where the uniforms are heavily tied to the public perception of their profession. Police officers are a particularly good non-medical example since there are uniformed and non-uniformed officers that play different roles playing on the different public perception of uniform and civilian clothing and the fact that without the uniform the police officer is not recognisable. Then the question arises if this should apply for doctors too. Does it make a difference if doctors have clothing that visually separate them from other people in the hospital and does this have an influence on the patient's experience of treatment. Other points to consider when addressing the role of attire is the depiction of doctors in the public sphere. This includes TV shows, books, news etc.

➢ Arguing against the statement is more difficult than it seems simply because you should make sure that you provide a diverse answer that addresses several aspects. On one hand, there is the connection of a specific attire to a specific professional role as described above. On the other hand, there is the question whether attire is relevant to influence the patient's experience to improve health outcome. The whole point of a placebo effect in this context is that it improves the outcome.

➢ Another point to consider when arguing against this statement is the power distribution that comes with the uniforms and whether that is something that is beneficial for the patient-doctor relationship.

➢ Arguing to the contrary, you can look at situations where a professionalization of the doctor-patient relationship can be beneficial. Now, to be clear, the relationship between doctor and patients should always be professional, but in the context of this question, you can use the role of attire and its role in establishing this professionalization. Examples for this include conversations about life-style changes and the role the patient can play in improving his/her own health, especially if this involves giving something up. In this case, attire can give the doctor legitimacy and a certain degree of authority.

"Medicine is a science of uncertainty and an art of probability."

➢ This statement basically addresses the fact that there is no such thing as certainty in medicine. People are different and individual and so is their experience of disease. For this reason, the statement argues that all a doctor can do in terms of approaching a sense of certainty, the doctor should weigh up different probabilities and possibilities of disease. The argument also suggests, that weighing up the different options of diagnoses is an art, rather than acquired knowledge. This suggests some degree of natural talent. It also provides a degree of contrast between the aspect of science that provides the theoretical basis for pretty much every decision we make in medicine and the art of the application of knowledge. It also acknowledges that science always contains a degree of uncertainty, even when individuals believe in the absolute truth of their theory/knowledge.

➢ Arguing to the contrary basically aims at increasing the perceived role of science and certainty versus that of art and uncertainty or flexibility. The main problem with this statement is the general perception associated with the words "science" and art. They naturally lie on different ends of a spectrum with science being associated with facts and certainty and art being associated with softer skills and an absence of certainty.

➤ If you choose to go into a more example oriented direction, there are several points you can raise to write a good and strong essay. On example is the treatment of infectious diseases with antibiotics, especially in severe cases. Often you will find that the disease is treated with a broad-spectrum antibiotic that is likely to target the causative agent based on local experiences and local occurrence of diseases. This is then later adjusted if necessary once a precise identification of the causative agent was possible. Other examples include the stratification of disease causes. One example here is smoking and lung cancer. Whilst it is generally accepted that smoking increases the risk of lung cancer, there are still non-smokers that get lung cancer and life-time smokers that do not. This pattern can be applied to a variety of parameters to result in similar results.

➤ In general, you can keep this essay very philosophical and abstract, or you can aim more at direct examples to illustrate your points. Bot options have strengths and weaknesses. A theoretical essay will stay more with the overall style of the statement, whilst a more example oriented essay will be easier to write and to keep track of. However, it will also be more difficult to find appropriate examples.

➤ In the conclusion, when you give your opinion, it pays to be very direct on one hand, but also to be very specific. Depending on which route you took for your main body arguments, this may be easier or more difficult. You can also pick up the idea of medicine being art again as this is an interesting point and ties in with the idea that medicine cannot be exclusively learned from books but should also contain a component of patient interaction.

"The New England Journal of Medicine reports that 9 out of 10 doctors agree that 1 out of 10 doctors is an idiot."

➤ This statement addresses how scientific research will never find complete acceptance in the field. It also suggests that no matter what is being published by even the most highly acclaimed scientific journals, there is always a risk of error. In the end, it illustrates that medical research usually is a game of probabilities as there is never complete certainty when it comes to the pattern of diseases or the optimal treatment of disease.

➤ On a face value level, this question is simple. It is very vague in its assertion, not defining which one of the 10 doctors think that the other is an idiot. Do they all think the same person is an idiot or do they think different persons are idiots? This an important issue to raise when answering this question as it presents a fundamental flaw of the question, especially if one is to apply it to general medical research and research practice. Even in the sometimes uncertain realm of medical research, parameters such as populations of subjects are always clearly defined, which is what gives any form of research value. If this was not the case, research would be completely arbitrary. Coming back to the question then, if all 9 doctors believe that that the one specific one of them is an idiot and they have no prior contact and no connection to each other, then chances are that this single doctor is actually an idiot. If, however, there is no pattern whatsoever to the claim that one doctor is an idiot, then that weakens the claim. Especially if the whole concept is then widened to a population level.

➤ Arguing to the contrary has different obvious points. You can either stay very close to the actual wording of the question which will lead you down a similar road as I have illustrated above, or you can use the question as a parable for the way we conduct scientific research. This will require you to have a good understanding of scientific method.

➤ If you decide to go down the scientific method pathway, you will have several things to point of. Firstly, is the definition of populations, as this is completely ignored in the question. In any form of research defining the pool of data you draw from is essential as only this will deliver accurate and usable information. It is all about reducing vagueness as much as possible. Secondly you need to define the research criteria. What exactly is meant by idiot in this case for example? Only if you formulate a clear-cut goal can you then acquire the data needed to come to a meaningful result. The term 'asking the right questions' comes to mind. Thirdly you need to ensure repeatability. For this you need to define your populations very broadly and in appropriate sizes. You must make sure that there is as little connection between the subjects as possible as this will reduce and bias from personal relationships.

➤ These two options should help you write a strong essay, especially since thy can be combined in essentially any way you choose.

"My father was a research scientist in tropical medicine, so I always assumed I would be a scientist, too. I felt that medicine was too vague and inexact, so I chose physics."

➢ There are several components to this question that you need to be aware of if you want to write a good essay. On one hand is the person Stephen Hawking himself. Being a world renowned theoretical physicist, gives the whole quote an almost comical note. This is something you should be aware of as you will always have to point out problems with the questions. Moving beyond this, there are several other points you should be aware of. One is the vagueness of the statement. This obviously is due to the fact that it is taken from what probably was a whole speech, rather than this single passage. Again, something you should point out. Then there is the subject matter of tropical medicine. Tropical medicine is in part still a very new field and a field which much room for exploration simply because there is such a wealth of different life forms in tropical areas that can cause diseases, some of which may never have been observed before. This necessarily adds to the perceived uncertainty. In addition, keep in mind that Stephen Hawking is now 75 years old, which places his father's professional career to the first half of the 20th century, a lot has happened in medicine since then. Secondly you should address the subject matter of physics. Whilst some fields in physics have very little uncertainty and vagueness, a lot of areas are very precise such as gravity or mechanics. So, it is important to make that distinction as physics is such a broad topic.

➢ When it comes to arguing to the contrary, there are several perspectives you can take. On one hand, you can argue that tropical medicine is more accurate than Hawking gives it credit for. An easy way to do this is to enlarge it to general medicine as the clear majority of general medical principles will still apply in tropical medicine, what will change will be different pathogens and the environmental factors influencing pathology and healing processes. If we accept that in general medicine is a fairly exact science, we can use that to support the same claims about tropical medicine.

➢ Another point of attack would be to point out the vagueness of some areas of physics. Easy targets here are String theory and relativity theory. Neither of those can be supported by non-mathematical evidence at this point and even the potential discovery of the Higgs boson in the Cern super collider does not provide enough answers to these questions yet. There are many other examples in the field of physics that are vague, that's why they have given rise to completely separate job description: the theoretical physicist.

➢ Finally, you can also consider Hawking's personal history with medicine. His suffering from ALS for decades and being bound to a wheelchair after far outliving any suggested life-expectancy it is understandable that he considers medicine as somewhat vague. This could well have influenced him in this statement.

END OF PAPER

Mock Paper B: Section 1

Question 1: B

When the total number of sides is even, the shapes are black; when the total number of sides is odd, the shapes are white.

Question 2: C

Start by calculating the area of wall that may be painted per tin of paint as 10 x 5 = 50m². Therefore to paint the whole area 1050/50 = 21 tins of paint are required per coat. As such to complete 3 coats it will cost Josh 3 x 21 x 4.99 = 314.37.

Question 3: C

A is a correct assumption as procession is a function of rotational motion. B is a necessary assumption or rather inference of the first sentence. The second sentence only says that an asterism can be used, not that it is the only possible method. Nothing is mentioned of navigating the Southern Hemisphere and therefore C is not a valid assumption.

Question 4: D

Recognise that "bank hours" refers only to hours that the bank is open – which Mon to Fri is 8 hours whereas it is only 6 hours on a Saturday. Although John needs the money by 8pm the bank closes at 5 and that 3 hours difference cannot be used. Hence working backwards John will need 8 hours on the Tuesday, 8 hours on the Monday, Sunday is closed, 6 hours on the Saturday, 8 hours on Friday and 8 hours on Thursday and 4 hours on the Wednesday. With a closing time of 5pm, the latest John can cash the cheque on Wednesday is 1pm.

Question 5: D

First thing to recognise here of course is that individual diamonds can be combined to form larger diamonds with the 5 x 5 diamond the biggest of them all. To avoid counting them all and risking losing count, instead deduced the number of triangles per corner and per side; then multiply up by 4.

Question 6: B

Let my current age = m and my brother's current age = g. The first section of this question can therefore be expressed as m + 4 = 1/3(g + 1) whereas the second half can be represented as 2(m + 20) = g + 20. Therefore this problem can be solved as simultaneous equations. Rearranged the second equation reads m = 1/2g - 10; when substituted into the first equation we form 1/2g – 10 + 4 = 1/3(g + 1). Expand and simplify to 1/2g – 6 = 1/3g + 1/3 → 1/6g = $6\frac{1}{3}$ which therefore means my brother's current age = $6\frac{1}{3}$ / (1/6) = 114/3 = 38. Which means that my current age = 1/2(38) – 10 = 9.

Question 7: D

A is categorically wrong as the first two paragraphs discuss how aneurysms produce inflammation which in turn blunts endothelial NO action. B is incorrect as it states aneurysms directly promote CVD, this is not a direct process. It is the blunted NO which directly produces the CVD. C can be ignored as nowhere are aneurysms categorised like this. E is incorrect as the text states that aneurysms reduce NO which will reduce vasodilation, thus increasing basal vasoconstriction and thus reducing blood flow. Leaving the correct answer of D which is of course true as observations are not transferable between species until tested scientifically.

Question 8: C

Any statement which refers to national or global figures is instantly incorrect as the text does not mention any statistical analysis has taken place. In order to produce national statistics from a small sample size such as this requires statistical analysis. Whilst E could possibly be true it cannot be stated as there are so many possibilities – perhaps the time of the survey was during rush hour in which case the majority of the traffic would have been travelling in the same direction anyway to reach an industrialised area.

Question 9: A
Black shapes demonstrate a reduction of 1 side and a transition into white, whilst white shapes demonstrate a gain in 1 side and a transition into black.

Question 10: A
This question can be solved quickly if you first realise that there is no need to calculate both volumes and subtract the larger from the smaller, instead only convert the television dimensions into metres and then calculate 60% of that.

Question 11: E
From the information provided all the flaws listed are valid since David's main point is that he has chosen the cheapest. A could be true as there is an additional cost of £3 for staying at Whitmore, therefore if the vehicle they are using achieves sufficient miles per gallon then travelling the extra few miles could cost less than £3 in terms of petrol. B again is possible which would argue against it being cheap, as would D. And if C is true then David's argument is flawed altogether.

Question 12: D
C is irrelevant as nowhere does the passage mention standards of modern medical practice. A may be incorrect as nowhere does the article explicitly say that animal testing is the only accepted method of drug approval. B categorically conflicts with the first sentence of the second paragraph.

Question 13: A
Begin by converting all the quantities into terms of items as that is the terminology used on the graph axis. Therefore 12 rugby balls = 6 items and 120 tennis balls = 24 items. Reading from the graph reveals their respective prices as £9 and £5. Therefore the total cost of products in the order is (6 x 9) + (24 x 5) = 174. Since this is significantly more than £100 the delivery charge is waived.

Question 14: D
Calculate the cost of 10 of everything as (2 x 5) x (10 x 7) x (5 x 9) = £125. Recall that delivery charge is waived at £100 and this therefore a trick question and no delivery charge is applied anyway.

Question 15: E
Tennis balls are sold in the largest pack and so they must be considered. Begin by dividing 1000/5 using the value from the first column = 200. As this is above the range 0 -99 look up the item value in the 100 -499 range where a £1 discount is applied per item. Therefore in actually fact 1000/4 = 250 items can be purchased which equates to a total of 250 x 5 = 1250 balls.

Question 16: B
Recognise that 120% profit is equivalent to 220% of the original price. In which case the initial purchase price = (1,320/220) x 100 = £600.

Question 17: A
Note that here the question uses the term item and therefore simply read the costs directly off the graph giving a total order cost of (2 x 2000) + (4 x 2000) + (6 x 2000) = 24,000. Recall though that he only pays tax on the amount over £12,000 which in this case is £12,000. Therefore he pays 12,000/4 = £3,000 tax.

Question 18: A
Note that the total number of black shapes is equal to the number of corners within the white shape. Hence with a five pointed start and five black shapes; A is the correct answer.

Question 19: E

First calculate an average complete one way journey time as 40 + 5 + 5 = 50 minutes. Deducting his breaks he works a total of 7 hours 20 or 440 minutes. Since the first train is already loaded his first run will only take 45 minutes leaving 395 minutes to complete his working day. 395/50 = 7 remainder 45. Note that 45 minutes is not enough to fully unload the train but it is enough to load the train and drive the distance. Therefore the driver will complete a total of 9 journeys equalling a distance of 198 miles.

Question 20: E

A is not actually a valid assumption as we do not know what proposal conservationists might be bringing to the local councils, they have only expressed their concern. They may well be bringing a proposal to ask for funding to rehome all the species in the affected environment. B is essential to the final paragraph whilst C must be assumed otherwise the councils would not be presenting these proposals at all.

Question 21: D

As there is not really information in the question to calculate the answer quickly. Instead consider each answer in term and calculate the differences to find the correct price difference in the question:

   A)   (3x 1) + (2 x 1.25) – (15 x 0.3) + (10 x 0.5) etc…

Question 22: E

Based on the information in the question options A - D are simply wrong. A is incorrect as antibiotic E has not affected growth at all. B is incorrect as the other antibiotics have significantly affected growth. E was the least effective antibiotic. C was not the most ineffective as it did disrupt growth slightly whereas E had no effect at all. D will now be taken and the experiment repeated with D at numerous concentrations to find the optimum dose.

Question 23: A

1L = 1000 cubic centimetres and therefore the total volume of air Laura needs to produce is 25 x 0.3 = 7.5L. With a total of 25 balloons she will take 25 x 0.5 = 12.5 seconds breathing in and a further $7.5/4.5 = 1\frac{2}{3}$ minutes inflating the balloons. This yields a total time of 1 minute 40 + 12.5 seconds = 1 minute 52.5 seconds or 112.5 seconds.

Question 24: B

Quickly represent the question schematically as (A = B) ≠ (C = D = E). We can now observe that A in fact supports George's argument, C also supports George's argument and D may well be true but it would have no effect in disrupting the argument, simply only imply D and E are both also equal to 0. However as E is equal to C it should therefore not equal B.

Question 25: B

This question is much less complicated than it sounds. Begin by just considering a single hour. Throughout the hour of 1 the hour hand will pointing at 1. Only during the 5th minute of that hour will the minute hand point to the 1 whereas every 5th second of the minute the second hand points to the 1. All these events will only coincide once. As there are 24 hours in a day 00:00 through to 23:59 this event will happen 24 times.

Question 26: B

As there are already to crosses on the board to only one nought it is noughts turn. James is forced to play B3 but then suppose crosses plays A1. James is then forced to block the diagonal by playing C3. However suppose then that crosses plays A3 leaving James to claim the winning move with C2. Therefore depending on the play it is possible for James to win although he cannot adopt a strategy to guarantee that he wins.

Question 27: D

The total number of sides of all the white shapes is divided by the number of sides of the black shape: 30/5 = 6 sides. Therefore the answer must comprise a 6 sided shape but note the answer is always in black.

Question 28: C

Whilst B may be true it is not a reason for dependence, only a supporting factor. Dependence implies that we have no choice but to use electricity. Hence A is wrong as gas is readily available; hence D is wrong for the same reason. This leaves the correct answer C which is the only statement which truly describes our absolute necessity for electricity – since electrical appliance by definition only function with electricity.

Question 29: B

First note that 27 guests plus Elin herself means that 28 people will be eating the 3 courses which will require a total of 28 x 3 = 84 glasses of wine. This is a total volume of 84 x 175 = 14.7L = 21 bottles. As wine is only sold in cases of 6, Elin will have to buy 24 bottles so as not to run out. Recall the buy one get one free offer so she only pays for 2 cases.

Question 30: E

Recognise that when rounded to the nearest 10 the shortest an episode could last is 35 minutes. Hence a total of 7 x 12 = 84 episodes would take a total of 84 x 35 = 2,940 minutes = 49 hours.

Question 31: E

Points A and B are the best exemplified through this passage. Often great discoveries come from accidental observations and then exact processes are refined through many experiments in a trial and error fashion until the correct methodology is achieved. The passage demonstrates how as our understanding of the world around us advance so too does our ability to provide healthcare. D can be observed in the passage as the 50/50 split.

Question 32: C

Whilst A and D are true they do not force the stranger to give him the sapphire – remember Jack can be given any stone for a truthful statement. B and C are both lies and will earn Jack nothing. Instead if Jack states E then the stranger has no choice to hand over the sapphire else it would be a false statement.

Question 33: A

Despite the enormous interest rate in Simon's current account it is only awarded twice, whereas in the saver account it is awarded 4 times. Hence earnings from the saver account = 100×1.5^4 = £506 whereas earnings from the current account would have stood at £361.

Question 34: D

The largest possible key can be obtained were the first two numbers are at a maximum because they are multiplied together → 9 x 9 = 81. Subtract the smallest number to yield 81 – 1 = 80 and again divide by the smallest number which is 1 hence 80 is the largest possible key.

Question 35: C

The use of coloured shapes in this question is simply a distraction and no pattern exists. Instead notice that when the total number of sides of all the shapes is even, the shapes are found outside the speech bubble; when the number of sides is odd, the shapes are found within the speech bubble.

END OF SECTION

Mock Paper B: Section 2

Question 1: D

As the question states that GLUT2 is ATP independent then answer A) active transport is instantly incorrect as it is ATP dependent.

Osmosis is applicable only to water molecules and is therefore incorrect.

Exocytosis refers to the movement of molecules out of a cell and is therefore incorrect.

Simple diffusion is incorrect as the question states that GLUT2 is essential for the process.

This leaves the correct answer of facilitated diffusion.

Question 2: E

In order to answer this question you must recall that anaerobic respiration in humans produces only lactate and energy, whilst in yeast the anaerobic respiratory process yields a molecule of ethanol and CO_2 per glucose molecule. Therefore there will be 0 mol of CO_2 produced in the human cell culture and you need only work out the moles of CO_2 produced by the yeast cell culture to calculate the difference. There is a total of 5.76/0.18 = 32 mol of glucose, of which half is supplied to the yeast cell culture. With a stoichiometric ratio of 1:1 in the anaerobic respiration equation a total of 16 mol of CO_2 will be produced.

Question 3: E

Firstly recall that endocytosis is a process of molecular transport into cells that result in vesicular formation. This question requires you to realise the special case of this which is phagocytosis – conducted by white blood cells in the ingestion of pathogens.

Question 4: E

All of the above statements are true of the Calvin cycle with regards to the Krebs cycle. As the main driver of photosynthesis we know that the Calvin cycle requires both CO_2 and light in order to conduct ATP dependent reactions. As opposed to the Krebs cycle in man however, the Calvin cycle adopts the use of NADPH as the intermediate in electron transport.

Question 5: D

Option d is one of only 2 graphs that demonstrate a quadratic relationship with the peak enzyme activity correctly placed – pepsin from the stomach close to pH 1, and trypsin secreted by the pancreas and therefore alkaline around pH 13. The curves traced in option c however are far too broad over the pH range to represent enzyme activity. As the pH scale is logarithmic, even a change of 1 or 0.5 can be devastating to enzyme activity.

Question 6: A

This question was taken directly from the BMAT syllabus where many examples are listed for different principles. Reading through the BMAT syllabus and highlighting these is a very good idea as well as learning the definitions listed.

Question 7: A

Initially the electron configuration of Mg is 2,8,2. In binding to two chlorine atoms it is effectively ionised to Mg^{2+} and it loses two electrons to leave a complete outer shell and thus the correct answer is 2,8.

Question 8: D

The first thing to note in this trace is that the m/z axis has been cut short. From looking up the mass of calcium in the periodic table one would expect to see the x axis centred around 40. However here the trace is only displaying those isotopes with valence 2 (z= 2) hence the values are half the size. Therefore (from the periodic tablE) when dividing the most abundant isotope of chromium by two, 52/2 = 26, we confirm that the outlier bar on the right is indeed the contaminant. Therefore to calculate the actual abundance of Mr 40 calcium ignore the chromium like so: 55/95 = 11/19.

Question 9: A
Begin by converting the total weight of arsenic into grams like so $15 \times 10^6 = 1.5 \times 10^7$. Then divide by the Mr of arsenic which is 75 (2sf) giving 2×10^5. Don't forget that the sample is at worst 80% pure. Therefore there will be a minimum of $(2 \times 10^5) \times 0.8 = 1.4 \times 10^5$ moles of pure arsenic.

Question 10: D
Recall that average atomic mass is calculated as the sum of (isotope mass x relative abundance). Therefore $28 = (26 \times 0.6) + (30 \times 0.3) + 0.1x$. Rearranging this equation reveals that $0.1x = 3.4$ and that the mystery isotope therefore has an atomic mass of 34.

Question 11: A
First recall that when a group 2 metal is reacted with steam a metal oxide is formed and therefore the following chemical equation can be drawn: $Mg + H_2O_{(g)} \rightarrow MgO + H_2$. Note the stoichiometric ratio which is simply 1. Next calculate that there is $72/24 = 3$ mol of hydrogen produced. Therefore assuming that there is 3 mol of all other reactants and the reaction is complete one would expect $3 \times 24.3 = 72.9$g of magnesium and $3 \times 18 = 54$g of steam. This is indeed the case and therefore the reaction is complete.

Question 12: B
The reducing agent is the species which is itself reduced in this instance from looking at the oxidation states we can see that that species is S^{2-}. As after the reaction has taken place it has an oxidation state of +6 which would require a loss of negative charge ie electrons.

Question 13: C
The highly stable bonds between carbon atoms, and between carbon and hydrogen atoms renders alkanes relatively unreactive. This is important to note as it highlights the major difference between alkanes and alkenes.

Question 14: A
Recall that current = charge/time. The question provides both charge and time in the correct units and so the calculation is relatively simple with no unit conversions required. Therefore current = $5/15 = 1/3 = 0.33$A. As the question states that the balloon has a negative charge it has therefore gained electrons. Given that a current is defined as a net movement of electrons, in this situation the current must be flowing into the balloon.

Question 15: D
Given that Power = IV it can be deduced that I = P/V. Recall that power given in Watts is a measure of the energy transferred per second and therefore has the alternative units Js^{-1}. When substituting these units into the power equation re-arranged for Amps it is revealed that $I = (Js^{-1})/V = A$.

Question 16: D
For a transformer that is 100% efficient power in must equal power out, recalling that P=IV. Therefore the transformer has a power output of $24 \times 10 = 240$W which is 80% of the initial input. As such the initial power input was $(240/80) \times 100 = 300$W.

Question 17: C
Begin by calculating the energy required to hoist the mass, this is calculated using the potential energy equation: mgh. Energy = mass x g x height = $20 \times 10 \times 30 = 6000$N. The power output of the motor is calculated as the joules dissipated per second = $6000/20 = 300$W

Question 18: D
In order to solve this problem recall that activity = decay constant x number of remaining atoms. Therefore the decay constant can be calculated simply as $0.36/6 = 0.06$.

Question 19: D

Recall that household electricity is available in the UK at 240V. Begin by calculating the wattage that the bulb is receiving as 0.5 x 240 = 120W. Given that the energy rating of the bulb is 80W, we can assume that this bulb is only 80/120 = 66% efficient.

Question 20: E

Begin by subtracting the integral from both sides producing $x - \int_{-z}^{z} 9a - 7 = \frac{\sqrt{b^3 - 9st}}{13j}$. Next multiply both sides

by 13j and square, rendering $[13j(x - \int_{-z}^{z} 9a - 7)]^2 = b^3 - 9st$. Finally subtract b³ from both sides and divide

by -9s leaving the correct answer: $\frac{[13j(x - \int_{-z}^{z} 9a - 7)]^2 - b^3}{-9s} = t$.

Question 21: C

The formula for calculating compound interest can be given as investment x interest rate^{years} or in short hand for this situation: $1687.5 = 500x^3$. Therefore in order to calculate the interest rate the above formula must be rearranged to $\sqrt[3]{1687.5/500} = 1.5$ revealing an interest rate of 50%.

Question 22: E

Begin by drawing your line of best fit, remembering not to force it through the origin. Begin fitting the general equation y = mx + c to your line. Calculate the gradient as $\Delta y/\Delta x$ and read the y intercept off your annotated graph.

Question 23: E

In order to start rearranging the fraction begin by adding m to both sides and squaring to yield $4m^2 = \frac{9xy^3z^5}{3x^9yz^4}$. Now it is clear to see that this can be most simply displayed in terms of powers. Therefore E is the correct answer.

Question 24: D

Non-normally distributed data doesn't demonstrate a 50-50 split of data points either side of the mean. Therefore standard data analysis techniques like normal range are inappropriate (as the formula for normal range is mean$\pm$ 1.96SD). Instead the interquartile range is used.

Question 25: D

Random chance is a large issue particularly in medicine. Clinical trials are inherently flawed as they only consider a very small percentage of the population which is far outweighed by the genetic variation demonstrated within the human genome. Therefore statistics must be used to transform sample data into data representative of the entire population.

Question 26: B

Begin by calculating the speed of the innermost well as the circumference of travel over time = 20 x 3.14 = 62.8m/s. Calculate the outermost well speed in the same manner = 40 x 3.14 = 125.6m/s. 125.6 – 62.8 = 62.8m/s faster.

Question 27: C

The question states that the repeat experiment is identical to the first in all aspects apart from the result. Therefore although a number of the options may be true like calibration bias, it would have been applied to both experiments and therefore should not affect the result. As such the difference in results is simply due to random chance.

END OF SECTION

Mock Paper B: Section 3

"Progress is made by trial and failure; the failures are generally a hundred times more numerous than the successes; yet they are usually left unchronicled."

➢ This statement aims at several aspects of science. On one hand, it aims at scientific method. It demonstrates that science itself is based on trial and error and that to come to the right answer we should test theories repeatedly, adjusting them all the time to become more precise and more in keeping with our results. In the end, it is very rare that a theory survives unchanged. It also stresses that the progress of science is slow and laborious as it requires a constant string of trial an error experiments before providing any results. The second component the statement addresses is the way the scientific progress is seen in the public and even amongst scientists. The common perception is that only success counts and if a theory cannot be proven it is a failure. This of course is a problem since every failure provides a new angle to start from on the hunt for success. Failure becomes necessary for success to be possible.

➢ Since this statement basically has two components, when arguing to the contrary, you will have to demonstrate either that failures stand in a different relationship to success or that the reporting of failures is equal to that of successes. Either is going to be difficult as the stamen itself forms a self-fulfilling prophecy. You cannot disprove it, provided it has some truth to it, since you will not find any evidence for it. So, you will have to focus on a more theoretical level to fund support to argue against the quote.

➢ You can argue that failures, being part of research arte always reflected to some extend in the presentation of data in research papers. They will also appear in the analysis components of any piece of research as failures are essential for the progress of research as it narrows the field of possible answers.

➢ Another perspective you can approach this topic from is to separate the failure and the success. Failure of one theory, even if it had been thought to be correct at some point will lead to evolution of a different idea that builds on the conceptual failures of the previous idea. Thereby, one idea facilitates the other and the failing of one concept will directly result in a new concept that then in turn will either remain a success or become a failure at some point down the line.

➢ You can also consider the role failure plays in our society. It is generally seen as a bad thing and as something to be avoided. This of course does also apply to the scientific community. But at the same time, failure can also provide a new stepping stone for future success, provided lessons are learned from the cause of the failure that can then be applied for future projects.

"He who studies medicine without books sails an uncharted sea, but he who studies medicine without patients does not go to sea at all."

➢ This statement aims directly at the connection between science and soft skills when it comes to the practice of medicine. It claims that medicine is more than just a science that can be learned by theories alone but has a large human component that gives the scientific aspect of medicine meaning. Without the application of the theoretical knowledge, the subject studied has no value at all, at least it cannot be called medicine.

➢ When addressing this statement, there are several tension points you should consider. Firstly, there is the uncharted sea. This symbol has several aspects. On one hand, it is threatening and dangerous as the sailor cannot know where difficult streams and lurking rocks are located. On the other hand, it also has a component of excitement and adventure, just think of the old explores Cook and Columbus etc. Secondly the symbol of not sailing at all. In this again, you can use the sailor metaphor to become fully clear on what he means. Imagine a sailor that has excellent navigational skills but lacks the courage to apply them and so wanders to the harbour every day to stare across the sea. All his skill is wasted as he never sets foot on the waves.

➢ In order to argue against this stamen, you should focus on the first part, the sailing an uncharted sea. This is because the second part holds a deep truth that is difficult to disprove. Even when it comes to medical research, you will have to interact with patients that you draw data from for your research. However, it is simple to argue why books play a vital role in medicine. In this case books are synonymous to all forms of theoretical learning. The main focus here should be that of safety of the patients. Without books it is only a matter of time until the doctor makes a mistake, crashing his proverbial ship on a proverbial sandbank. Since the focus of medical treatment is the improvement of the patient's condition or quality of life, uncertainty and adventurism have no role in this. At this point it is essential to keep the text on a general level, as medical progress does also come from ignoring the common wisdom. Remember the theory of 4 humours from the Middle Ages, if it hadn't been for somebody breaking with this common wisdom and basis of teaching, modern medicine would never have been born...

➤ If you write an essay about this topic, make sure that you have a very clear position that will give you a good basis to argue from. Also make sure you have fully understood the statement. Due to the use of metaphors this can be tricky, but on the other hand, if you have understood the question, you can use similar metaphors and they will tie in nicely with the question. This will then give your whole essay a smoother appearance and make it better to read.

'"Medicine is the restoration of discordant elements; sickness is the discord of the elements infused into the living body"

➤ To understand this statement, you have to understand Leonardo da Vinci. Being an Renaissance artist and scientist, artist and architect, he had a very varied background but also lived in the late 15th and early 16th century which will obviously have influenced his perception of medicine. The idea of discordant elements that are infused in the body and that have to be rebalanced is clear evidence of that since it basically rephrases the theory of the 4 humours that was the basis of pretty much all school medicine pretty much up until the 19th century, when pathogens were discovered and described in their properties to cause disease. In general, however, the statement is to be understood in a sense that disease represents a damaging influence on the body, who's default is health, and the job of medicine is to rectify this influence to restore health.

➤ When arguing against this stamen, there are several possible angles of attack. On one hand, there is the historical aspect of the 4 humours mentioned above. This is pretty straight forwards since you can easily demonstrate why da Vinci would be influenced by this theory and how this theory was inherently false. On the other hand, you can attack the idea of corruption through diseases causing influence by a more general discussion of disease patterns. Whilst it is true that infectious diseases are cause by the insertion of pathogens into the healthy organism, there are a vast amount of diseases that are not. One good example are genetic diseases. Especially those that are inherited in a recessive pattern meaning that parent generations must be carriers and therefore be 'corrupted' as well without displaying the actual disease. If you want to go down the mutation route as well, you can point out that not all change causes negative outcomes since mutations form the basis of evolution and thereby the basis of how we as a species came to be.

➤ The second point of attack to argue against da Vinci here is the role of medicine. Whilst it is generally true that the aim of medicine is to cure the patient, sometimes this is either not possible due to a lack of ability of the medical profession, i.e. we just don't have a cure, or it is not desirable since the risk to the patient if undergoing treatment outweighs the risk of the disease or the benefit of treatment. Good examples here are chemotherapy in the frail and elderly. Another example is that of mutations as the motor of evolution as mentioned above.

➤ To the last part of the question, this statement still holds some truth to modern medicine, consider for example cancer that can be caused by poisonous external influences such as smoking or radiation, in this case the treatment will involve on one hand the removal of the negative stimulus, if possible, and on the other hand the treatment of the negative impact this stimulus has left.

"Modern medicine is a negation of health. It isn't organized to serve human health, but only itself, as an institution. It makes more people sick than it heals."

➤ With this statement, some background knowledge can be very helpful. Ivan Illich was a Croatian-Austrian Priest and philosopher that lived during the 20th century. He is generally known for is critic of the institutions of Western culture such as schools or in this case modern medicine. Looking at the statement itself, it is clear, that the basic message is that medicine has no interest in curing humans but rather prolongs their suffering to sell them as much treatment as possible to fund its own interests.

➤ In order to argue against this stamen, it can be helpful to detect components of truth in it that can then be refuted. One point that can be raised in connection to this statement is that of medicalisation. By labelling everything that does not conform 100% with the ideal of health in medical terms produces a population of sick people that then require treatment.

➤ Another point where the statement holds true is in different health care systems such as the one in the US where maintaining a sick status provides continued income to the doctor and the medical professionals involved in treatment. This is less of an issue in publicly funded environment such as the NHS where there is a stricter regulation of resources and therefore less option for artificial prolongation of treatment requirements.

➤ Arguing against the statement is fairly easy, especially when arguing from the perspective of the NHS. In the NHS, healthcare is provided free of charge for residents and there are no direct barriers in place to block access to health care. This in itself proves Illich wrong since it would serve the institution to make health care a luxury item that comes with the associated price tag.

➤ Arguing that the primary duty of the doctor is not to prolong life is more difficult, since two of the ethical pillars of the medical profession call for doctors not to do harm and to act in the patients' best interest, both of which aim at the prolongation of life in the majority of cases. There are some exceptions to the prolonging life idea, and it is probably safest to approach this part of the question from that angle as it will ensure that you stay on the right track and don't end up in a direction you didn't want to go.

➤ Limitations to the idea of prolonging life are pretty much all the cases falling under palliative care where the idea is to remove suffering and providing symptomatic relief rather than curing the dieses causing the symptoms. Common examples here are cancer in the elderly that are not fit enough to undergo chemotherapy or surgery. Other examples are incurable diseases such as inoperable brain tumours etc.

➤ In this question again, it helps very much to have a clear idea of what you think about the issue. It will make it easier to structure your answer appropriately and it will ensure that you don't navigate yourself into uncertain waters which is fairly easy with this topic, especially when the idea of prolonging life or not is being introduced.

END OF PAPER

Mock Paper C: Section 1

Question 1: D

There are three different options for staying at the hotel. They could either pay for three single rooms for £180, one single and one double room for £165, or one four person room for £215.

Subtracting the cleaning cost for one night would leave:
£180-(3x£12) = £144
£165-(2x£12) = £141
£215-£12 = £203

The cheapest option is one single and one double room and they want to stay three nights, giving £141x3 = £423.

Question 2: D

Glass one starts with 16ml squash and 80ml water. Glass two starts with 72ml squash and 24ml water. 48ml is half of 96ml so 8ml squash and 40ml water is transferred to glass two. Glass two now contains (8+72 = 80ml squash) and (24+40 = 64ml water). Glass two now has a total of 144ml and half of this is transferred to glass one. Glass one now has (40+8 = 48ml squash) and (32+40 = 72ml water). Therefore glass one has 48ml squash and glass two has 40ml squash.

Question 3: B

B is the main conclusion of the argument. Options A and D both contribute reasons to support the main conclusion of the argument that the HPV vaccination should remain in schools. C is a counter argument, which is a reason given in opposition to the main conclusion. Option E represents a general principle behind the main argument.

Question 4: B

The speed of the bus can be calculated using the relationship: Speed $=\frac{\text{distance}}{\text{time}}$

$\frac{3\text{ km}}{0.2\text{ h}} = 15$ kmh^{-1}

The bike speed is therefore ($\frac{4}{5}$ x 15 = 12 kmh^{-1}). Considering that the bus leaves 2 minutes after the bike, it is now possible to write an expression, where d is the distance travelled when the bus overtakes the bike:

$\frac{d\text{ km}}{12\text{ km/h}} = \frac{1}{30}\text{h} + \frac{d\text{ km}}{15\text{ km/h}}$

This expression can be solved by multiplying each term by (12 kmh^{-1} x 15 kmh^{-1}):
15d km = 6 km +12d km
3d km = 6 km
d = 2 km

Therefore, the bus overtakes the bike after travelling 2 km.

Question 5: B

Firstly, determine who will move up to set one. Terry, Bahara, Lucy and Shiv all have attendance over 95%. Alex, Bahara and Lucy all have an average test mark over 92. Terry, Bahara, Lucy and Shiv all have less than 5% homework handed in late. Therefore, Bahara and Lucy will both move up a set. Secondly, determine who will receive a certificate. Terry, Bahara, Lucy and Shiv have absences below 4%. Alex, Bahara and Lucy have an average test mark over 89. Bahara and Shiv have at least 98% homework handed in on time. Therefore, only Bahara will receive a certificate.

Question 6: C

Firstly, construct two algebraic equations: A-18=B-25 and A=$\frac{5}{6}$B

Solve these two equations as simultaneous equations by substituting $\frac{5}{6}$B for A in equation 1:

$\frac{5}{6}$B-18=B-25

7=$\frac{1}{6}$B

B=42

Put B=42 back into equation 2: A= 42 x $\frac{5}{6}$

A=35

Question 7: D

I need to make 48 scones, which makes up 8 batches.
8 batches would take: 35+ 7(25+10) +25 = 305 minutes

I need to make 32 cupcakes, which makes up 4 batches.
4 batches would take: 15+ (4x20) =95 minutes

I need to make 48 cucumber sandwiches
This would take (8x5) = 40 minutes

Adding 305, 95 and 40 minutes is 440 minutes in total. 440 minutes is equivalent to 7 hours and 20 minutes. Adding 7 hours and 20 minutes to 10:45am leads to 6:05pm so I will be finished at 6:05pm.

Question 8: D

The volume of a pyramid is given by the equation:

$v = \frac{a^2h}{3}$ where v=volume, a=base and h=height

Rearrange to work out the height for each pyramid: $h = \frac{3v}{a^2}$

Pyramid	Base edge (m)	Volume (m³)	Calculation:	Height (m)
1	3	33	$\frac{3 \times 33}{9}$	11
2	4	64	$\frac{3 \times 64}{16}$	12
3	2	8	$\frac{3 \times 8}{4}$	6
4	6	120	$\frac{3 \times 120}{36}$	10
5	2	8	$\frac{3 \times 8}{4}$	6
6	6	120	$\frac{3 \times 120}{36}$	10
7	4	64	$\frac{3 \times 64}{16}$	12

The tallest pyramid is 12m and the smallest is 6m. Subtracting the height of the tallest pyramid from the height of the smallest pyramid leaves 6m.

Question 9: A

Work out the two wages by substituting the information provided into the formula:
Jessica's wage is: 210 + 42 - 3.2 = 248.8
Samira's wage is: 210 + 78 - 8.8 = 279.2

Subtracting 248.8 from 279.2 leave 30.4 so the difference between their wages is £30.4.

Question 10: C

The main conclusion is C. A and B both represent reasons to support the main conclusion of the argument. Option D represents an assumption that is not stated in the argument but is required to support the main conclusion that research universities should strongly support teaching. Option E is a counter argument that provides a reason to oppose the main argument.

Question 11: D

D is the main conclusion of the argument. A is a general principle of the argument, but the argument is more specific to the use of helmets rather than the wider concept of danger in sport and the responsibilities of the governing bodies to sports players. Options B and C are reasons to support the main conclusion. Option E is an intermediate conclusion, which acts as support for the next stage of the argument and as a reason to support the main conclusion.

Question 12: D

There are 10 passengers on the tube at the final stop. At stop 5 there were twice the number of passengers on the tube so 20 passengers were at stop 5. At stop 4, there were $\frac{5}{2}$ times the number of passengers at stop 5 so 50 passengers were present at stop 4. At stop 3, there were $\frac{3}{2}$ times the number of passengers at stop 4 so 75 passengers were on the tube. At stop 2, there were $\frac{6}{5}$ times the number of passengers at stop 3 so 90 passengers were present at stop 2. Similarly, at stop 1, there were $\frac{6}{5}$ times the number of passengers at stop 2 so at the first stop 108 passengers got on the tube.

Question 13: E

➢ Some students born in winter like English, Art and Music
➢ There is not enough information to tell whether some students born in spring like both Biology and Maths.
➢ We don't know what the students born in spring think about Art.
➢ We don't know what the students born in winter think about Biology.
➢ There is not enough information to know whether this is true or not.

Subject	Time of Birth		
	Spring	Autumn	Winter
English	Everyone likes	Everyone likes	Everyone likes
Biology	Some like	No one likes	
Art		Everyone likes	Some like
Music			Everyone likes
Maths	Some like		

Question 14: A

The main conclusion is option A that some works of modern art no longer constitute art. B is not an assumption made by the author as the main conclusion does not rely on *all* modern art being ugly to be valid. C is not an assumption because the argument does not rely on artists studying for decades to produce pieces of work that constitute art. This point is simply used to support the main argument. Options D and E are stated in the argument so are not assumptions. A is an assumption because it is required to be true to support the main conclusion, but is not explicitly stated in the argument.

Question 15: E

Reducing the price of the sunglasses by 10% is equivalent to multiplying the price by 0.9. the price of the sunglasses is successively reduced by 10% three times and so the price on Monday is 0.9^3 the price of the sunglasses on Friday. 0.9^3 is equal to 0.729 and so the price of the sunglasses on Monday is 72.9% of the price of the sunglasses on Friday.

Question 16: C

It is easier to write out this calculation in the following format:

a b 7 –
   a b
_____

5 6 5

From the above subtraction it is clear that b must be equal to 2 because 7 minus 2 is equal to 5, which is the unit term of the answer. It is now possible to rewrite the calculation with 2 substituted for b:

a 2 7 –
   a 2
_____

5 6 5

From the above calculation it is possible to gauge certain facts. A must be greater than 5 because 1 is carried over to the second term:

a ^{1}2 7 –
   a 2
_____

5 6 5

It is now clear than a must be equal to 6 because 12 minus 6 is equal to 6, which is the tens value of the answer.

Question 17: E

Look at the flat cube net and note the shapes that are adjacent to each other. Sides that are joining on the net will be beside each other on the formed cube. Work through to deduce option E can be fromed from the cube net shown.

Question 18: E

The H shape is comprised of 12 squares. The shape's area of 588 can be divided by 12 to give 49, which is the area of each individual square. The square root of 49 is 7 and so the side length of each individual square is 7cm. The perimeter of the shape is comprised of 26 sides and the length of each side is 7 so the perimeter of the shape is 182cm.

Question 19: E

The information provided about the child needs to be inserted into the BMI formula: BMI=$35 \div 1.2^2$

1.2 squared is equal to 1.44 and it may be easier to work out 3500 divided by 144. The answer needs to be worked out to 3 decimal places for an answer required to 2 decimal places. The answer to 3 decimal places is 24.305 and so the BMI to 2 decimal places is 24.31.

Question 20: C

It is important that the information is inserted into the formula given for calculating the BMR of a woman rather than a man:

BMR= (10 x weight in kg) + (6.25 x height in cm) – (5 x age in years) -161
BMR = (10 x 80) + (6.25 x 170) – (5 x 32) – 161
BMR= 800 + 1062.5 -160 -161

The BMR of the woman in the question is therefore 1541.5 kcal

Question 21: D

This time, the information needs to be inserted into the formula for calculating the BMI of a man:

BMR= (10 x weight in kg) + (6.25 x height in cm) – (5 x age in years) + 5
BMR= (10 x 80) + (6.25 x 170) – (5 x 45) +5
BMR= 800 + 1062.5 -225 +5

The BMR of the man in the question is therefore 1642.5 kcal. The man does little to no exercise each week. It is therefore required to multiply 1642.5 by 1.2, which gives a daily recommended intake of 1971 kcal.

Question 22: B

Slippery Slope describes a series of loosely connected and increasingly worse events that lead to an extreme conclusion. A is not a flaw because the author does not predict a series of undesirable outcomes. C is not a flaw. It is unlikely that correlation has been confused with cause if the American school did not change other aspects of the school day although this is not explicitly stated in the argument. D is not a flaw. A circular argument assumes what it attempts to prove and this is not the case in this argument. E is a counter argument rather than a flaw. B is the flaw in the argument. Just because moving start times later worked in one school in America does not mean that it will work in all other cases.

Question 23: D

Options A and E, if true, would weaken the argument. If the class is more disrupted this will be detrimental to learning, as will less effective teaching. B does not strengthen the main conclusion, which is based on improvement in academic achievement levels rather than activity levels. C does not strengthen the argument as the school curriculum makes no difference to the argument about the science behind teenage brains. If D is true then it suggests that the improvement in grades is a direct effect of the later school starts rather than a mere correlation.

Question 24: B

The main conclusion is that EnergyFirst is expected to expand its customer base at a rate exceeding its competitors in the ensuing months. A does not directly contradict the main argument. It demonstrates a flaw in the argument in that it ignores the fact that other companies may be stronger in other areas and attract customers by other means. However, it does not serve to weaken the main argument. C does not contradict the main conclusion; EnergyFirst could still expand its customer base at the fastest rate even if there is not much competition between energy companies. D would not weaken the argument as it refers to the rate of new customer intake rather than the number of new customers attracted. E, if true, would strengthen the argument because it suggests that visual advertising would attract new customers. B would weaken the main argument because if it were true then investing the most money in advertising would not serve to attract the most customers.

Question 25: A

Option B points out a flaw in the argument, which attributes the healthier circulatory system of vegetarians to diet, but ignores other potential contributory factors to a healthy circulatory system such as exercise. C is not an assumption: the health benefits of a vegetarian and omnivorous diet are not discussed; rather the argument is centred on the negative health ramifications. D is stated in the argument so is not an assumption and option E is a counter argument, not an assumption. Option A is required to support the main conclusion but is not stated in the argument so is an assumption made in the argument.

Question 26: A

First, calculate the number of hours spent flying and waiting. It takes 24 hours in total from Auckland to London, 11.5 hours from London to Calgary and 8 hours from Calgary to Boston. In total this amounts to 43.5 hours of flying and waiting. Boston is 16 hours behind Auckland and so when Sam arrives in Boston it will be 27.5 hours ahead of 10am. The time in Boston will therefore be 13:30 pm.

Question 27: B

This question requires you to find the lowest common multiple. This is the product of the highest power in each prime factor category.

$18 = 3^2 \times 2$

$33 = 3 \times 11$

$27 = 3^3$

Therefore, 3^3, 11 and 2 need to be multiplied together which equals 594 seconds between simultaneous flashes. 5 minutes or 300 seconds needs to be subtracted from 594 in order to find the length of time until the next flash. The time that they will next flash simultaneously is 294 seconds.

Question 28: B

Firstly, calculate the number of students who play each instrument. 21 students play piano, 12 play violin and 3 play saxophone. Point 1 is true because the sum of 21 piano students and 12 violin students is 33, which is 3 more than the total number of students in the class. Therefore, at least 3 students must play both piano and violin. Point 2 is true because only 12 students actually play the violin so there cannot be more than 12 students playing both piano and violin. Point 3 does not have to be true because some of the 9 students that do not play piano may play the violin.

Question 29: D

One way of answering this question is to set out the result after each game:

	Neil	Simon	Lucy
Start	50	50	50
Game 1	100	25	25
Game 2	50	50	50
Game 3	25	25	100
Game 4	12.5	12.5	125
Game 5	6.25	15.625	128.125

After game 5 Lucy has £128.13, however the question is asking how much money Lucy gains. The difference between 128.125 and 50 is 78.13, so Lucy gains £78.13.

Question 30: C

Option A may explain why young drivers are involved in more accidents but does not need to be true for the main conclusion to hold. B would weaken the argument if true as drivers that spend more time driving will have a greater chance of being involved in accidents regardless of age. D is not an assumption, but if true may weaken the argument as it attributes the accidents to unsafe cars rather than unsafe driving. E is irrelevant to the main conclusion: it does not matter whether the young drivers are male or female; arguably steps should still be taken to reduce the number of accidents. Option C represents an assumption that is not stated in the argument but is required to support the main conclusion.

Question 31: D

The total weight of all of the apples is 6 multiplied by 180g, which equals 1080g. The highest value the heaviest apple could take would occur if all of the other 5 apples weighed the same as the lightest apple. 5 multiplied by 167g, the weight of the lightest apple, is 835g. The difference between the weight of all of the apples (1080g) and 835g gives the highest possible weight of the heaviest apple, which is 245g.

Question 32:

In A the banner has not been flipped. In C the crescent is black and the square is grey. In D the teardrop has not been flipped and neither has the L shape or the black staircase shape. In E the banner is grey, the teardrop and crescent are white and the L shape is grey.

Question 33: E

If we make x the number of sheep sold on day 1, it is possible to write an expression for the profit made on both days:

$2(\frac{7}{8} \times 112)x = 112x + 3528$

$(98 \times 2x) = 3528 + (112x)$

$84x = 3528$

$x = 42$

The number of sheep sold on day 1 was therefore 42. Since twice the number of sheep were sold on day 2 as day 1, then the total number of sheep sold across the two days is equal to 42 multiplied by 3, which is 126 sheep.

Question 34: B

The main conclusion is that we should not wait for proof of climate change

A and D are reasons to support the main conclusion

C is an analogy

E is a counter argument

Question 35: B

The mean is the sum of all of the numbers divided by the number of terms. From the information, we know that the sum of the first 8 numbers divided by 8 is equal to 44 plus the sum of the first 8 numbers all divided by 10. An expression for this can be written like this:

$$\frac{\text{sum of 8 numbers}}{8} = y = \frac{\text{sum of 8 numbers} + 44}{10}$$

Two equations can be derived from the above expression:

10y = sum of 8 numbers +44

8y = sum of 8 numbers

If we subtract the second equation from the first, we are left with: 2y=44 → y=22

The value of y and the average of both sets of numbers is therefore 22.

END OF SECTION

Mock Paper C: Section 2

Question 1 : D

Statement 1 is false. Sucrose is a disaccharide formed by the condensation of two monosaccharides (glucose and fructose)

Statement 2 is false. Lactose is a disaccharide formed by condensation of a glucose molecule with a galactose molecule

Statement 3 is true. Glucose has two isomers: alpha-glucose and beta-glucose

Statement 4 is true

Statement 5 is true

Question 2 : C

Statement 1 is true. High temperatures and pH extremes cause a permanent alteration to the highly specific shape of the active site so that the substrate can no longer bind and the enzyme no longer works

Statement 2 is false. Amylase is produced in the salivary glands, pancreas and small intestine

Statement 3 is true

Statement 4 is false. Bile is stored in the gall bladder, but it does travel down the bile duct to neutralise hydrochloric acid found in the stomach

Statement 5 is true. Fructose is sweeter than glucose so smaller amounts can be used in food used in the slimming industry

Question 3 : C

The combining of food with bile and digestive enzymes occurs in the duodenum of the small intestine. In the ileum of the small intestine, the digested food is absorbed into the blood and lymph. The digested food then progresses into the large intestine. In the colon, water is reabsorbed. Faeces are then stores in the rectum and leave the alimentary canal at the anus.

Question 4: C

Statement 1 is true

Statement 2 is true. For example the drug curare, a South American plant toxin which is used in arrow poison, stops the nerve impulse from crossing the synapse and causes paralysis and can stop breathing

Statement 3 is false. The sheath provides insulation for the nerve axon and increases the speed of impulse transmission

Statement 4 is false. The peripheral nervous system includes motor and sensory neurons carrying impulses between receptors, effectors and the central nervous system. The CNS consists of the spinal cord and the brain

Statement 5 is true. A reflex arc travels from sensory neuron to relay neuron to motor neuron and is an innate mechanism designed to keep the animal safe. For example, it allows a person to quickly draw their hand away from a flame.

Question 5 : C

Statement 1 is true

Statement 2 is false. The transition metals are both malleable and ductile, they conduct heat and electricity and they form positive ions when reacted with non-metals.

Statement 3 is true. Thermal decomposition is a reaction whereby a substance breaks down into two or more other substances due to heat. When a transition metal carbonate is heated, metal oxide and carbon dioxide are produced. The carbon dioxide can be collected and will turn limewater cloudy.

An example of this reaction is: $CuCO_3 \rightarrow CuO + CO_2$

Statement 4 is false. Transition metal hydroxides are insoluble in water

Statement 5 is true

Question 6 : E
There are 9 Sulphur atoms on the left so there must by 9 on the right. Therefore, the values of B and C must add to make 9. This can be written as an equation: B+C=9

It is now useful to try to balance the Oxygen atoms: 4A+36 = 10+4B+4C+14

Simplify to give: 12 = 4B+4C-4A

Equation 1 can now be substituted into equation 2 to give: 12 = (4x9)-4A
24 = 4A
A = 6

There are 6 Potassium atoms on the left. This means that there must also be 6 potassium atoms on the right so B must by 3. As shown in equation 1, B and C add to make 9 so C must be 6.

$\underline{5}$ PhCH$_3$ + $\underline{6}$ KMnO$_4$ + $\underline{9}$ H$_2$SO$_4$ = $\underline{5}$ PhCOOH + $\underline{3}$ K$_2$SO$_4$ + $\underline{6}$ MnSO$_4$ + $\underline{14}$ H$_2$O

Question 7: B
Statement 1 is true. Males have one X chromosome so if the allele is present they will be affected. Females have two X chromosomes so both need to be affected to be red-green colour blind as the condition is recessive
Statement 2 is true because according to the Punnett square below half of the children will have the homozygous recessive tt genotype and so will be non-rollers.

	T	t
t	Tt	tt
t	Tt	tt

Statement 3 is true because all of the male children will inherit an X chromosome from the mother which will carry the colour blind allele.

Question 8: B
Start by multiplying each term by ax to give: a(y+x)=x^2+a^2

Expand the brackets: ay+ax=x^2+a^2

Subtract ax from both sides: ay=x^2+a^2-ax

Lastly, divide the both sides by a to get: $y = \frac{x^2+a^2-ax}{a}$

Question 9: A
This question requires the use of the equation: $C = \frac{n}{v}$ where C= concentration, n= moles and v=volume

Convert 25cm^3 into litres to get 0.025 litres and plug the values for concentration and volume into the equation to get the number of moles: $0.1 = \frac{n}{0.025}$ so n=0.0025

This question also requires the use of the equation: $n = \frac{m}{Mr}$ where m=mass, n=moles and Mr= molecular mass
The molecular mass is the sum of one calcium and two chlorine atoms which is equal to 111gmol^{-1}.

Inserting the molecular mass and number of moles into the above equation can be used to calculate the mass of calcium chloride: $m = 0.0025 \, x \, 111 = 0.28$g

Question 10 : C

Solve as simultaneous equations

Start by substituting $x = \frac{y}{3}$ into equation B.

This gives $y = \frac{18}{y} - 7$

Multiply every term by y to give:

$0 = y^2 + 7y - 18$

Factorise this quadratic to give:

$0 = (y+9)(y-2)$

Where the graphs meet, y is equal to 2 and 9

y=3x so the graphs meet when x = 6 and x = 27

Question 11: D

Statement 1 is false because the pulmonary artery carries deoxygenated blood from the right ventricle to the lungs

Statement 2 is true. This property of the aorta allows it to carry blood at high pressure and is why it pulsates

Statement 3 is false because the mitral valve, otherwise known as the bicuspid valve, is between the left atrium and left ventricle

Statement 4 is true

Question 12: D

The Ar of Carbon is 12, Hydrogen is 1 and Oxygen is 16. Therefore, 12g of carbon is 1 mole of carbon; 2g of H is 2 moles of hydrogen and 16g of O is 1 mole of oxygen. The empirical formula is therefore CH_2O. The molecular weight is 30 gmol^{-1}, which goes into 120 gmol^{-1} exactly 4 times. The empirical formula must therefore be multiplied by 4 to obtain the molecular formula so the molecular formula is $C_4H_8O_4$.

Question 13: B

To win one game, Rupert must win one squash game and one tennis game. In order to calculate the probability one winning one game it is necessary to add the probability of winning one tennis game and losing one squash game to the probability of losing one tennis game and winning one squash game. The following calculation must be performed:

$(\frac{3}{4} \times \frac{2}{3}) + (\frac{1}{4} \times \frac{1}{3}) = \frac{7}{12}$

Question 14: C

The numbers can all be written as a fraction over 36:

$0.\dot{3}$ is the same as $\frac{12}{36}$ 0.75 is the same as $\frac{27}{36}$

$\frac{11}{18}$ is the same as $\frac{22}{36}$ $\frac{62}{72}$ is the same as $\frac{31}{36}$

0.25 is the same as $\frac{9}{36}$ $\frac{7}{7}$ is the same as $\frac{36}{36}$

Ordering them from lowest to highest gives: $\frac{7}{36}$; 0.25 ; $0.\dot{3}$; $\frac{11}{18}$; 0.75 ; $\frac{62}{72}$; $\frac{7}{7}$

Therefore the median value is $\frac{11}{18}$

Question 15 : E

This question requires use of the equation: Percentage yield $= \frac{actual\ yeild\ (g)}{predicted\ yield\ (g)}$ x 100

If all of the benzene were converted to product (100 percent yield) then 20.5g of nitrobenzene would be produced: 13g C_6H_6 x $\frac{1\ mol\ C6H6}{78g\ C6H6}$ x $\frac{123g\ C6H5NO2}{1\ mol\ C6H5NO2} = 20.5g\ C_6H_5NO_2$

However, only 16.4g are actually produced. Using the equation we can now calculate the percentage yield: $\frac{16.4g}{20.5g}$ x 100 = 80% yield

Question 16 : C

Statement 1 is true

Statement 2 is false because infrared has a longer wavelength than visible light

Statement 3 is true

Statement 4 is false because gamma radiation and not infrared radiation is used to sterilise food and to kill cancer cells

Statement 5 is true because darker skins contain a higher amount of melanin pigment, which absorbs UV light

Question 17: B

This question requires the use of the equation:

P=mv where p=momentum, m=mass and v=velocity

The total momentum before the collision is equal to the sum of the momentum of carriage 1 (12000 x 5) and carriage 2 (8000 x 0), which is 60,000 kg ms^{-1}. Momentum is conserved before and after the collision so the total momentum after the event also equal 60,000 kg ms^{-1}. The carriages now move together so the combined mass is 20,000kg. Using the equation again, the total momentum (60,000 kg ms^{-1}) divided by the total mass (20,000 kg) gives the velocity of the train carriages after the crash, which is equal to 3 ms^{-1}.

Question 18: C

Statement 1 is false. In a nuclear reactor, every uranium nuclei split to release energy and three neutrons. An explosion could occur if all of the neutrons are absorbed by further uranium nuclei as the reaction would escalate out of control. Control rods that are made of boron absorb some of the neutrons and control the chain reaction.

Statement 2 is false. Nuclear fusion occurs when a deuterium and tritium nucleus are forced together. The nuclei both carry a positive charge and consequently, very high temperatures and pressures are required to overcome the electrostatic repulsion. These temperatures and pressures are expensive and hard to repeat and so fusion is not currently suitable as a source of energy.

Statement 4 is true. During beta decay, a neutron transforms into a proton and an electron. The proton remains in the nucleus, whereas the electron is emitted and is referred to as a beta particle. The carbon-14 nucleus now has one more proton and one less neutron so the atomic number increases by 1 and the atomic mass number remains the same.

Statement 5 is false. Beta particles are more ionising than gamma rays and less ionising than alpha particles

Question 19 : E

Firstly, deal with the term in the brackets: 3^3=27

$(x^{\frac{1}{2}})^3 = x^{1.5}$

$(3x^{\frac{1}{2}})^3 = 27x^{1.5}$

Next, divide by $3x^2$: $\frac{27}{3} = 9$

$\frac{x^{1.5}}{x^2} = x^{-0.5} = \frac{1}{\sqrt{x}}$

Answer= $\frac{9}{\sqrt{x}}$

Question 20 : E
Statement 1 is true
Statement 2 is true. Decomposers in the soil break down urea and the bodies of dead organisms and this results in the production of ammonia in the soil
Statement 3 is true
Statement 4 is true

Question 21: A
Write $\frac{\sqrt{20}-2}{\sqrt{5}+3}$ in the form $p\sqrt{5} + q$

Firstly, multiply the term by $\frac{\sqrt{5}-3}{\sqrt{5}-3}$ (ie 1) and write $\sqrt{20}$ as $2\sqrt{5}$

This gives: $\frac{10-6\sqrt{5}-2\sqrt{5}+6}{5-9}$

This simplifies to: $\frac{16-8\sqrt{5}}{-4}$

This simplifies to: $2\sqrt{5} - 4$

Therefore p= 2 and q= -4

Question 22: E
The question is asking for which of the statements are *false*
Statement 1 is true
Statement 2 is true
Statement 3 is false. Ionic compounds do conduct electricity when dissolved in water or when melted because the ions can move and carry current. On the other hand, solid ionic compounds do not conduct electricity.
Statement 4 is true. Alloys contain different sized atoms, making it harder for the layers of atoms to slide over each other.

Question 23: A
The equation for a circle, with centre at the origin and radius r is $x^2 + y^2 = r^2$
The equation of this circle is therefore $x^2 + y^2 = 25$
Solve the problem using simultaneous equations or by drawing the line onto the graph.
$x^2 + (3x-5)^2 = 25$
This simplifies to $10x^2 - 30x = 0$
$10x(x - 3) = 0$
So x=3 or x=0 where the two graphs intersect

Question 24: D
Statement 1 is false. Heat energy is transferred from hotter to colder places by convection
Statement 2 is true
Statement 3 is true. Radiation can travel through a vacuum like space
Statement 4 is false. Shiny surfaces are poor at reflecting and absorbing infrared radiation and dull surfaces are good at absorbing and reflecting infrared radiation

Question 25: C
Statement 1 is true
Statement 2 is false. The melting and boiling points increase as you go down the group
Statement 3 is true
Statement 4 is false. Chloride is more reactive than bromine so no displacement reaction occurs
Statement 5 is true

Question 26: C

ABC and DBE are similar triangles because all of the angles are equal.

Therefore:

$$\frac{BE}{BC} = \frac{DE}{AC}$$

This is the case because the side length of the small and large triangles are in proportion to each other. Substitute the side lengths into the expression:

$$\frac{4}{6} = \frac{DE}{9}$$

DE=6cm

Question 27: E

This question requires the use of the equation:

$v^2=u^2+2ah$ where v=final velocity, u=initial velocity, a=acceleration and h=height

From the information provided in the question, we know that v=0ms^{-1}, u=40ms^{-1} and a=-10ms^{-2}. Inserting these values into the equation gives:

0=1600 + 2(-10h)

The maximum height reached is therefore 80m

END OF SECTION

Mock Paper C: Section 3

'The NHS should not treat obese patients'

Explain what this statement means. Argue to the contrary. To what extent do you agree with the statement?

The statement argues that free health care should not be given to patients with a BMI of 30 or more. This essay will consider both perspectives before arriving at a conclusion.

There are several arguments to support the treatment of obesity by the NHS. The first is that it is in accordance with the definition of a disease; namely that is reduces life expectancy, negatively impacts normal body function and can be induced by genetic factors. Obesity often has a genetic basis, for example the melanocortin-4 receptor polymorphism and leptin receptor deficiency, which shift the homeostatic balance towards weight gain and are associated with hyperphagia and obesity. Obesity can also be a major feature of certain syndromes such as Prader-Willi syndrome, Bardet-Biedl syndrome and Cohen syndrome. If obesity is either classified as a disease or is an unavoidable ramification of certain syndromes then surely it should be treated by the NHS just the same as any other disease.

Moreover, if the NHS refuses to treat obese patients, it will become difficult to decide where to draw the line. Should smokers or people who drink alcohol also be denied free health treatment and how many cigarettes or units per week should qualify? Should all obese people be denied free health treatment or just in cases where it is not an unavoidable secondary result of certain syndromes? Obesity is often a consequence of mental illnesses such as depression and it may be hard to differentiate cause from effect.

On the other hand, obesity in certain cases could be considered as a self-induced condition rather than an actual illness. Individuals arguably exercise a degree of free will and are responsible for the amount of calories that they consume and the amount of exercise that they do. There is an argument that obesity is driven by structural changes in the environment and is a mass phenomenon influenced by advertising and propaganda. Perhaps societal changes in the outlook towards healthy living are required to address the obesity problem.

Many NHS organisations already ration surgery for overweight patients and will not for example pay for joint or hip replacements for patients with a BMI of over 30. Surely NHS funds and taxpayers money is better spent on people who make an effort to maintain a good level of health, for instance patients who are subject to largely unpreventable and serious diseases such as certain cancers.

I would suggest that each case should be considered on an individual basis and that obesity treatments should be included on the NHS where they may act to significantly improve the patient's life in the longer term.

'We should all become vegetarian'

Explain what this statement means. Argue to the contrary, that we should not all become vegetarian. To what extent do you agree with this statement?

This statement is saying that everyone should stop eating meat. This essay will consider both perspectives before arriving at a conclusion.

Some animals are raised in poor living conditions. Circumstances can be cramped and due to growth rate maximisation, animals can develop serious joint problems. Pig tails are cut, chickens have their toenails and beaks clipped and cows are dehorned without painkillers. The slaughter process can also be stressful and inhumane. Halal meat is not stunned before the jugular vein is slit and death is not instantaneous. It could be considered unethical to kill animals for food in this way when vegetarian options are available. Moreover, if farmers grew crops in place of livestock, this would generate more food and potentially alleviate world hunger.

Farming meat also has environmental implications. The overgrazing of livestock entails significant deforestation, which destroys natural habitats and endangers wild species. Enteric fermentation generates huge greenhouse gas emissions and ammonia and hydrogen sulphide leach poisonous nitrate into the water.

A vegetarian diet also has notable health benefits. Diets high in animal protein can cause excretion of calcium, oxalate and uric acid, which contribute to the development of kidney stones and gallstones. Vegetarians absorb more calcium: meat has a high renal acid content which the body neutralises with calcium leached from bones, which can weaken them. A diet rich in legumes, nuts and soy proteins can improve glycaemic control in diabetics. Moreover, growing crops instead of farming livestock can reduce antibiotic use and minimise the development of resistance.

However, there are advantages to eating meat. Meat contains healthy saturated fats that enrich the function of the immune and nervous system. Meat is the best source of vitamin B12 required for nervous and digestive system function and is a better source of iron than vegetables (the body absorbs 15-35% of heme iron found in meat compared to only 2-20% of the non-heme iron found in vegetable sources). Most plants do not contain sufficient levels of essential amino acids.

Moreover, a vegetarian diet can actually have negative environmental consequences. For example, some herbicides utilised on genetically modified crops are toxic to wild plants and animals are often killed during harvest. Eating meat could be considered as natural rather than cruel or unethical. Moreover, the problem of world hunger could partly be attributed to economics and distribution as opposed to insufficient amounts of food.

I would argue that it is ethically acceptable to eat meat so long as it is raised in a satisfactory way. It provides important nutrients, especially for growing children. However, it would be better if we reduced the amount of meat we eat in order to reduce the environmental impact of enteric fermentation and deforestation.

'Certain vaccines should be mandatory'

Explain what this statement means. Argue to the contrary. To what extent do you agree with the statement?

Vaccines are antigenic substances derived from the infectious microorganism itself that provide immunity against a disease. The statement argues that some vaccines should be compulsory. This essay will consider both perspectives before arriving at a conclusion.

Vaccines can protect the individuals that receive them against terrible debilitating diseases. Moreover, vaccines can also protect others in the population. If a certain proportion of the population are protected, herd immunity can be achieved. This means that people who cannot be vaccinated, for instance if they are immunocompromised or undergoing chemotherapy, will not contract the disease. Vaccines can also protect later generations. For instance, mothers vaccinated against rubella reduce the chance of their unborn children acquiring birth defects such as loss of vision, heart defects, cataracts and mental disabilities. Some vaccines have completely eradicated diseases for example the last case of Smallpox occurred in Somalia in 1977. Rinderpest, a disease of cattle, has also been eradicated and the instance of Polio has been substantially reduced.

Although many vaccines are available on the NHS and are funded by the taxpayer, they ultimately cost less to administer than the expense involved in time off work to care for a sick child, long term disability care and medical costs.

Nonetheless, vaccines sometime have serious and occasionally fatal consequences. About one in a million children are at risk of anaphylactic shock. The rotavirus vaccination can result in a type of bowel blockage known as intussusception; and the DPT and MMR vaccines have been associated with seizures, coma and permanent brain damage. Some physicians have raised concerns over the ingredients used in vaccinations. For example, thimerosal has been linked to autism, aluminium taken in excess can cause neurological harm and formaldehyde is a carcinogen that can result in coma, convulsions and death.

It could also be argued that the decision to be vaccinated should constitute a personal medical decision and individuals should be allowed to exert freedom of choice. There are also religious objections to vaccinations. For example the Amish object to vaccines and mandatory vaccinations. The Catholic Church is also opposed to the ingredients of certain vaccinations. For example, the MMR vaccine is cultivated in cells derived from two foetuses aborted in the 1960s.

However, the chance of serious side effects is incredibly small and furthermore the ingredients in vaccines are safe in the tiny amounts used: the exposure of children to aluminium is higher in breast milk than it is in vaccines. The FDA (food and drug administration) requires vaccines to be tested for up to 10 years before they are licensed and even after licensing, they continue to be monitored. In my view, the wider benefits of vaccines outweigh the minimal risk of poor side effects. In addition, it could be argued that personal decisions should be restricted when they affect the health of others. Therefore, I am supportive of certain vaccinations being mandatory.

'Compassion is the most important quality of a healthcare professional'

Explain what this statement means. Argue to the contrary. To what extent do you agree with the statement?

The statement argues that in careers involved in caring for the sick; kindness and empathy for the patients is the most important professional attribute. I will provide reasons for why this might be the case, whilst also discussing the importance of a sound scientific knowledge. I will then decide which quality I believe to be the most important.

A lack of compassion in care homes and hospitals could be held partly responsible for inexcusable cases of patient neglect. For example, care home members have been mocked and tortured and in hospitals, patients have been left surrounded in their own urine and forced to drink water from flower vases. Arguably this neglect has arisen from a lack of care and compassion from the healthcare professionals. However, at the same time it must partly be attributed to understaffing, lack of resources and training. Moreover, it is difficult to assess someone's level of compassion and it is uncertain whether this is something that can actually be taught.

A greater level of compassion would lead to better diagnoses. A large aspect of healthcare involves listening and communicating to patients. If a doctor has more empathy, patients are more likely to trust their doctor and disclose more personal information. An empathetic manner has also been shown to reduce patient anxiety and lead to faster patient recovery.

On the other hand, too much empathy could actually hamper healthcare professionals. Doctors and other health workers often require a degree of objectivity in order to make optimal decisions that may go against the patient's wishes. A level of detachment would also help professionals to remain calm in stressful clinical situations. Clearly, it is desirable for doctors and other healthcare professionals to have a detailed and comprehensive medical knowledge contributing to faster diagnoses, more skilled treatments and faster recoveries.

I would argue that scientific knowledge is the most important quality of a doctor especially because it is a necessity in order to practice medicine. However, compassion is also a highly important quality in a healthcare worker and is what separates an adequate doctor or nurse from an exceptional one.

END OF PAPER

Final Advice

Arrive well rested, well fed and well hydrated

The BMAT is an intensive test, so make sure you're ready for it. Unlike the UKCAT, you'll have to sit this at a fixed time (normally at 9AM). Thus, ensure you get a good night's sleep before the exam (there is little point cramming) and don't miss breakfast. If you're taking water into the exam then make sure you've been to the toilet before so you don't have to leave during the exam. Make sure you're well rested and fed in order to be at your best!

Move on

If you're struggling, move on. Every question has equal weighting and there is no negative marking. In the time it takes to answer on hard question, you could gain three times the marks by answering the easier ones. Be smart to score points- especially in section 2 where some questions are far easier than others.

Make Notes on your Essay

Some universities may ask you questions on your BMAT essay at the interview. Sometimes you may have the interview as late as March which means that you **MUST** make short notes on the essay title and your main arguments after the essay. This is especially important if you're applying to UCL and Cambridge where the essay is discussed more frequently.

Afterword

Remember that the route to a high score is your approach and practice. Don't fall into the trap that *"you can't prepare for the BMAT"*– this could not be further from the truth. With knowledge of the test, some useful time-saving techniques and plenty of practice you can dramatically boost your score.

Work hard, never give up and do yourself justice.

Good luck!

Acknowledgements

I would like to express my sincerest thanks to the many people who helped make this book possible, especially the 15 Oxbridge Tutors who shared their expertise in compiling the huge number of questions and answers. I am also indebted to *David Bailey* for always being there when I needed a helping hand or a listening ear and finally to my parents, *Anil and Ranjna* for always believing in me- even when I didn't.

Rohan

About UniAdmissions

UniAdmissions is an educational consultancy that specialises in supporting **applications to Medical School and to Oxbridge**.

Every year, we work with hundreds of applicants and schools across the UK. From free resources to our *Ultimate Guide Books* and from intensive courses to bespoke individual tuition – with a team of **300 Expert Tutors** and a proven track record, it's easy to see why UniAdmissions is the **UK's number one admissions company**.

To find out more about our support like intensive **BMAT courses** and **BMAT tuition** check out www.uniadmissions.co.uk/bmat

Your Free Book

Thanks for purchasing this Ultimate Guide Book. Readers like you have the power to make or break a book – hopefully you found this one useful and informative. If you have time, *UniAdmissions* would love to hear about your experiences with this book.

As thanks for your time we'll send you another ebook from our Ultimate Guide series absolutely <u>FREE</u>!

How to Redeem Your Free Ebook in 3 Easy Steps

1) Find the book you have either on your Amazon purchase history or your email receipt to help find the book on Amazon.

2) On the product page at the Customer Reviews area, click on 'Write a customer review'

Write your review and post it! Copy the review page or take a screen shot of the review you have left.

3) Head over to www.uniadmissions.co.uk/free-book and select your chosen free ebook! You can choose from:
- ➤ The Ultimate UKCAT Guide – 1250 Practice Questions
- ➤ The Ultimate BMAT Guide – 800 Practice Questions
- ➤ The Ultimate TSA Guide – 300 Practice Questions
- ➤ The Ultimate LNAT Guide – 400 Practice Questions
- ➤ The Ultimate NSAA Guide – 400 Practice Questions
- ➤ The Ultimate ECAA Guide – 300 Practice Questions
- ➤ The Ultimate ENGAA Guide – 250 Practice Questions
- ➤ The Ultimate PBSAA Guide – 550 Practice Questions
- ➤ The Ultimate FPAS SJT Guide – 300 Practice Questions
- ➤ The Ultimate Oxbridge Interview Guide
- ➤ The Ultimate Medical School Interview Guide
- ➤ The Ultimate UCAS Personal Statement Guide
- ➤ The Ultimate Medical Personal Statement Guide
- ➤ The Ultimate Medical School Application Guide
- ➤ BMAT Past Paper Solutions
- ➤ TSA Past Paper Worked Solutions

Your ebook will then be emailed to you – it's as simple as that!
Alternatively, you can buy all the above titles at **www.uniadmisions.co.uk/our-books**

UKCAT Intensive Course

If you're looking to improve your UKCAT score in a short space of time, our **UKCAT intensive course** is perfect for you. It's a fully interactive seminar that guides you through all 5 sections of the UKCAT.

You are taught by our experienced UKCAT experts, who are Doctors or senior Oxbridge medical tutors who excelled in the UKCAT. The aim is to teach you powerful time-saving techniques and strategies to help you succeed for test day.

➢ Full Day intensive Course
➢ Copy of our acclaimed book "The Ultimate UKCAT Guide"
➢ Full access to extensive UKCAT online resources including:
➢ 2 complete mock papers
➢ 1250 practice questions
➢ Online on-demand lecture series
➢ Ongoing Tutor Support until Test date – never be alone again.

Timetable:

➢ **1030 - 1200:** Section 1
➢ **1200 - 1330:** Section 2
➢ **1330 - 1400:** Lunch
➢ **1400 - 1515:** Section 3
➢ **1515 - 1615:** Section 4

➢ **1615 - 1700:** Section 5
➢ **1700 - 1730:** Summary
➢ **1730 - 1800:** Questions

The course is normally £195 but you can get **£ 10 off** by using the code *"BKTEN"* at checkout.

www.uniadmissions.co.uk/ukcat-crash-course

£10 VOUCHER:

BKTEN

BMAT Intensive Course

If you're looking to improve your BMAT score in a short space of time, our **BMAT intensive course** is perfect for you. It's a fully interactive seminar that guides you through sections 1, 2 and 3 of the BMAT.

You are taught by our experienced BMAT experts, who are Doctors or senior Oxbridge medical tutors who excelled in the BMAT. The aim is to teach you powerful time-saving techniques and strategies to help you succeed for test day.

➢ Full Day intensive Course
➢ Copy of our acclaimed book "The Ultimate BMAT Guide"
➢ Full access to extensive BMAT online resources including:
➢ 4 complete mock papers
➢ 800 practice questions
➢ Fully worked solutions for all BMAT past papers since 2003
➢ Online on-demand lecture series
➢ Ongoing Tutor Support until Test date – never be alone again.

Timetable:

➢ **1000 – 1030:** Registration
➢ **1030 – 1100:** Introduction
➢ **1100 – 1300:** Section 1
➢ **1300 – 1330:** Lunch

➢ **1330 – 1600:** Section 2
➢ **1600 – 1700:** Section 3
➢ **1700 – 1730:** Summary
➢ **1730 – 1800:** Questions

The course is normally £195 but you can get **£ 10 off** by using the code "*BKTEN*" at checkout.

www.uniadmissions.co.uk/bmat-course

£10 VOUCHER:

BKTEN

Medicine Interview Course

If you've got an upcoming interview for medical school – this is the perfect course for you. You get individual attention throughout the day and are taught by Oxbridge tutors + senior doctors on how to approach the medical interview.

- Full Day intensive Course
- Guaranteed Small Groups
- 4 Hours of Small group teaching
- 2 x 30 minute individual Mock Interviews + Written Feedback
- Full MMI interview circuit with written feedback
- Ongoing Tutor Support until your interview – never be alone again

Timetable:

- **1000 - 1015:** Registration
- **1015 - 1030:** Talk: Key to interview Success
- **1030 - 1130:** Tutorial: Common Interview Questions
- **1145 - 1245:** 2 x Individual Mock Interviews
- **1245 - 1330:** Lunch
- **1330 - 1430:** Medical Ethics Workshop
- **1445 - 1545:** MMI Circuit
- **1600 - 1645:** Situational Judgement Workshop
- **1645 - 1730:** Debrief and Finish

The course is normally £295 but you can get £35 off by using the code *"BRK35"* at checkout.

www.uniadmissions.co.uk/medical-school-interview-course

£35 VOUCHER:

BRK35